Teaching with
The Norton Anthology of
American Literature
SEVENTH EDITION

A Guide for Instructors

Teaching with
The Norton Anthology of
American Literature

SEVENTH EDITION

A Guide for Instructors

Bruce Michelson
UNIVERSITY OF ILLINOIS AT URBANA-CHAMPAIGN

W. W. NORTON & COMPANY
New York • *London*

The text of this book is composed in Fairfield Medium
with the display set in Barnhard Modern

ISBN 978-0-393-92992-8

W. W. Norton & Company, Inc., 500 Fifth Avenue, New York, NY 10110
www.wwnorton.com

W. W. Norton & Company Ltd., Castle House,
75/76 Wells Street, London W1T 3QT

Contents

Acknowledgments

A good instructor's guide is a continuing process, evolving from conversations, suggestions, and a great deal of direct observation. In the following pages, many fine teachers have made their mark, letting us see what they do as they refresh the literature and culture of North America for new generations of students. *Teaching with the Norton Anthology of American Literature* owes all of these hard-working imaginative people a great debt of thanks. We hope that you will continue to share with us, and with one another, to keep our literary histories relevant and alive.

Instruction is empowered by memory—of great moments in the classroom when our own teachers and friends opened possibilities to us, and convinced us that this profession is supremely worthwhile. We remember Roy Baker, Frank Hodgins, Richard Barksdale, and Carol Kyle—teachers.

CHAPTER 1

———

Getting Started

Was there ever a stranger moment at which to be teaching American literature and the legacy and the value of the printed word?

As teachers, we have daily reckonings now with the fact that no culture before our own has tried so hard to undermine the human attention span; to subvert the craft and the effort of sustained conversation about complex subjects; to convince us that our own minds should be everywhere and anywhere but here and now. Though nothing is gained by being grumpy about all this, nothing is gained by ignoring the truth either. Your students know it, probably better than you do; and that truth is there, in the room with us, every time we open a book together and focus our eyes on something as archaic as an ink-marked page of American poetry, drama, or prose.

In the pocket, the dashboard, the briefcase, the private lair, this interfacing gear grows slicker, faster, and more seductive. Content seems to drown in electronic dazzles of light and noise, hyperlinks, flipping channels, and fast-forward. Not long ago, our university lost a wonderful student, killed by a young driver who was "multitasking" at fifty miles an hour, too distracted by onboard toys to notice something so mundane, so unregenerately unvirtual, as a boy on a bicycle out in the afternoon air. We can all tell stories like this, of casualties in what seems like a ramifying contest against consciousness itself. The technologies we cope with every day—and yes, also exploit every day—are morphing too quickly for published analysis to keep up—too quickly even for satire. Today's rueful, extravagant joke, about news-video "crawls" downloaded straight into the brain, or picture-within-picture for the corner of every American eye, could be tomorrow's R&D project and the end-cap hot item for next year's holiday shopping.

So in other words we are in a fix—which also, in a sense, means business as usual. Crosswinds of one sort of another are always buffeting the bow of literary studies and the teaching of cultural history. The value and use of "American lit" as a college subject were questioned vigorously when the enterprise began in earnest more than a century ago, and every social and political upheaval has had an impact on the canon, the syllabus, and the conversations in the classroom. To teach literature well requires a sustained encounter with your own motives: what you really think you're doing, and what you hope your students might remember, long after, from this experience in your company. Literature, culture, politics, race, gender, class conflict, faith, the meaning of "literacy," "history," "nation," "people"—on a good campus the air is alive with these questions; and when the roster is full of inquisitive and independent-minded students, issues of this kind can situate and energize a voyage together into the cultural past.

All of which means that to teach a course using the Seventh Edition of *The Norton Anthology of American Literature* (NAAL), or any other vast and well-constructed anthology, you need to have an idea, an abiding assumption about where you and your students are, in a cultural context, and where you can go in each other's company, with awareness and respect for the complexities of our present and the uncertainties of our technological and cultural future. In other words, an idea rather than an agenda—more agile, more open to unforeseen possibilities, a strategy for good-faith inquiry. NAAL has been used with great success in many different instructional and cultural situations, and the Seventh Edition responds to requests and suggestions that have come in from hundreds of experienced teachers. NAAL is a big, rich, thoughtful collection—a resource and touchstone for courses in history, American studies, and cultural studies in both college and high school English classrooms. Priding themselves on their independence and sensitivity to changing cultural contexts and student interests, instructors of American literature and culture often develop their own strategies and styles in moving through this trove of material. In this guide, several kinds of courses are suggested and developed; but there are many resources here that can be selected, mixed, or adapted in countless other ways.

When we engage a swath of literary history, or open questions about ideas and crises in American cultural life, finding our own way as instructors and students is part of the pleasure. Even when uncertainty reigns about how to describe America, or history, or culture or how to decide which writers to spotlight and which to ignore, some intentions do seem to remain steady. One of these is a hope that our students will achieve informed, open-minded responses to authors we encounter together and to larger questions that take shape in an extended experience with American literature:

- What relationship can we plausibly and beneficially achieve with texts that are proposed as part of a cultural inheritance?
- What blend of credence and robust skepticism should we lend to our own ideas of "literacy," especially in an age of hypermedia and other sensory engagements?

- What can imaginative works offer, in terms of lasting value, in an age of newness and change, when even the latest, fastest computer on which you write is likely to be a relic in a matter of months?

As teachers, we probably want our students to appreciate a variety of literary styles and to speculate intelligently on relationships among these styles and the historical situations in which these works took shape. We probably want our students to think effectively about thematic and stylistic connections among texts. We want our students to encounter the lucidity and emotional power that can be found in American literary utterance. Perhaps we also want them to recognize an element of the irrational, or even a touch of complacency, or intellectual or moral blind spots that can also turn up in these works. No matter what conception of the American past may evolve in the give and take of a good class, intellectual independence is something that most of us hope to "teach"—lucid, patient affirmation of the self against or within the pressures of culture, including perhaps the culture of the classroom, and delight in the potentialities of the printed word.

This instructor's guide to *The Norton Anthology of American Literature,* Seventh Edition, is therefore intended to help with the following challenges:

- Deciding what your course is going to be about and recognizing implications of that decision;
- Choosing and presenting texts consistent with those intentions;
- Leading provocative, informed discussions about those texts;
- Choosing appropriate subjects for papers, essay examinations, and independent work.

Planning a Course: Preliminary Considerations

Individual personalities and enthusiasms—in other words, our own personalities—have much to do with success in a survey of authors and themes. So do time constraints. Since survey courses in American literature have been around for about a hundred years, there is some established wisdom that has circulated about how *not* to plan a survey tour, if you want students to stay with you and with this material for fifteen weeks or longer.

It can be tempting to think of an American literature survey as a kind of flu shot against twenty-first-century barbarism. Wouldn't it be nice if we could perfect a one-time inculcation of all the important names, dates, and "-isms," so that students wouldn't lack such reference points when they take more specialized courses later on or go out into the world and never look back at "Am Lit" again? Such an education would be inert, however, if it conveyed no sense of the vigor with which some of these texts have been debated and set apart as special. Inciting curiosity about this material seems essential to achieving a lasting presence in a student's mind.

Though your students may come to you without an inborn or conditioned zest for reading Paine's "The Crisis" or Bryant's "To a Waterfowl," they can wonder—and they do—why readers at other times have found these works compelling. Without presenting such texts as obsolete, we can open them as old sources of intensity and speculate on the transience or permanence of that spirit or cultural frame of mind. A survey course can offer reasons, even if they are only speculative, for why such literary works have remained stubbornly with us, or have been recovered for close, compassionate reading, after a long absence from our collective attention.

Amid controversies that have also been around for a long time, American literature courses can (and do) still go forward without directly facing the question of what literature, or in this case American literature, is or has come to mean. Perhaps to avoid pedagogical chaos and outbreaks of back-row nihilism, or perhaps out of weariness, some of us seem to affirm, or rather to concede, that "literature" is whatever gets included in literary anthologies or shelved under that heading in the bookstore at the mall. At a conference not long ago one of our elder colleagues, a scholar of great distinction, referred to his own teaching strategy as "tying a knot in the end of the rope and just hanging on."

But uncertainty can be an advantage too, if we want students to engage directly with the open question of who and what we are. Because your students may want to engage such issues, you may find it provident to reopen them regularly during the term. *Why* are we reading this material? Why might a young nation or an established culture yearn for a list of classics, a canon that everybody can agree on and respect? What are the values by which some literary books are valorized and some are not? In constructions and reconstructions of our literary heritage, there are odd-looking choices to account for—especially, perhaps, in regard to texts that date from before the Civil War. After the American Revolution and before the great revolution in publishing that took fire in the 1840s—high-speed steam-powered presses, cheap paper, telegraphs and railroads, easy long-distance shipping, and better copyright laws—the new American books published in any given year could all fit comfortably on a single library table. If you wrote a good play or readable poems in those early years and subsidized the printing (as most early American authors had to), the competition for publicity was not keen compared to now. Are these old works privileged merely because they are scarce? Some of our canonical texts were indeed huge best sellers like Stowe's *Uncle Tom's Cabin*, but anemic print runs were common for new books by Emerson, Child, and Fenimore Cooper before 1845. William Cullen Bryant's most famous collection of poems sold fewer than three hundred copies in its first two years in the shops. Not exactly a stunning blow to the cultural status quo. And what about Bradford's *Of Plymouth Plantation* and Edward Taylor's dozens of poems? None of these were published until centuries after these writers were gone.

To sum up: whatever else we might be doing, we are certainly not teaching the Top Hits of the last few centuries. So as teachers we face a stubborn question: how some of these recovered texts, which obviously shook no worlds on their first appearance, can be important to us now.

Although our students may not seem to us especially well read or culturally literate, they can be quick to perceive differences between exploring a body of literature and pressing it into other service. If one objective of a college literature course is to help students improve as makers of distinctions and askers of questions, then they need to acquire certain skills that have been taught for generations in good humanities courses but that are rarely expressed in the college catalogs:

- Acuity and sensitivity in the art of reading;
- Practice in the arts of adult-level writing and conversation;
- A heightened and complicated sense of what comes after what, and possibly *because* of what, in the onward flow or tumult of cultural history.

When teaching the survey as a large lecture or in small sections, instructors often report that they change strategy and fundamental assumptions every time around. And it goes without saying that experienced and highly successful instructors have often winced, in retrospect, over things they may have said from the podium: Great Profundities that turned ludicrous as soon as they rebounded off the walls. In reviewing your own assumptions as you begin planning your course, you might want to spend a few minutes thinking over the following questions, because they can underlie decisions (conscious or otherwise) that shape a syllabus and class presentations:

- Should this course center on *answers* or on *questions*? We often tell students that a course can help them begin thinking about a complex and evolving arrangement of cultural experiences and that if their thinking continues (as it should) long beyond the end of the course, they should experience at a certain point the pleasure of rejecting some or all of what gets said in this classroom.
- In a personal or a guided quest for cultural literacy, do some perceptions naturally and helpfully come before others? Everyday and professional realities, realities that students must be ready to face, seem to require a measure of familiarity with "major" and "canonical" authors. Familiarity doesn't have to mean reverence; literate, passionate antipathy can sometimes work just as well to bring a student into an independent, intense relationship with a challenging author, text, or literary period. As the poet Richard Wilbur has remarked, "All revolutions in art are palace revolutions"—in other words, performed by brilliant people who understand what they are rising up against. To dismiss the canonical and the major author idea out of hand may be to deny students their chance to join that conversation.
- Has the question of an American cultural identity, discoverable in our literary heritage, been settled or laid aside? If each generation of readers redefines the literary heritage and infuses it with its own values and imagination, then a survey course can be designed to open this issue and keep it alive rather than close it down.

- Can a survey course, in itself, be interesting as cultural practice? There are more than four thousand four-year colleges and universities in the United States, about two thousand community colleges, and many thousands of public and private high schools. Most of the collegiate campuses have at least one or two historical courses in American literature; many of these classes are large. It is a reasonable bet, therefore, that when you and your students open NAAL to discuss Bradstreet or Douglass or Wharton, legions of other students and their instructors at that moment are doing pretty much the same thing all around the country. In itself, the survey course is a standard American cultural practice—possibly a rite of passage. It is not just an inquiry into cultural history but also an actual part of its making, its transformation, and its continuance. If you comment about this to students early in the term, you can provoke interesting responses and a heightened attention to what you are doing together.

The Small Class: Special Considerations

If you review student questionnaires about humanities courses, you may see a correlation between how much high-quality discussion students experienced in a given class and how much they valued it and feel they learned from it. Your students may want to talk about a lot of things, including the course itself as well as specific authors and readings. If you're doing a literary history course and you want to take advantage of this willingness to participate, then you will have balances to work out—between getting historical facts sufficiently into mind and helping your group speculate about the assigned material rearrange it, play with it, and achieve some kind of direct and durable connection with it. Tromping through an anthology chronologically may seem unimaginative, but the process can work well if you and your students pull back once in a while and open some freewheeling dialogue about where you are. What kinds of questions and uncertainties are they facing just now about specific literary and cultural moments or the value of the tour?

Though a reading list and a discussion sequence probably have to be established right away, certain decisions about strategy might wait until, say, the second week of the term, when you have a better sense of the energy and tone of your class. You might ascertain if there are pockets of special interest in the room: enthusiasms for particular writers, periods, or issues. You could get a sense of this by handing out index cards on the second day (or whenever enrollment has stabilized) and asking students to write something about other English courses that they have taken, the best college course they have had so far (or high school class, if they are college freshmen), their plans or options for a major, and some strong personal interest or achievement that they feel comfortable mentioning, academic or otherwise. With a smaller class, you can pick up cues from their answers and develop a sense of who in your group might be attracted to a particular writer, cultural predicament, or large-scale issue.

If you do see a pattern of such interests, you might think about asking each student to be a resource person on a particular subject (or writer or literary era), or on a recurring and evolving question, or on some topic parallel to literary concerns (architecture, race relations, the status of women, religious minorities, book publishing, and technical innovations). Students need room to choose, so you might want to hand out a list of available subjects, with one or two standard resources listed for them to consult for a few hours sometime in the opening weeks of the term. Students may not be ready or willing to chime in with deep-background information every time a question comes up; but if you and they feel comfortable with their offering insights once in a while, then you can hope for these benefits: more voices participating in class discussion, better opportunity for some students to connect to the class, better preliminary thinking by students, and more enthusiasm in regard to the design and writing of major papers.

If a plan like this seems incompatible with your students or your own design for this small class, then you might want to try other options that can work well with groups of fewer than thirty people.

Teaching the Art of the Question

Some students may tell you (in an office visit or, alas, when the course is over) that they don't talk in class because they "don't have anything say." Some students are just naturally quiet, of course; and their silence doesn't signify boredom, hostility, stupidity, or lack of preparation. One common problem, however, that can injure their efforts and morale and your ability to keep the class moving is their belief that "anything to say" means pronouncements and grandiose summaries rather than measured, provocative questions about the material or ways of reading it. Students are sometimes driven into unhappy silence by previous courses, where a human jukebox of semiuseless observations has convinced them that class participation amounts to a game of Getting the Last Word. If you can convince students that one or two well-aimed questions per week can be wonderful contributions to a class, valued not only by the instructor but also by peers who were hoping that somebody would ask that, then you will be doing them a service. The craft of conversation is important to survival in adult professional life, and if some of your students can grow comfortable with the notion that in many situations asking is wiser and more humane than telling, that practice may stay with them long after their textbooks have fallen apart or been sold back to the bookstore.

A Course as a Process of Discovery

There may be correspondence between the size of a given section and the percentage of students who feel puzzled by any variance from a march through time. But with a smaller group, some of the nonlinear arrange-ments, outlined elsewhere in this guide, may be easier to contrive.

Even with larger groups, instructors can successfully open a course with some "big" work: major in terms of its sales, its mass-cultural impact, its stay-ing power in the academic mind, and its durable appeal to a larger public. The NAAL excerpts from *Uncle Tom's Cabin* can be a good choice, if you want to open questions that subsequent readings could help answer. Where do the moral values that inform this book come from, and how could this novel find such a huge receptive audience? If a creed or a body of religious thought lies at its heart, shaping not only the personages in the story but the narrative itself, what roots do these qualities have in the American literary experience? What are the sources of the novel's ideas of goodness, of evil, of salvation and damnation, of the well-lived life and the subtle ways in which well-intentioned people fall into terrible error? What kind of cultural land-scape makes it possible for a novel, a tale about people who in a strict sense never existed and about events that never took place, to figure centrally in an immense political and moral upheaval? In other words, you could work backward from a book of this magnitude, laying the groundwork for a recon-sideration of Calvinism, the Enlightenment, romanticism, transcendental-ism, and the evolving idea of the writer, the imaginative text, and the individual self—not as closed historical issues but as perceptions, crises, and questions that carry forward and shake the foundations of the country.

Adventures of Huckleberry Finn, included complete in NAAL, could also work well, considering that this novel's status as a required text in many high school and college curricula is still hotly debated. How did this mean-dering tale of a river trip, a novel attacked as immoral soon after it appeared at the end of the nineteenth century, achieve such high placement in scholastic and popular lists of the "best" American novels? If the staying power of this mass-market adventure story suggests something about Amer-ican culture (as it really is or was, or as we want to imagine it is or was), then what are those qualities that it suggests, and where else in our literature might we see them in evidence?

The Lecture Course: Special Considerations

In undergraduate sections ranging from a dozen students up to hundreds, American literature survey courses seem to flourish. With high-tech support in our lecture halls, and because many of us have lectured often enough to have memorized our orations, we can move around a big room, ask ques-tions, work for actual discussion, apply active-learning strategies, and make the gathering feel smaller and more human in scale than it really is. Tech-nology and cautious theatrics: these things can help—up to a point. But a lecture is still a lecture, and when you try to lead a group through many authors and complex issues in American cultural history, there are times when you may have to explain at length, and students may have to listen, if the alternative is TV talk-show exchanges of enthusiastic ignorance.

In a smaller class, discussion can be freewheeling at times without creating anxiety among your students. In the large lecture, however, the interesting sidelight, the digression, or the periodic discussion that intrigues some students can lose others and cause them to fear that you're rambling or that all of what's being said must be reverently remembered. To try to allay such worries, you might consider producing "lecture summaries" and making them available online and at a local copy shop. These summaries should not be transcripts of the lectures, and you would have to make clear that they are not a substitute for coming to class and taking notes. Rather, such summaries could provide core considerations, major dates, names, events, and key questions, so that students could actually think with you when an interesting question was posed rather than sweat to catch up with whatever was being declaimed just before. Such lecture summaries could be drawn out of your own presentations, and the copy shops will be eager to accommodate you and your students—provided copyright laws are respected.

Using the *NAAL* Web Site

Designed to help for students extend their exploration of American literature and develop subjects for writing and research, this free Web site offers additional pedagogical materials and connections to authoritative resources on the Web. Included on the site are quick-reference timelines, historical-literary outlines, maps, self-grading quizzes, and searchable "exploration" sections that provide generative questions and projects that help students draw connections, close-read texts, and link texts to contexts for 120 of the anthology's authors. In addition, nearly every author in the anthology appears with a brief biography and annotated links to other Web sites. These materials can be used in countless ways. An instructor can assign explorations as writing assignments; students can use the entire site as a sort of "electronic workbook" and as a way into current literary criticism on specific authors and problems.

CHAPTER 2

Planning the Historical Survey Course

NAAL is organized chronologically by the birth dates of the authors. Although as teachers we often construct required reading lists that loosely follow such an order, chronology in and of itself doesn't provide historical perspective. Historical approaches to teaching American literature should do more than sequence; they should empower students to ask questions about lives and values and styles of thought and expression; about ethnic, literary, geographical, and political environments; and about powerful beliefs in the minds of readers that American authors were trying to engage.

In teaching an historical survey, we can see ideas unfold and flourish in our literary culture. From the selections written before the Civil War you can choose works related to specific historical events; these events can inform the presentation of readings and give students a good basis for exploring questions in class or developing writing topics. Such an approach encourages students to situate literary works in the context of American history courses they may have taken. After the Civil War, as American literature develops an expanding variety of voices, themes, and degrees of connection to actual events, you can emphasize that diversity while teaching the individuality of writers and a rich array of aesthetic movements.

As you plan, you may need to guess how much literary history you will end up teaching and how much history of a more basic sort you'll need to impart. Contrary to horror stories about how little American college students know of the major events in the development of Western civilization, you may find that most of your students actually do have, or can quickly acquire, passable familiarity with Puritanism, the Enlightenment, romanticism, and transcendentalism, although they may have more stubborn problems with

10

murkier formulations such as realism, naturalism, aestheticism, and literary modernism. They probably know, or can reacquire, the dates of the American Revolution and the Civil War; and they likely know about the settling of New England and the Spanish Southwest, about the Industrial Revolution, westward expansion, slavery, and the displacement and decimation of native peoples. What they may lack, and what historical surveys can begin to give them, are the voices relating and responding to these cultural moments.

Such an approach, however, does not have to be a tour through arcane or antiquated "-isms." The period introductions in NAAL do a fine job of describing historical and cultural landscapes through which a literary history survey course must move, and your own presentations, therefore, do need to be grounded in the numbing assumption that the only way to read each writer is as a mouthpiece for some supposedly dominant idea system or list of aesthetic stipulations. The poorer essays that you will read this year and the most inert answers on midterm tests and final examinations may reflect this unhappy misapprehension: the teacher describes the zeitgeist (preferably in twenty-five words), and the student applies it, forcibly if necessary, to every writer whose career happens to fall within the conventional dates of a literary period.

For such reasons, it seems important to present literary history as a lively interaction between prevailing values (or moral conflicts) of a given time, on the one hand, and individual minds and talents, on the other, emphasizing distinctions among those minds and differences in how they each engage with a historical predicament. Most students and teachers, it seems likely, would rather read Bradstreet as a many-sided sensibility responding to Puritanism than as an undifferentiated voice of that culture and creed. If the idea is only to find romanticism or abolitionist ideology in Stowe, rather than see Stowe as an individualized writer working amid a landscape of romanticism and moral crisis, then there would really be no need to read Stowe after hearing a general description of American romantic thought or a summary of mid-nineteenth-century politics and race relations. In fact there would be little need to read anything other than the author headnotes.

To teach the historical survey now is to take on a compound responsibility: to offer students background and context and to investigate authors as remarkable individuals within it. If we can accomplish something like this, we stand a chance of avoiding hypocrisies that students intuitively recognize and resent: the implicit notion that everyone (except, of course, an elite contemporary "us") has been a hopeless mental prisoner of easily summarizeable value systems and that what we do in reading back through American historical periods is hear that system reverberate in the words of any and every given writer. You won't lose conscientious students if you can engage, at least now and then, with paradox instead and with contradictions that we seem to assume are essential to selfhood and modern literary identity. If we begin planning a historical survey course from the idea that the American self is and has been commonly defined in terms of internal conflicts, ambivalence, and some sort of dialogue between reason and received ideas on the one hand and emotions and irrational urgencies on the other, then we can bring some of these texts to life as literature and discover in them lasting relevance and appeal. One key objective, then, can be to look for a humanizing, unhomogenized mix of motives, aspirations, and values.

If you have been teaching for a while, you know that many of your students haven't accepted the possibility that modern identity involves a measure of turmoil. Such students could be both comforted and inspired by a recognition that even in eras that seem overwhelmed by dogmas and idea systems (e.g., Puritanism, transcendentalism, literary naturalism), something in the self may stand apart; and that a text offering access to that unreconciled presence within is a text worth remembering.

Accordingly, as you move from one literary era to the next and offer your own review of how historical and cultural situations have evolved around individual writers, you might want to talk about particular situations in regard to the act of writing itself and about what, at those times, it meant to read something. For instance: in talking about the religious and political tumult of seventeenth-century Europe and the conditions that propelled thousands of English Puritans to try to establish a theocratic colony in the New England wilderness, you can lose students in a footrace through historical events that do not successfully open up the texts of that period, however huge those events might seem. American students in this sometimes overwhelming "information age" can gain imaginative entry into the seventeenth century if attention is paid to the printing and literacy revolutions that made the Reformation possible. For the first time in history, those revolutions allowed direct engagement of the ordinary citizen with the sacred text; consequently, new theologies developed and spread, including theologies that placed immense importance on that encounter between mind and text and on the urgencies of reading right. In other words, the northeast coast of the United States was being settled at a time when, as never before, the printed word and its interpretation energized not only personal and community life but also the private encounter with belief and divine will.

Similarly, a discussion of the literary scene of mid-nineteenth-century America benefits from attention to the technology and business of book publishing in those years: the sudden move to the mass production of books, thanks to the rotary press and the reliable sheet feeder, and the ability to cheaply and easily ship those books deep into the American heartland, thanks to the web of railroads. Quite quickly, authorship in America offered an unprecedented chance for high profit, large-scale cultural impact, and real celebrity, not just in the United States but also elsewhere in the English-speaking world. A look at literary modernism and postmodernism will seem more plausible to students if it takes notice of situations in which they themselves are reading: a context in which colleges and universities are major presences in the establishment of literary value and taste and in which film and television have a very great impact on what gets written, published, and noticed by the larger culture.

As suggested earlier, the historical survey course is also a good place for spending some time talking about what literary history has been in the last century and in the thousands of survey classes taught on our campuses up to this moment. Reviewing this development need not mean condescending to it or congratulating ourselves for achieving some eleventh-hour wisdom that generations of benighted students and instructors had never glimpsed before. If the historical roots of the survey lie in an early-twentieth-century wish to acculturate an increasingly diverse population and stave off chaos by requiring a kind of collective homage to a sequence of supposedly heroic (and mostly white male) American authors, then at the millennium's end, one valid subject for us to discuss is the survey itself, and the cultural work that it can do, and the right of students to participate in reviewing and defining that mission. This need not be a posture: you may find that your students take the course much more seriously if they understand themselves to part of a collective process rather than audience for an overperformed ritual.

The suggested readings listed here promote a presentation of important historical situations, of the rise and transformation of literary eras and values, of the complex engagement between individual talents and their immediate contexts, and of a literary legacy. The teaching notes for individual authors included in this guide are intended to help address these questions.

Suggested Readings

Volume A: Beginnings to 1700

NATIVE AMERICAN LITERATURE—ORIGINS

The Iroquois Creation Story
Pima Stories of the Beginning of the World
Native American Trickster Tales

LITERATURE OF EXPLORATION AND EARLY COLONIZATION

Columbus: "Letter to Luis de Santangel"; "Letter to Ferdinand and Isabella"
Harriot: *A Brief and True Report*
Smith: *The General History of Virginia*

LITERATURE OF WITNESS AND ENCOUNTER

Casas: *The Very Brief Relation*
Cabeza de Vaca: *The Relation*

NEW ENGLAND PURITAN WRITERS

Bradford: *Of Plymouth Plantation* ["The Mayflower Compact"]
Winthrop: "A Model of Christian Charity"; *The Bay Psalm Book*
Bradstreet: "The Prologue"; "Contemplations"; "The Flesh and the Spirit"; "The Author to Her Book"; the elegies to her three grandchildren; "Here

Follows Some Verses upon the Burning of Our House"; "As Weary Pilgrim"
Wigglesworth: *The Day of Doom*
Rowlandson: *A Narrative of the Captivity and Restoration*
Edward Taylor: "Psalm Two"; *Preparatory Meditations* (including "Prologue"); "The Preface"; "Upon Wedlock, and Death of Children"; "Huswifery"; "A Fig for Thee, Oh! Death"
Sewall: *The Diary*

RESISTANCE TO BAY COLONY VALUES

T. Morton: *New English Canaan*
Roger Williams: *The Bloody Tenet of Persecution;* "A Letter to the Town of Providence"

THE NEW ENGLAND PURITAN VISION: CRISIS, REVIVAL, AND METAMORPHOSIS

Mather: *The Wonders of the Invisible World;* "*Galeacius Secundus*: The Life of William Bradford"; "*Nehemias Americanus*: The Life of John Winthrop"
Calef: *More Wonders of the Invisible World*
Sewall: "The Selling of Joseph"

NATIVE PEOPLES AND THE NEW ARRIVALS

Bradford: *Of Plymouth Plantation*
R. Williams: *A Key into the Language of America*
Rowlandson: *A Narrative of the Captivity and Restoration*
Cluster: "A Notable Exploit": Hannah Dustan's Captivity and Revenge

WOMEN IN THE NEW WORLD

Bradstreet: poems
Winthrop: *The Journal*
Rowlandson: *A Narrative of the Captivity and Restoration*
Mather: "The Trial of Martha Carrier"

Volume A: American Literature 1700–1820

PURITANISM IN THE EIGHTEENTH CENTURY

Knight: *The Private Journal*
Byrd: *The Secret Diary*
Edwards: *Personal Narrative;* ["Sarah Edwards's Narrative"]; "A Divine and Supernatural Light"; "Letter to Rev. Dr. Benjamin Colman"; "Sinners in the Hands of an Angry God"

FEDERALISM, DEISM, AND THE ENLIGHTENMENT SPIRIT

Franklin: "The Way to Wealth"; "Information to Those Who Would Remove to America"; "Remarks Concerning the Savages of North America"; *The Autobiography*
J. Adams and A. Adams: letters
Paine: *Common Sense*; "The Crisis, No. 1"; *The Age of Reason*
Jefferson: The Declaration of Independence; *Notes on the State of Virginia*
Hamilton and Madison: *The Federalist*
Freneau: "On the Emigration to America and Peopling the Western Country"; "The Wild Honey Suckle"; "The Indian Burying Ground"; "On the Religion of Nature"
Tyler: *The Contrast*

WOMEN WRITERS IN THE ENLIGHTENMENT AND THE NEW REPUBLIC

Murray: ["History of Miss Wellwood"]
Foster: *The Coquette*
Tenney: *Female Quixotism*

SLAVERY, IDENTITY, AND PERSONAL ETHICS

Byrd: *The Secret Diary*
Woolman: *The Journal*
Crèvecoeur: *Letters from an American Farmer* (Letter IX)
Jefferson: The Declaration of Independence
Equiano: *The Interesting Narrative*
Freneau: "To Sir Toby"
Wheatley: "On Being Brought from Africa to America"; "To the University of Cambridge, in New England"; "Thoughts on the Works of Providence"; "To S. M., a Young African Painter, on Seeing His Works"; letters
S. Morton: "The African Chief"

NATIVE AMERICANS AND THE WHITE IMAGINATION

Occom: "A Short Narrative of My Life"
Franklin: "Remarks Concerning the Savages of North America"
Freneau: "The Indian Burying Ground"

COLONIAL AMERICAN WOMEN AND THE PREVAILING ETHOS

Knight: *The Private Journal*
Byrd: *The Secret Diary*
Edwards: "On Sarah Pierpont"
J. Adams and A. Adams: letters
Foster: *The Coquette*

Tenney: *Female Quixotism*
Cluster: Women's Poetry: From Manuscript to Print
Murray: "On the Equality of the Sexes"

Volume B: American Literature 1820–1865

The New American-ness of American Literature

Irving: "Rip Van Winkle"; "The Legend of Sleepy Hollow"
Sedgwick: *Hope Leslie*
Sigourney: "Death of an Infant"; "The Suttee"; "The First Slave Ship"; "To a Shred of Linen"; "Two Old Women"
Bryant: "Thanatopsis"; "To a Waterfowl"; "The Prairies"
Schoolcraft: "Elegy"; "Lines Written at Castle Island"; "Two Songs"; "Moowis, the Indian Coquette"
Child: *Letters from New-York*
Emerson: "The American Scholar"; "The Divinity School Address"; "Self-Reliance"; "Thoreau"; "Letter to Walt Whitman"
Hawthorne: "Young Goodman Brown"; "Wakefield"; "The May-Pole of Merry Mount"; "The Minister's Black Veil"; *The Scarlet Letter*
Longfellow: "A Psalm of Life"; "The Slave Singing at Midnight"; *Evangeline*; "The Fire of Drift-wood" "The Jewish Cemetery at Newport"; "My Lost Youth"
Poe: "The Raven"; "Annabel Lee"; "Ligeia"; "The Fall of the House of Usher"; "The Black Cat"; "The Philosophy of Composition"
Melville: "Hawthorne and His Mosses"; *Moby-Dick*; "Bartleby, the Scrivener"; *Billy Budd, Sailor*

American Transcendentalism

Emerson: *Nature*
Fuller: "Summer on the Lakes, in 1843"
Thoreau: *Walden*

Narratives of Westward Expansion

Fenimore Cooper: *The Last of the Mohicans*
Parkman: *The California and Oregon Trail*
Memorial of the Cherokee Citizens
Kirkland: *A New Home*
Clappe: *California, in 1851 and 1852*

Literature of a House Divided

Lincoln: "A House Divided"; Gettysburg Address; Second Inaugural Address
Stowe: *Uncle Tom's Cabin*
Brown: *Narrative*

Thoreau: "Resistance to Civil Government"; "Slavery in Massachusetts"; "A Plea for Captain John Brown"

Douglass: *Narrative of the Life*

Whitman: *Drum-Taps* poems

Melville: "The Paradise of Bachelors and The Tartarus of Maids"; *Battle-Pieces*

Dickinson: 39; 124; 202; 225; 260; 340; 347; 372; 521; 576; 648; 760; 764; 857; 935; 1263; 1668; 1773 (poems about being alienated)

F. Harper: "To Mrs. Harriet Beecher Stowe"; "The Slave Mother"; "Bury Me in a Free Land"; "Two Colored People in America"

Cluster: Slavery, Race, and the Making of American Literature

PUBLIC VALUES AND DEMOCRATIC PROSPECTS

Lincoln: Second Inaugural Address

Douglass: "What to the Slave Is the Fourth of July?"

Whitman: "Preface to Leaves of Grass"; *Leaves of Grass* ["Song of Myself"]; "Letter to Ralph Waldo Emerson"; "From Pent-up Aching Rivers"; "Facing West from California's Shores"; "Scented Herbage of My Breast"; "Crossing Brooklyn Ferry"; "Out of the Cradle Endlessly Rocking"; "As I Ebb'd with the Ocean of Life"; "When Lilacs Last in the Dooryard Bloom'd"; "Democratic Vistas"

Stoddard: "Lemorne *Versus* Huell"

Dickinson: 67; 112 194; 279; 320; 339; 340; 365; 395; 407; 411; 448; 466; 519; 521; 576; 632; 675; 764; 817; 1353; 1577; 1593; 1668; 1773 (poems about struggle, triumph, and vision)

Davis: "Life in the Iron-Mills"

Volume C: American Literature 1865–1914

REGIONALISM AND LOCAL COLOR WRITING

Harte: "The Luck of Roaring Camp"

Harris: "The Wonderful Tar-Baby Story"; "How Mr. Rabbit Was Too Sharp for Mr. Fox"

Jewett: "A White Heron"

Freeman: "A New England Nun"; "The Revolt of 'Mother'"

Chesnutt: "The Goophered Grapevine"; "The Wife of His Youth"

Garland: "Under the Lion's Paw"

Austin: "The Walking Woman"

Zitkala Ša: "Impressions of an Indian Childhood"; "The School Days of an Indian Girl"; "An Indian Teacher among Indians"; "The Soft-Hearted Sioux"

AMERICAN LITERARY REALISM

Ruiz de Barton: *The Squatter and the Don*

Twain: *Adventures of Huckleberry Finn*; "Fenimore Cooper's Literary Offenses"

Bierce: "An Occurrence at Owl Creek Bridge"; "Chickamauga"
James: *Daisy Miller*; "The Real Thing"; "The Beast in the Jungle"; "The Figure in the Carpet"
Hopkins: *Contending Forces*
Wharton: "The Other Two"
Cahan: *The Imported Bridegroom*, "A Sweat-shop Romance"
Sui Sin Far: "In the Land of the Free"

NARRATIVES OF MINORITY STRUGGLE AND RESISTANCE

Ruiz de Burton: *The Squatter and the Don*
Native American Chants and Songs
Winnemucca: *Life Among the Piutes*
Washington: *Up from Slavery*
Chesnutt: "The Passing of Grandison"
Eastman: *From the Deep Woods to Civilization*
Hopkins: *Contending Forces*
Cahan: *The Imported Bridegroom*
Wells-Barnett: "Mob Rule in New Orleans"
Du Bois: *The Souls of Black Folk*
Johnson: *Autobiography*
Dunbar: "An Ante-Bellum Sermon"; "We Wear the Mask"; "Frederick Douglass"; "Harriet Beecher Stowe"
Wovoka: "The Messiah Letter"
Zitkala Ša: "Impressions of an Indian Girlhood"; "The Soft-Hearted Sioux"
Corridos
Cluster: Debates over "Americanization"

LITERARY NATURALISM

Chopin: *The Awakening*; "At the 'Cadian Ball"; "The Storm"
Freeman: "A New England Nun"; "The Revolt of 'Mother'"
Gilman: "The Yellow Wall-paper"
Du Bois: *The Souls of Black Folk*
Norris: "Fantaisie Printanière"
S. Crane: *Maggie*; "The Open Boat"; "The Black Riders"; "War Is Kind"
Dreiser: *Sister Carrie*
London: "To Build a Fire"; "The Mexican"
H. Adams: *The Education*

Volume D: American Literature 1914–1945

LITERARY NATURALISM IN AMERICAN VERSE

Masters: poems
Robinson: "Luke Havergal"; "Richard Cory"; "Miniver Cheevy"; "Mr. Flood's Party"
Sandburg: poems

MODERNIST THEMES

A. Lowell: poems

Stein: *The Making of Americans*

Frost: "Mending Wall"; "The Death of the Hired Man"; "After Apple-Picking"; "The Oven Bird"; "Birches"; " 'Out, Out-' "; "Nothing Gold Can Stay"; "Stopping by Woods on a Snowy Evening"; "Desert Places"; "Design"; "Neither Out Far Nor In Deep"; "The Gift Outright"; "Directive"; "The Figure a Poem Makes"

Anderson: *Winesburg, Ohio*

Stevens: "The Snow Man"; "A High-Toned Old Christian Woman"; "The Emperor of Ice-Cream"; "Disillusionment of Ten O'Clock"; "Sunday Morning"; "Anecdote of the Jar"; "Thirteen Ways of Looking at a Blackbird"; "The Idea of Order at Key West"; "Of Modern Poetry"

Loy: "Parturition"; "Brancusi's Golden Bird"; "Lunar Baedeker"

Williams: "Portrait of a Lady"; "The Widow's Lament in Springtime"; "Spring and All"; "To Elsie"; "The Red Wheelbarrow"; "The Dead Baby"; "The Wind Increases"; "Death"; "This Is Just to Say"; "A Sort of a Song"; "The Dance"; "Landscape with the Fall of Icarus"

Pound: "Hugh Selwyn Mauberley"

Eliot: "The Love Song of J. Alfred Prufrock"; "Tradition and the Individual Talent"; *The Waste Land*; "The Hollow Men"

O'Neill: *Long Day's Journey into Night*

McKay: poems

Porter: "Flowering Judas"

Cummings: "Buffalo Bill 's"; "the Cambridge ladies who live in furnished souls"; " 'next to of course god america i' "; "i sing of Olaf glad and big"; "anyone lived in a pretty how town"; "pity this busy monster,manunkind"

Toomer: *Cane*

Fitzgerald: "Winter Dreams"; "Babylon Revisited"

Faulkner: *As I Lay Dying*

Hemingway: "The Snows of Kilimanjaro"

Hughes: "The Negro Speaks of Rivers"; "Mother to Son"; "Theme for English B"

Boyle: "The White Horses of Vienna"

Cluster: World War I and Its Aftermath

FORMAL AND TECHNICAL EXPERIMENTATION

Pound: "A Pact"; "In a Station of the Metro"; "Villanelle: The Psychological Hour"; *The Cantos*

H. D.: "Oread"; "Leda"; "Fragment 113"; "Helen"; "The Walls Do Not Fall"

Moore: "Poetry"; "To a Snail"; "Bird-Witted"; "The Mind Is an Enchanting Thing"

Eliot: "Burnt Norton"

Dos Passos: *U.S.A.* ["The Big Money"]

Faulkner: *As I Lay Dying*

H. Crane: "Chaplinesque"; "At Melville's Tomb"; *The Bridge*
Cluster: Modernist Manifestos

Social and Political Writing

Glaspell: *Trifles*
Chandler: "Red Wind"
Hurston: "The Eatonville Anthology"; "How It Feels to Be Colored Me"
Larsen: *Quicksand*
S. Brown: poems
Hughes: "I, Too"; "Mulatto"; "Song for a Dark Girl"; "Visitors to the
    Black Belt"; "Madam and Her Madam"; "Madam's Calling Cards";
    "Silhouette"
Steinbeck: "The Leader of the People"

The New Negro Movement

McKay: poems
Hurston: "The Gilded Six Bits"
Larsen: *Quicksand*
Toomer: poems
S. Brown: poems
Hughes: poems
Cullen: poems
R. Wright: "The Man Who Was Almost a Man"

Women Writers, Minority Writers, and the American Realist Legacy

Cather: *My Ántonia*, "Neighbour Rosicky"
Porter: "Flowering Judas"
Bulosan: "Be American"

Volume E: American Literature since 1945

Rather than apply historical labels to contemporary writers, you might choose a few who suggest the various gatherings and traditions representative of later-twentieth-century literature.

Postwar African American Writers

Ellison: *Invisible Man*
Baldwin: "Going to Meet the Man"
Morrison: "Recitatif"
Baraka: *Dutchman*
Clifton: "miss rosie"; "homage to my hips"; "wishes for sons"
Reed: *The Last Days of Louisiana Red*; "Neo-HooDoo Manifesto"
Bambara: "Medley"

Komunyakaa: "Facing It"; "My Father's Love Letters"; "Slam, Dunk, and Hook"
Walker: "Everyday Use"

Southern Writers

Warren: *Audubon*
Welty: "Petrified Man"
T. Williams: *A Streetcar Named Desire*
O'Connor: "The Life You Save May Be Your Own"; "Good Country People"
Komunyakaa: "Song for My Father"; "Nude Interrogation"
Walker: "Everyday Use"

American Jewish Writers

Malamud: "The Magic Barrel"
Bellow: *The Adventures of Augie March*
Paley: "A Conversation with My Father"
Ginsberg: *Howl*
Levine: poems
Rich: poems
Roth: "Defender of the Faith"
Spiegelman: *Maus*

Postwar American Drama

T. Williams: *A Streetcar Named Desire*
Miller: *Death of a Salesman*
Baraka: *Dutchman*
Shepard: *True West*
Mamet: *Glengarry Glen Ross*

Writers of the Postwar East Coast

Cheever: "The Swimmer"
Updike: "Separating"
Beattie: "Weekend"

Narrative Experimentation

Kerouac: *Big Sur*
Le Guin: "Schrödinger's Cat"
Barthleme: "The Balloon"
Pynchon: "Entropy"
Carver: "Cathedral"
Apple: "Bridging"
Spiegelman: *Maus*
Powers: "The Seventh Event"
Vollmann: "Red Hands"
Cluster: Postmodern Manifestos

Postwar Native American Writers

Momaday: *The Way to Rainy Mountain*
Vizenor: "Almost Browne"
Silko: "Lullaby"
Harjo: "When the World As We Knew It Ended"
Erdrich: "Grief"; "Fleur"
Alexie: "At Navaho Monument Valley Tribal School"; "Crow Testament"

Latino and Latina Writers

Anaya: *Bless Me, Ultima*
Anzaldúa: "Towards a New Consciousness"
Alvarez: ¡Yo!
Ríos: poems
Cisneros: "Woman Hollering Creek"
Cervantes: poems

Grouping Individual Poets

From the contemporary poets included in NAAL, here are a few who demonstrate a variety of themes, techniques, and traditions.

Penn Warren
Roethke
Bishop
Berryman
R. Lowell
Brooks
Wilbur
Clifton
Kerouac
J. Wright
Simic
Howe
Rich
Plath
Graham
Collins

Exploring Individual and "Signature" Poems

Roethke: "My Papa's Waltz"
Bishop: "In the Waiting Room"; "The Moose"; "One Art"
Hayden: "Middle Passage"
Jarrell: "The Death of the Ball Turret Gunner"; "Well Water"
Berryman: *Dream Songs* (especially 1; 14; 40)
R. Lowell: "Memories of West Street and Lepke"; "Skunk Hour"; "For the Union Dead"

Brooks: "kitchenette building"; "the mother"; "a song in the front yard"
Wilbur: "Love Calls Us to the Things of This World"; "The Mind-Reader"
Merrill: "Dead Center"; "Family Week at Oracle Ranch"
Ginsberg: *Howl*
J. Wright: "Autumn Begins in Martins Ferry, Ohio"; "A Blessing"
Sexton: "Sylvia's Death"
Snyder: "Riprap"; "Straight-Creek—Great Burn"
Rich: "A Valediction Forbidding Mourning"; "Diving into the Wreck"
Plath: "Lady Lazarus"; "Daddy"
Baraka: "An Agony. As Now."
Lorde: "The Woman Thing"; "Black Mother Woman"
Pinsky: "The Figured Wheel"; "The Want Bone"
Dove: *Thomas and Beulah*

POETS EXPLORING THE DIVERSITY
OF CONTEMPORARY AMERICAN LIFE

Hayden
Brooks
Levertov
Merrill
Ginsberg
Rich
Baraka
Lorde
M. Harper
Ortiz
Harjo
Dove
Ríos
Cervantes
Song
Lee

CHAPTER 3

A Course in Traditions, Minority Voices, and Literary Diversity

The literature of the United States encompasses many ways of imagining experience. As the latest edition of NAAL once again makes clear, our literary diversity is a treasure, and as an instructor you may decide that it warrants more attention and development in your course than chronological surveys usually allow. The Seventh Edition features an especially fine representation of eighteenth- and nineteenth-century American women writers, Latina and Latino writers, Asian American writers, Native American voices and authors, and recent texts from other North American minority communities. NAAL can also help students explore populist and vernacular voices that both express and transcend gender and ethnicity. These voices contribute to a literary chronicle of working-class experience in the United States.

It is no secret, however, that as a community of teachers, we are in the midst of important conversations about identity politics and its relationship to literary study, and that there are competing perspectives about where, in a course about traditions and diversity, the emphasis should fall: on the text, on the historical moment, on long-term or timeless political and moral concerns. No instructor's guide can presume to solve such riddles. For thinking about them on your own, we can offer only this proposition: if we want our students to remain engaged with literary texts, then those texts do have to be approached with the thought that they are something more than repositories of themes. In other words, the advice in this chapter is organized around the assumption that a key purpose of a course in literary traditions and literary diversity is to explore the text rather than situate it—to help students talk about voice, style, poetics, and rhetorical strategy and

24

understand how community affiliation, minority status, or other pressures on a given artist affect the choice and ordering of words on the page. The range of voices in NAAL do much more than allow mapping out of an array of divergent political and moral positions. They enrich, complicate, and expand our collective power to imagine and to tell.

Strong central questions for a course in traditions and diversity, therefore, can be questions about poetics:

- How might differences in gender, in ethnicity, in social power, and in historical circumstances affect literary imagination and style?
- Where and how do we see minority or marginalized voices challenging or complicating the prevailing aesthetic values of their own time and the literary legacy they inherit?
- In terms of style, structure, and imaginative possibilities, how do these works extend or resist the idea of an American literary tradition?

Questions like these can help tie a course together, but there are hard choices to make: if you decide to structure your course as an exploration of literary diversity, and of contrasting or competing poetics, you will need to decide on a limited array of communities and traditions to emphasize and to select authors who represent them well. Necessitated by the time constraints of the academic year, those choices can be painful; but if you can describe that selection process at appropriate moments in your class discussions and presentations, your students will understand why you have made certain choices and how as readers they themselves can explore further on their own.

A Course or Unit about Gender and American Poetics

One enduringly relevant "traditions" exploration is the evolution of gender-related discourses in American poetry and prose: there are two strong traditions here, sometimes at odds, sometimes complementary, and students are often delighted to explore them together. There are moments in our literary history when male-promulgated assumptions about negotiating experience and creating literary art are challenged openly by women writers or are subverted with wit or are repudiated with a bold move in new aesthetic and epistemological directions. In American letters, these revolutionary women continue to have enormous impact on the way we think and write. In a long story running from Winthrop through Emerson and Whitman and on into twentieth-century male poets, fiction writers, and literary critics, there is an emergent masculinist poetics that favors thematic and moral finality, a dominion over worldly experience not unlike what Emerson valorized in "The Poet"—the author as bard, as namer, as prophet. But starting with Bradstreet an alternative tradition emerges that women writers through Fuller, Dickinson, Hurston, Welty, Bishop, Rich, and many others draw on and transform, a tradition that emphasizes an "us" rather than

Edward Taylor's and Emerson's masculinist "I." This feminist tradition values intense yet open-ended engagement with experience rather than final or reductive moralizing. This American feminist poetics accepts and celebrates collectivity, indeterminacy, living without "knowing," a tomorrow replete with more possibilities rather than confined by yesterday's answers.

Some core questions for a course in gender and American poetics:

- What do various canonical American male writers assume to be the intention of imaginative literature? Where are those assumptions made clear?
- Compared to the values implicit in Bradford, Winthrop, and Mather, how is Bradstreet a radical writer? How do nineteenth-century American women poets continue her quest?
- Consider the way that romantic and transcendentalist American male poets end their poems. Why is there such emphasis on a firm philosophical or spiritual conclusion? How do women writers of the same period respond to that expectation?
- In the twentieth century, where do we see authors of either gender learning from the American feminist poetics that Bradstreet, Fuller, and Dickinson pioneered? Where do we see women writers affirming and resisting values that trace back to Emerson?

A Course or Unit about American Minority Voices

From NAAL's substantial collection of minority authors and voices, it is not difficult to assemble a syllabus representing African American, Native American, Jewish American, and Latina and Latino communities. Again, the challenge is to organize such a course around compelling questions, questions that your students will find intellectually and culturally interesting. Good students will enjoy complication; they will value paradoxes and special predicaments that allow writers to emerge as individuals as well as constituents of a tradition. Here are some large-scale questions that can provide continuity as well as complexity in an encounter with literature by American minorities:

- When minority writers work within or against a dominant literary culture, how does a minority "literary tradition" take shape? Does it begin in a large-scale cultural movement? Can traditions arise, over time, from the creativity of isolated artists?
- What connections do we see between such literary traditions and popular culture or folk practices?
- How do American minority writers convey in their texts an understanding that they are participating in a tradition or resisting one?
- How is a concept of minority literary traditions useful to us in writing about or discussing American literature?

- What dialogue do these minority writers maintain, willingly or otherwise, with the dominant culture or the literary mainstream of their own time?

Throughout most of the history of the United States, the printing presses, the bookshops, the literary reviews and journals were predominantly controlled and operated by people who were white and male; the potential audience, with the education and affluence to be readers, was also mostly white, and from the middle of the seventeenth century on, the language of North American literary discourse was overwhelmingly English. What are the challenges here for minority American writers who seek access to such an audience and market, and what accommodations, in any given historical moment, might have to be made?

A Course about Marginality and Inclusion

For intellectually adventurous students, you can construct an exciting course that finds additional dimensions in concepts like marginality, minority, and diversity. Some of your students may come to your class already puzzled as to whether there can be an "American literature" at all, as opposed to a Babel of competing values and voices, a chaos forced into shape and continuity by scholars and teachers. That question is difficult and serious— and in discussing it with your class or organizing a syllabus to investigate it, you might want to develop the possibility that in America, everyone can feel like an outsider, and that many American writers, regardless of ethnicity or gender, have struggled with marginalization, alienation, or exclusion. Paradoxically, this powerful feeling of being outside seems to unite many authors into a large-scale community. Does a collective sense of exclusion provide a tradition that includes us all?

Therefore, you could develop a unit or a course that compares traditions and discourses of marginality—in other words, a marginalized status as a conscious artistic decision or as a lasting or inescapable predicament. In such a unit, you could explore differences between, for example, Thoreau's deliberate choice to write from the physical and social isolation of Walden Pond, to dramatize himself as an eccentric, and the kind of crisis that his contemporary Frederick Douglass faced throughout his life. As a black slave at birth, and subsequently as a fugitive, and later as an African American author in the company of white abolitionists, with a measure of acceptance in white literary culture, Douglass had none of the freedom that Emerson or Thoreau enjoyed to take up or put aside a constructed public identity. For educated white American men in New England, marginality was an artistic option, a way of achieving an individual voice. However, they could make that decision with confidence in their own literary authority and social position, a confidence that nineteenth-century women writers, and writers from ethnic and racial minorities, could not share.

These traditions of marginality—in which artists adopt or affect a marginalized status, or seem to feel deeply and inescapably alienated from every community, or are categorized by others, regardless of what they do or say, as belonging to a specific minority—persist throughout the nineteenth and twentieth centuries. Bellow, Baldwin, Ellison, Ginsberg, Rich, Momaday, and many other modern writers, over the course of their careers, dissented from constituencies within a minority to which they supposedly belonged and paid a price for doing so. In a nation and a culture that place such value on individuality, how is isolation or marginalization to be avoided by a writer with an independent mind?

Some core questions for a course or unit on marginality and inclusion:

- For specific writers and historical periods before romanticism, what were the consequences of writing from a minority or marginalized position? How do the conditions that created the marginalization compare with the predicaments of marginalized American authors after 1850?
- When nineteenth-century popular and official culture begins to celebrate rugged individualism and independence, how do these values empower marginalized artists or complicate their situation?
- Since the 1970s, much has been said about "radical chic" in American popular culture—an affectation of marginalized or outlaw status for the purpose of achieving celebrity and profit. Your students will think of many examples. If this is indeed a presence in our culture, where are its historical roots, and what might the consequences of a quest for cultural diversity and inclusion be?

A Unit on American Persuasion and Polemic

Another way to organize a syllabus is to group writers who share a particular rhetorical or political style or intention. The tradition of the jeremiad and the polemic go back to the Bay Colony, and in the nineteenth century a passionate didacticism becomes a powerful presence in American poetry and fiction. Winthrop, Edwards, Paine, and Jefferson; Emerson, Stowe, Fuller, Whitman, Douglass, Du Bois, and Ellison—in following this tradition, students can explore varieties of rhetoric intended to change minds quickly and utterly as well as the interactions between the freewheeling individual imagination and moral imperative.

Some core questions for a unit on American persuasion and polemic:

- In the opening century of European settlement, the dominant published literary form was the sermon. As New England opens to the Enlightenment, the Federal period, and American romanticism, where does the sermon tradition show itself in imaginative literature?
- From Edwards's "Sinners in the Hands of an Angry God" onward through Whitman's *Leaves of Grass*, flagrantly didactic passages turn up in the midst of novels, poems, and plays. How are these didactic

passages integrated into secular imaginative works and with what degree of success?

- When American minority and women authors moralize on the printed page, what rhetorical strategies do they employ?
- In modern American literature, have imagination and polemic parted company? If so, why? If not, can you give examples of poems, fiction, or plays that are didactic as well as imaginative?

Suggested Readings

Alternative Voices and American Literary Diversity

Volume A: Beginnings to 1700

EUROPEAN MALE LITERARY PRACTICES AND POETICS

Bradford: *Of Plymouth Plantation*
T. Morton: *New English Canaan*
Winthrop: *The Bay Psalm Book*
Cabeza de Vaca: *The Relation*
E. Taylor: "Psalm Two"; "Prologue"; "Meditations" (8; 16; 38; 150); "The Preface"; "Upon Wedlock, and Death of Children"; "Huswifery"; "A Fig for Thee, Oh! Death"
Mather: *The Wonders of the Invisible World*
Calef: *More Wonders of the Invisible World*

ALTERNATIVE WAYS OF TELLING: NATIVE AMERICAN TRADITIONS

Stories of the Beginning of the World
Native American Trickster Tales

ORIGINS OF AN AMERICAN POETICS BY WOMEN

Bradstreet: "Contemplations"; "The Flesh and the Spirit"; "The Author to Her Book"; elegies for her grandchildren; "Here Follows Some Verses upon the Burning of Our House"; "To My Dear Children"

Volume A: American Literature 1700–1820

POLITICS AND WHITE AMERICAN MALE VOICES

Edwards: Personal Narrative; ["Sarah Edwards's Narrative"]; "A Divine and Supernatural Light"; "Letter to Rev. Dr. Benjamin Colman"; "Sinners in the Hands of an Angry God"
Franklin: "The Way to Wealth"; "Information to Those Who Would Remove to America"; "Remarks Concerning the Savages of North America"; *The Autobiography*
Jefferson: The Declaration of Independence; *Notes on the State of Virginia* ("Query XVII")

Paine: "The Crisis"
Crèvecoeur: *Letters from an American Farmer*
J. Adams: letters to A. Adams

American Men Creating Women's Voices

Tyler: *The Contrast*

Responses and Resistance by Women; Minority Perspectives

Knight: *The Private Journal*
Occom: "A Short Narrative of My Life"
A. Adams: letters to J. Adams
Equiano: *The Interesting Narrative*
Stockton: poems
S. Morton: poems
Murray: "On the Equality of the Sexes"
Wheatley: poems
Foster: *The Coquette*
Tenney: *Female Quixotism*

Volume B: American Literature 1820–1865

Gender, Romanticism, and American Poetics

Poetry

New England "Men of Letters"

Bryant: "Thanatopsis"; "To an American Painter Departing for Europe";
    "The Prairies"
Emerson: "The Poet"; "Experience"
Whittier: "The Hunters of Men"
Poe: poems; tales; "The Poetic Principle"
Longfellow: poems

American Gay and Women Poets

Sigourney: poems
Schoolcraft: poems
F. Harper: poems
Dickinson: poems, especially 225; 269; 372; 303; 411; 448; 479; 519;
    591; 620; 1168; 1353; 1675; 1773
Whitman: "Preface to Leaves of Grass"; *Leaves of Grass* ["Song of
    Myself"]; "Out of the Cradle Endlessly Rocking"

Fiction

"Men of Letters"

Irving: "The Legend of Sleepy Hollow"
Hawthorne: "The Minister's Black Veil"; "Young Goodman Brown";
    "Rappaccini's Daughter"
Poe: "Ligeia"; "The Fall of the House of Usher"; "The Black Cat"
Melville: "Bartleby, the Scrivener"; "The Paradise of Bachelors and the
    Tartarus of Maids"; "Benito Cereno"; "John Marr and Other Sailors"

American Women Writers

Sedgwick: *Hope Leslie*
Stowe: *Uncle Tom's Cabin*
Fern: *Ruth Hall*
Davis: "Life in the Iron-Mills"
Stoddard: "Lemorne *Versus* Huell"

American Persuasion and Polemic

"Men of Letters"

Emerson: "Nature"; "The American Scholar"; "Fate"
Thoreau: "Resistance to Civil Government"; *Walden*; "Slavery in Massa-
    chusetts"; "Walking"; "A Plea for Captain John Brown"
Poe: "The Philosophy of Composition"
Lincoln: "A House Divided"; Gettysburg Address; Second Inaugural
    Address

Women Writers

Child: Letter XXXIV ["Women's Rights"]
Fuller: "The Great Lawsuit"
Fern: "Male Criticism on Ladies' Books"

Minority Voices

Apess: "An Indian's Looking-Glass for the White Man"
Petalesharo: Speech of the Pawnee Chief
Truth: Speech to the Women's Rights Convention
Jacobs: *Incidents in the Life of a Slave Girl*
Douglass: *Narrative of the Life*; "What to the Slave Is the Fourth of July?"
Zitkala Ša: "Why I Am a Pagan"

Men, Women, and Travel

Kirkland: *A New Home*
Clappe: *California, in 1851 and 1852*

Volumes C and D: American Literature 1865–1914 and 1914–1945

MINORITY VOICES IN AMERICAN FICTION

Ruiz de Burton: *The Squatter and the Don*
Chesnutt: "The Goophered Grapevine"; "The Wife of His Youth"
Hopkins: *Contending Forces*
Cahan: *The Imported Bridegroom*; "A Sweat-shop Romance"
Larsen: *Quicksand*

WOMEN WRITING MODERN AMERICAN FICTION

Jewett: "A White Heron"
Chopin: "At the 'Cadian Ball"; *The Awakening*
Freeman: "A New England Nun"; "The Revolt of 'Mother'"
Gilman: "The Yellow Wall-paper"
Wharton: "Souls Belated"
Porter: "Flowering Judas"
Cather: *My Ántonia*; "The Sculptor's Funeral"; "Neighbour Rosicky"

LITERATURE ON THE THEME OF MARGINALITY AND INCLUSION

Charlot: ["He has filled graves with our bones"]
A. Cooper: "Woman Versus the Indian"
Washington: *Up from Slavery*
Eastman: *From the Deep Woods to Civilization*
Wells-Barnett: "Mob Rule in New Orleans"
Sui Sin Far: "In the Land of the Free"
Du Bois: *The Souls of Black Folk*
Oskison: "The Problem of Old Harjo"
Johnson: *Autobiography of an Ex-Colored Man*
Zitkala Ša: "Impressions of an Indian Girlhood"; "School Days of an
    Indian Girl"; "An Indian Teacher among Indians"; "The Soft-Hearted
    Sioux"
Bulosan: "Be American"

AMERICAN WOMEN POETS, 1914–1945

A. Lowell
H. D.
Moore
Millay

AFRICAN AMERICAN POETS AND PROSE WRITERS, 1914–1945

McKay
Toomer
S. Brown
Hughes
Cullen

R. Wright
Hurston

The Native American Experience

Black Elk: *Black Elk Speaks*

Volume E: American Literature since 1945

Voices of Diversity and Inclusion, 1945 to the Present

Fiction by Women

Welty: "Petrified Man"
Paley: "A Conversation with My Father"
O'Connor: "The Life You Save May Be Your Own"; "Good Country
   People"
Kingston: *Tripmaster Monkey*
Beattie: "Weekend"
Tan: *The Joy Luck Club*
Lahiri: "Sexy"

Fiction by African Americans

Ellison: *Invisible Man*
Baldwin: "Going to Meet the Man"
Baraka: *Dutchman*
Reed: *The Last Days of Louisiana Red*; "Neo-HooDoo Manifesto"
Morrison: "Recitatif"
Bambara: "Medley"
Walker: "Everyday Use"

Fiction by Native Americans

Momaday: *The Way to Rainy Mountain*
Vizenor: "Almost Browne"
Silko: "Lullaby"
Erdrich: "Fleur"
Alexie: "Do Not Go Gentle"

Fiction by Latina and Latino Americans

Anaya: *Bless Me, Ultima*
Alvarez: *¡Yo!*
Cisneros: "Woman Hollering Creek"

Poetry by Women

Bishop: "The Fish"; "The Bight"; "At the Fishhouses"; "Questions of
   Travel"; "The Armadillo"; "In the Waiting Room"; "One Art"
Levertov: "To the Snake"; "In Mind"

Sexton: "The Truth the Dead Know"; "Sylvia's Death"; "The Death of Fathers"

Rich: "Snapshots of a Daughter-in-Law"; "'I Am in Danger—Sir—'"; "A Valediction Forbidding Mourning"; "Diving into the Wreck"

Plath: "Morning Song"; "Lady Lazarus"; "Daddy"

Oliver: "Poppies"; "Hummingbird Pauses at the Trumpet Vine"

Howe: "The Nursery"; "My Broken Heart"

Glück: "The Drowned Children"; "Appearances"; "Vespers"; *October*

Graham: "Call in Fear"; "When the World As We Knew It Ended"

Poetry by African Americans

Hayden: "Middle Passage"; "Homage to the Empress of the Blues"

Brooks: "kitchenette building"; "a song in the front yard"

Baraka: "A Poem for Willie Best"

Lorde: "Coal"; "The Woman Thing"; "Black Mother Woman"

Clifton: "wishes for sons"; "blessing the boat"; "moonchild"

M. Harper: "American History"; "Martin's Blues"

Komunyakaa: "Facing It"; "Jasmine"

Dove: *Thomas and Beulah*

Poetry by Native Americans and by Latina and Latino Americans

Ortiz

Harjo

Ríos

Cervantes

Contemporary Literature by Asian Americans

Tan: *The Joy Luck Club*

Song: "Beauty and Sadness"; "Lost Sister"; "Chinatown"; "Heaven"

Lee: "The Gift"; "Persimmons"; "Eating Alone"; "Eating Together"

The Southern Tradition

The southern tradition is represented in NAAL by the following authors:

Beginnings to 1700

Smith

American Literature 1700–1820

Byrd

Jefferson

AMERICAN LITERATURE 1820–1865

Brown
Douglass

AMERICAN LITERATURE 1865–1914

Twain
Harris
Chopin
Washington
Wells-Barnett

AMERICAN LITERATURE 1914–1945

Porter
Hurston
Faulkner
Wolfe

AMERICAN LITERATURE SINCE 1945

Penn Warren
Welty
T. Williams
Dickey
O'Connor
C. Wright
Walker
Komunyakaa

American Literature and Representations of Gender

If you are interested in examining representations of lesbian and gay experience, you will need to make this category more visible for students. The following list includes writers believed to be lesbian or gay, writers whose work raises questions concerning what Adrienne Rich has called "compulsory heterosexuality," and writers who have produced works of interest in the study of cultural representations of lesbian and gay experience.

Volume A: Beginnings to 1700 and American Literature 1700–1820

Representations of Pocahontas in Smith suggest that colonization follows the paradigm of heterosexual conquest.

Bradford: *Of Plymouth Plantation* (Book II, Chapter XXXII) establishes Bradford's concept of sexual deviance.

Sewall: *The Diary* offers a sometimes comic portrait of a thoughtful man trying to reconcile firm Calvinist beliefs, an elderly man's romantic inclinations (toward Mrs. Winthrop), and a wish for worldly comfort and prosperity.

Byrd: *The Secret Diary* represents marriage as an economic pact, a source of power and convenience for men, and a source (to Byrd) of amusing rivalry and domestic skirmish, in which African Americans are the pawns and casualties.

Bradstreet (poems) and J. Adams and A. Adams (letters): these writings celebrate loving heterosexual relationships as the paradigm for the republic.

Volume B: American Literature 1820–1865

Irving: "The Legend of Sleepy Hollow" pits the "masculine," ignorant Brom Bones against an "effeminate" or asexual and scholastic Ichabod Crane; the real relationship in the story may not be Ichabod's heterosexual interest in Katrina Van Tassel but rather the rivalry between the men, ending in a caricature of erotic conquest.

Emerson: "The Poet," which helped shape American aesthetics for generations, codifies a poetics of dominion over experience, of an agonistic relationship between the male "bard" and a vast and essentially female natural order.

Hawthorne: *The Scarlet Letter* contrasts the erotic and even sadomasochistic relationship between Dimmesdale and Chillingworth with the very different sort of passion between Dimmesdale and Hester Prynne.

Poe: "The Sleeper," "The Raven," "Annabel Lee," and other elegiac poems seem to celebrate dead women as the ideal subject for the poet and the ideal consorts for the truly sensitive male lover; "Ligeia" seems to construct heterosexuality as a form of death.

Fuller: "The Great Lawsuit" critiques the reality of modern American bourgeois marriage.

Thoreau: how much does misogyny or unconventional sexuality figure into *Walden*, which, according to its opening chapter, offers essentially economic advice to "poor students" and supposedly genderless counsel on how to live "deliberately"?

Whitman: the *Calamus* poems contrast powerfully with the *Children of Adam* poems.

Melville: "Hawthorne and His Mosses" depicts the pervasive single-sex world of Melville's fiction. The *Moby-Dick* selections foster discussion of power structures and love relationships among this company of men, thousands of miles from women and standard family life.

Dickinson: 199, 249, 986, and others suggest both homoerotic and heteroerotic themes. Her poems, which avoid a discourse of domination in regard to worldly experience, constitute an eloquent rebellion against Emersonian poetics.

Volume C: American Literature 1865–1914

Twain: like the relationship between Dimmesdale and Chillingworth in Hawthorne's *The Scarlet Letter*, the relationships between Huck and Tom and Huck and Jim in *Adventures of Huckleberry Finn*, as Leslie Fielder observed many years ago, may exemplify a homoerotic bond that turns up frequently in American narratives by male writers: Hawkeye and Chingachgook, Ishmael and Queequeg, Jay Gatsby and Nick Carraway, Chief Bromden and Randall McMurphy.

James: *Daisy Miller* and *The Beast in the Jungle*, along with other narratives, raise questions about male narcissism, the social and sexual predicament of upper-class, late-century women, and the fate of heterosexual and homosexual eroticism in the Gilded Age.

Jewett: rejecting the requirement of "compulsory heterosexuality," Sylvy, in "A White Heron," refuses to tell the heron's secret to the attractive male hunter.

Chopin: the enduring feminist novel *The Awakening* can be read as a critique not merely of an exhausted bourgeois existence but of all conventional descriptions and confinements of sexuality.

Freeman: in "A New England Nun," Louisa Ellis rejects overwhelming social and economic pressures to marry.

Volume D: American Literature 1914–1945

A. Lowell, Stein, H. D., and H. Crane: all offer poems with homoerotic themes and radical critiques of conventional (post-Emersonian) ways of seeing and dominating experience.

Volume E: American Literature since 1945

T. Williams: *A Streetcar Named Desire* explores various forms of modern sexuality, socially sanctioned and otherwise.

Baldwin: "Going to Meet the Man" is a narrative of a white racist, his memory of a lynching, and a forbidden sexuality entwined with both the bigotry and the crime.

Duncan, Merrill, Ginsberg, Rich, and Lorde: all bring gay perspectives to poems about contemporary life.

CHAPTER 4

A Course in Major
American Authors

To thoughtful teachers in any season, "major authors" rarely signifies an immutable array of Greats. A browse through old American literature collections and college reading lists will provide plenty of evidence that each generation challenges and changes the Parnassus, lifting up new writers and nudging others down the slope. When Stowe died in 1896, *Uncle Tom's Cabin* was commonly regarded as America's *Les Misérables*; only thirty years later, high-profile professors were condescending to it as misshapen, sentimentalist, and hopelessly mass-market. Two generations further on, Stowe's best seller was back on the lists of national classics and available in half a dozen scholarly editions. Toward the end of his career, the discriminating Henry James declared that the best novelist then writing in the English language was Hugh Walpole—an author whose works didn't break into anyone's retrospective "top hundred" for the twentieth century. And Twain enthusiasts have seen the reputation of some of his works whipsaw up and down like stocks on an over-the-counter exchange. Other examples of shifting valuations will occur to you—and the lesson that they teach is clear.

Such realities, however, need not be grounds for debunking any selection of great American texts, and a "major authors tour," mixed with a little healthy and playful skepticism, can be stronger and more pleasurable for good students than either a solemn presentation of the timelessly sublime or a protracted exercise in iconoclasm. If we are having luck in fostering honest conversation in the classroom, then these worries over majorness and greatness may take care of themselves. For our own good as teachers, and for the continued worth of the discussions we encourage about American cultural history, we need vigorous participation from our students—and a survey course runs no great risk of collapse if it welcomes that participation at the outset and sustains it throughout the term.

If that intention makes sense, you might consider opening your course with a discussion of how literary worth is determined and how modern Western culture has deliberated issues like the ones above. Who makes those choices? Why should they have an impact? What cultural forces and aesthetic values might be in play, and how much should they matter? What about mass appeal, as measured by sales in a given year or over several decades? What about popularity of another sort—among professors in literature departments and regular mention in august histories of American letters? What is the effect of big-budget Hollywood screen versions, with high-profile stars? Students will have impressions to share—and if in sharing them and in noting the strengths and limitations of these modes of selections, they see the whole process as a complex and open-ended one, then so much the better.

In a major authors survey, as in a more general historical tour, we can present some of these canonical writers as figures who have been regarded as important—by other well-known writers who came after and either adapted from them or quarreled with them, or by influential critics and historians, or by a large and steady reading public, as was true for Longfellow and remains true for Melville, Twain, Douglass, Cather, Ellison, and many others. In a semester-long course, you might open with some authors who have been recently added to the lists of the Famous and talk about why they might have been rediscovered. You may also want to add writers whose place on the major authors lists is still controversial. Again, the inclusion of a few such writers encourages students to think not just about literary meaning but also about the open-endedness of creating and recreating an American canon and about the ways in which we use such texts to conduct a dialogue with ourselves about ourselves.

Presenting a course as a study of major authors makes it possible to read and discuss more of each writer's work. This approach does not require eliminating the historical context or the literary history within which any given writer wrote, although such a course usually emphasizes the development of each writer's career rather than broad historical and cultural contexts. If you require students to read the excellent NAAL period introductions, you can allocate class time to intensive discussion of writers and individual works.

The major authors model works well in a multicourse curriculum in which first-year students take an introduction to literature course and upper-division students study literary periods in detail. The major authors course can be an intensive reacquaintance with writers that students have read before, either in high school or elsewhere on your campus, and an incentive to read other writers who were contemporaries of these major figures or who owe them a literary debt.

As a start, you might find it useful to review your own ideas or intuitions about majorness. Some of the words we might casually resort to, in explaining choices of certain writers over others—great, universal, enduring, and major itself—can be cloudy, evasive. Your students are sure to have questions of their own: How did this particular author become major? Is his or her greatness open to debate? Is there a "dictionary" somewhere that establishes criteria for inclusion or does inclusion of any particular author reflect the opinions of many readers over a long stretch of time? Why do there appear to be so many major American authors in one brief period (e.g., 1820–65), and so few in other eras (e.g., 1620–1820)? If the theaters were open and thriving in America during the Gilded Age, why don't anthologies include those plays?

One way to open up questions about literary reputation is to allow students to choose a favorite author who is not on the syllabus and ask them to write about this author's literary value. Asking questions like these can help keep the conversation refreshingly open-ended and encourage students to consider that this whole issue of majorness and greatness is one in which they can participate as informed and thoughtful adults. At one of the opening sessions, you might want to see if your class can evolve its own tentative criteria. If you help them keep track by writing their suggestions on the board, you may end up with a list like the following regarding authors we could call major:

- They still appeal to a variety of readers, and serve as points of reference in conversations about cultural history.
- They wrote works that influenced more than one other major author.
- They contributed at least one acknowledged "masterpiece" to American literature.
- They sustained a literary career beyond a single tour de force.
- They were pioneers or innovators in subject matter, literary tradition, technique, or genre.
- They have also been recognized as influential literary critics or historians.

Phrases like "major authors" and one of its classroom variants, "major-minor authors," can add to students' confusion. We might need to distinguish between "major," meaning "significant" in some way, and "major" as "mainstream." One of the larger challenges in teaching the major authors course is helping some students reconsider assumptions that major always equals "Euro-American" or "male" and that women, Native American, African American, and other minority writers—because they take up fewer pages in NAAL and most other comprehensive anthologies—are certified "minor" writers.

Suggested Readings

Volume A: Beginnings to 1700

There are several authors here whose voices have echoed strongly in recent reconstructions of cultural history.

Columbus
Cabeza de Vaca
Smith
Winthrop: "A Model of Christian Charity"
Bradstreet
E. Taylor

Volume A: American Literature 1700–1820

Most of these writers have been touchstones in American literary history courses and comprehensive anthologies since the beginning of the twentieth century.

Edwards
Franklin: including *The Autobiography*
Jefferson: including *Notes on the State of Virginia* and The Declaration of Independence
Tyler: *The Contrast*

Volume B: American Literature 1820–1865

These are some of the seminal figures and perennial favorites in descriptions of the American Renaissance.

Emerson: including *Nature*
Hawthorne: including *The Scarlet Letter*
Poe
Stowe
Thoreau: *Walden*
Douglass: *Narrative of the Life*
Whitman
Melville: including *Billy Budd, Sailor*
Dickinson

Volume C: American Literature 1865–1914

Since this was a period remembered better for narrative and nonfiction prose than for poetry and drama, the usual choices are influential novelists of the realist tradition and essayists on social moral questions. Since the republic's awareness of its own diversity was increasing in these years, however, it makes sense to include voices from communities recently recognized by centers of literary power and production.

Twain: including *Adventures of Huckleberry Finn*
Native American Chants and Songs
James
Chopin

Washington
Wharton
Du Bois

Volume D: American Literature 1914–1945

Again, an accumulation of older anthologies and cultural histories provides good evidence of who can be, or was, regarded as major in the age of American high modernism.

Cather
Frost
Stevens
W. C. Williams
Pound
Eliot
O'Neill
Hurston
Fitzgerald
Faulkner
Hemingway
Hughes
Steinbeck

Volume E: American Literature since 1945

The closer we come to the present, the greater the controversy. We have celebrities here, and prize winners, and classroom favorites, and figures who command vigorous attention in American high schools as well as in scholarly journals and conferences.

PROSE

T. Williams
Malamud
Ellison
Bellow
Miller
O'Connor
Momaday
Walker
Beattie

POETRY

Roethke
Bishop
R. Lowell

Brooks
Wilbur
Ashbery
J. Wright
Rich
Dove

A Broader American Canon?

Part of the fun of teaching and reviewing a parade of major writers is encouraging your students to second-guess it. Below are listed some NAAL works that can not only lengthen a list of The Greats but also enrich our conception of the culture that these "Great" works are about.

Volume A: Beginnings to 1700

Stories of the Beginning of the World
Native American Trickster Tales
Bradford
T. Morton

Volume A: American Literature 1700–1820

Crèvecoeur
Equiano
Stockton
S. Morton
Foster

Volume B: American Literature 1820–1865

Irving
Sedgwick
Sigourney
Schoolcraft
Fuller
Fern
Brown
Davis

Volume C: American Literature 1865–1914

Native American Chants and Songs
Lazarus
Jewett
Freeman
Chesnutt
Eastman

Hopkins
Cahan
Dreiser
S. Crane
Dunbar

Volume D: American Literature 1914–1945

Stein
Anderson
H. D.
Moore
Porter
R. Wright

Volume E: American Literature since 1945

Prose

Welty: "Petrified Man"
Le Guin: "Schrödinger's Cat"
Anaya: *Bless Me, Ultima*
Kingston: *Tripmaster Monkey*
Silko: "Lullaby"
Powers: "The Seventh Event"

Poetry

Kunitz
Olson
Hayden
Berryman
Levertov
Ammons
Merrill
Merwin
Sexton
Plath
Lorde
Clifton
Simic
Pinsky
Komunyakaa
Graham

Works by Noncanonical Writers Especially Suited for a Major Authors Course

Volume A: Beginnings to 1700

We can look for works that focus on exploration and discovery in other locales than the New England coast or what became the Spanish colonies in North America.

Wigglesworth: *The Day of Doom*

Volume A: American Literature 1700–1820

For this period, one of the best sellers of the age (Paine) might be played off against compelling works from the margins.

Occom: "A Short Narrative of My Life"
Paine: *Common Sense*; "The Crisis," No. 1
Wheatley: poems

Volume B: American Literature 1820–1865

As Emerson and others around Concord take up the public project of imagining and defining an American public and an array of national values, what traditions and social realities are they including, and what are they leaving out?

Bryant: poems, especially "The Prairies"
Schoolcraft: poems
Apess: "An Indian's Looking-Glass for the White Man"
Jacobs: *Incidents in the Life of a Slave Girl*
Brown: *Clotel*
Davis: "Life in the Iron-Mills"

Volume C: American Literature 1865–1914

Here we can revisit writers who were eased out of the limelight after their careers ended or who were regarded as "regional" in ways that kept them on the margins.

Harte: "The Luck of Roaring Camp"
Harris: "The Wonderful Tar-Baby Story"; "How Mr. Rabbit Was Too Sharp for Mr. Fox"
Garland: "Under the Lion's Paw"
Gilman: "The Yellow Wall-paper"
Austin: "The Walking Woman"

Volume D: American Literature 1914–1945

In America between the wars, what else was going on besides high modernism?

Black Elk: *Black Elk Speaks*
Masters: poems
Hurston: "The Eatonville Anthology"; "How It Feels to Be Colored Me"
Cummings: poems
Toomer: *Cane*
Wolfe: "The Lost Boy"
Boyle: "The White Horses of Vienna"

Volume E: American Literature since 1945

As we approach the present, who's major and who's not becomes a cloudy issue. Here are some strong candidates not listed earlier.

PROSE

Cheever: "The Swimmer"
Baldwin: "Going to Meet the Man"
Updike: "Separating"
Roth: "Defender of the Faith"
Dillard: *Pilgrim at Tinker Creek*
Pynchon: "Entropy"
Powers: "The Seventh Event"

POETRY

Oppen
Jarrell
Wilbur
Snyder
Pinsky
Oliver
Erdrich: "I Was Sleeping Where the Black Oaks Move"
M. Harper
Song
Lee

CHAPTER 5

A Course about Genres and American Literary Themes

This chapter offers reading lists for a course emphasizing the development of specific genres of American writing:

The personal and historical account
Forms of poetry
Narrative fiction
The drama

A course of this kind can be organized to open several large-scale questions:

- In a given historical moment, how do favored genres reflect and converse with conventional thought and cultural values?
- How does a specific literary work follow, resist, or reinvent standard forms and rules of the genre?
- In the American traditions, why do certain genres gain dominance, at various times, for the exploration of moral, political, philosophical, or spiritual themes?
- In a literature with a proliferation of genres and a sizable inheritance from European literary traditions, what constitutes originality or creativity?

In discussing literary history, what are the advantages and drawbacks of imagining an evolution of American genres, a process by which new experiments develop from an accumulated legacy? Does an American cult of newness or a succession of cultural innovations in England and western Europe complicate our wish to see each powerful new text as related to whatever came before?

A course that pays special attention to the development of American genres may need to look carefully at the literary circumstances of each author—meaning his or her formal or informal cultural experience, the strength (in that historical moment) of indigenous and imported literary models and influences, the availability of other texts, the supporting community and intended audience, the clarity or uncertainty (at that time) of the function and responsibilities of authorship. Luckily, we can keep at least two different dialogues going in such a course: an investigation of literary history from the perspective of the literary circumstances of the author and a freer and (to some students at least) more pleasurable review of American genres from our viewpoint, whereby texts are read as engaged in a dialogue (author-intended or not) with a long sequence of other texts.

Suggested Readings: Genres

Volume A: Beginnings to 1700

Indigenous Narratives before the Coming of the Europeans

Stories of the Beginning of the World
Native American Trickster Tales

The Age of Discovery and Colonization

Columbus
Casas
Cabeza de Vaca
Harriot
Smith
Bradford
T. Morton
Winthrop
R. Williams
Rowlandson
Mather
Calef

Poetry

Bradstreet
Wigglesworth
E. Taylor

Sermons, Philosophical and Theological Inquiry

Winthrop
E. Taylor: "God's Determinations"
Mather
Calef

Political Nonfiction Prose

Bradford
R. Williams

Volume A: American Literature 1700–1820

Historical Chronicles and Personal Accounts

Knight
Byrd
Edwards: *Personal Narrative*; "Sarah Edwards's Narrative"
Occom
Franklin
Woolman
Crèvecoeur
Jefferson
Equiano

Poetry

Turell
S. Morton
Stockton
Freneau
Wheatley

Sermons, Philosophical and Theological Inquiry

Edwards: "Sinners in the Hands of an Angry God"; "A Divine and Supernatural Light"

Prose Fiction

Webster
Tenney

American State Papers and Political Nonfiction Prose

Franklin
Crèvecoeur
Paine
Jefferson

The Federalist
Murray: "On the Equality of the Sexes"

DRAMA

Tyler

Volume B: American Literature 1820–1865

FICTION

Irving
Fenimore Cooper
Sedgwick
Hawthorne
Poe
Stowe
Brown
Melville
Stoddard
Davis

JOURNALS AND LETTERS

Child
Whitman
Dickinson

LITERARY ESSAYS

Emerson
Child
Hawthorne
Poe
Fuller
Whitman
Melville

LYRIC POETRY

Bryant
Schoolcraft
Longfellow
Whittier
Poe
Whitman
Harper: "Bury Me in a Free Land"
Dickinson

PERSONAL NARRATIVE

Kirkland
Jacobs
Brown
Douglass

PHILOSOPHICAL ESSAYS

Emerson
Thoreau

TRAVEL ACCOUNTS

Child
Fuller
Fern
Clappe

POLITICAL NONFICTION PROSE

Apess
Lincoln
Fuller
Truth
Brown
Fern
Thoreau
Douglass
Memorial of the Cherokee Citizens
Harper: "The Colored People in America"

Volume C: American Literature 1865–1914

THE FOLK TRADITION IN AMERICAN LITERATURE

Harris
Chesnutt
Corridos

HUMOR

Twain
Harris
Chesnutt, "The Goophered Grapevine"

LITERARY CRITICISM

Twain
Howells
James

LOCAL COLOR

Twain
Harte
Harris
Jewett
Garland
Austin: "The Walking Woman"
S. Crane

LYRIC POETRY

Lazarus
S. Crane: "The Black Riders"; "War Is Kind"
Dunbar

LITERARY NATURALISM

Bierce
Chopin
Gilman
Howells
Norris
S. Crane
Dreiser
London

PUBLIC AND POLITICAL WRITING

A. Cooper
Washington
Wells-Barnett
Du Bois

REALISM

Ruiz de Burton
Twain
James
Hopkins
Howells
Wharton
Cahan
Far

REGIONALISM

Jewett
Chopin

Freeman
Chesnutt
Austin
Oskison
Zitkala Ša

NATIVE AMERICAN ORAL LITERATURE

Navajo Night Chant
Chippewa Songs
Cochise
Charlot
Ghost Dance Songs
Wovoka

AUTOBIOGRAPHY AND PERSONAL NARRATIVE

H. Adams
Winnemucca
Washington
Eastman
Gilman
Zitkala Ša

Volume D: American Literature 1914–1945

AFRICAN AMERICAN FICTION

Larsen
Hurston
Toomer
R. Wright

DRAMA

Glaspell
O'Neill

EXPERIMENTAL PROSE

Stein
Dos Passos
Faulkner
Cluster: Modernist Manifestos

AFRICAN AMERICAN LYRIC POETRY

McKay
S. Brown

Hughes
Cullen

POPULIST AND FOLK LYRIC POETRY

Masters
Sandburg

LONGER POEMS

Pound
H. D.
Eliot
H. Crane

MODERNIST LYRIC POETRY

Robinson
A. Lowell
Frost
Stevens
W. C. Williams
Pound
H. D.
Moore
Eliot
Millay
Cummings
H. Crane

REALIST FICTION

Cather
Anderson
Chandler
Porter
Hurston
Fitzgerald
Dos Passos
Faulkner
Hemingway
Steinbeck
Bulosan

SOUTHERN FICTION

Porter
Hurston
Faulkner
Wolfe

Native American Autobiography

Black Elk

Volume E: American Literature since 1945

Drama

T. Williams
Miller
Baraka
Mamet

American Jewish Fiction

Malamud
Bellow
Roth

Fiction from and about New York City

Cheever
Malamud
Ellison
Bellow
Updike
Beattie

Southern Fiction

Welty
O'Connor
Walker

African American Fiction

Ellison
Baldwin
Morrison
Bambara
Reed
Walker

Native American Fiction

Momaday
Vizenor
Silko
Erdrich
Alexie

LATINO/LATINA FICTION

Anaya
Alvarez
Cisneros

FANTASY/SCIENCE FICTION

Le Guin
Vonnegut
Pynchon

ASIAN AMERICAN FICTION

Kingston
Tan

FICTION IN THE REALIST MODE

Cheever
Malamud
Bellow
Baldwin
Updike
Carver
Walker

FICTION IN EXPERIMENTAL MODES AND STYLES

Kerouac
Paley
Le Guin
Barthelme
Pynchon
Bambara
Apple
Beattie
Spiegelman
Powers
Vollmann

POSTMODERN NONFICTION PROSE

O'Hara: "Personism: A Manifesto"
Sukenick: "Innovative Fiction/Innovative Criteria"
Anzaldúa: "How to Tame a Wild Tongue"

ASIAN AMERICAN POETRY

Song
Lee

AUTOBIOGRAPHICAL AND CONFESSIONAL POETRY

Roethke
Bishop
Berryman
R. Lowell
Levertov
Merrill
Ginsberg
Sexton
Rich
Plath
Simic

THE BEATS

Ginsberg
Snyder

AFRICAN AMERICAN POETRY

Hayden
Brooks
Lorde
Clifton
M. Harper
Komunyakaa
Dove

LATINO/LATINA POETRY

Ríos
Cervantes

WOMEN POETS

Bishop
Sexton
Rich
Plath
Lorde
Graham
Harjo
Glück
Dove
Song

SHORT LYRICS

Jarrell
Wilbur
Ammons
Merwin
J. Wright
C. Wright
Simic
Howe
Pinsky
Collins
Komunyakaa
Glück
Graham

LONGER POEMS

Wilbur
Merrill
Ginsberg
Rich
Gluck
Dove

NATIVE AMERICAN POETRY

Ortiz
Harjo
Alexie

NATURE AND LANDSCAPE POETRY

Niedecker
Penn Warren
Roethke
Bishop
Wilbur
Ammons
Merrill
J. Wright
Snyder
Oliver

NEW YORK SCHOOL

O'Hara
Ashbery

"Projective Verse"

Olson
Levertov

Protest and Political Poetry

R. Lowell
Levertov
Ginsberg
Rich

Experimental Poetry

Oppen
Duncan
Creeley

Suggested Readings: Themes

Any catalog of major themes in American literature, and of works in which those themes appear, will necessarily be incomplete and reductive. The following lists refer to themes that are characteristic of, though not necessarily exclusive to, the American experience.

The Problem of American Identity

This theme so pervades American literature that it might serve as a basis for organizing an entire course, especially for students interested in American history and culture. Following are lists of some of the works in NAAL grouped by the issues they raise.

Volume A: Beginnings to 1700 and American Literature 1700–1820

THE NEW WORLD AND ITS LANDSCAPE

Stories of the Beginning of the World
Casas: "The Coast of Pearls"
Harriot: *A Brief and True Report*
Smith: "A Description of New England"
Bradford: *Of Plymouth Plantation*
R. Williams: *A Key into the Language of America*
Rowlandson: *A Narrative of the Captivity and Restoration*
Crèvecoeur: *Letters from an American Farmer* (Letter X)
Freneau: "On the Emigration to America and Peopling of the Western Country"; "The Indian Burying Ground"; "On Mr. Paine's Rights of Man"
Wheatley: "On Being Brought from Africa to America"

ACHIEVING A PERSONAL VOICE IN THE BAY COLONY

Bradstreet: poems
E. Taylor: poems
Sewall: *The Diary*

PRIVATE PAPERS AS A WAY OF KNOWING

Sewall: *The Diary*
Knight: *The Private Journal*
Byrd: *The Secret Diary*
Woolman: *The Journal*
J. Adams and A. Adams: letters

THE SELF AND DIVINE REVELATION

Bradstreet: "Contemplations"; "To My Dear Children"
Wigglesworth: *The Day of Doom*
E. Taylor: poems
Mather: *The Wonders of the Invisible World*
Edwards: *Personal Narrative*; "A Divine and Supernatural Light"
Woolman: *The Journal*
Wheatley: "Thoughts on the Works of Providence"

INVENTING THE SELF IN THE EIGHTEENTH CENTURY

Occom: "A Short Narrative of My Life"
Franklin: "The Way to Wealth"; *The Autobiography*
Equiano: *The Interesting Narrative*
Tyler: *The Contrast*

PUBLIC DISCOURSE AND THE FORMATION OF A NATIONAL CHARACTER

Crèvecoeur: *Letters from an American Farmer*
Stockton: poems
Paine: *Common Sense*; "The Crisis," No. 1; *The Age of Reason*
Jefferson: The Declaration of Independence; *Notes on the State of Virginia*
The Federalist Papers
Murray: "On the Equality of the Sexes"

Volume B: American Literature 1820–1865

FICTION, POETRY, AND THE QUESTION OF AMERICAN IDENTITY

Irving: "Rip Van Winkle"; "The Legend of Sleepy Hollow"
Cooper: *The Pioneers*
Sedgwick: *Hope Leslie*
Sigourney: "Our Aborigines"
Bryant: "The Prairies"
Schoolcraft: "To the Pine Tree"

Defining the American Intellect

Emerson: "The American Scholar"; "The Divinity School Address"; "Self-Reliance"; "The Poet"; "Fate"; "Letter to Walt Whitman"
Fuller: "The Great Lawsuit"

Problems of Self-Knowledge

Hawthorne: "Young Goodman Brown"; "The Minister's Black Veil"; *The Scarlet Letter*
Stowe: *Uncle Tom's Cabin* (especially Chapters III, IX, XX)

Fantasy, Dreams, and the Private Self

Poe: poems; "Ligeia"

Slavery and the Achievement of Selfhood

Jacobs: *Incidents in the Life of a Slave Girl*
Brown: *Narrative*
Douglass: *Narrative of the Life*; *My Bondage and My Freedom*
F. Harper: poems

The Self Triumphant

Emerson: "Self-Reliance"
Longfellow: "A Psalm of Life"; "Excelsior"
Thoreau: *Walden* (especially "Economy"; "Where I Lived"; "Spring"; "Conclusion")
Whitman: *Leaves of Grass* (especially "Song of Myself"; "Live Oak, with Moss")
Melville: *Benito Cereno*
Dickinson: 194; 207; 395; 409; 411; 466; 475; 519; 598; 817; 1163

The Self as Contingent or Imperiled

Whitman: "Facing West from California's Shores"; "When Lilacs Last in the Dooryard Bloom'd"
Melville: *Moby-Dick* (Chapter I); "Bartleby, the Scrivener"; *Billy Budd, Sailor*
Dickinson: 202; 260; 320; 339; 347; 348; 355; 446; 576; 591; 620; 656; 764; 1096; 1263; 1665; 1715; 1733
Davis: "Life in the Iron-Mills"

Volume C: American Literature 1865–1914

In post–Civil War works, the question of American identity joins with other compelling issues. Here are some works useful for addressing issues of personal identity in the modern era.

Twain: *Adventures of Huckleberry Finn*
James: *Daisy Miller*; "The Beast in the Jungle"
Chopin: *The Awakening*
Gilman: "The Yellow Wall-paper"
Freeman: "A New England Nun"
Washington: *Up from Slavery*
Chesnutt: "The Wife of His Youth"
Eastman: *From the Deep Woods to Civilization*
Du Bois: *The Souls of Black Folk*
Oskison: "The Problem of Old Harjo"
Chippewa Songs
Zitkala Ša: "Impressions of an Indian Childhood"; "The School Days of an Indian Girl"; "An Indian Teacher among Indians"
H. Adams: *The Education*

Volume D: American Literature 1914–1945

Black Elk: *Black Elk Speaks*
Masters: poems
Robinson: poems
Frost: poems (especially "The Gift Outright"; "Directive")
Sandburg: "Chicago"
Larsen: *Quicksand*
McKay: poems
Cather: "The Sculptor's Funeral"
Hurston: "How It Feels to Be Colored Me"
Cummings: "Buffalo Bill 's"; " 'next to of course god america i"; "i sing of Olaf glad and big"
Toomer: *Cane*
Fitzgerald: "Babylon Revisited"
Dos Passos: *U.S.A.*
H. Crane: *The Bridge*
Hemingway: "The Snows of Kilimanjaro"
S. Brown: "Mister Samuel and Sam"; "Master and Man"
Hughes: "Visitors to the Black Belt"; "Madam and Her Madam"; "Freedom"; "Madam's Calling Cards"

Volume E: American Literature since 1945

Prose

Bellow: *The Adventures of Augie March*, chapter 1
Miller: *Death of a Salesman*
Paley: "A Conversation with My Father"
Baldwin: "Going to Meet the Man"
Momaday: *The Way to Rainy Mountain*
Reed: *The Last Days of Louisiana Red*
Kingston: *Tripmaster Monkey*

Poetry

Penn Warren: "American Portrait: Old Style"
Bishop: "The Armadillo"
R. Lowell: "For the Union Dead"; "Skunk Hour"
Wilbur: "Love Calls Us to the Things of This World"
Ginsberg: *Howl*; "A Supermarket in California"; "Sunflower Sutra"
Rich: "Diving into the Wreck"

The Individual and the Community

Bradford: *Of Plymouth Plantation*
Mather: *The Wonders of the Invisible World*
Calef: *More Wonders of the Invisible World*
Jefferson: The Declaration of Independence
Hawthorne: "Young Goodman Brown"; "The May-Pole of Merry Mount";
    "The Minister's Black Veil"; *The Scarlet Letter*
Thoreau: "Resistance to Civil Government"; *Walden*
Douglass: *Narrative of the Life*
Whitman: *Song of Myself*
Melville: *Moby-Dick*; "Bartleby, the Scrivener"; *Billy Budd, Sailor*
Twain: *Adventures of Huckleberry Finn*
James: *Daisy Miller*; "The Beast in the Jungle"
Jewett: "A White Heron"
Chopin: *The Awakening*
Freeman: "A New England Nun"; "The Revolt of 'Mother'"
S. Crane: "The Bride Comes to Yellow Sky"; "The Blue Hotel"
Oskison: "The Problem of Old Harjo"
Zitkala Ša: "Impressions of an Indian Childhood"; "The School Days of
    an Indian Girl"; "An Indian Teacher among Indians"; "The Soft-
    Hearted Sioux"
H. Adams: *The Education* (Editor's Preface; Chapters I, XIX)
Cahan: "A Sweat-shop Romance"; *The Imported Bridegroom*
Masters: poems
Robinson: poems
Frost: "The Pasture"; "Mending Wall"; "The Death of the Hired Man";
    "Departmental"; "Neither Out Far Nor in Deep"
Anderson: *Winesburg, Ohio*
Eliot: "The Love Song of J. Alfred Prufrock"; "Tradition and the Individ-
    ual Talent"
Cummings: "the Cambridge ladies who live in furnished souls"; "anyone
    lived in a pretty how town"; "pity this busy monster, manunkind"
Ellison: *Invisible Man*
Morrison: "Recitatif"

The Problem of Literary Authority

Bradstreet: "The Prologue"; "The Author to Her Book"

E. Taylor: "Prologue"; "Meditation 22"; "Upon a Wasp Chilled with Cold"; "Huswifery"

Edwards: *Personal Narrative*; "Sinners in the Hands of an Angry God"

Franklin: "The Way to Wealth"

Wheatley: "To Maecenas"; "To the University of Cambridge, in New England"; "To S. M., a Young African Painter, on Seeing His Works"

Irving: "The Legend of Sleepy Hollow"

Emerson: "The American Scholar"; "The Divinity School Address"; "Self-Reliance"; "The Poet"

Hawthorne: *The Scarlet Letter* ("The Custom-House")

Poe: "The Philosophy of Composition"

Fuller: "The Great Lawsuit"

Thoreau: *Walden*

Douglass: *Narrative of the Life*

Whitman: "Preface to Leaves of Grass"; *Song of Myself*; "Trickle Drops"; "Here the Frailest Leaves of Me"; "As I Ebb'd with the Ocean of Life" "Letter to Ralph Waldo Emerson"

Melville: "Hawthorne and His Mosses"; *Moby-Dick*

Dickinson: 202; 348; 411; 449; 519; 764; 1263; 1577; 1715

Twain: *Adventures of Huckleberry Finn* (Chapter I); "Fenimore Cooper's Literary Offenses"

H. Adams: *The Education* (Editor's Preface; Chapter I)

Washington: *Up from Slavery*

Chesnutt: "The Goophered Grapevine"

Gilman: "The Yellow Wall-paper"

Du Bois: *The Souls of Black Folk*

Black Elk: *Black Elk Speaks*

Stein: *The Making of Americans*

Frost: "Directive"; "The Figure a Poem Makes"

Stevens: "A High-Toned Old Christian Woman"; "Thirteen Ways of Looking at a Blackbird"; "Of Modern Poetry"

W. C. Williams: "Portrait of a Lady"; "The Red Wheelbarrow"; "A Sort of a Song"; "The Dance ('In Brueghel's great picture, The Kermess')"

Moore: "Poetry"; "The Mind Is an Enchanting Thing"

Eliot: "The Love Song of J. Alfred Prufrock"; "Tradition and the Individual Talent"

McKay: "Outcast"; "If We Must Die"

Ellison: *Invisible Man* (Prologue)

Paley: "A Conversation with My Father"

Pynchon: "Entropy"

Bambara: "Medley"

The American Dream

Columbus: letters
Smith: "A Description of New England"; "New England's Trials"
Native American Trickster Tales
T. Morton: *New English Canaan*
Winthrop: "A Model of Christian Charity"
Franklin: "The Way to Wealth"
Equiano: *The Interesting Narrative*
Irving: "Rip Van Winkle"
Emerson: *Nature*
Hawthorne: "Young Goodman Brown"
Fuller: "The Great Lawsuit"
Thoreau: *Walden* (Chapters 1, 2)
Douglass: *Narrative of the Life*
Whitman: *Leaves of Grass* ["Song of Myself"]
Davis: "Life in the Iron-Mills"
Twain: *Adventures of Huckleberry Finn*
James: *Daisy Miller*
Jewett: "A White Heron"
Chopin: *The Awakening*
Garland: "Under the Lion's Paw"
Masters: poems
Cather: "Neighbour Rosicky"; *My Ántonia*
Anderson: *Winesburg, Ohio*
Fitzgerald: "Babylon Revisited"
Dos Passos: *U.S.A.*
H. Crane: *The Bridge*
Steinbeck: "The Leader of the People"
Ellison: *Invisible Man* (Chapter I)
Miller: *Death of a Salesman*
Updike: "Separating"
Mamet: *Glengarry Glen Ross*

The American Landscape

Bradford: *Of Plymouth Plantation* (Book I, Chapters IX, X)
T. Morton: *New English Canaan* (Chapter XIV)
Knight: *The Private Journal*
Byrd: *The Secret Diary*
Crèvecoeur: *Letters from an American Farmer*
Jefferson: *Notes on the State of Virginia*
Freneau: "On the Emigration to America and Peopling the Western
    Country"
Irving: "The Legend of Sleepy Hollow"
Cooper: *Last of the Mohicans*
Bryant: "Thanatopsis"; "The Prairies"
Thoreau: *Walden*

Whitman: *Leaves of Grass* (section 33); "Crossing Brooklyn Ferry"
Twain: *Adventures of Huckleberry Finn*
Jewett: "A White Heron"
Garland: "Under the Lion's Paw"
London: "To Build a Fire"
Cather: "Neighbour Rosicky"
Frost: "The Wood-Pile"; "Birches"; "'Out, Out-'"; "Design"; "Directive"
Sandburg: "Chicago"; "Fog"; "Grass"
Niedecker: "Lake Superior"
Penn Warren: "Bearded Oaks"
R. Lowell: "The Quaker Graveyard in Nantucket"; "Skunk Hour"
Brooks: *A Street in Bronzeville*
Ginsberg: "Sunflower Sutra"
Kerouac: *Big Sur*
J. Wright: "A Blessing"
Snyder: "Milton by Firelight"; "August on Sourdough, A Visit from Dick
    Brewer"; "Falling from a Height, Holding Hands"
Momaday: *The Way to Rainy Mountain*

Immigration and Wandering

Bradford: *Of Plymouth Plantation*
Franklin: "Information to Those Who Would Remove to America"
Crèvecoeur: *Letters from an American Farmer* (Letter III)
Equiano: *The Interesting Narrative*
Freneau: "On the Emigration to America and Peopling the Western
    Country"
Wheatley: "On Being Brought from Africa to America"
Bryant: "To an American Painter Departing for Europe"; "The Prairies"
Thoreau: "Walking"
Whitman: *Song of Myself*; "Crossing Brooklyn Ferry"
Memorial of the Cherokee Citizens
Davis: "Life in the Iron-Mills"
Ruiz de Burton: *The Squatter and the Don*
Twain: *Adventures of Huckleberry Finn*
Native American Oratory (especially Cochise)
Winnemucca: *Life Among the Piutes*
Lazarus: "In the Jewish Synagogue at Newport"; "1492"; "The New
    Colossus"
Cahan: *The Imported Bridegroom*, "A Sweat-shop Romance"
Eastman: *From the Deep Woods to Civilization*
Garland: "Under the Lion's Paw"
Oskison: "The Problem of Old Harjo"
Cather: "The Sculptor's Funeral," *My Antonia*, "Neighbour Rosicky"
Hughes: "Visitors to the Black Belt"; "Notes on Commercial Theatre";
    "Vagabonds"
Malamud: "The Magic Barrel"

Ginsberg: *Howl*; "A Supermarket in California"
Roth: "Defender of the Faith"
Kingston: *Tripmaster Monkey*
Alexie: "The Exaggeration of Despair"

Family Relationships

Cabeza de Vaca: *The Relation* (especially ["The Malhado Way of Life"]; ["Our Life among the Avavares and Arbadaos"]; ["Customs of That Region"])
Bradstreet: "To the Memory of My Dear and Ever Honored Father Thomas Dudley Esq."; "To Her Father with Some Verses"; "Before the Birth of One of Her Children"; "To My Dear and Loving Husband"; "A Letter to Her Husband, Absent upon Public Employment"; "Another [Letter to Her Husband, Absent upon Public Employment]"; "In Reference to Her Children"; "In Memory of My Dear Grandchild Elizabeth Bradstreet"; "In Memory of My Dear Grandchild Anne Bradstreet"; "On My Dear Grandchild Simon Bradstreet"; "To My Dear Children"
Wigglesworth: *The Day of Doom*
Rowlandson: *Narrative of the Captivity and Restoration*
E. Taylor: "Upon Wedlock, and Death of Children"
Sewall: *The Diary*
Byrd: *The Secret Diary*
J. Adams and A. Adams: letters
Irving: "Rip Van Winkle"
Hawthorne: "Young Goodman Brown"; "Rappaccini's Daughter"; *The Scarlet Letter*
Fuller: "The Great Lawsuit"
Stowe: *Uncle Tom's Cabin*
Jacobs: *Incidents in the Life of a Slave Girl*
Brown: *Clotel*
Douglass: *Narrative of the Life*
Stoddard: "Lemorne *Versus* Huell"
Twain: *Adventures of Huckleberry Finn*
H. Adams: *The Education* (Chapter I)
James: *Daisy Miller*
Jewett: "A White Heron"
Chopin: *The Awakening*
Freeman: "The Revolt of 'Mother' "
Gilman: "The Yellow Wall-paper"
Cahan: *The Imported Bridegroom*; "A Sweat-shop Romance"
Wharton: "The Other Two"
Du Bois: *The Souls of Black Folk*
Dreiser: *Sister Carrie*
Zitkala Ša: "Impressions of an Indian Childhood"; "The School Days of an Indian Girl"
Masters: poems

Cather: *My Ántonia*; "The Sculptor's Funeral"; "Neighbour Rosicky"
Frost: "The Death of the Hired Man"; "Home Burial"; "Birches;
　"'Out, Out-'"
Anderson: *Winesburg, Ohio* (especially "Mother")
O'Neill: *Long Day's Journey into Night*
Cummings: "my father moved through dooms of love"
Faulkner: *As I Lay Dying*
Wolfe: "The Lost Boy"
Hughes: "Mother to Son"
Steinbeck: "The Leader of the People"
Roethke: "My Papa's Waltz"
Welty: "Petrified Man"
Cheever: "The Swimmer"
R. Lowell: "My Last Afternoon with Uncle Devereux Winslow"
Brooks: "a song in the front yard"
O'Connor: "The Life You Save May Be Your Own"; "Good Country People"
Ginsberg: "To Aunt Rose"
Sexton: "Little Girl"; "The Death of the Fathers"
Rich: "Snapshots of a Daughter-in-Law"
Barthelme: "The Balloon"
Plath: "Daddy"
Updike: "Separating"
Walker: "Everyday Use"
Beattie: "Weekend"
Silko: "Lullaby"
Ríos: "Madre Sofía"
Cervantes: "Uncle's First Rabbit"
Song: "Lost Sister"

Race, Segregation, and Slavery

Casas: *The Very Brief Relation*
Cabeza de Vaca: *The Relation*
Smith: *The General History of Virginia*
Bradford: *Of Plymouth Plantation* (Book I, Chapters IX, X; Book II,
　Chapter XIX)
R. Williams: *A Key into the Language of America*
Rowlandson: *A Narrative of the Captivity and Restoration*
Byrd: *The Secret Diary*
Occom: "A Short Narrative of My Life"
Franklin: "Remarks Concerning the Savages of North America"
Woolman: *The Journal*
Crèvecoeur: *Letters from an American Farmer* (Letter IX)
Jefferson: The Declaration of Independence
Equiano: *The Interesting Narrative*
Freneau: "The Indian Burying Ground"; "To Sir Toby"

Wheatley: "On Being Brought from Africa to America"; "To S. M., a Young African Painter, on Seeing His Works"; letters

The Cherokee Memorials

Apess: "An Indian's Looking-Glass for the White Man"

Emerson: "Last of the Anti-Slavery Lectures"

Longfellow: "The Slave's Dream"

Lincoln: "A House Divided"; Second Inaugural Address

Stowe: *Uncle Tom's Cabin*

Jacobs: *Incidents in the Life of a Slave Girl*

Thoreau: "Resistance to Civil Government"; "Slavery in Massachusetts"

Douglass: *Narrative of the Life*; "What to the Slave Is the Fourth of July?"

Whitman: *Song of Myself*

Melville: *Benito Cereno*

Twain: *Adventures of Huckleberry Finn*

Native American Oratory

Harris: "The Wonderful Tar-Baby Story"; "How Mr. Rabbit Was Too Sharp for Mr. Fox"

Jewett: "The Foreigner"

Washington: *Up from Slavery*

Chesnutt: "The Goophered Grapevine"

Eastman: *From the Deep Woods to Civilization*

Du Bois: *The Souls of Black Folk*

Oskison: "The Problem of Old Harjo"

Native American Chants and Songs

Zitkala Ša: "Impressions of an Indian Childhood"; "The School Days of an Indian Girl"; "An Indian Teacher among Indians"

Black Elk: *Black Elk Speaks*

Hurston: "The Eatonville Anthology"; "How It Feels to Be Colored Me"

Toomer: *Cane*

S. Brown: poems

Hughes: poems

Cullen: poems

R. Wright: "The Man Who Was Almost a Man"

Hayden: poems

Ellison: *Invisible Man*

R. Lowell: "For the Union Dead"

Brooks: poems

Baldwin: "Going to Meet the Man"

Lorde: poems

Clifton: poems

Harper: poems

Walker: "Everyday Use"

Komunyakaa: poems

Dove: *Thomas and Beulah*

Gender Issues: Women's Lives, Work, and Vision

Winthrop: *The Journal*

Bradstreet: "The Prologue"; "The Flesh and the Spirit"; "The Author to Her Book"; "Before the Birth of One of Her Children"; "To My Dear and Loving Husband"; "A Letter to Her Husband, Absent upon Public Employment"; "Here Follows Some Verses upon the Burning of Our House"

Rowlandson: *A Narrative of the Captivity and Restoration*

Sewall: *The Diary*

Mather: "The Trial of Martha Carrier"

Knight: *The Private Journal*

Byrd: *The Secret Diary*

Edwards: ["Sarah Edwards's Narrative"]

J. Adams and A. Adams: letters

Jefferson: The Declaration of Independence

Irving: "Rip Van Winkle"

Sedgwick: *Hope Leslie*

Sigourney: "Death of An Infant"

Schoolcraft: "Sweet Willy"; "Moowis, the Indian Coquette"

Hawthorne: "Rappaccini's Daughter"; *The Scarlet Letter*

Poe: "The Raven"; "To ———. Ulalume: A Ballad"; "Annabel Lee"; "Ligeia"; "The Fall of the House of Usher"; "The Philosophy of Composition"

Fuller: "The Great Lawsuit"

Stowe: *Uncle Tom's Cabin*

Fern: *Ruth Hall*

Jacobs: *Incidents in the Life of a Slave Girl*

Whitman: "Preface to Leaves of Grass"; *Song of Myself*; "Letter to Ralph Waldo Emerson"

Melville: "The Paradise of Bachelors and The Tartarus of Maids"

Dickinson: 112; 207; 269; 347; 348; 355; 409; 519; 600; 620; 656; 675; 764; 857;1263; 1353; 1577

Davis: "Life in the Iron-Mills"

Twain: *Adventures of Huckleberry Finn*

Harte: "The Luck of Roaring Camp"

H. Adams: *The Education* (Chapter XXV)

Chippewa Songs

James: *Daisy Miller*; "The Real Thing"; "The Beast in the Jungle"

Winnemucca: *Life Among the Piutes*

Jewett: "A White Heron"

Chopin: "At the 'Cadian Ball"; "The Storm"; *The Awakening*

Freeman: "A New England Nun"; "The Revolt of 'Mother'"

A. Cooper: "Woman Versus the Indian"

Gilman: "The Yellow Wall-paper"; "Why I Wrote The Yellow Wall-paper?"

Dreiser: *Sister Carrie*

S. Crane: *Maggie*

Oskison: "The Problem of Old Harjo"

Zitkala Ša: "Impressions of an Indian Childhood"; "The School Days of an Indian Girl"; "An Indian Teacher among Indians"; "The Soft-Hearted Sioux"

Masters: "Trainor, the Druggest"; "Margaret Fuller Slack"; "Lucinda Matlock"

A. Lowell: "The Captured Goddess"; "Venus Transiens"; "Madonna of the Evening Flowers"

Frost: "The Death of the Hired Man"; "Home Burial"

Anderson: *Winesburg, Ohio*

W. C. Williams: "The Young Housewife"; "The Widow's Lament in Springtime"; "To Elsie"; "The Dead Baby"

Pound: "The River-Merchant's Wife: A Letter"

H. D.: "Leda"; "Helen"; "The Walls Do Not Fall"

O'Neill: *Long Day's Journey into Night*

Millay: poems

Cummings: "the Cambridge ladies who live in furnished souls"

Toomer: *Cane* ("Fern")

Dos Passos: *U.S.A.* ["The Big Money"]

Faulkner: *As I Lay Dying*

Hughes: "Mother to Son"; "Song for a Dark Girl"; "Madam and Her Madam"; "Madam's Calling Cards"

Boyle: "The White Horses of Vienna"

Niedecker: poems

Roethke: "Frau Bauman, Frau Schmidt, and Frau Schwartze"

Welty: "Petrified Man"

Bishop: "In the Waiting Room"; "The Moose"; "One Art"

T. Williams: *A Streetcar Named Desire*

Hayden: "Homage to the Empress of the Blues"

Malamud: "The Magic Barrel"

Ellison: *Invisible Man* (Chapter I)

Brooks: poems

Levertov: poems

O'Connor: "The Life You Save May Be Your Own"; "Good Country People"

Ginsberg: "To Aunt Rose"

Sexton: poems

Rich: poems

Plath: poems

Updike: "Separating"

Lorde: poems

Clifton: poems

Walker: "Everyday Use"

Beattie: "Weekend"

Silko: "Lullaby"

Alvarez: *¡Yo!*

Dove: *Thomas and Beulah*

Ríos: "Madre Sofía"

Tan: *The Joy Luck Club*

Erdrich: "Fleur"
Cervantes: poems
Song: poems

Politics and War

Stories of the Beginning of the World: "The Story of the Flood"
Columbus: letters
Casas: *The Very Brief Relation*
Cabeza de Vaca: *The Relation*
Bradford: *Of Plymouth Plantation*
Rowlandson: *A Narrative of the Captivity and Restoration*
Franklin: *The Autobiography* (especially Part Three)
J. Adams and A. Adams: letters
Paine: *Common Sense*; "The Crisis," No. 1; *The Age of Reason*
Jefferson: The Declaration of Independence
The Federalist
Freneau: "On Mr. Paine's Rights of Man"
Wheatley: "To the Right Honorable William, Earl of Dartmouth"; "To His
    Excellency General Washington"
Irving: "Rip Van Winkle"
Hawthorne: "My Kinsman, Major Molineux"
Lincoln: "A House Divided"; Gettysburg Address; Second Inaugural
    Address
Thoreau: "Resistance to Civil Government"
Douglass: "What to the Slave Is the Fourth of July?"
Whitman: *Drum-Taps*; "When Lilacs Last in the Dooryard Bloom'd"
Melville: *Battle-Pieces*; *Billy Budd, Sailor*
Memorial of the Cherokee Citizens
Bierce: "An Occurrence at Owl Creek Bridge"
Native American Oratory
Eastman: *From the Deep Woods to Civilization*
S. Crane: *War is Kind*
Lowell: "September, 1918"
Alan Seeger: "I Have a Rendezvous with Death . . ."
Native American Chants and Songs
Black Elk: *Black Elk Speaks*
Roth: "Defender of the Faith"
Jarrell: "The Death of the Ball Turret Gunner"; "Second Air Force"
R. Lowell: "For the Union Dead"
Brooks: "The White Troops Had Their Orders But the Negroes Looked
    Like Men"; "The Blackstone Rangers"
Komunyakaa: "Facing It"
Cluster: Writing in a Time of Terror: September 11, 2001

CHAPTER 6

Teaching Notes for Authors and Works: Volume A, Beginnings to 1700

Because NAAL contains excellent period introductions, author headnotes, and bibliographies at the end of each volume, these teaching notes emphasize the following:

- Comparisons among individual authors
- Ways of relating literary works to large-scale questions that may work for you as central issues in your course

The main purpose here is to suggest ways to *introduce* material to intelligent, reasonably mature readers who may not initially feel any bond with it or see an access into it. These notes, which are arranged chronologically following the NAAL tables of contents, also suggest ways of encouraging students to think across periods and genres and to sense the development of literary traditions at given historical moments.

Since the mid-1980s, scholars have grown accustomed to talking about "the literature of the Discovery" as a literature about cultural conflict. In bringing together these works from the century or so before the English colonies really began to take root, we have found a compelling drama in the opening encounters between a European and a Native American ethos and about the effect that each wider culture had on the other. Nonetheless, some of your students, who probably know little of that academic dialogue, will have questions like the following in mind:

- How is this material American literature or even a significant precursor of American literature? Much of it was written by Europeans who never thought of themselves as belonging to any place other than their homeland; much of the rest wasn't really "written" in the strict sense at all, but spoken by members of cultures without written language— and in contexts that no commentary can make fully accessible to most of us. And all of this indigenous material was set down—or over-heard, translated, and transcribed by outsiders—a long time ago.

- If many of these works were never even published (in the modern sense) until recently and were not written for publication, then what sort of "reading" are we engaged in here? Are we reading as a literary public? As antiquarians? As intruders?

- Since much of this material was not originally written in English and had no direct impact on later writers who used English—and since this is (in all likelihood) an "English" or "American Studies" class, labeled as such in the catalog, why are we bothering with it? Are we paying po-litically expedient homage before getting on with the real course?

Actually, bewilderment of this kind can be a resource. It can help open up not just honest access to material from early historical periods, but also core issues related to the creation, teaching, and learning of literary history.

This section can also help students reconsider the idea that the most interesting early writings from North America, writings in which the con-tinent and its indigenous people had an impact on the consciousness of the European visitor, were all products of the English explorations and migrations. A drama begins here: a hub-bub of voices in different lan-guages, from different places, the verbal record of what Franklin later described as a "great mixing of peoples from the whole Atlantic basin" and as "a many-sided process of influence and exchange that ultimately pro-duced the hybrid cultural universe of the Atlantic world." Indeed, as the Native American creation narratives indicate, the continent was already "peopled" when the Europeans arrived, and the languages of the native inhabitants of the Americas would also contribute to this hybrid cultural universe. One good effect of including this section in your syllabus is that students can glimpse American experience as multicultural from the beginning, with an array of European peoples encountering a variety of nations already here.

To give students a sense that this many-voiced beginning of American lit-erature is not a dead-end historical moment, you might briefly jump ahead to Cervantes's poem "Visions of Mexico While at a Writing Symposium in Port Townsend, Washington," from Volume E. Here is a living Latina American writer writing in English as the dominant language of the United States, yet reopening for herself the colonial experience and speculating on its connections to her own, and our own, identity. The "Beginnings to 1700" collection invites students to encounter the possibility that Ameri-can literature is more fluid than these boundaries; it invites students to cross them.

Literature before 1620

STORIES OF THE BEGINNING OF THE WORLD

As Arnold Krupat writes in his introductory notes to these creation stories, both the Iroquois and the Pima narratives included here are in a Western chronological sense misplaced, since these versions date from the nineteenth and early twentieth centuries. However, including creation stories in the "Literature to 1700" period of NAAL is pedagogically appropriate. First, these written narratives are transcriptions or translations of oral stories whose origins long precede such transcription. Second, the Iroquois and Pima narratives present a worldview that contrasts markedly with the worldview the colonizers brought with them. Although these mythological narratives do not address the relatively more recent historical period of contact with the European invaders, they serve as representations of early Native American culture. Teaching them side by side with European narratives of invasion and colonization allows students to view their own reading as encounters of cultures as well as of historical persons.

Instructors who assign these materials in an American literature course will probably be coming to them from Western cultural perspectives on mythological or cosmological origins and on narrative forms and elements. And students will probably be in the same situation. Is there a way for most of us to teach Native American materials in the American literature classroom without expertise in these cultures?

The answer has a great deal to do with what we, as teachers, assume that a survey course is about, on the most basic level. A survey, or an introduction, can mean a paying of perfunctory attention or it can mean the opening of a longer acquaintance, deepening and broadening over the years, with many different texts that now belong, or that might belong, in a diverse culture's conversation with itself about its own nature. If you have the latter intention in mind, then two mistakes to avoid in regard to these early Native American materials are probably obvious: (1) a cursory glance that conveys, implicitly or otherwise, the sense that these texts are somehow beside the point; and (2) a presumptuous "analysis" or dramatized empathy, either of which can work the same kind of harm.

We are still rethinking, as a culture, nearly everything having to do with our relationship to these recovered materials: how to read them, in what sort of context, and why. The best strategy, therefore, may be to keep such questions open with your class, assuring students that such issues are not to be dismissed quickly or lightly and that their participation is needed to help move our collective thinking forward. Good strategies for reading these Native American materials, in the very Euro-American context of a modern college or high school classroom, will take shape if literary culture and history can be presented as something changeful, alive, and available to all who read patiently and in good faith.

One influential essay on teaching Native American texts is Barre Toelken and Tacheeni Scott's "Poetic Retranslation and the 'Pretty Languages of

Yellowman,'" in Toelken, ed., *Traditional Literatures of the American Indian: Texts and Interpretations* (1981), a volume that offers many strong suggestions and perspectives. Without discouraging readings by cultural outsiders, Toelken draws our attention to complications of approaching Native American texts across barriers of translation and dislocation. His encouragement to us, to try to proceed in spite of these obstacles and in full cognizance of them, is worth bearing in mind:

> I have encouraged—even forced—my students in recent years to go beyond mere reading of native literature and into the troublesome, frustrating, and often impossible task of recovering something of the original. "But what if we can't speak Tsimshian?" they ask: "How are we to presume we can reconstitute the original presentation properly?" My response is to suggest that—using the materials at hand—we can at least come closer to real presentation than is now provided for us in the awkwardly serviceable and often primitive-sounding prose translations of linguists who were not anyhow as involved in the study of live literature as in the recovery of almost moribund languages. (69)Another good essay about the complications of reading these texts in English translations, and in the context of the American college campus, is Paula Gunn Allen's "Kochinnenako in Academe," in Robyn Warhol and Diane Price Herndl, eds., *Feminisms* (1991). Allen proposes a "feminist-tribal" approach to Native American narrative, which allows readers to understand the kinds of agency that Native American narratives give women. For Allen, these stories can be read as about balance rather than conflict, about agency rather than heroism, and about background rather than a possibly overvalued foreground. The art she speaks of, running counter to Western expectations, is about a "living web of definition and depth" and emphasizes the "importance of balance among all elements." As Allen describes it, "tribal art functions something like a forest in which all elements coexist, where each is integral to the being of the others." See also Allen's *The Sacred Hoop: Recovering the Feminine in American Indian Traditions* (1986).

Obviously there are limits to how much contextualizing material can be included in anthologies covering four hundred years and many North American voices. Nonetheless, the help in this guide, along with the headnotes and other Native American materials in NAAL can take us fairly far—at the very least into a recognition that other cultures were present, active, and imaginatively engaged at the time of European settlement. Students should understand that the American experience was being looked at passionately, and from many perspectives, as European and native cultures encountered one another.

The Iroquois Creation Story

Because of the shifts in context and expectations required to engage with these works, it is important to devote some class time to a close reading of them. But close reading, the way one closely reads Bradstreet or Eliot, will not take students where they want (or expect) to go—that is, to a full understanding of the human sensibility in these texts. That may have to wait, and you may need to reassure your students that patience and comfort with uncertainty are required of all mature readers who seek to move across time, landscape, and large cultural barriers. As you assign other Native American texts, these will create an intertextuality, and instructors will receive much help from the headnotes and introductory materials in NAAL in providing the historical and oral/literary contexts for Native American stories and storytellers.

For this first experience with Native American mythology, you might encourage your students to read comparatively, bearing in mind the creation stories that most of them already know and scrutinizing the differences between these Native American creation myths and accounts from other cultures. Two interesting differences to note right away: first, these Native American stories do not enforce a distinction that most students are used to—a distinction between the Creator and world created—and second, these stories do not talk about a world somewhere else—an Eden, a Mount Ararat, or some other landscape far away from the experience of the listener or reader. The world spoken of is a world that is right here, to be gazed on and known firsthand as the tale is told again and again.

These differences matter because, for most of your students, reading these stories will require acknowledging certain habits of mind, habits of imagining and telling, that are culturally contingent and yet rarely recognized by us as paradigms, as ways of organizing not just experience, but also our narratives about experience.

As an exercise to stimulate discussion and an awareness of such differences, construct with students a visual "map" or interpretive sketch of the events of the Iroquois Creation Story. You will probably develop a diagram with a vertical axis: the woman who conceived (note Krupat's reference to one version in which she conceives parthenogenetically) begins in the "upper world" but falls to the "dark world," where "monsters" collect enough earth to make a seat for her, on which she gives birth to the twins, the good mind and the bad mind. In *Native American Literature* (1985), Andrew Wiget provides a useful diagram that suggests connections between specific events in origin stories and genres of Native American oral narrative. The twins transform the earthen seat, the Great Island that the monsters have created for the woman who fell, into a world that begins to resemble a world of humans rather than of mythical people; indeed, the story ends with the twins retiring from the earth, as the creation has been accomplished. Wiget's diagram maps three "generations" of beings: the original parent (the woman who fell from the sky), the twins (one of whom, the good mind, creates the earth and, by deceiving the bad mind, sets in motion the "nature of the system" we know as the world), and the first people with souls (who come to inhabit the universe).

Within these three levels, numerous narratives are possible; the Iroquois Creation Story that students have before them is only one variant of a story whose main elements may be relatively fixed but whose details change in its communal and participatory retelling. Communal participation results from viewing creation as a process of descent rather than as a one-time construction in a single god's image.

Students may also read the creation account in the Book of Genesis and compare elements: descent in the Iroquois story suggests a process of creation rather than the completed act of a single creator; the woman who fell from the sky may have become parthenogenetically pregnant, thereby linking the origins of the world to women (or to an asexual being capable of parthenogenesis) rather than to a patriarchal god (note that the Iroquois were matrilineal); and the monsters in the "dark world" are benign compared with the devils that inhabit Western conceptions of hell, and these monsters actually help the falling woman give birth. The good twin creates "two images of the dust of the ground in his own likeness," unlike the single male image the Western god creates in Genesis, where the female image is later created from a rib of the male.

Another exercise that helps open up the Iroquois Creation Story for Western-oriented students involves making a list of the characters in the myth and trying to determine each one's particular contribution, without which the creation would not be complete. While a Western narrative might suggest that the woman who fell from the sky and the good twin are "central" characters, the Iroquois story highlights the importance of the other characters and the interdependence of all. The turtle, for example, who offers to endure the falling woman's weight and who enlarges to become an island of earth is essential to the origin of the world, as are the contrivances of the bad twin, without whom we would not have mountains, waterfalls, reptiles, and the idea that even the good twin's powers are limited (as are those of humans). This suggests that there is no human agency without help from a variety of participants and that all creative powers must know their limits. If possible, read Wiget's beautiful interpretation of the story of the woman who fell. He says, in part, that [t]he Earth-Diver is the story of the Fortunate Fall played out against a landscape more vast than Eden and yet on a personal scale equally as intimate. It is a story of losses, the loss of celestial status, the loss of life in the depths of the sea. But it is also the story of gifts, especially the gift of power over life, the gift of agriculture to sustain life, and the gift of the vision to understand man's place as somewhere between the abyss and the stars.

Pima Stories of the Beginning of the World

These stories focus on two prevalent themes in Native American creation myths: the "woman who fell from the sky" and the "emergence" of the world. One of the images that distinguishes the emergence narrative, connecting the Pima myth to it, is Juhwertamahkai poking a hole in the sky with his staff and emerging through this hole into another dimension, where he begins his act of world creation anew. Some scholars have suggested that this movement is a metaphor for the numerous migrations of Native American peoples, and that these myths may implicitly record those migrations.

In discussing this story, students might try some comparisons, locating similarities and differences between Iroquois and Pima myths and among other Native American and Western versions of "genesis." Unlike the

Judeo-Christian tradition, which favors one story of origin, Native American traditions offer many creation stories, as if this wide and fecund world required many exploits to get it going.

At first glance, the Pima Story of the Creation resembles the narratives of the Book of Genesis more closely than the Iroquois story. In the Pima, as in Genesis, the world begins "in the beginning" with a person who floated in the darkness; in Genesis, the spirit of God hovers over the darkness. Even so, recognizing the perils of the transcription is crucial to "reading" the opening of this story, for the language of the English transcription itself echoes the language of Genesis—and those echoes could have been wished for by the English-speaking translator as much as inherently there in the original text. Later on the story ceases to resemble Genesis. Indeed, Juhwertamahkai makes several mistakes in the process of creating the world. Unlike the Western god, whose destruction of the world by flood is blamed on human behavior, Juhwertamahkai takes a trial-and-error approach to creation, starting over or letting the sky fall each time the creative act sets in motion a process that will not sustain life. As the headnote points out, he makes the world four times before he is satisfied with his creation, establishing the number four (corresponding to north, south, east, and west) as significant in Native American cosmology.

The Pima Story of the Creation includes the birth of Coyote, the trickster of many Native American legends, and the arrival of Seeurhuh, or the elder, who in this story seems to move the creation into a world of negotiation between powerful personages who "claimed to have been here first," perhaps suggesting the process of relating stories about the organization of the social world into native cultures.

In the Pima Story of the Flood, Seeurhuh, or Ee-ee-toy, and Juhwertamahkai seem to engage in a struggle—not about creation but about *recreation*. This is an interesting theme and a promising basis for a conversation.

Questions for discussion:
- In the Pima stories, what details indicate imbalance in a social order, a cause for turmoil?
- Although Juhwertamahkai has already created people, Ee-ee-toy makes a man of his own, arming him with bow and arrow. Can we say why? The arrival of the flood is linked to the birth of a child from the young man who turns into a pregnant woman; the birth produces springs that "would gush forth from under every tree and on every mountain." What can we say are the themes that bring the flood and the birth together?
- Juhwertamahkai and Ee-ee-toy, and the person/animal Toehahvs (Coyote) face directions that may signify territories or tribal lands, and they make new dolls, or persons, to replace those who have drowned. Juhwertamahkai deliberately makes dolls that will not survive, "because he remembered some of his people had escaped the flood thru a hole in the earth, and he intended to visit them and he did not want to make anything better than they were to take the place of them." Why this emphasis on impermanence and imperfection?

- Can the Story of the Flood be understood as an attempt to explain and understand death as well as the origins of the world? How are these two enormous facts of human experience, life and death, brought into order or contact by these stories?

CHRISTOPHER COLUMBUS

Using Columbus to get the course started and open questions about the "literary" status of personal accounts and letters written centuries ago in languages other than English, and in immensely different cultural situations, can be ideal, because Columbus became a huge figure in the mythology of the Americas. You could loosen the class up with a quick review of old and newer artifacts of that legend: the cities, rivers, and countries named after him, the countless statues in public parks and squares, the two handsome tombs (he is buried in grand style in Havana and also in Seville, and there is still no settlement to the dispute over which church has the real remains!), and the two big-budget films released in 1992 to mark the five hundredth anniversary of the San Salvador landing. The literary impact of Columbus shows up in the hagiographic biography by Washington Irving; the once-popular epic poem by Joel Barlow; and even the jokes in Twain's *Innocents Abroad,* in which European guides expect American tourists to be floored by the sight of any object related to the Great Discoverer. All this can raise student interest in trying to hear the actual voice (more or less) of the actual human being who started the whole drama of European conquest and settlement.

Reading these letters as showing us a figure of deep and unresolved conflict reveals an element of psychological familiarity in Columbus. There is piety here, and covetousness, and self-righteousness, and pride, and political servility and manipulation, and these mingled inclinations and drives, even when seen through the thick distorting glass of so much intervening time, can make him seem eminently real. If one of your course objectives is to make these readings memorable and accessible, then attention to these very familiar contradictions can take the discussion in good directions.

Questions for Discussion:
- What happens if you read Columbus's 1493 letter with his 1503 letter, in which he complains bitterly of his own abandonment and betrayal and reveals his disillusionment with the experience of colonization?
- What do these letters suggest about the relative value of kings and great cities, the power of Spanish explorers, and the relative "importance" of the "people without number" who already inhabit the islands?

BARTOLOMÉ DE LAS CASAS

The selection from Casas's *Very Brief Relation* will open up interesting questions about assumptions held by Spanish explorers in their treatment of the Native Americans and challenge the notion that all these explorers were blind to the human worth of the people they encountered or mindless apologists for colonialism.

Questions for discussion:

- If we speculate on Casas's motives as a writer, what can we say? He witnesses horrors in the Spanish treatment of native peoples, and the moral outrage expressed by this rough-and-tumble soldier-adventurer seems to be based in Judeo-Christian teachings and ethics.
- Casas's *Very Brief Relation* can be seen as the opening of a long and important dialogue in the literature of North America, as writers on this continent try to reconcile political and social practice with religious values and to close the rift between professed creeds and actual practice. In other courses, have your students encountered other, later authors who base their interventions on similar principles? A bit of foreshadowing in regard to the ways in which America will quarrel with itself can be effective here.

ÁLVAR NÚÑEZ CABEZA DE VACA

Amid the legacy of exploration histories and reports, Cabeza de Vaca, even in translation, achieves a voice that actually sounds unique and human, and students may respond strongly to the sense that finally, among all of these accounts, a distinct personality is in evidence. His interest in detail is different: he writes of customs and people with respect and genuine curiosity. His *Relation* attempts to present the native peoples' way of life as much as possible from the inside.

Questions for discussion:

- What moments do you find in Cabeza de Vaca's *Relation* that suggest unorthodox thinking for his time and culture, an imaginative and independent wanderer?
- This is the first author we encounter who shows a measure of interest in the lives of women and who makes some headway in understanding and communicating with various American Indian groups. What passages in his narrative do you find especially interesting as early attempts at good-faith intercultural encounter?
- One remarkable glimpse of how Native Americans respond to Cabeza de Vaca's respectful curiosity about their way of life emerges in [The Falling-Out with Our Countrymen], where the local people refuse to believe that Cabeza de Vaca and his group were from the same race as the "Christian slavers." What ironies are embedded in this episode, as Cabeza de Vaca tells it?

THOMAS HARRIOT

As noted in the comments on Cabeza de Vaca, encounters between the Spanish explorers and the American Indians reveal contradictions within the conquest that cause moral and imaginative crisis for some of these writers. This internal contradiction may seem more muted to students in early English narratives, but there are enough similarities between Spanish and English encounters to suggest patterns.

After reading Cabeza de Vaca, students may find Harriot less perceptive or curious about the native peoples he encounters. You might ask students to look for signs in Harriot's text of seeing the world from fresh perspectives: early in his *Brief and True Report*, he writes, "In respect of us, they are a poor people, and for want of skill and judgment in the knowledge and use of our things, do esteem our trifles before things of greater value."

Questions for discussion:
- In Harriot's view, what does Native American mythology, as he encounters and interprets it, demonstrate to him about these peoples?
- When Harriot dismisses as absurd the Native American belief that "a woman was made first, who by the working of one of the gods, conceived and brought forth children," what values and assumptions are implicit in his judgment?

JOHN SMITH

Smith is an imaginative writer, a dramatist and self-dramatist as well as a chronicler and advocate for European settlement. With Smith, many students may find themselves in comfortable territory—not just because Smith, an Englishman, has become part of the American mythology but also because his narrative is different, and more familiar in shape and pace, than the others encountered thus far. Students may want to look at *The General History of Virginia* as an American adventure story and observe ways in which it configures actual events and experiences to appeal to a London audience. The moment of encounter has passed, for Smith, and the shift to settlement and exploitation has begun. Indeed, Smith's job was to make the Americas safe for colonial growth, and as his *General History* demonstrates, when "trade and courtesy" failed, he resorted to force.

Smith's account of Pocahontas may be highly fictionalized, and students may want to take note of another instance of this archetypal story of a young woman who crosses cultural boundaries and changes the world. If students want to talk about the Disney restyling of this story, or Terence Malick's spectacular *The New World* (2005), or other ways in which the "history" has been reworked to reflect values of other times in our cultural heritage, why not encourage them?

Questions for discussion:
- Smith's explorations unfolded during a golden age of English theater. What hints of theatrical thinking do you see in Smith's account of his own adventure?
- As a cultural myth in the United States, Pocahontas does not come down to us in the way that La Malinche does in Mexico. How do we account for the difference? In Mexico, the myth of a treacherous Doña Marina represents the betrayal of one culture to another—but this is a founding story for a nation where native peoples and Europeans have commingled. In the myth of La Malinche, she betrays Mexico itself, yet

Mexico is in a sense descended from that betrayal. What are the ironies in that story, and how do they compare to implicit ironies in this tale of John Smith and an Indian princess?

NATIVE AMERICAN TRICKSTER TALES

The headnotes to this section will be invaluable for your students and should be read carefully, not just for their cautions and suggestions about historical context but also as a basis for considering whether "literature" can have any stable description across times and cultures and whether transformations worked by the passage of time and change of context and language are invariably a loss, harm, or gain.

One cautious generalization that we can begin with is that these stories are about change, about shape-shifting: change in physical form; change in relationships among natural and supernatural creatures (including human beings); changes of mind and intention. Furthermore, from a European perspective these narratives seem to shape-shift in terms of mood and mode: farce gets mixed up with the sacred; bawdiness and scatological humor break out in places where a listener from outside these cultures might least expect them. There are elements in these stories that can make them seem like caricatures of a creation story; there are also tales here that seem didactic or etiological—lessons in how to be careful and how the natural world came to be as it is.

How can we account for this? If you live in a subsistence culture in the midst of a vast natural landscape and, therefore, see indications, every day, that creation is an ongoing process rather than something that happened far away and long ago, what might be the effects of that on the way that stories are told? In other words, if you perceive the events and consequences of one of these trickster tales as timeless or as a process that not only continues but involves the participation of the teller and listener as the story happens as a literary and cultural event, how might those very different assumptions affect the shaping of a narrative?

Students could have much to say, therefore, about the way that the world is categorized and stabilized by certain basic structures in narratives constructed in the European tradition and the way that emotional and psychological experiences are blended in some of these Native American texts. Even so, to go from that generalization, or from any other, into conventional close reading or a hunt for parallels or universal themes and motives is to move in a direction that the headnotes caution us against. No amount of academic guidance, in the context of a broader and ongoing survey, can prepare us to read and understand a Chinook tale from a Chinook perspective, a Navajo tale from a Navajo point of view, and so on, because the very ideas of telling, of listening, of fiction, of truth, and of belief can vary so much among Native American cultures.

Questions for discussion:
- We can take guidance from the recurring emphasis on change, on shape-shifting, and talk also about the shape-shifting of literary texts—Native

American or otherwise—from the oral to the written, from one culture to another; from the popular world to the solemnity of academe; from the notepad or the popular edition to the portable Hall of Fame that an anthology can signify to many students. These Native American story-tellers and listeners seem to participate in the making of the world by the very act of saying, by repeating reverently and irreverently, and adapting boldly; by conserving lore and visions, dreams and wisdom; and by giving them new shapes for new cultural situations. What are the fundamental differences between that idea of telling, and of hear-ing, and the assumptions we commonly have in mind as we look at a printed text in a classroom?

• Later on, when students consider contemporary Native American writ-ers like Leslie Marmon Silko and Louise Erdrich, they will see writers on a quest to accomplish something akin to what these ancestors did: to keep old tales alive by reconfirming their relevance and making them new. A discussion that entertains such problems can broaden into important considerations for your students as they negotiate these texts or wonder about the process and ritual of the survey course and what they themselves are being asked to do, and are doing on their own, as they infuse these deeply foreign yet deeply American texts with their own imagination. Where else in their cultural experience do they encounter that paradox: the strange-sounding or strange-looking text or work of art that is nonetheless inherently from our own world, our own expanded and diverse contemporary culture?

Literature between 1620 and 1700

To open this period, you could ask students first to imagine the passage from seventeenth-century England to the New World: the violence and dis-ruptions of the old country and the unknown terrors of the new one; the loss of home, of kinship, of worldly possessions (these ships were very small), of so much that matters to one's personal and cultural identity. It's also a good idea to spend some time on the sheer physical risk of this kind of disloca-tion. The Roanoke Colony had been wiped out without a trace; a year after the landing at Plymouth Rock, half of the *Mayflower* Pilgrims were dead. Religious warfare raged in Europe; civil war would soon break out in the En-glish homeland, and a succession of religious upheavals and political changes over the previous half century had claimed tens of thousands of lives.

If you're hoping that your students will find ways to empathize with the New England Puritan mind and not regard the whole group as grumpy, hopelessly repressed, inhuman zealots, then it may be a good idea to estab-lish what mortality meant to these people, how very close at hand it was, and how it could affect all phases of life—not just belief but ideas of family, of career, of the worth of any human action or enterprise.

The Massachusetts Bay Colonists were primarily, though not exclusively,

Puritan in ideology, which meant that most believed in the literal authority of the Bible. They saw the Bible as a topological model for their own lives (Puritan writers use biblical metaphors to explain the Puritan condition; they often refer to themselves, for example, as Israelites, and the New World becomes Canaan). You will probably need to outline several basic tenets of Puritan thought: original depravity (we are born sinners), limited atonement (no worldly ritual or prayer will ensure salvation; no human action or gesture of faith obliges the Almighty to respond), and predestination (God has chosen his elect before we were born).

For the sake of keeping this a *literature* course and avoiding disappearance into theological arguments that very few of us are competent to handle properly, you might want to approach predestination (if you approach it at all) as an example of the rigorous logic that flourished in Reformation theology, partly as a result of the unprecedented empowerment of the reader and the exhilaration and terror of trying to discern Divine Will on our own. From the perspective of ordinary life and the writing of imaginative literature, predestination is almost a moot point, and students who go round and round with the matter run the risk of doing so at the expense of attention to the texts you are reading together.

Here a few key matters:

- Puritans viewed the Bible as God's covenant with them; they saw themselves as a Chosen People and identified strongly with the tribes of Israel in the Book of Exodus. In reading both Testaments, they concluded that God, though sometimes arbitrary in His power, is neither malicious nor capricious.
- Doers of evil suffer and are destroyed; true believers and doers of good may suffer as well, as worldly misfortune is both a test of faith and a signifier of God's will.

In sum, covenant theology taught that although no human being can ever know for certain whether or not he or she is among the saved, the only hope lay in rigorous study of Scripture; relentless moral self-examination; and active, whole-hearted membership in these congregations.

Again, if we are looking for lasting cultural effects, ways in which this theological system, and the consciousness it shaped, continue down through many generations and cultural moments, then it's worth backing away at the end of your summary to ask students to speculate on what those effects might be. The list you come up with might run something like this:

- With no central religious authority, and an expectation that each member of the community should encounter Scripture and theological prose firsthand, New England Puritanism would be strongly influenced by a drive toward solidarity and consensus and by a championing of individual thought. These conflicting values would become clear in the collision between the Colony's elders and Anne Hutchinson, less than ten years after the founding of Boston.

- An emphasis on individual responsibility, on a direct and personal relationship with God, and on the acquisition of knowledge in anticipation (or hope) of the coming of Divine Grace could be a powerful force for the education of women, and eventually for their political and social equality.
- A belief that salvation required, and would be signified by, achievement of absolute integrity among faith, worldly conduct, private life, and the spoken and written word would eventually figure centrally in the rise of abolitionist sentiment: race slavery becomes not an economic expediency or a social problem to be overlooked and eventually remedied but a mortal sin, threatening the moral condition of the society and every individual within it. The long-term effects of this kind of thinking are enormous. Nearly two centuries later, *Uncle Tom's Cabin* was constructed around a similar proposition.
- A belief in a special destiny and a conviction that what was unfolding in New England was the last and best hope of the Christian world. Cataclysmic changes in London in the middle of the seventeenth century and the erosion of solidarity in the colony after the Restoration and with the passage of years would bring those convictions into crisis at century's end.
- A special emphasis on reading correctly—not only holy texts but commentaries and the events of ordinary life. The New England Puritans were an intellectual people who believed firmly in portents, symbols, and the significance of all that happened in private and public life.

WILLIAM BRADFORD

Of Plymouth Plantation is an excellent foundation for the study of colonial American literature, as it offers a portrait of hopes and expectations central to the New England Puritan mind, and it shows us how an idea of destiny, and an expectation that all worldly experience is meaningful and must be "read," organizes Bradford's account of the colony's first years. Everything seems to matter: prosperity, misfortune, natural events, even outbreaks of indecency, which your students will probably find hilarious. If you are hoping to demonstrate key qualities of the seventeenth-century Puritan consciousness, assumptions and beliefs that echo down through New England literature for hundreds of years, those qualities are strongly evident in Bradford.

The earlier selections from *Of Plymouth Plantation* help students visualize the practical and spiritual concerns of the earliest colonials. In trying to find a harbor (Book I, Chapter X), the "lusty seaman" on board the shallop reminds the pilot to row "or else they were all cast away." Bradford's account reveals the necessity for self-reliance among the first Puritan settlers; only after they reach "the lee of a small island" can they afford to give thanks to God "for His mercies in their manifold deliverances." Students may be surprised to discover how secular and pragmatic the Puritans had to be in the process of creating their spiritual New World. In Book I, Chapter IV, Bradford cites physical hardships, premature aging, lack of control over their children, and only last (if not least) their hope of "propagating and advancing the gospel of the kingdom of Christ" as the Puritans' reasons for "removing" to the "vast and unpeopled countries of America." How does Bradford's text challenge undergraduate students' preconceptions of the Puritans and their literature?

Among the selections from *Of Plymouth Plantation*, [The Remainder of Anno 1620] deserves special attention in class discussion. Bradford writes that the document was "occasioned partly by the discontented and mutinous speeches that some of the strangers [non-Puritans aboard the *Mayflower*] amongst them had let fall from them in the ship." How does what Bradford calls "the first foundation of their government in this place" establish a Puritan community from the beginning as one that excludes "strangers"? What evidence is in the compact that even before landing the Puritans defined themselves as an elect group? And what implicit effect does writing and signing the Mayflower Compact have? Putting their first agreement into written form was an act of major significance for the Puritans, who believed in the Bible's literal truth and authority. Written words, from the beginning of American culture, carry the associative power of God's word.

Questions for discussion:
- What does the writing of the Mayflower Compact indicate about the importance of divine authority?
- How do these excerpts from *Of Plymouth Plantation* recall later moments or patterns of thought in American history, even in our own time? Compare Book I, Chapter IV, with Book II, Chapter XXXII, as early attempts to rationalize colonial life. Where do we see Bradford's logic come under pressure?
- As Bradford records successive years in his history, he continues to convey a pattern of rise and fall, of end prefigured in the beginning. In "[Proposed Removal to Nauset]," he describes the split in the church that resulted from the removal, and characterizes the "poor church" as "an ancient mother grown old and forsaken of her children." Do the selections from Book II in particular suggest an altered view of our colonial origins?

THOMAS MORTON

Morton makes a wonderful pairing with Bradford, especially if you want to focus on relationships between cultural values and literary style. Morton, as the headnote tells you, was anything but a Puritan, and his intentions in settling at Merrymount were worldly pleasure and profit, not the fulfillment of grand destinies or the founding of the New Jerusalem. We know little about his life, but his prose speaks volumes.

Questions for discussion:
- Read aloud a few opening lines from the Morton selection. When the student gets lost in the forest of show-off prose and esoteric allusions,

build some questions from that confusion: is this kind of writing actually meant to communicate clearly? Could it be intended to strike a posture and convey a certain kind of social position and comradeship? Morton seems to know what he is doing, and he is sending his London audience a message that unlike these dour and austere colonists, he is "one of us," an urbane Englishman who loves a good time, fancy dress, courtly manners, and florid writing styles.

- If your students are coming to you with some experience of Renaissance English literature, urge them to stop worrying about the allusions that break out everywhere in Morton. Instead ask them if they can say what this prose *sounds* like? If somebody says Shakespeare, you have a good connection to build on; you're closer to the mark if they say Sir Toby Belch or Falstaff, affable rascals who escape blame and accusations not by denying the charges against them but by being charming and by engaging in farce as an act of self-defense. Morton knows what he is doing: in retelling the taking of his settlement by Standish and the other Puritans, Morton makes the event a slapstick encounter between good-natured revelers and a sneaking band of Malvolios who threaten to close down all good times in the New World.

- As you move in a bit closer: do Morton's allusions and metaphors come from a different storehouse than do Bradford's or Winthrop's? The earlier Puritan writers (with the exception of Bradstreet, whose refreshing independence and range we shall look at it in a moment) have turned away from the classical (favored by Shakespeare, Donne, Jonson, and most of the best writers of the English high Renaissance) and draw their metaphors chiefly from Scripture. Compared to Morton's, their prose is as plain and clear as the dress they favored—and a stop with *New English Canaan* will bring home the fact that the difference between the Puritan sensibility and that of the non-Puritan English middle class affected the choice of words and the workings of the imagination.

John Winthrop

"A Model of Christian Charity" gives students the earliest example of a Puritan sermon delivered in the New World (or, technically, en route to the New World, because Winthrop delivered it while still board the *Arbella*). Students can comment on the image patterns by which Winthrop characterizes the community he envisions, and they can discuss the discursive form of this sermon as an example of the key literary genre of seventeenth-century Puritan culture. If students in a historical survey course are beginning to wonder whether these early writings have any resonance in our own time or show us any literary motifs or imaginative habits that continue to this day, then it's worth spending time with the City on a Hill metaphor, unpacking its meaning, looking for its analogues in Judeo-Christian history, and noticing where similar core beliefs—that Boston or Chicago or the whole United States is a beacon for humanity and the destiny of the world—continue to show up in our own culture and public discourse.

Questions for discussion:

- Winthrop's *Journal* offers examples of typology and evidence of principles of exclusion and special mission, principles that animated the government and the collective ethos of the Bay Colony. How can we account for the fervor of Winthrop's reaction against Anne Hutchinson and her doctrine of personal conscience, which would seem, from some perspectives, quite in keeping with the general religious tenets of the colony?

- Why does Winthrop go to such lengths to seek evidence that Hutchinson is dangerously wrong and has lost favor with God? What are the implications, and possible dangers, that can arise from that kind of close reading of worldly experience?

- We have here a famous public speech and also a private journal. One of these documents was widely known in Winthrop's own time; the other was not published until centuries after. In constructing a literary history, how much should these differences figure into our thinking as we try to identify landmarks in a cultural past?

THE BAY PSALM BOOK

From the first book published in English-speaking North America, these versified psalms were recited and sung in Puritan church services and other gatherings for generations after. These poems influenced New England writers from an early age; and in the twenty-first century the *Bay Psalm Book* can tell us much about the tastes and objectives of colonial New England with regard to the printed word. Felicity and delight were not what these verses were for. The great causes were personal salvation and the education and unity of imperiled congregations—and lines "hammered out foursquare" (to borrow a phrase of Robert Lowell's) could root deep in the mind and also represent the austerity and simplicity that signified righteous living for the first waves of Bay colonists.

But despite their firm importance in American cultural and literary history, these poems may require some careful situating when they are brought into the classroom. For at least three decades there has been controversy about applying essentially secular aesthetic analysis to religious texts, the ethics and intentions of teaching "The Bible as literature" generating the most heat. Obviously sensitivity about this practice will vary from place to place and year to year—and with the *Psalm Book*, as with *The Day of Doom* and the devotional writings of Jonathan Edwards, you may need to open this issue with your class, and explain what you're intending to do together, before you launch into an engagement with any of these poems. If your group is comfortable with trying to search for underlying aspirations and purposes, I'd recommend centering on psalms that will strike chords of recognition among some of your students, psalms that are regularly recited, in their King James version or one of various modern translations, in many different religious and public ceremonies. The obvious choices are Psalms 19 and 23 and the two versions of Psalm 100.

Questions for discussion:

- Read aloud one of the *Bay Psalm Book* psalms and then read aloud the same psalm in the King James version—the Church of England translation that was fresh and authoritative at the time of the Bay Colony's founding. You might try several readings until your class is comfortable that they have found the appropriate sound of each version, revealing the poetry in each. What are the differences in language and effect?
- The King James translation was, in its time, the most meticulous and scholarly effort ever undertaken to render the Old and New Testament into English, with fidelity to Latin, Greek, and Hebrew sources. Versification of a prose source almost always requires a manipulation of that source—but the Puritans were also fervently committed to knowing and promulgating Scripture as accurately as possible. Comparing these versions of the psalms, where do you see moments that the *Psalm Book* undertakes this kind of manipulation for the sake of rhyme and meter, striving to keep faith with the meaning of the original text? What are the results?
- As the NAAL introductions make clear, one crucial motive for the founding of the Massachusetts Bay Colony was pilgrimage into a new and Promised Land, for the founding of a "city on a hill" cleansed of old values and practices. How do the colony's versified psalms exemplify that wish?

ROGER WILLIAMS

Some of your students could be stunned by this encounter with Williams, one of the first voices in an American liberal tradition, emerging suddenly in the midst of the New England seventeenth century. You can have a vigorous dialogue about a clash of values and ethics here—Williams versus Winthrop is the obvious face-off. But in a course about literature and culture, the energy of such a conversation could be channeled along the way into an encounter with Williams as a stylist, building his prose and framing his arguments in a difficult context. Drawing from, and also resisting, the assumptions and tropes that characterize the discourse of other colonists, Williams is one of the first American authors to assume an especially powerful imaginative and intellectual position—within a culture, and on the edge of it, quarreling as kin.

Questions for discussion:

- If you begin with the brief "Letter to the Town of Providence," you can obviously read it with Winthrop's "A Model of Christian Charity." Williams and Winthrop admonish their respective communities by recourse to history and analogy. Read aloud three or four sentences from Williams, beginning with "It hath fallen out sometimes" (bottom of page 186), and compare them to Winthrop's lines beginning with "Thus stands the cause between God and us" (middle of page 157). What are the differences in the analogies that they choose?

- The introduction to *A Key into the Language of America* also uses analogies and comparisons to describe the native peoples of New England. What are the implications of Williams's choices? How do they resist conventional Bay Colony thinking about these peoples?
- At other places in *A Key into the Language of America*, Williams adopts the "1, 2, 3" enumeration of propositions and perceptions, an organizational form favored by Puritan homilists. Why might he do this—and what does he do stylistically to set himself apart from the tradition of the homily?

Anne Bradstreet

Bradstreet can be a breakthrough moment in a survey or major authors course. After a sequence of historical accounts that may be interesting chiefly as artifacts rather than as living and compelling literature, we suddenly come upon creative genius, a writer whose verse still seems limpid, courageous, and profound and who would command substantial space in any good anthology of Anglo-American verse. As one delighted student recently described the discovery of Bradstreet: "Finally, I can hear one of these writers breathing!"

Bradstreet's poetry may "breathe" because it presents a conflict, a conflict that may have been inherent in living a secular and a spiritual life in a Puritan colony. In the small city of Boston (never more than a few thousand people in her lifetime), she was a public figure, a leader in her congregation, and eventually the wife of the governor. She was also a mother and a grandmother, and as such she had to reconcile Holy Writ with human love, and human fear, for her immediate and extended family. And in Bradstreet's verse we can hear as well the voice of a woman pleased by the richness of non-Puritan English literature, by the sometimes outlandish art of Renaissance verse, and by the whole alluring and dangerous heritage of the Western imagination.

Questions for discussion:
- It's been suggested often that there at least two voices here, sometimes in harmony, sometimes in contradiction. One of those voices, whom you might call "Mistress Bradstreet," is the poet-voice who speaks as she ought, in full accord with religious doctrine, public duty, and conventional belief. The other voice, "Anne," is the woman who loves, grieves, fears, feels pride, and experiences the full range of emotions and curiosities that the teachings of her faith were supposed to put to rest. In the drama of her poems, sometimes one side of her seems to win out and sometimes the other; sometimes a reassuring harmony is reached and sometimes not. Look over the set of Bradstreet poems in NAAL, and ask yourself which of them, in their titles, seem to suggest one voice or the other. When you settle in to read these poems, do you find any surprises—discontinuities between the voice that seems implicit in the title and the voice or voices that emerge in the actual poem?

- Read aloud "The Author to Her Book," a poem that employs a metaphor that is downright dangerous, especially in a poem from a colony where women could be severely punished for adultery. Why might Bradstreet make that choice—and how does the tone and the context of the poem provide some validation and protection?
- The darkening mood of the three elegies for her grandchildren, a sequence in which the doctrinal consolations seem to console less and less, will also catch the attention of your class and increase receptiveness to the great poems of family love and domestic life. Read these poems aloud, in sequence, listening for that change of mood, and then look carefully to see what language choices and rhetorical strategies establish those contrasts. Who is speaking in which poem—Mistress Bradstreet, or Anne, or both?
- Pause over "Before the Birth of One of Her Children" and offer some background about the enormous medical risks of bearing a child in the seventeenth century, noting the frequency with which young women died of "childbed fever" and the situation of orphans in a near-subsistence culture with no social services. How does knowing that Bradstreet was looking at very real possibilities, alter our understanding of the intention and tone of the poem?
- What does "The Prologue" reveal about Bradstreet's struggle to locate literary authority within herself? Is she really as self-deprecating as a quick first reading of the poem might suggest? How does she assert her own achievement despite the poem's apparent apologetic tone? What are the several meanings of the line "It is but vain unjustly to wage war" in the context of Bradstreet's self-assertion?
- Is Anne Bradstreet a true Puritan writer?

Michael Wigglesworth

The Day of Doom may present difficulties for students unless you suggest what to look for as they read. This was the first New England bestseller, a fact that will astound some members of your class, and you can ask them to speculate on why it lasted so long and did so well. What does it tell us about what New England Puritans thought a poem was for?

In some ways this is a tale of terror that makes use of some of the same horrifying surprises and rhythms that propel our endlessly popular gothic fiction. The surprise twist makes a reappearance in works centuries after, like *Uncle Tom's Cabin*, in which St. Clair, as a decent and supposedly Christian and humane sort of slave-holder, is almost ready to free his slaves when without any warning he is stabbed and killed, bringing doom not only to himself but to his entire household.

Questions for discussion:
- In the poem, what specific evidence can you find of important tenets of Puritan theology? How can we characterize Wigglesworth's contrast between the saved and the damned? Read aloud stanzas 107–8 on page 226 in which a plea goes up from well-intentioned mortals, people who

were planning to seek salvation more vigorously. Why might Wigglesworth single out this group, to give them voice—and also to let us hear
the divine response?
- How can we summarize the portrait of hell in this poem, and what passages here suggest the nature of family relationships in Puritan New
  England society?
- How might Bradstreet's "Here Follows Some Verses upon the Burning
  of Our House, July 10th, 1666" pick up a different sound or implication, once we've been made aware of how soon after Wigglesworth's
  poem of 1662 it was written?

MARY ROWLANDSON

A *Narrative of the Captivity and Restoration* can fascinate students and
help them make thematic connections among several Puritan writers. Students will want to speculate about Rowlandson's purpose in writing this narrative: is it a personal account or essentially didactic—or are the purposes
mingled here? Rowlandson's story will come alive for your class not merely
because it includes mayhem and heartbreaking suffering but also because
Rowlandson shows us a conflicted sensibility. Her conflict grows straight
out of two Puritan premises: first, that the Indians are agents of Satan,
emblems of the Philistines, and the unforgivable enemies of her own Bay
Colony group; and second, that as a Puritan she is obligated to look steadily
and carefully at worldly experience and understand fully what it signifies.
Therein lies the conflict: though she suffers terribly among her captors and
sees much to confirm her impression of some of them as creatures from
hell, she encounters others who do not seem so, who indeed seem capable
of humanity and even of charity.

Questions for discussion:
- How does the narrative compare with other Puritan works that show
  triumph or redemption after suffering?
- What do the poems of Bradstreet and the *Narrative* of Rowlandson,
  when looked at together, suggest about the fears and anxieties that
  shadowed ordinary life for women in Puritan society?

EDWARD TAYLOR

Taylor's extended metaphors and intricate poetic forms are not evidence
of showing off like a Cavalier poet back in England. His devotional verses,
most of which were kept private in his lifetime, demonstrate the energy and
intellectual focus that characterized spiritual introspection among the Puritans of New England. You can get your students to focus their attention on
Taylor's use of poetic form by asking them first to describe the stanzaic patterns of any of the Preparatory Meditations and then to examine his development of conceits, his elaborate controlling analogies adapted from the
metaphysicals. "Prologue" works well for line-by-line analysis, especially by
way of contrast with Bradstreet's poem of the same title, as it clearly shows

Taylor's awareness that his spiritual salvation and his poetic imagination depend on each other.

One of Taylor's personal quests, as a Puritan pastor, is to demonstrate to himself over and over again that his mind and heart are truly open to divine grace, and one demonstration of that openness is the capacity to see evidence of that grace everywhere in worldly experience. Accordingly, there are poems here that show a mind in crisis, in a quest of inspiration, consolation, complete faith—not a mind in peaceful possession of all these virtues.

Questions for discussion:
- Looking at "The Preface" from *God's Determinations*: What is the relationship between "nothing man" and "Might Almighty"? What kind of coherence is Taylor seeking, in his repetition of "nothing" and "might," "all might," and "almighty" throughout the poem?
- Several of these poems make reference to children. In what spirit and with what intentions are they invoked?
- Comparing Bradstreet's "To My Dear and Loving Husband" with Taylor's "Huswifery" can demonstrate the major differences between these two preeminent Puritan poets. Bradstreet is interested in worldly life; she seems aware of love as a physical tie; she views heaven as a consequence of human faithfulness; she chooses imagery from daily life and classical mythology. In Taylor's contemplation of the spinning wheel in motion, doing its work, who or what is missing—and why?

Samuel Sewall

Of the judges who presided at the Salem witch trials, Sewall is remembered as the most intellectually rigorous and courageous. We have a sampling here of his private thoughts and some of his more stunning public utterances. Sewall seems a slow, thorough thinker, willing to acknowledge error in his own life and his community and to accept consequences. If students are surprised by the moral conclusions of "The Selling of Joseph," published at a time when Boston economic and religious life were largely oblivious to race slavery, they can be encouraged to think about how Sewall arrives at this controversial affirmation: through exegesis, the same kind of rigorous reading and interpretation of Scripture that had propelled the Puritan quest and community through much of the seventeenth century.

Questions for discussion:
- How does the devotional and meditative content of Sewall's diary compare with themes and intentions in Edward Taylor's poems?
- What relationship can we discern among Sewall's commitment to "great exercise of mind," "Spiritual Estate," and his interest in ordinary daily life?
- We have indications here of a Puritan temperament and intellect both on duty and off and struggling for reconciliation among the various sides of the self. How does Sewall's diary complicate our thinking about personal life, public responsibilities, spiritual obligations, and human

relationships in Puritan society more than sixty years after the colony's founding?

COTTON MATHER AND ROBERT CALEF

The headnote to Mather points out that *Magnalia Christi Americana* remains an important Puritan document for its portraits of Bradford and Winthrop, but your students may find more to excite them in the excerpts from *The Wonders of the Invisible World*, Mather's history of the Salem witch trials. They may judge him harshly for his militant enthusiasm for these inquests and executions. As the best-remembered justifier of this persecution, he is often presented as a hysterical last gasp of Puritan fervor before the Enlightenment washed up on New England shores. That might not be fair to Mather, and if students read the excerpts from *Magnalia*, you could have a good and more balanced discussion of Mather's concept of greatness and its deep connection with goodness.

New to NAAL, the excerpt from Robert Calef's *More Wonders of the Invisible World* is interesting as a direct response to Mather but also as an early instance of an anomaly that will grow in complexity and difficulty as publishing booms in later centuries and as technologies allow private interactions to become almost instantly public and even global at the touch of a button. Calef publishes a Mather account that Mather himself had not yet published; and drawing Mather into an exchange of letters, he publishes those as well—and there is no clear indication that Mather had anticipated that his heated reply to an Ipswich neighbor would end up in print, in the bookstalls of the London metropolis, as part of Calef's attack on the trials. E-mail and the web create this kind of confusion and trouble every day, and students might enjoy thinking about Calef and Mather as an early signal of what was to come, the shattering of boundaries between public and private writing.

Questions for discussion:
- Compare Mather's biographical writings to contemporary biography: in a supposedly true representation of a personality and a life, what do we look for now, compared to what Mather was seeking as he reviewed the lives of the colony's founders?
- In *Wonders of the Invisible World*, read aloud the sentences beginning "We know not, at least I know not, how far the delusions of Satan" (bottom of page 309) and comment on their reasoning and the tone. In modern retrospect, Mather is often represented as a depraved witch hunter. But he was also a scholar and a scrupulous logician. Is there a convergence or conflict here of different motives and habits of thought?
- Calef might qualify as the first American investigative journalist. History may have absolved him, but how do his methods compare to those you seen in play in investigative journalism today?

CLUSTER: "A NOTABLE EXPLOIT":
HANNAH DUSTAN'S CAPTIVITY AND REVENGE

Obviously it's easy to sit comfortably in twenty-first-century armchairs and pass moral judgment on an "exploit" involving people in desperate circumstances more than three hundred years ago, an exploit that comes down to us through muddled and sketchy oral accounts and embellished retellings. The story of Hannah Dustan provides a touchstone for explorations in that art: the infusion of the past with the imagination of a given historical moment. In his private pages Samuel Sewall tells the story brusquely, and with a wry undertone that flickers elsewhere in his prose; Mather pours on the adjectives from the same bin he exploits in *Wonders of the Invisible World*; Carver gazes back through the lens of the Enlightenment; and Thoreau writes it all again as nearly-idle thoughts on a river excursion.

Questions for the discussion:

- Compare a couple of important allusions in two accounts: Mather's reference to the story of Jael and Sisera in the Book of Judges in the Old Testament and Carver's closing praise of Dustan for her "Amazonian intrepidity." Check the details of the story of Jael and Sisera (in which a righteous woman does her duty by killing an enemy king in the night, while he sleeps, by driving a tent peg into his temples) and find out something about the Amazons as figures in Greek mythology. Why does Carver turn to the classical, and Mather to Scripture, to set Dustan in an historical and literary context?
- Whittier breathes romantic life into the account, going so far as to invent dialogue. Is this going too far? If Mather is telling a tale of righteous retribution and Carver a tale of Amazonian courage, what kind of story is Whittier trying to tell?
- Of the various accounts, Thoreau's may seem the most peculiar—and it is possible that some prior knowledge of Thoreau and *Walden* and Concord Transcendentalist thought can help us understand the motives and temperament that are in evidence here. What about the proportions of this narrative? Why does Thoreau focus so much attention, ultimately, on the natural setting through which Hannah flees after the killings? Why the final attention on that still-living apple tree? In the historical record, and the reimagining of that history, what matters most to Thoreau?

CHAPTER 7

Teaching Notes for Authors and Works: Volume A, American Literature 1700–1820

The previous chapter opens with a summary of basic tenets and lasting intellectual and imaginative effects of New England Puritanism. As you move forward from the turn of the eighteenth century, you might need to emphasize to your students that Puritanism did not evaporate, as a powerful religious, moral, and literary presence, right after the Salem witch trials; or with the end of the Great Awakening; or with the unpacking, on American shores, of a few popular texts from the English and continental Enlightenment. The eighteenth century and the first years of the nineteenth can be effectively presented as an ongoing interaction between an Age of Reason and an Age of Faith, a time when new ideas and older ones commingled in sharp minds and strong American literary texts. We begin to shift attention southward, toward colonies where other values were growing and local culture was taking different directions. The colonists visit each other, compare, and experiment with the pluralism and empiricism that played a major role in the thinking of the Revolutionary period, and the intellectual and imaginative courage that supported a new literature for a new republic.

SARAH KEMBLE KNIGHT

Knight writes as one of our first homegrown tourists, traveling down the East Coast with a keen eye and a playful curiosity. Students may enjoy the secular truculence of her voice and want to compare it to Rowlandson's, perhaps speculating on what may be happening to the status and voice of colonial women. Students might be puzzled by the apparent strangeness of New York to Knight's Boston sensibility, especially now, when the territory between Beacon Street and Manhattan can seem like one amalgamated supercity.

Questions for discussion:
- What insights does Knight offer about different cultures flourishing in what we now regard as close proximity and about the challenge of forging one nation out of these differences and the attendant mutual suspicions?
- How would we describe Knight as a moment in the evolution of a feminist voice on this continent? What are the implications of seeing independently, of establishing a distance between the self and the worlds one visits, and of reporting one's judgments crisply in words, even if only in a "private" journal?
- A larger and more ungainly question that could be posed now and revisited later is, in constructing a history of American feminist discourse, do we transform Knight somehow when we bring her journal into the light and situate it with works that, unlike it, were written for public reading and response?

William Byrd

Students sometimes need reminding that not everyone who settled in the New World in the seventeenth century was a Puritan, and that we give special emphasis to the Bay Colony because of its inhabitants' uncommon fervor and outpouring of printed eloquence and not because they were here alone. Down the coast, in climates that seemed milder in spirit as well as in weather, colonies flourished with considerably more attention to worldly gain and comfort and less worry about matters that were overwhelming in the culture of New England: salvation, absolute fidelity to Scripture and religious principle, reconciliation of all dimensions of the self. Byrd goes to church like every Virginia public man of his time—but when he quit those precincts his devotional thinking seems to quit as well. A man of action—politician, businessman, slaveholder, patriarch—Byrd compartmentalizes his own existence in ways that can amuse and astound. And as for his inner life, his scrutiny of his own soul—at times is hard to see those episodes as more than another sort of callisthenic "dance," a brief exercise in toning up.

Questions for discussion:
- What happens if we compare Sewall's *The Diary* with Byrd's *The Secret Diary*? How does the Virginian Byrd's view of life differ from that of his New England Puritan counterpart? In form and apparent intention, Byrd's regular writing in his "secret diary" resembles the Puritan practice of introspection and meditation. But students will find it a refreshing contrast.
- Have a look at Byrd's favorite repetition at the end of his entries, about "good health, good thoughts, and good humor, thank God Almighty." Is this a prayer? If so, is it the sort of prayer that Bradstreet, Winthrop, or Taylor would offer?

- Again, we face an open and complex question that came up with regard to Sarah Kemble Knight or Samuel Sewall—the transformation, much later, of private discourses into components of a public and collective literary heritage. If none of these three writers had large numbers of readers or literary followers in their own time or for generations after, how should we think of them as presences in the American canon?

JONATHAN EDWARDS

The Edwards selections in NAAL can be introduced as visits to the highest, fullest achievement in New England Puritan prose but also as the epitome of the male Puritan mind: in New England literature before 1750, only Bradstreet ranks with him in creating, on the printed page, a passionate, intellectual, complex, yet integrated sensibility.

Students should understand that even this long after his death, Edwards still ranks as a major American philosopher and theologian—a rigorous, systematic thinker. His brimstone sermons are more widely read by modern undergraduates than are his careful readings of scripture and the natural world or his gentle personal narratives. The contrast in his tone can cause problems: conditioned by contemporary pop culture, some students may assume that any preacher with a fiery delivery is a hypocrite. It may be important, therefore, to make clear from the start that Edwards lived what he believed, and that the blameless life (which has withstood generations of skeptical review), the rhetoric, the devotion to family, and the relentless scholarship and theological inquiry coalesce into an integrated self and into the first great intellect to emerge in Puritan New England.

A reading of "Personal Narrative" allows us to contrast the Puritan Edwards to the Quaker John Woolman; it also shows us Edwards responding to the richness and theological challenge of Enlightenment thinking. Edwards took on the challenge of organizing and strengthening Calvinist theology to meet eighteenth-century scrutiny, a scrutiny based in logic, in science, and in a belief that the individual mind, propelled along by healthy skepticism and common sense, could find its way to truth. The contrast between Edwards and Franklin and the response of Edwards to the likes of Franklin offer a dramatic opposition and a way to move from the New England Puritans to the secular world of the Federalists.

If you decide not to have students read all of the Edwards selections, you can make headway reading "Sinners in the Hands of an Angry God," not as a work of antisecular fanaticism but as a triumph of relentless logic and powerful belief. The earlier sermon, "A Divine and Supernatural Light," helps provide a context, a demonstration that those same commingled intentions—to read Scripture accurately, to follow logic wherever it might take you, and to believe wholeheartedly—could guide a Puritan consciousness to a vision of grace and peace and to a vision of damnation.

Questions for discussion:
- In analyzing "Sinners" in the classroom, consider tracing the evolution of semantic meaning in the sermon. Edwards takes a verse from

Deuteronomy as his text: "Their foot shall slide in due time." Paying the verse exegetical attention, he achieves this interpretation: "There is nothing that keeps wicked men at any one moment out of hell, but the mere pleasure of God." Hereafter, the logic moves relentlessly, and the passion of the sermon rises with it. Even in the "Application," where attention turns from the "they" of the Old Testament to the "you" of the congregation before him, he never lets up on his relentless, Scripture-founded inquiry, and the tone of "Sinners" remains one of enlightened compassion, not condescension or wild accusation. What connections can we make between the intellectual genius of the sermon, its relentlessness and its rhetorical power, and far gentler discourses for which Edwards is also remembered?

- In "A Divine and Supernatural Light" and the short sketch of Sarah Pierpont (the woman who became his wife), Edwards tries to define religious conversion and describe its outward signs and inner life; "Sinners in the Hands of an Angry God" terrifies the unconverted—and like Huck Finn, students may feel that hell has more interesting literary possibilities than heaven. What are the challenges of writing about the supremely beautiful? In "A Divine and Supernatural Light" and in the tribute to Sarah Pierpont, Edwards tries to find words for the infusion of the Holy Spirit. Read passages from these works aloud and look for moments of success and struggle in conveying these themes.

Cluster: Native Americans: Contact and Conflict

This cluster, as one of a pair providing a sample of Native American public discourse from the eighteenth and nineteenth centuries, plunges us into a contemplation of media power, crucial in the construction of history and the survival of swaths of human experience. By 1820, white Americans had the iron presses; the huge new Fourdrinier machines for making abundant paper; the roads and boats and soon the railroads for moving the printed word all over the settled regions. Moreover, the towns and villages of the United States communicated in only a handful of languages, not scores or hundreds of dialects with no easy transcription to the page. As a result, the voices of the Native American spokesmen (they are all male at this point) come down to us with strange and unsettling resonations: the others, the strangers, are the ones who transcribe and promulgate, and they do so on their own terms.

Samson Occom is the rarity in this first group, as one who assiduously mastered English, taught in it, and wrote in it—and later in life came to have second thoughts about his accommodation to white ways and Christian practice; the others are brought into our language and our medium— print—by white men with uncertain credentials and motives. In another place in this guide I suggest that ascribing quaintness to the speech of a people you mean to displace is a common and effective strategy: elegize the unwanted others out of the way, mourn for them while they're still above the earth. It's not surprising that Chief Logan's Spartan epitaph for himself and his people became so famous in its time and after—it's an apt inscription for a monument for the dead, not a call to engage with the living. Pontiac and Tecumseh and Red Jacket were also defeated leaders, and the ritualized utterance that they leave behind also has an inevitable aura of elegy to it. One challenge to us, now, as we read through this thick scrim of time and emotionally inflected transcription, is to breathe life into this discourse and not hear it as outtakes from a Cooper novel or a Hollywood film from the forties or the fifties.

Questions for discussion:
- Read aloud the final paragraph of the speech of Pontiac (page 440) and the closing lines of Logan's message, as set down by Jefferson (page 444). Between oral discourse and written discourse, what are the crucial differences in reaching and holding the attention of an audience? How does each passage reflect its provenance as *spoken* literature rather than as words created for print?
- Pontiac offers a speech about mission and destiny, and he does so by means of a story about "the Indian" and "the Master of Life." How should we think of this story—as a kind of Scripture, like an episode from the Old Testament? As a fable, rather than as a retelling of history or an established myth? In other words, how does Pontiac use personal imagination and the collective past to reach his listeners at a moment of crisis?
- Red Jacket and Tecumseh in their respective speeches (again, as translated and transcribed), make frequent reference to "brothers" and brotherhood. Why such emphasis, at that historical moment, upon fraternity and unity?

BENJAMIN FRANKLIN

For your students, the transition to Franklin may be quite easy. They have known Franklin since the second grade as a benign and grandfatherly American icon, and (for the first time since Morton!) they are now in the company of someone with a modern-style sense of humor. Overall, Franklin is going to seem, particularly in contrast to the Puritans, refreshingly contemporary, and a good way to begin engaging with him is to ask why he strikes us that way.

What could be shocking about Franklin, from the point of view of a Jonathan Edwards or any fervent New England Puritan, is his breezy acceptance of unreconciled conflicts and discontinuities in his own system of values. The Puritan quest for complete integrity among all of one's words, public actions, private life, and cherished principles is replaced by a quest for maximum worldly effectiveness and exemplary citizenship—and the condition of the soul seems to have little to do with his plan.

One can begin with a look at the famous rules that he lays out for himself in *The Autobiography* as a method for achieving a kind of perfection. With delight, students will notice the hedge about "venery"—to be used "rarely" for purposes other than "health or procreation," meaning that it's okay to go on a tear once in a while, provided you do it discreetly and don't disturb others. And they may jump at the paradox inherent in trying to "imitate" both "Jesus and Socrates," as if there were no differences between these moral models and as if such "imitation" weren't in itself a problem in trying to achieve "humility." When Franklin encounters such dilemmas (as he does here), he escapes with a wink and a joke. Students will have much to say about that as an intellectual and moral strategy and about whether or not a Puritan thinker would ever allow himself or herself an evasion of that kind.

Franklin's life and his "instruction" through his *Autobiography* transform daily routine into something resembling a religious practice. Practical life itself seems to become his secular or deistic "religion," governed by precepts, self-discipline, and a consistent desire for worldly self-improvement, so that Franklin's work can be seen as both deriving from Puritan religious method and reacting against it. You might need to make clear that materialism and greed evidently aren't the motives that propel Franklin but an assumption that civic, intellectual, scientific, and charitable action constitute the only self worth caring about and the only self that the Almighty (who Franklin imagines as somebody much like himself—busy, intellectual, reasonable, benign, undogmatic, and forgiving) cares about either. Students will have fun considering the implications of Franklin's use of the word "erratum" in describing moral failings and his refusal to use the word "sin."

Questions for discussion:
- What similarities and essential differences can we see between Franklin's "Project of arriving at moral Perfection" and the Puritan practice of rigorous introspection and meditation? Franklin writes that "daily Examination would be necessary," and he uses a "little Book," duly lined, "on which Line and in its proper Column I might mark by a little black Spot every Fault I found upon Examination to have been committed respecting that Virtue upon that Day." What is familiar about this practice—and what makes it radically new?
- How does *The Autobiography* reveal Franklin to be an eighteenth-century man? In what ways does he adapt what he calls the "Age of Experiments" to political and personal life?
- What does Franklin's plan for the "union of all the colonies" have in common with his thinking about other matters? Franklin is motivated by the advice he receives to "invite all wise men to become like yourself"—and students can get a clear picture of Franklin as both a self-made man and a "self-invented" one. Franklin offers his life as a blueprint, a repeatable experiment, evidence that an American can resolve the confusion involved in being a colonial by inventing himself or herself as a new kind of person.
- Franklin's other prose both confirms and enlarges on his self-portrait as a rational man. Discuss Franklin's use of satire, especially in "Rules by Which a Great Empire May Be Reduced to a Small One," as an eighteenth-century rhetorical device. Compare the form of "Rules" with the numbered, discursive, rational forms that William Bradford

attempts (see *Of Plymouth Plantation*, Book I, Chapter IV) and Jonathan Edwards perfects (see especially "Sinners in the Hands of an Angry God") and evaluate the power of Franklin's work. If we discern the serious theme behind each satirical observation, what can we say about Franklin's logic here, about its process and its underlying assumptions?

JOHN WOOLMAN

Read in conjunction with the Jonathan Edwards materials, Woolman's *Journal* extracts can help students see that many core values of Puritanism endured throughout New England as deism gained favor and flourished in the thinking of writers who belonged to very different congregations. In reading Woolman's *Journal*, students may wonder what was so alien about the Quakers that the Puritans felt a need to persecute them. This curiosity may lead into a good discussion of similarities and differences between Woolman's beliefs and those of the major writers of the Bay Colony.

Woolman's emphasis on the inward life or "inner light" of the Quakers may recall the development of individual voice in the poetry of Anne Bradstreet rather than the didactic poetry of Taylor or Wigglesworth. Woolman's *Journal* suggests a yearning for faith connected more to feeling than to the kind of "delight" that Edwards celebrates, a delight borne of rigorous reasoning and close reading of Scripture. Ask students to think about connections among the expression of self-reliance in Bradford's *Of Plymouth Plantation*, the description Woolman offers of "inward life," and the assumptions that promoted Franklin's popularity in Quaker Pennsylvania.

Questions for discussion:
- What does Woolman mean when he writes that "true religion consisted in an inward life?"—and how is this different from the theology of Edwards?
- What are the ways in which Woolman's *Journal* illustrates a split within colonial religious and philosophical thought and a different orientation toward worldly experience?

J. HECTOR ST. JOHN DE CRÈVECOEUR

Letters from an American Farmer meditates on the now-famous question "What is an American?" If there is a measure of truth in the old adage that one universal American trait is the constant reopening of this very question, then a very long and culturally important discussion may begin here with Crèvecoeur's attempt to make an answer. Crèvecoeur asserts that in America "the rich and the poor are not so far removed from each other as they are in Europe" and implies that the United States has been founded as a classless society. Crèvecoeur also notes the near barbarousness of some of the pioneers and finds strength and cultural promise in that lack of a European-style sophistication. Indeed, as his narrative reveals in Letter XII, he prefers to accommodate himself to life with the Indians more than with some of the Europeans who have become settlers in the American woods.

A variety of European philosophers and historical crises seem to influence Crèvecoeur's thinking, and it might be worth asking your students to suggest what these are. There are moments when he sounds like Hobbes, like Locke, even like Rousseau—and students may want to discuss this correlation. Throughout a discussion of Crèvecoeur, asking students to locate both his assumptions and his contradictions will help them read the letters in their historical context and identify their significance for present-day readers.

Letter IX offers an implicit contradiction to Crèvecoeur's affirmation in Letter III that "we know, properly speaking, no strangers," when he describes coming on the caged African who has been left to die. The letter ends with his report that when he asked why the slave had been punished in this manner, "they told me that the laws of self-preservation rendered such executions necessary." Letter X, in which he writes about the mortal conflict between a black snake and a water snake, seems a rather gloomy parable, and students may want to speculate on its implications. If we read this parable as being about the relationship between power and corruption, then, given the brief span of years the letters cover (from about 1769 to 1782), we might observe that it didn't take long for Crèvecoeur to arrive at a view of American life that more accurately reflected the contradictions inherent in the creation of the United States than the utopian vision reflected in Letter III, particularly when he writes, "we have no princes, for whom we toil, starve, and bleed; we are the most perfect society now existing in the world."

Questions for discussion:
- Is this a body of thought that grows out of American experience or is his thinking, and his hope, imposed on American experience or adapted to it from some other culture or body of wisdom?
- In response to Crèvecoeur's question "What is an American?" some students may want to ask, what does he mean by an American?

JOHN ADAMS AND ABIGAIL ADAMS

In the letters of John and Abigail Adams, students can see the rare intersection of public and personal life in colonial America and evidence of an intimate relationship between two people. Organize class discussion of the letters by asking students to list the various conflicts that each of these writers reveals in his or her letters: Abigail is concerned with smallpox, a lack of pins, and other domestic troubles; she fears war with England; she's afraid that others might read her letters; and she takes pride in her connection to John's work. John is concerned about keeping his private identity alive, even as he attends to the affairs of the new Continental Congress and labors to ensure the survival of a new country. Both are capable of praising and chiding in the same letter and of complaining about the other's lack of attention or expression of feeling. John's letter of July 20, 1776 (less than three weeks after the signing of The Declaration of Independence), opens, "This has been a dull day to me," because a letter he had expected to receive from Abigail did not arrive.

John and Abigail Adams transcend the formal requirements of eighteenth-century letter writing and allow feeling to interrupt form. Indeed, Abigail statedly prefers those letters in which John transgresses conventional form, writing about one of his letters, in hers of July 21, 1776, that "I think it a choise one in the Litterary Way, . . . yet it Lacked some essential engrediants to make it compleat." She wants from John more personal discourse and more words "respecting yourself, your Health or your present Situation." These letters exist within the dual contexts of personal relationship and political change, and the rapid shifts in the discourse reflect the way attention to audience changes the use of language, even in the late eighteenth century.

THOMAS PAINE, THOMAS JEFFERSON, *THE FEDERALIST*, AND THE DECLARATION OF INDEPENDENCE

Throughout the 1700–1820 period, we have been observing the way in which each shift in thinking retains old forms. The need that the Mayflower Puritans felt for a document to clarify and stabilize their shared values is the earliest example of this. In the writings of the Federalist period, the pattern continues. Madison, in *The Federalist* No. 10 (1787), argues that one advantage of union is "its tendency to break and control the violence of faction." His concern that factions be controlled by a union laid out in writing suggests his close kinship with Puritan thought in regard to the authority of the written word.

Like Franklin's *Autobiography*, The Declaration of Independence is a blueprint, an experiment that the French would soon emulate, and another important moment in the invention of an American polity and identity. Yet students may not do more than skim it outside of class, because they read it in high school or because they feel that they are somehow "living" it. It has the aura of a sacred text, and you may find it necessary to discuss, the legitimacy of looking at The Declaration as a literary work, a work with special rhetorical qualities and power, a work that was actually written by human beings, not dictated from the heavens. Ask your students to consider the way it "invents" history, as Franklin invents his own life in *The Autobiography*. Do they see a resemblance, in sheer use of the English language, between The Declaration and the sermon form, especially in "Sinners in the Hands of an Angry God?" Compare the language with Franklin's in "The Way to Wealth." Whatever else you teach from Jefferson and the Federalist era, The Declaration of Independence is a central work that can be read closely with students.

OLAUDAH EQUIANO

Equiano's *Interesting Narrative* gives students a new perspective on life in the American colonies. Although the original version of The Declaration of Independence includes a reference to the slave trade (see the changes Jefferson notes in the text included in his *Autobiography*) and although during the writing of the Constitution the prohibition of the slave trade was discussed, stipulations concerning slavery were omitted from the Constitution, and Congress was formally prohibited from abolishing the slave trade for at least twenty years. That is the historical context in which Equiano was writing, and the narrative provides a rare and stirring firsthand account of life in Africa, the internal African slave trade (Equiano's own father owned slaves), and conditions on the slave ships themselves.

The American world that Equiano depicts enshrines the merchant. King, the Philadelphia merchant, eventually keeps his promise and allows Equiano to buy his freedom. Equiano does so by becoming a merchant himself. Cargo thus becomes central to Equiano's freedom; he begins as "live cargo," becomes a trader in various goods, and literally reverses his fortunes. Unlike the authors of later slave narratives, such as Frederick Douglass, Equiano does not achieve freedom by finding his voice. Neither does he feel compelled to keep silent. By including his manumission papers in his narrative, he seems to suggest that, indeed, it is only a reversal of fortune, not his own power, that has produced his freedom, for the "absolute power and domination one man claims over his fellow" that allowed Robert King to emancipate Equiano equally allowed other white men to enslave freeman Joseph Clipson.

Question for discussion:
- One of the first questions you might raise with students concerns the inclusion of Equiano's narrative in NAAL. What makes it interesting as "American" literature?

CLUSTER: WOMEN'S POETRY: FROM MANUSCRIPT TO PRINT

This cluster of eighteenth-century women poets—most of whom had all but vanished from American literary history before their recovery by NAAL—offers a very good opportunity for your class to step back from close analysis, take a breath, and engage instead with some larger issues. As you know, your students live in a moment when "publishing" can be a back porch with a global reach, sometimes intentionally, sometimes not. A personal narrative, a joke, a poem, a polemic, a short video uploaded with the click of a key to MySpace or YouTube might reach nobody or millions of people, and there's no sure way of knowing in advance where these documents will end up. Most of the poets gathered into this cluster wrote for family, or circles of friends, and if they published in their own lifetime, these chapbooks were handprinted in small runs paid for by the author or someone close—they were keepsakes rather than "editions" or "books" in the modern sense of these words.

Even so, the poems collected here can be sorted out, at least for a start, into poems that seem like performances or obligatory works and poems that seem more intimate, less ceremonial. Odes to General Washington and demonstrations of craft, like samplers of embroidery, commingle here with poems to husbands and special friends. As a first step, you could ask your students to try sorting the poems themselves and to debate which poems should go into which stack. Afterward, a discussion could build on questions like the following:

- Are there are differences in voice, in sound, between the "public" poems and the private ones? If so, how could you describe those differences?
- Mercy Otis Warren's "To A Patriotic Gentleman" seems to be caught in a predicament of sorts: it's a poem to a friend who has asked for a performance, a show of poetic skill, and also, implicitly, for a commentary on both poetry and friendship. Where and how in the poem does Warren blend a response to those demands? When Anna Bleecker's poem addressed to "Peggy" turns to General Washington about a dozen lines from the end, what is the effect?
- A couple of these poems portray the poet as under psychological stress: for example, Warren's "A Thought On the Inestimable Blessing of Reason," Bleecker's "On the Immensity of Creation," and Faugères's elegy "To Aribert." Each of these poems follows conventional forms—quatrains, rhymed couplets, rime royal. What relationships do you sense among that formality, the tone, and the emotional effect of each poem?
- Which of these poets strikes you as achieving the most original style or sound, and why?

JUDITH SARGENT MURRAY

NAAL7 offers broader experience with Murray than was available in previous editions, and students can compare her prose and her themes as she moves from a polemic about gender inequality into didactic fiction following a classic eighteenth-century pattern. Before settling in to discuss the gender politics that energize both of these texts, it's worth spending some time with the tone and rhetoric of the essay and its epigraph poem and also with the voice, or voices, that students might discern in the excerpt from "History of Miss Wellwood." The tone in "On the Equality of the Sexes" is subtle and blended, and it may take your class a while to hear some of its components, the playfulness and wit mixed in with the combativeness and rage. By this point in the course, students should be developing a sense of how to hear various rhetorical strategies, how to listen to the rhymed couplets and relatively simple language of Murray's verse in the epigraph as opposed to the declamatory classical style put on by Sarah Morton. They may also be able to hear the exuberance and the agility in that first, almost endless onrush of a paragraph, that torrent of rhetoric and rhetorical questions with which Murray overwhelms a supposedly male reader. What stereotypes is she playing with here, in the very structure of her prose? When does she good-humoredly seem to give ground, concede small points or admit the truth of cliché characterizations of women to move around or to pass these minor issues to get to major ones? Where does the tone change—and at what points is the reader, put at "his" ease by the easy flow of this mostly genial and civil argument, caught by surprise?

If you follow with "History of Miss Wellwood" in a survey course in American literature, it would be well to set the narrative in context before you launch into the excerpt and to take note especially of the stubborn perennial best seller that first appeared right around the same time: Susanna Row-son's *Charlotte: A Tale of Truth*, which went through two hundred editions before 1900. In many ways a cruder stylist than Murray, Rowson offered a fable with a similar plot and moral—stunned by first love, a naive young woman is deceived by a cad and left destitute and disgraced as an unwed mother. Hearkening back to Samuel Richardson's elaborate epistolary novel *Clarissa* (another sad, admonitory narrative of gentle trusting women and unscrupulous men), Murray pours on the style in the personal letters that take up most of the space in her tale. In an age of "texting" and e-mail courtship and confession, students will probably marvel at the elaborate-ness of all this telling. That curiosity can be a starting point for exploring the following questions:

- Why are these letter writers accorded such eloquence? In reading these fictional, intimate letters now, what are the pleasures and frustrations? Do they give us a vicarious experience of people as they were? Of peo-ple as we *wish* they were? Is Murray striving for absolute realism, or might she have something else in mind?
- The story comes to a happy ending—more or less—because of an inter-vention; our narrator acts as a go-between. What are the underlying assumptions here about the nature of a "good" marriage? What are the prospects for this couple, out beyond the final pages of the text?

These are important matters to dwell on: when we get to Emerson, students will be able to see, thanks to Murray, that the discourse of human liberty has more than one tradition within it, more than one way of accomplishing its purpose. When Fuller comes up in the sequence of your readings, be sure to stop and do some comparison to Murray and see how the two of them gang up on the likes of Emerson, offering a Fabian, supremely mobile prose strat-egy in contrast to his more ponderous forward movement. When you come to talk about differences between male poetics and female (or feminist) poetics in the American tradition, a comparison of these rhetorical styles will serve that discussion well.

PHILIP FRENEAU

In a provocative mix of voices, Freneau's early poetry addresses the social and historical events of his day and attends to both moral issues and small details from nature, in anticipation of the romantic poems like *The House of Night* and "On Observing a Large Red-Streak Apple." "On the Emigration to America and Peopling the Western Country" and "On Mr. Paine's Rights of Man" derive their force from their historical situation. The poems sug-gest that the American Revolution made the development of American poetry possible, and yet, as noted in the NAAL headnote, Freneau was not "the father of American poetry."

Ask students to think about what limits Freneau. Freneau's brand of elo-quence as it survives in his poetry (he also wrote political pamphlets) has not appeared to be as lasting in its significance as our country's founding documents; the political covenant and the autobiography absorb almost all of the literary energy available during the Revolutionary and Federal periods and serve as the major literary genres of the late eighteenth century. Still, Freneau's choice to respond to political and social conditions in "To Sir Toby," written about slavery (although he addresses a sugar planter in Jamaica rather than a southern slaveholder), demonstrates his faith in the power of language used in the service of political and social change. This faith has its roots in the Puritan belief in the literary authority of the Bible, but it also anticipates the First Amendment to the Constitution and the idea that freedom of speech is the most important freedom, because it is speech that leads to freedom itself.

PHILLIS WHEATLEY

Wheatley is a fascinating poet, for she reflects Puritan influence, wrote poetry that imitates Alexander Pope, and was the first African American to publish a book. Wheatley writes about liberty as an abstract or spiritual condition rather than as freedom from slavery. In "On Being Brought from Africa to America," the kind of enslavement she seems most concerned with is that of her former ignorance of Christianity and redemption. Her letters provide a valuable addition about her life, documenting her correspondence with abolitionist groups in England and America and with other Africans in servitude in America. The correspondence continues to suggest that she views spiritual salvation as "the way to true felicity," as she expresses in her letter to Arbour Tanner, but also that she is aware of the needs of both Africans and American Indians. Her letter to Samson Occom comes closest to revealing the development of Wheatley's voice as an advocate for the natural rights of blacks.

Wheatley makes a connection between achieving exalted language in poetry (or in art, as in "To S. M., a Young African Painter, on Seeing His Works") and rising on "seraphic pinions." Wheatley resembles the earlier colonial writers (such as Wigglesworth and Edward Taylor) is whose writings personal concerns and personal voice are largely absent, but the powerful images of "rising" and racial uplift will reappear in black prose and poetry from Booker T. Washington to Countee Cullen.

"To the Right Honorable William, Earl of Dartmouth" and "To Maecenas" can be looked at as a good deal more than polished performances in a borrowed genteel mode, an African American woman working in a form perfected by Pope, Cowley, Lee, and a score of other British Augustans. When Wheatley addresses Dartmouth and Maecenas, she addresses individuals who achieved (as she says of Maecenas) a "partial grace," who lived lives of talent and achievement but who somehow exist on the periphery, either of history or cultural memory or the mainstream of contemporary action. Terence and Virgil were "happier" in the arts than was Maecenas; Dartmouth did "once deplore" injustice, but he has taken sides against freedom now, as the revolutionary movement in America rises to what Wheatley portrays as irresistible strength.

Questions for discussion:

- Ask students to compare Wheatley with Bradstreet as poets on public subjects. What explains the absence of personal voice in Wheatley?
- Is her emulation of eighteenth-century British poets a kind of performance or does this poetic style allow her both to achieve and to evade a distinct literary voice?
- As Wheatley frames her address, she reveals something of herself, as if to achieve some commonality with the individual she speaks to. What does she turn to within herself and why?

Royall Tyler

At last, a play! Even if you haven't been moving through NAAL chronologically, logging time with explorers and historians and sermonizers and folktales, you may need to pause and engage the class, right away, with the oddities of reading a play, and what kinds of imaginative leaps might be necessary to enjoy and understand a text that was meant to be acted and heard and written more than two centuries ago. Because this is a comedy and a satire, a work meant to inundate a happy audience from a proscenium stage, some boundaries might need to be broken and inhibitions let go when we open it as a text in a classroom, several hundred pages into a daunting anthology.

In class discussion of *The Contrast*, a point of arrival might be the play's quest to affirm a separate, superior American identity and an ethos of pragmatism and rough-hewn Yankee nobility while borrowing heavily from the drama traditions of England, the culture from which *The Contrast* supposedly turns away. Is Tyler trying to have it both ways? Is it legitimate for him to play by the rules of the cultural tradition that he wants to scorn? The conversation might engage with these paradoxes if it starts from the familiar— what students recognize as archetypes in the opening scenes and the major characters, and the oddities in those archetypes as they are exploited even now. The first American comedy opens with two lively young women and a conversation centered on fashion, "shopping," and "visiting." Exactly how unusual is this? Do Lettia and Charlotte have posterity in the suburban shopping malls now and on the screens at the cineplexes? The superficiality and materialism of the American young are major clichés in our culture, and in the stories that Hollywood spins of that culture—with this extra spin, that the stories on the screen can influence the values and behavior of the real people in the audience. When students see modern-day analogues for this opening scene, do they also see cues here for how it should be played? If one were staging *The Contrast* for a twenty-first-century audience, what would one have these young women sound like? How fast would one have them talk? And how much attention would an audience end up paying to what they said? In other words, if the dialogue of the first scene is bright patter of talk among intimates, what are the conventions of listening to it?

This last question can open up a consideration of the dynamics of stage comedy, and of how *The Contrast*, as a performed work, can strike the ear and the mind. If speed is essential not only for getting through that first scene but for understanding the temperament of the people on the stage, then that speed runs counter to the habits of people in classrooms working their way laboriously through a text, slowing down to decode and evaluate every speech, every joke. If young people in our own moment are expected to speak in codes and patterns that affirm an in-group and a generation, then how well do you suppose Tyler, a man of thirty when he wrote this play, understood the special discourses of young women in his time?

The second scene—between Maria and her father, Van Rough—can also be nudged for familiar patterns. The encounter will be familiar to students who have been through some Shakespeare comedies or the Jane Austen novels, which come a bit later than *The Contrast*—a sensitive, courageous young woman sparring with a loving but stodgy and obtuse father about marriage. This is supremely familiar territory, and the stuff of comedy since the Renaissance, and a dilemma that we still exploit: young love and exuberance defying custom and parental rules. What kind of suspense is established at the end of Act I? There might be at least two varieties: a simple sort, having to do with whether these women will know and get whatever they want—but also a richer sort as well, a suspense about whether this play will at some point become American, affirm a sensibility or offer us heroes and heroines who do not come from the collections that populated standard comedies in England and on the Continent.

Charlotte is the sister of Colonel Manly, a hero of the Revolutionary War, a friend of the great Lafayette, and a prime specimen of the honest and virile new Yankee. You might point out that Manly's name is itself borrowed from the English tradition, that William Wycherley nearly a century before Tyler had established a "Manly" as a brash "Plain Dealer" cutting a swath through London foppery and pretense. Students will see other resemblances: the strong stoic type, unpolished yet keenly intelligent, turns up everywhere in our popular literature as the handsome prince, rescuer of damsels in the distress of impending bad marriage. Manly and Maria have met on their own, without the manipulations of elders of chaperones, and a bit like the young in Crèvecoeur's *Letters from an American Farmer* they love and ultimately marry without regard to background or community approval. Dimple, the insidious fop in pursuit of Maria, is duly driven from the scene: ask students to suggest what progeny Dimple has in novels or films that they have recently seen.

But then a larger question might take shape. Class discussion could now center on the admiration we affirm, or the lip service we pay, to simple styles and virtues. Here we are, back at the very beginning of American drama and the genre that would eventually give birth to American film and television, and already there is this championing of the simple, good-hearted, untutored, fashionless hero, not "rough" like Van Rough in his insensitivity but rough in his surfaces, with an inherently good nature shining through. But this is a play in a theater, aimed assumedly at people of fashion, and the popular cult of the simple hero is strong in a contemporary America that spends more money on clothes, cosmetics, and status symbols than any other culture on earth.

Question for discussion:
- When as a public we watch and value plays of this kind, what are we really doing?

Hannah Webster Foster

Undergraduates in American literature courses typically read one "tale of seduction" from the Big Three at the end of the eighteenth century: Brown's *The Power of Sympathy*, Rowson's *Charlotte, A Tale of Truth*, or Foster's *The Coquette*. NAAL offers Foster's novel for the first time in the Seventh Edition. All three of these works are fiercely and forthrightly didactic; all of them owe a debt to Samuel Richardson and other British novelists who wrote fiction (ostensibly) to teach moral lessons to the reading public, and especially to young women. And although an age of literary innocence may have passed and contemporary audiences might not take a fable like this as seriously as Rowson and Foster intended, these books stand at the headwaters of a popular tradition that your students will recognize quickly. For all the strangeness they might find in the structure and cadences of an epistolary novel, they will probably recognize that what we have here is something akin to a "soap," and that this cast of characters has plenty of kin on the television networks and out at the multiplex. The beautiful, bright, but superficial and self-indulgent heroine; the "good" suitor, a bit too earnest and plodding to hold her attention; her confidants, offering good advice that she doesn't take seriously enough; the handsome, charming cad and his partners in a war of the sexes; distant parents and visiting gossips—this is familiar ground, and probing the novel first for its pop-culture analogues and archetypes can help students understand, subsequently, what's different about *The Coquette*, the risks and advantages inherent in this kind of storytelling, the aesthetic and organizational decisions that set this novel apart.

Because there are a lot of characters here, another way into the narrative is to ask students to help you list them on the blackboard and speculate about why all these people are needed to get the story told—what roles are played, for example, by Lucy Freeman (later Lucy Sumner), by Charles Deighton, Julia Granby, Mrs. Richman, and others who seem to be on the periphery of the main action. Also, you might want to observe that unlike the letters in Richardson's *Clarissa*—perhaps the ultimate epistolary novel of the Enlightenment era and the most formidable ancestor of *The Coquette*—the letters in Foster's novel open with no clear indication as to whom they are from. Unless you cheat and look at the end of each letter, each one, at least for a while, is a puzzle to be worked out: whose voice is this, and how skilled is Foster in establishing and sustaining differences between one character's style and another?

Another question might be lurking in the room at the outset of a discussion, and it might be well to get it aired out sooner rather than later: why is it so often the case, in these admonitory fables about chastity and watching out for seducers, that the sexual encounter quickly produces a child, and that the descent of the "fallen" heroine into desperation and death is so swift? These are questions that can be approached historically as well as morally: death in childbirth, or soon after, was a real and terrible prospect, especially for women with no money, no family, and no access to care; the social systems of the Western world offered little forgiveness or support for young women with children out of wedlock; and from a moral perspective, once the precious innocence was lost, there was little hope for recovery of any sort, short of the grave.

For many students, the only real surprise in the plot of this novel might be that Eliza falls into an illicit and disastrous relationship with the despicable Sanford after he is married, and after Eliza has acquired plenty of evidence that his motives are all wrong. Students may want to spend some time with the longest letters in *The Coquette,* especially with the long letter from Julia Granby (Letter XLVI) in which the seduction of Eliza is revealed—not by Eliza or by Sanford but by discovery, secondhand. They may also want to discuss the way that Eliza's sordid death at the inn, along with that of her infant daughter, is handled with a *third*-hand report in Letter LXXI: Granby's report of a brother's account of someone else's account of the final hours. Why handle the big scene in this way? What might be gained with regard to maintaining an aura of dignity or gentility in a story about sex, betrayal, and catastrophe?

If your class takes a liking to *The Coquette* and is willing to join you in prowling out farther, into speculations about self-expression in the eighteenth century and in our own moment, you can ask them to ponder letters as acts of performance—for the self as well as for the person you write to. Do your students actually write letters anymore? If so, in what circumstances? What are the stylistic differences that they sense in their *own* writing, depending on the medium (the letter, the e-mail message, the blog, the text message) and to whom they're writing (the close friend, the acquaintance, the teacher, the parent, the "significant other")? Written in ink with a quill pen on paper and sent by slow mail, the letter was a ritual of self-expression and also of self-discovery. Students might want to look closely at a letter from Reverand Boyer to his friend Selby (e.g., Letter XL) or Lucy's letter to Eliza (Letter XLIX) in which Lucy comments that the recent action has been much like a novel. Where do we see evidence of self-consciousness in these characters, as they create, on paper, these eloquent narratives of their own lives?

TABITHA TENNEY

An emotional young woman, an unscrupulous suitor, and a good-hearted young man whom we come to root for—we are in familiar territory here, for such triangles of love go back a long way in the history of English comedy. This is also the stuff of soap opera: concealed intentions, emotional breakdowns, messages found and read by the wrong person. Tenney is playful about her own characters and plot, constructing a story that has it both ways: satirizing romantic and sentimental fiction but also delivering that same kind of story, with even a measure of suspense along the way. Three generations before Tenney, Henry Fielding had played the same sort of game in *Joseph Andrews* and *Tom Jones*; twenty years after *Female Quixotism*, Washington Irving would do it all again, in compact form, in "The Legend of Sleepy Hollow," a work that can be compared in interesting ways to *Female Quixotism*.

Questions for discussion:

- Ask your students to take a look at the letters and notes that Dorcas, O'Connor, and Philander leave for one another in these chapters. The letter seems endangered now as a resource in courtship, a weapon in the wars of love: the text message, the curt email, and the cell phone conversation may have irretrievably taken the place of the carefully penned epistle. Consider these letters as performances of style, as displays of true or contrived feeling. What cultural rituals are enacted here? How do we account for the style that each writer takes on when he or she writes one of these letters? What might have been gained, or lost, with the decline of this kind of writing?

- Ask students to size up Dorcas as a personality. The introduction to the excerpt explains that she is being pursued by O'Connor, who is mainly interested in her money. Is Dorcas in love with O'Connor? Is she chasing after emotional intensity for its own sake? Where are the cues for understanding what Dorcas really wants in this narrative that is written from her point of view?

- Is there anything distinctly American about this story as Tenney tells it? With what details does she distinguish it from, say, a comic romance set in Jane Austen's English countryside? Are the differences confined to props, supporting characters, and place names? Or do we sense an effort here to create American characters as well?

CHAPTER 8

Teaching Notes
for Authors and Works:
Volume B,
American Literature
1820–1865

One way of creating a context for discussing early-nineteenth-century authors is to analyze closely with students several works related in theme. You might ask students to read "Rip Van Winkle" (see discussion of Rip's dream below) in conjunction with "Young Goodman Brown" (another story that shows the male protagonist waking from a dream), "Bartleby, the Scrivener" (where Bartleby's "dead wall revery" becomes a variation on the dream motif), and Thoreau's "Resistance to Civil Government" (in which he describes his night in jail as "a change [that] had to my eyes come over the scene"). Students have heard the phrase *American Dream* used as a cliché; beginning in the nineteenth century with works in which American dreams actually figure in the plot helps them look for new meanings in the theme. In these four works the dreamers share confusion concerning the nature of reality. Your students should keep in mind the larger historical context—the abolitionist movement; early manifestations of the women's rights struggle in the temperance society; the emerging American economic system; the near extinction of the American Indians in the settled Northeast and Midwest; and the various conflicts with Canada, Britain, and Mexico—as they study a literature that explores the power of the imagination and struggles with or evades the conflicts at the center of early-nineteenth-century American social and political life.

By the 1850s there was definitely some quality about the new literature that was *American*. Even though many of our early-nineteenth-century writers may have turned inward—to the world of romance, Gothic fantasy, dreams, idealized portraits of the West and the American Indians, or to the microcosm of individual perception, or to the single-sex universe of

Melville's sea fiction—even the transcendentalist Thoreau, in separating himself from society at Walden Pond, tries to give imagery of the waking literal—and literary—body. Is an American identity the creation of a few early-nineteenth-century dreamers or does it result from rhythms of dreaming and waking, of separation and engagement, of evasion and confrontation?

As the literature of the 1820–65 period shows, writing helps Emerson, Hawthorne, Dickinson, and others discover who they are in what they see and the language they find to express that vision. What we are exploring, in part, as we read American literature is the development of ways of thinking and seeing the world as well as ways of imagining and creating the self. In rejecting the rationality of the Enlightenment, early-nineteenth-century writers were evolving their own vision. Thoreau, in *Walden*, exchanges Enlightenment thinking for mystical enlightenment. Can students see this period's writers' rejection of rationality as part of a pattern in American literary history? The Puritans were typological; the eighteenth-century writers exalted reason and logic, but the early-nineteenth-century writers were analogical in their way of seeing. Perhaps the emergence of an "American" imaginative literature in the early nineteenth century may itself be seen as evidence of evolution in epistemology. Once writers became capable of inventing metaphors for their own imagination or for telling stories about either private or public life, they became equally capable of exploring the meaning of their experience and of defining it as "American."

In one sense, Transcendentalism took the separatism of early-nineteenth-century writers to its limit, yet "Nature" and *Walden* both show us that the transcendentalist theory of language is the basis for another American spiritual movement. In fact, every prior moment of separation in colonial and American literary history may be seen in retrospect as a variation on that pattern. When the Puritan reliance on God's word seems in need of strengthening, Edwards rewrites the Bible; when theology fails to solve material problems, Franklin invents a language with which to address the common people and to create himself as a blueprint; when Britain no longer speaks for the colonists, Jefferson writes a document that enacts the very independence it declares; and in the early nineteenth century, Emerson calls for a literary separation ("We have listened too long to the courtly muses of Europe," from "The American Scholar") and for an American poet capable of finding the language for the "as yet unsung" American experience ("Yet America is a poem in our eyes," from "The Poet"). The evolution from typology to logic to analogy is progressive, even though the early-nineteenth-century writers were the first to see the pattern. The "forms of being" change and the theories of language change, but American writers become increasingly aware of their powers to name themselves and thus to write themselves into being. From Rip Van Winkle's dream to Adrienne Rich's "dream of a common language," the meaning of both American identity and American literary history are intimately tied to the evolution of an American language.

By the end of their study of the first two volumes of NAAL, students can see that while American writers may continue after the Civil War to struggle with language and literary forms that will make it possible for them to write an American literature, from the Revolution on they look to themselves for their literary authority and to their own experience for the emotional and aesthetic power of their work. Despite Stowe's comment about taking dictation from God, American writers after the Federal period no longer have even the illusion, as Edward Taylor had written, "that Thou wilt guide my pen to write aright." Nineteenth-century authors make creative literature out of the economic and spiritual self-reliance of which Franklin and Emerson wrote. Nevertheless, the prohibitions against writing and speaking that American white women and black and Native American men and women suffered throughout the 1620–1865 period in American history would mean that many Americans, then and now, continued to be silenced and that the act of writing for white women and for black writers would reflect acts of heroic rebellion.

Washington Irving

"Rip Van Winkle" is a good place to open the 1820–65 period, and we can analyze it closely. If this story is the first "American Dream" in American literature, we can talk about the implications of that dream. Students make connections between the confused state of mind the earliest colonists must have experienced and Rip's confusion on "waking" to discover that he is a citizen of a new country, an event that must have seemed to many to have taken place overnight. In one central passage in the story that recurs almost as a template in later American literature, Rip asks, "Does nobody here know Rip Van Winkle?" Irving writes, "The poor fellow was now completely confounded. He doubted his own identity, and whether he was himself or another man. In the midst of his bewilderment, the man in the cocked hat demanded who he was, and what was his name?" Rip's reply echoes with contemporary resonance to undergraduate students: "'God knows,' exclaimed he, at his wit's end; 'I'm not myself—I'm somebody else—that's me yonder—no—that's somebody else, got into my shoes—I was myself last night, but I fell asleep on the mountain, and they've changed my gun and every thing's changed, and I'm changed, and I can't tell what's my name, or who I am!'" The story suggests that, like Rip, we may be deeply confused and years behind in accepting or understanding our own history and destiny. The new country begins in uncertainty; the new American's sense of identity falters, then gains confidence, much as the tale itself shows Rip, by the end, invested with new authority and self-assurance.

But what is the nature of that authority? For Rip, who becomes "reverenced" as a storyteller, a "chronicle of the old times 'before the war,'" is the same person who, twenty years earlier, owned the "worst conditioned farm in the neighbourhood" and was "ready to attend to any body's business but his own." It is only after history catches up with Rip, in a sense, and he manages to wake up after the Revolution that he finds his vocation. Is the story in some sense Irving's meditation on imaginative literature before and after the American Revolution? What happens to Rip's cultural identity that makes it possible for the townspeople to produce their first storyteller? The story seems to document the transition between the moment in which the new country had a potential chronicler (Rip Van Winkle) but no history to the moment just a "dream" later when its new identity gave it both a story-teller and a story to tell. Like the moment of the decline of Puritanism and the emergence of Enlightenment thinking that we see in Franklin's *Autobiography* (where Franklin respects the general form of Puritan introspection but dramatically alters its content), there is a similar moment of transition between pre-Revolutionary and post-Revolutionary thinking for the new American Rip Van Winkle. That the village inn should have changed only the red coat of King George to the blue coat of George Washington on the sign that used to stand over it (and that now advertises the Union Hotel) suggests that, in Irving's view, the "singularly metamorphosed" country may have undergone radical change in some ways, but that in other ways it may have changed very little indeed.

At the end of the story, Irving turns Rip's confusion into a joke at Dame Van Winkle's expense: "But there was one species of despotism under which he had long groaned, and that was—petticoat government." Here Irving establishes a theme that would become characteristic of much nineteenth-century fiction, in which the male character represents simple good nature, artistic sensibility, and free spirit and the female character signifies the forces that inhibit that sensibility. Dame's "curtain lectures" vie only with Puritan sermons in their severity, and it is her "dinning" voice, her tongue that was "incessantly going," that Irving blames for silencing the budding artist in Rip. ("Rip had but one way of replying to all lectures of the kind. . . . He shrugged his shoulders, shook his head, cast up his eyes, but said nothing.") American fiction seems to begin, therefore, in the silencing of Dame Van Winkle—for Rip's real victory is not the one he wins over the British, but the one he wins as a result of Dame's death. One might speculate that for Irving—as for Fenimore Cooper, Poe, Hawthorne, and Melville—the real American Dream is of a world in which women are either silent, dead, or in some other way excluded from the sphere of action.

If students are interested in reading Irving for allegorical resonance or for the indication (or betrayal) of certain archetypal fears in the emerging American male author, then "The Legend of Sleepy Hollow" can provide them with more possibilities along this line. What if we read the conflict between Ichabod and Brom Bones as suggesting somehow a larger opposition—between Ichabod as the product of a new-style book learning that conceals but does not eliminate foolishness and superstition and Brom Bones, who flat-out refuses intellectuality and intellectual pretensions and who makes his way through the world on personal intuitions and common sense? Ichabod reads and reasons and teaches, but he cannot escape his childish fears; Brom says no! in thunder to Ichabod's kind of thinking—is it significant then that this horseman of his is headless? About two hundred years before Irving wrote this story, Anne Hutchinson was banished from the Bay Colony for trusting her own mind and heart above any printed word or reasoned argument; playfully or otherwise, has her spirit made its return in Irving's story? Does the last line of the story suggest, perhaps, that the story itself celebrates a buoyant distrust of the spoken and printed word? If the students remember Anne Hutchinson, you might ask a question like this: to what extent are latter-day antinomians and headless horsemen heroic figures in American imaginative literature? Such a question is worth keeping in mind as we move forward from Sleepy Hollow.

JAMES FENIMORE COOPER

You have selections here from a writer known for sprawling works, and care is required to raise the chances that students will read him sympathetically, and find enjoyment in a novelist who was very popular for more than a century as a writer of adventure stories and historical epics of the American past. You might want to open with some notes about that popularity, observing perhaps that later nineteenth-century writers (famously including Mark Twain) saw Fenimore Cooper was a ponderous romantic legacy that realism had to push out of the way, just as British realism had to rise up against Sir Walter Scott.

Fenimore Cooper remained a rite of passage for young American boys until the middle of the twentieth century; and his grander yarns, in which Hawkeye (Natty Bumppo, the old hunter in these excerpts) was young and a superhero in buckskins, did much to shape not only the popular conception of the eastern woods in the French and Indian War and the Revolution but also popular ideas of what Indians were like and how to tell the Noble Savages (mostly Delawares and Mohegans in these tales) from the skulking, villainous Hurons.

Back before academics began to fuss about literary modes and schools, Fenimore Cooper was engaged in doing several kinds of cultural work at once in these novels about Natty and the early days of settlement in the neighborhood of Otsego Lake, Lake George, and Lake Champlain. He was writing an epic of sorts, emulating the classic purposes of Virgil's epic: to lay claim to a heroic heritage; to infuse a landscape with an aura of grandeur and elegy; to inspire his contemporaries with paragons of various virtues.

But Fenimore Cooper was also writing romance, in emulation of Scott, who had imbued Scotland with magic, legend, and melancholy beauty, making a lot of money in the process. And Fenimore Cooper was also a man of political and social causes: environmentalist ethics burst forth at times in these novels, as do moments of prophecy. As you read more closely, you might talk at some length about Fenimore Cooper's slow-developing sentences; his delight in the carefully composed tableau; and the affinity of such a style to the dark, emotion-charged, ceremonial canvases of the Hudson River School of painters, to which Cooper was closely allied.

The sequence of the NAAL selections respects the chronology in which the Leatherstocking Tales were written—roughly in reverse order with regard to Natty's age. In *The Pioneers* the great hunter and scout is an old man, a living, tristful relic; in *The Last of the Mohicans,* set almost half a century earlier, Natty is in his prime. A series that began as an elegy for a fading past—of exploits and unspoiled wilderness—becomes an imaginative return to those bygone glorious days, and an example of fully indulgent romantic storytelling.

Questions for discussion:

- It's worth telling your students that the floods of pigeons, slaughtered with cannons and so thick that they blot out the sky, are indeed the passenger pigeons that were driven to extinction in the opening decades of this century. The chapter can be read as an early moment in American environmental literature—but before we do that, what can we say about the paradox of Natty's life, as one of the *first* pioneers in this valley?
- Chapter III of *The Last of the Mohicans* introduces Natty (Hawkeye) and Chingachgook—already familiar figures for readers who know *The Pioneers*—and a new character, the young and powerful Uncas. And almost nothing happens except an extended conversation. What are the purposes and effects of inserting this chapter of discussion in the opening pages of an adventure story?
- As the notes make clear, Hawkeye often asserts that he is a man "with no cross in his blood"—in other words, that he is completely white. But Hawkeye in these stories is often presented as a true inheritor of the best of the American Indian tradition. What cultural uneasiness might underlie Fenimore Cooper's presentation of his hero—and his hero's assertions about himself?

CATHARINE MARIA SEDGWICK

NAAL provides two interesting "core sample" chapters from a long, convoluted, and ambitious historical novel—really a more ambitious reimaging of the early decades of the Bay Colony than the colonial sketches of Hawthorne and even *The Scarlet Letter*. Epic narratives were doing very well in Britain and America alike, and Walter Scott and James Fenimore Cooper were grand figures on the literary scene—figures to be resisted as well as emulated.

Hope Leslie dates from the later 1820s, the center period of Fenimore Cooper's work on the Leatherstocking Tales, and about a decade after two of Scott's big hits, *Rob Roy* and *Ivanhoe*. Complex stories of intrigue, star-crossed and secret love, revenge and feuds and battles and massacres horrific and picturesque at once—these were standard fare for Cooper and Scott. What wasn't standard at all, however, is Sedgwick's emphasis on strong, cool-headed women as figures of agency rather than comely prizes to be rescued and protected again and again, like Cora in *The Last of the Mohicans* or Rebecca in *Ivanhoe*.

A couple of other cultural and historical realities should be borne in mind to understand the configurations of Sedgwick's project and the individuality of her achievement. In American fiction, the ennobling of the Indian was a motif that waited until the Indians were almost completely gone from the

East Coast and the Piedmont, and readers of these novels, in safe parlors and at snug firesides, could dream their way into these narratives without worrying that actual Native Americans in inconvenient numbers might actually show up at the front door. Also something else has shifted, which the headnotes mention: Calvinism has evolved or eroded into a less restrictive sort of faith. Unitarianism has taken hold in the environs of Boston, and romantic intuitive belief in the beneficence of nature and the brotherhood of humankind has spread from Germany and France through England to the domesticated woodlands of the American East, where it flourished. When Hope Leslie and Magawisca affirm, at their emotional parting, that a benign divinity oversees and welcomes them all, they are neither of them thinking like seventeenth-century Calvinists but are rather joining together in a kind of affirmation that your students may have already seen in "Thanatopsis" and other Bryant poems and will see soon (perhaps) in Longfellow and the Fireside Poets.

Questions for discussion:
- These chapters offer us enormous helpings of dialogue and monologue, and students may wonder whether these exchanges and orations are realistic or congruent with good writing in any era. It might be well to stop and consider right away the oratorical or operatic quality of the interaction between Digby and Everell—if only to contextualize similar arias between Hester Prynne and Edward Dimmesdale in Hawthorne's classic twenty years later. How should we eavesdrop on these speeches? Should we feel discomfort at their apparent staginess or unreality, or do they succeed in carrying us into a different, heightened level of experience and expectations?
- Magawisca's monologue about the English siege of her village and the courage of her own mother is a tour de force of eloquence—flawless unhesitating English prose from a Native American girl who has had no formal schooling and who has learned English as a second language. Read aloud the section beginning on page 1017 with "Honour! was it, Everell—ye shall hear." What literary or cultural echoes do you sense in this narrative? In other words, does its literary ancestry extend back farther than the tradition of the English novel? What might the emotional effects be, on us as readers, if those echoes are called forth in the mind?
- Take a step back from these chapters and look at them in the context of other literary works that you have read from this period, roughly 1800 to 1830. Think about poets and novelists—or think forward to Emerson if you have encountered the transcendentalists before. What qualities in these chapters identify them clearly as belonging to a work of this time?

LYDIA SIGOURNEY

New to NAAL, Lydia Sigourney built her career and her considerable reputation in a moment when poetry, as a cultural practice, faced obligations that were every bit as conflicted as those which faced her contemporary

Bryant, her predecessors Freneau and Phillis Wheatley, and even Anne Brad-street. As romantic values collided with the old imperative that poetry be pub-lic in some dimension, speaking for a town, a region, a country as well as for the self, Sigourney produced verse that sometimes seems highly rhetorical, fulfilling a public duty, and that at other times seems to be "overheard," as John Stuart Mill, schooled in Wordsworth and the British romantics, declared that all poetry should be. As is also true for Bryant and Longfellow, there are moments in Sigourney's work where she writes on subjects that in a strict sense she knows little or nothing about, and a first encounter with her poems will require us to account for and evaluate those efforts.

Questions for discussion:
- Sigourney's voice as a poet shows a great deal of variety: she can be plain and also ornate; she can speak softly and also turn out oratory and polemic. Which poems in this set seem to be most different from each other in language-choice and sound and why?
- The poem "The Suttee" is about a Subcontinent Indian practice of immolating wives on the funeral pyres of their husbands. Read the final ten lines of this poem aloud. What hints are there that Sigourney has people other than Hindu men and women on her mind?
- Compare "To the First Slave Ship" to Longfellow's "The Slave Singing at Midnight." What are the similarities and differences in strategy here, as these two poets address a national emergency?
- "To a Shred of Linen" seems to stand apart from other poems in this set, not only for subject but also for cadence. How would you describe Sigourney's voice here, compared to the voice you hear in "Fallen Forests?"
- There are several poems in this set about Native Americans, invoked or addressed as a vanished race. One obvious danger of elegizing like this, as Bryant does in "The Prairies," is that the subject can diminish into a mere excuse for elegiac poetry—the ruin or the chance gravestone as a pretext for a good, long romantic sigh. How does Sigourney resist that degradation in these poems?

WILLIAM CULLEN BRYANT

Celebrating romantic intuition, heartfelt inspiration, and the American wilderness as a great book of unread wisdom Bryant was an important pioneer in the quest to build a uniquely American poetic voice. Whether or not he would qualify as such a poet by standards Emerson laid down when Bryant was well along in his career—well, that's a matter for you and your students to talk about vigorously when you get to Emerson. Right now, your students may want to learn some survival skills with regard to Bryant—for instance, how to tell a Bryant poem from one by Whittier or Longfellow or Wordsworth or any of the other romantics they might be reading. That's a final exam ID type of question but addressing it can inspire a search for the Bryant sound, his cadences, and his tastes.

There is a civility to Bryant, and a simplicity of theme that underlies what might seem (especially in "Thanatopsis" and "The Prairies) a daunting tide of language. One way of breaking through is to ask a student to read aloud the opening dozen lines from either poem and then to say, in a shorter and simpler sentence, what Bryant says there. If you try it with the opening two stanzas of "To a Waterfowl," one of your students will eventually cook them down to nothing more than "Where are you going?" That exercise ought to provoke some interest in how to take all this rhetorical display: is Bryant a showoff? Is he merely laying thick romantic sauce over simple observations? That can be an abiding question for a visit to Bryant—what effects he might be after, and how we can enjoy him.

Ask your students to compare "Thanatopsis" with Freneau's "The House of Night." Which of Bryant's poems look to eighteenth-century values, both in philosophy and in aesthetics? You can closely analyze "The Prairies" in class, for this poem is the most clearly "American" of the Bryant selections in NAAL. Even so, memories of Sarah Morton (if "The African Chief" has been read before Bryant) will cause students to wonder what the core intention is here—a mystical breakthrough into understanding of these bygone Indian nations, these enigmatic mound builders about whom Bryant has no clues but the landscape and its telltale shapes? Or a pretext to write, on a small scale, an American *Aeneid*, and thus claim for ourselves some reassuring romantic ghosts in our wilderness and some oblique claim to an ancient, heroic, and tragic tradition?

What marks the poem as American? You can discuss the way Bryant draws his imagery from the Great Plains, takes as his subject the "dilated sight" of the romantic perceiver, and associates the source of perception with change in the "forms of being." The mixture of styles, philosophies, and attitudes toward poetry that students find in "The Prairies" helps them see that evolution in thinking and writing takes place slowly. Some might argue that the "British" elements in Bryant's poetry contribute greatly to its beauty and power, and that they reflect one valid response to the confusion the new Americans must have felt after the Revolution and also serve as a tribute to the enduring cultural and emotional content of the new country's relationship to things British, despite the change in our form of government.

Questions for discussion:
- What happens if we imagine ourselves out of class for a moment— much like one of Bryant's original readers, generations before he was brought into the classroom—and settle back and just hear the language in Bryant's lyrics without worrying about finding the verb and tracking the subordinate clauses? Is redundancy and opulence always a drawback in art? Has anyone listened to a symphonic work from right around this time—by Beethoven or Schubert? What about redundancy and opulence there—or in the enormous paintings that British and American landscape artists (like Thomas Cole) were turning out? In other words, can we engage with this poem more happily if we see it as in keeping with other art from that moment?

- In "The Prairies," Bryant is confronted with a challenge to his imagination and his mission: with nothing to go on but a huge grassy mound, and with no knowledge of the people who built it, he dreams a dream of their glory and downfall. What traditions does he draw on to do that work? Is it legitimate for a white New England poet to try something like this? What kind of faith or complacency would sustain or justify that effort—for Bryant as an artist and perhaps for others who read him?
- New to NAAL is Bryant's short poem to Thomas Cole, departing for Europe. The poem is a valedictory but also an admonition. Bryant is worried about something—what? And how does that concern help us to understand other works by this poet?

WILLIAM APESS

Both Occom and Apess were Christian preachers, and both worked as missionaries to and reformers of American Indian peoples. Furthermore, in both of the texts in NAAL, Occom and Apess are addressing a white audience; Apess, however, is much more direct in criticizing the audience he is addressing.

Ask students to comment on the image of the looking glass. In one sense Apess's essay holds a mirror up to his Euro-American audience, but that mirroring also creates a rhetorical form of encounter, thus linking Apess's text with the "Beginnings to 1700" period of NAAL and hinting at several new ways to interpret this trope in light of the history of native Americans in the nineteenth-century United States.

For the looking glass also shows his audience the reality of the lives of Indians, particularly of women and children in poverty. "Let me," he writes, "for a few moments turn your attention to the reservations in the different states of New England," thus asking his audience to encounter in a literal sense the lives he describes for them and in a spiritual sense the racism they have condoned and that Apess deems responsible for the material condition of the Indians' lives. The looking glass thus becomes both self-reflexive and reflective of the racialized "others" in American history—a history that for Apess includes African Americans as well as American Indians.

In some ways the rhetoric of Apess's text may seem uncomplicated, perhaps partly because the arguments he raises to counter racism may be familiar to students in your class. He argues that Euro-Americans use skin color to racialize the difference and hence the inferiority of both Native Americans and African Americans; he reminds his audience that there are by far more skins of color in the world than there are skins of white (he cites a ratio of fifteen to one); he makes his audience aware of the theory that Jesus Christ and the Apostles were themselves persons of color; and he protests the double standard that has allowed white men to marry Native American women but has not allowed Native American men "to choose their partners among the whites if they wish." Many of these and other points of his argument actually seem quite forward looking for 1833, anticipating analyses of racial formation in our own time. And Apess cites Scripture to underscore his reasoning.

In another way, his rhetorical strategy is complex and provocative. After all, as a Christian Indian, he is himself the product of a particular aspect of white culture, the aspect he now invokes to affirm his perspective. Thus as he addresses his white audience, he himself becomes a looking glass; in Apess, his Christian audience can see their own creation and their own best selves taken as gospel and then held back up to them. Point out to students that Apess does not base his essay on Scripture and in fact does not even quote from the Bible early in his text. It is only later, when he is looking for support for his own argument, that he quotes. Examine the particular passages he includes; these passages become the ultimate moments of encounter with the self for his Euro-American audience, for they have ostensibly served as models for New England character. When he examines them, he states his purpose, namely "to penetrate more fully into the conduct of those who profess to have pure principles and who tell us to follow Jesus Christ. . . . Let us see if they come anywhere near him and his ancient disciples." The act of examining the principles of Christ—including especially "Thou shalt love thy neighbor as thyself" and "Let us not love in word but in deed"—becomes the rhetorical act of holding up the looking glass, but in effect, the Indians themselves are what Apess wants his audience to see when they look in a mirror. "Thou shalt love thy neighbor as thyself" becomes, in Apess's text, "Thou shalt see thy neighbor as—and in—thyself."

Apess's text thus becomes an emblem of American literature viewed as encounter: without the meeting of Native American and Christian cultures in Apess himself, he would not be speaking texts in a language that can be transcribed (but rather, perhaps, be an orator of Native myths or songs). What he has to say, as a product of that encounter, is conveyed by the word "looking glass." Thus the history of relations between Indians and whites explains the emergence of Apess's text: encounter serves as a figure for another creation myth, this one for a Native American's creation of American literature and his implied white reader.

JANE JOHNSTON SCHOOLCRAFT

A recently recovered poet, Schoolcraft was also a writer and translator of prose narrative from the Ojibwe tradition, the lineage of her mother. Somewhat like Louise Erdrich in our own time, Schoolcraft was challenged and empowered by her life on cultural and geographic borders. Of mixed heritage, she lived and wrote in sparsely settled regions around the Great Lakes—essentially an American frontier—and she constructed her literary and cultural identity from a blending of traditions. The Ojibwe language and heritage she learned orally and at home. But through an Irish father proud of his past, a mingling of native and European peoples in villages around Lake Michigan, and a strengthening inflow of print from the Northeast, Schoolcraft also learned to be a proficient writer in the dominant language and culture of the new nation.

At other places in this guide I have suggested that the tempering and complication of a life between worlds, or a life lived from more than a single perspective and in more than one heritage, can make a great difference in shaping the voice of a sensitive and talented author. Though we are only in the early stages of understanding Schoolcraft and her response to various aspects of American and Native American cultures, you might want to try that general principle at the outset of a discussion. Some of Schoolcraft's poems she wrote in Ojibwe first and then in English; other works seem to be firmly in a tradition running back through white American literature as far as Bradstreet; still others seem to be sites where those different pasts and voices clash or reconcile.

One other perspective you might begin with: when Schoolcraft turns to the cultural work of transcribing, preserving, and promulgating prose tales from the Ojibwe oral tradition, she chooses a voice that seems to defy a practice of white writers in their translations and transcriptions of Native myths, chants, and oratory, and a focus on those differences can do much to set her work apart.

Questions for discussion:
- Because elegies can provide insight into the values and voices of a poet, you might begin with the two elegies to the lost child, comparing them to each other and then to Bradstreet's elegies to her grandchildren, if you have Volume A of NAAL handy. "Sweet Willy" was written more than eight years after Schoolcraft's first elegy on the same death; what differences do you notice, not only in mood, but also in allusion? Would you know that the first poem was written by a Native American woman? How about the second? What are the clues you're responding to? Though Schoolcraft probably never knew Bradstreet's elegies, do you see similarities in purpose here with regard to the implicit responsibilities of the elegist and how those duties are met or resisted?
- The Ojibwe tale "The Little Spirit" can be associated with a vast and worldwide tradition that includes the medieval chanson de geste as well as the modern pop-culture obsession with young superheroes. Describe the voice that Schoolcraft takes on to tell this story. How does it compare to the style you see in transcriptions of Native American trickster tales (Volume A of NAAL)? What can you say about the mood of this story compared to those others? Does a personality emerge herein the "Boy-man" or in the teller of the story?
- Read aloud "Two Songs" in their English versions and also "My lover is tall and handsome." Schoolcraft here is transcribing and interpreting short Ojibwe works about love. As you connect these works together and read them also in light of "Moowis, the Indian Coquette" and the two elegies, what can you say about Schoolcraft's own sensibility, as it is implied here, on the subject of love? What do these works do to represent Ojibwe life to outsiders and Schoolcraft herself to a larger world?

CAROLINE STANSBURY KIRKLAND

Sketches of the Michigan outback, offered with modesty and breeziness: Kirkland can seem unconscionably "light" to your students if you're also guiding them through sonorous elegies by Sigourney and Bryant, or if you've recently been through prose with overtly high-serious designs, writers like Paine, Jefferson, Crèvecoeur, John Adams, and other prophetic (male) authors from around this time. But in that difference, that comparative lightness of Kirkland, an important perception might be lurking: unlike Crèvecoeur and these other men who intend to describe or *pre*scribe American character and destiny, Kirkland belongs to a different poetics and represents an important feminist or protofeminist strategy for engaging with the world as found. Like Dickinson, like Fanny Fern, like Margaret Fuller in "Summer on the Lakes," Kirkland describes what she sees without forcing it into configurations and meanings. No Michigan or American "type" or archetype emerges here, as this is a realm that is still very much in the process of inventing itself. And there is no final judgment on this wilderness as a place of paradise or promise or perdition. This refusal to assert dominion over experience, and this willingness to keep the conversation open-ended, situates Kirkland within a very important contrarian poetics in nineteenth-century American literature.

Questions for discussion:
- Read the paragraph beginning " 'Tis true there are but meager materials for anything which might be called a story" (bottom of page 1070). Is this a candid statement of purpose (or lack of purpose) for Kirkland's sketches? Or a coy one?
- On the bottom of page 1076, read the lines beginning with "It is surprising how many such people one meets in Michigan" and compare it to the long paragraph in Crèvecoeur's "What Is an American" in which he describes a ride past an array of farmers scattered in the American wilderness. What differences do you see in theme and voice when you compare these passages?
- On the top of page 1073, Kirkland closes an account with the line "I seriously advise any of my friends who are about flitting to Wisconsin or Oregon, to prefer a heavy lumber-wagon." How "serious" in advising her readers about choosing the right conveyance does she seem at this point? What cues are you reading to gauge that mood, and how does this moment affect your response to the rest of the sketches in this selection?

LYDIA MARIA CHILD

As a literary form, the formal, polished travel letter is nearly gone, overwhelmed to the point of extinction by video travelogues, endless supplies of blogs and digital images, and the rising truth of Mark Twain's observation well over a hundred years ago that "now everybody goes everywhere." Though Child was writing from "home," publishing about New York in a New York-based abolitionist journal, she was also implicitly writing back to her *real* home, the Boston environs where she grew up, the literary and intellectual Boston that at that moment was dominated by Emerson, Channing, Longfellow, Fuller, Alcott, Washington Allston—a powerful set of cultural leaders. Even so, the power was beginning to shift: the rising economic might and raucous cultural diversity of New York were creating a new literary center for the American East. Bryant was there, and soon afterward Whitman and many other voices would rise up strongly from the environs of the lower Hudson River.

Part of the pleasure of reading these recovered letters, then, lies in how much Child takes on here, and the implicit ambition of spanning different realms and perspectives. There is anguish here, at the squalor and desperation faced in New York by thousands of new immigrants, at the rapaciousness she feels in the air of Wall Street; but in those same streets Child also feels the excitement and the unquenchable optimism that will propel Whitman's *Song of Myself* only a few years after.

Though Child was not at the center of the transcendental circle, she obviously shares that movement's core sentiments and aspirations, and if your class is coming to Child after an encounter with Emerson, you could open the conversation by looking at these letters as the record of a philosophical experiment: what happens if you take the joys and affirmations of *Nature* in your satchel as you prowl the rough neighborhoods of a turbulent metropolis, a long way from the consolations and peace of the Concord woodlands?

Questions for discussion:

- Look carefully at the paragraph on the bottom of page 1081 beginning "There *was* a time when all these things would have passed by me," a paragraph that soars like Emerson, Thoreau, or Whitman. Consider how the letter began. How does it get to this point? In other words, what are the strategies by which Child moves from one perception or mood to the next without sounding contradictory or incoherent?
- On pages 1086–87, Child offers an account of two immigrant burial grounds. Read from "Following the railroad, which lay far beneath our feet" down to the end of the letter and describe her purposes in describing and contrasting these two visits.
- "That the races of mankind are different, spiritually as well as physically, there is, of course, no doubt," says Child, in a long and urgent meditation on the science of the time, and especially on phrenology as a way of sorting out human beings. What are Child's purposes in facing this "science" and its implications? How should we read this long passage now, when phrenology has lost its position in modern scientific thought?

RALPH WALDO EMERSON

A chronological semester-long run through American literature, moving from the opening years up to around 1870, will often hit the brakes right here: three hundred years covered in the first few weeks—and then a long sojourn in the Age of Emerson, looking at a swarm of writers who responded directly to his work or who joined him in his engagement with values and crises that energized New England and national cultural life. If you are focusing on the conscientious newness and American-ness of American literature in the early nineteenth century, any of the essays in NAAL will help you develop that theme. One way or another, Emerson is a lodestone at the center of American writing for his generation and decades after.

Whatever your model of course organization, the first and biggest challenge that might face you, with regard to engaging and enjoying Emerson, is a tour through *Nature*. Regarded by many scholars as the cornerstone of Emerson's thought and the transcendental revolution, it's also the hardest essay for students to get through. There are long forays into abstraction here, expositions of reasoning that seem to follow no logic, and a "form" that seems circular. If you begin here, you may need to proceed with patience— or to suggest that your students concentrate on specific passages rather than worry about getting the whole argument down pat. Somewhat disparagingly, people often observe that Emerson paragraphs and essays work just as sensibly backward, sentence by sentence, as they do forward. There might be some truth in that—Emerson's idea of an idea, and his idea of intellectual process, have very little in common with Edwards and systematic Calvinism.

Because Emerson can produce casualties in these opening paragraphs, it might be useful to read the "Introduction" with your students during the class period, before you turn them loose on the entire essay. One of the initial affirmations, that "Every man's condition is a solution in hieroglyphic to those inquiries he would put. He acts it as life, before he apprehends it as truth" (top of page 1111), can seem opaque, but as you talk together about this perception, seeking moments in personal experience that might illuminate what Emerson is saying, your students will see that for Emerson nature includes nearly everything about our own "condition." He breaks down boundaries between self and body, between our own feeling and the natural world, with the result that he achieves a spiritual vision of unity with nature: "I become a transparent eye-ball. I am nothing. I see all. The currents of the Universal Being circulate through me; I am part or particle of God" (bottom of page 1112).

From the perspective of teaching Emerson, it's worth pausing over sentences like the following: "Each particle is a microcosm, and faithfully renders the likeness of the world" (top of page 1125). How can he say such a thing? Does the proposition become clearer and more plausible when we combine it with another observation on the bottom of page 1118, "Who looks upon a river in a meditative hour, and is not reminded of the flux of all things? Throw a stone into the stream, and the circles that propagate themselves are the beautiful type of all influence." Emerson often connects with us by this strategy, by reaching, suddenly, for mutual common experience, for the everyday perceptions that everyone shares.

From here, you can begin to speculate about propositions that seem to provide the shape and continuity of Emersonian thought: (1) that our observation of the finite ripples on the water leads us to "see" the ripples that ease out into infinity, (2) that the concentric circles made by the ripples themselves form a series of analogies, and (3) that in the act of throwing one stone we can manage to touch an infinitely enlarging sphere. These perceptions can help us sort out some related ideas that "man is an analogist, and studies relations in all objects" (top of page 1119) and that "the world is emblematic. Parts of speech are metaphors because the whole of nature is a metaphor of the human mind" (pages 1120–21) or that "Empirical science is apt to cloud the sight . . . a dream may let us deeper into the secret of nature than a hundred concerted experiments" (bottom of page 1133).

The Poet

"The Poet" makes an argument for the continuing value of poetry, an argument that remains compelling in the early twenty-first century. The essay also reflects a distinctly male sort of poetics that can be contrasted very effectively, later on in the course, to the way American women writers from Fuller through Dickinson, and onward to Plath and Rich, choose to engage with the world.

Since Emerson was also a poet, we can read this essay—and all of them, perhaps—as if we were reading the work of a poet; we can respond to individual sentences and to Emerson's specific expression of particular ideas much as if we were trying to close read a lyric poem rather than a sequence of firmly and intricately interconnected propositions. In this essay, we begin with his central idea that all of us "stand in need of expression. In love, in art, in avarice, in politics, in labor, in games, we study to utter our painful secret. The man is only half himself, the other half is his expression" (bottom of page 1181). Asking students to respond to this idea can lead into a discussion of voice, one of their own specific tasks as undergraduates as well as the ongoing task of American writers throughout our literary history. Emerson suggests that the poet possesses both a complete vision and the tool—language—for expressing what we would all understand if we were just given the analogies for doing so. The poet finds those particular analogies (metaphors, similes, images) that allow us to understand what we might have been on the verge of seeing, never see fully or truly without the analogies themselves.

"Words are also actions, and actions are a kind of words" (bottom of page 1182). This idea may generate some controversy for students, unaccustomed to viewing language as action. Ask students to explain what it might mean to see the world as "put under the mind for verb and noun" (top of page 1187). Doing so might help them achieve a recognition about the relationship between words and actions and between words and the motions of consciousness.

This is a powerful manifesto for the liberation of poetry from all custom and restraint; but ask students to look closely at lines like these: "The man is only half himself, the other half is his expression" (bottom of page 1181) and "the religions of the world are the ejaculations of a few imaginative men" (top of page 1192). Here and throughout the essay, Emerson's poetics is aggressively male: all about gaining dominion over experience, playing Adam, naming all things in the natural world, or playing some version of the wild bard that Emerson imagines as powerfully male primordial spirit and force in Anglo-Saxon poetry. It's not just the imagery in the essay that shows this male inflection: it is this assumption that the highest and best engagement with worldly experience is agonistic, a struggle to say the profoundest and most permanent possible thing, and to have the Last Word. What about a poetics based on dialogue with experience rather than dominion over it? What about a poetics in which each poem is not proffered as the last word or the last poem but as momentary perceptions in and of a particular moment? What about a poetics in which a certain mutuality, rather than domination, is the hoped for relationship to the world?

If students are curious about the masculine inflection of Emerson's idea of verse and the poet, this is a great time to turn to Emily Dickinson, reading half a dozen of her poems together, and fairly quickly. When students ask whether they "add up" to a consistent theme or aesthetic vision, why not ask where this requirement of emotional and thematic unity comes from, this premise that all the poems from a complex and changeful sensibility have to add up to some overarching and final profundity? That idea comes from Emerson, and in Dickinson we see the most brilliant resistance to the idea that Emerson's "Poet" describes the Poet, for all times and for both genders.

John Brown

To forthright resistance of race slavery Emerson was a latecomer; Thoreau and others in the transcendental communities of Boston and Concord were speaking out years before he joined in. The capture of Brown at Harper's Ferry in 1859 brought forth many essays supporting him and compared to Thoreau's "A Plea for Captain John Brown," Emerson's contribution seems warily abstract. Toward the end, however, it warms up in ways that can astound—for example, the paragraph that begins "All women are drawn to him by their predominance of sentiment. All gentlemen, of course, are on his side" (bottom of page 1212). Is Emerson serious here? Swept away by his own rhetoric? Or is some special quality of his reasoning, or self-presentation, in evidence here that we have seen before?

Fate

The late essay "Fate" will elicit controversy among your students and give them a glimpse of Emerson responding to the current events and spirit of his own times. Throughout the essay, Emerson variously defines fate as the laws of the world, as what limits us, and as unpenetrated causes; he writes that "once we thought, positive power was all. Now, we learn, that negative power, or circumstance, is half. Nature is the tyrannous circumstance" (top of page 1218). Contrast what he says here about nature with the book *Nature* itself. How do your students respond to Emerson's position that the "fate" of our limitations cannot be transcended, except by accepting it and building "altars" to the "Beautiful Necessity"? Is there no hope for reform in the world if "the riddle of the age has for each a private solution" (top of page 1214)? Is Emerson asking us to accept what he himself terms the "complicity" of "race living at the expense of race" because "Providence has a wild, rough, incalculable road to its end," and therefore, it is futile to "whitewash its huge mixed, instrumentalities" (bottom of page 1215)? Is there no hope for environment or the "nurture" side of Emerson's portrait of nature? He writes of the ditch digger that "he has but one future, and that is already predetermined in his lobes, and described in that little fatty face, pig-eye, and squat form. All the privilege and all the legislation of the world cannot meddle or help to make a poet or a prince of him" (bottom of page 1216). Is Emerson's own essay itself an example of "organization tyranniz-ing over character"? If we accept the "Beautiful Necessity" of things, are we enshrining elitism, the New England Brahminism of ideological caste and class? Allowing your students to challenge Emerson is one way of teaching them to take his ideas seriously, to be critical as well as appreciative; it is a way of allowing them to participate in the shaping of ideological debate that characterizes American cultural history.

The Poems

Northrop Frye was famous for remarking that Wordsworth's "Preface" to the *Lyrical Ballads* was an important moment in the formation of the roman-tic sensibility but that as a guide to the actual poems of Wordsworth it rated "only a B plus." A good way of engaging with the poems is to ask a similar question, reading them in light of "The Poet." Aesthetic and philosophical principles can lead in one direction, personal temperament in another. If your students find poems like "Each and All" a bit austere in sound, declam-atory rather than convincingly a "song," you might observe that Emerson, born and raised in the environs of Boston, and schooled at Harvard to be a parson, not a wild bard, may have carried forward certain personality traits that even his own avowals of freedom and wildness could not displace. When he writes an ode to Bacchus, the god of wine and intoxication and excess, he rhymes, writing some of the tightest and most formal stanzas in this set of poems! No paradox there? Should we regard these poems as some sort of failure of nerve? Or can we enjoy a tension here, between the aspi-rations and exhortations that the poems offer and the rhetorical dignity that they enact?

Questions for discussion:
- When your students have built up a body of experience with Emerson as a poet, aesthetician, observer of nature and humanity, philosopher, and theologian, you're ready to open an especially important question: does Emerson, in each sentence, mean what he says, as Edwards or Winthrop or any of the great Puritan theologians or homilists "meant" every sentence they wrote? If not, then how should we read him?
- If the above questions lead to an impasse, try another key sentence or two from "Self-Reliance," a declaration of intellectual freedom perhaps—but also a source of trouble for interpreting his written work:

"A foolish consistency is the hobgoblin of little minds, adored by little statesmen and philosophers and divines. With consistency a great soul has simply nothing to do. He may as well concern himself with his shadow on the wall. Out upon your guarded lips! Sew them up with packthread, do. Else, if you would be a man, speak what you think today in words as hard as cannon balls, and to-morrow speak what to-morrow thinks in hard words again, though it contradict every thing you said to-day. Ah, then, exclaim the aged ladies, you shall be sure to be misunderstood. Misunderstood! It is a right fool's word. Is it so bad then to be misunderstood? Pythagoras was misunderstood, and Socrates, and Jesus, and Luther, and Copernicus, and Galileo, and Newton, and every pure and wise spirit that ever took flesh. To be great is to be misunderstood" (top of page 1168). How shall we read an essayist who might mean what he says only "today?"

- And a broader question beyond these two: Jefferson provides us with a declaration of political independence; Franklin affirms our independence from any single dogma or body of systematic thought, exhorting us to make our own systems—preferably on the model of his own. If we try reading Emerson as a declaration of complete intellectual independence, then in what spirit should we read Emerson—or anybody else who offers wisdom or values? In other words, is rebellion against Emerson himself, moment to moment or overall, a supremely Emersonian act?

NATHANIEL HAWTHORNE

Hawthorne can present a special challenge, because students can feel that reading his work is little more than a quest for the "moral" or a protracted game of "find the secret sin." Confusing his Puritan subjects and themes with his own values, they can wrongly conclude that Hawthorne is himself a Puritan, a grumpy refuser of transcendental optimism. They may also need help in understanding how allegory figures into an appreciation of Hawthorne and in discerning differences between stories that seem predominantly or essentially allegorical and stories in which allegorical dimensions are part of a larger experience or meditation.

Though "Young Goodman Brown," "The Minister's Black Veil," and "Rappaccini's Daughter" all invite students to go hunting for allegories, each of these stories ultimately frustrates that hunt. In each of these stories, if you ask students to identify the "good" character, they will eventually come around to qualifying their initial response. If students can grow comfortable with a possibility that Hawthorne, as an author and a modern human being, asks complex questions rather than deals in reductive answers, they will enjoy reading him all the more and understand better his importance to American fiction.

With "Rappaccini's Daughter," students can have fun teasing out parallels between the Garden of Eden and Rappaccini's garden. But beyond those parallels lies another enigma: who is the real serpent in this garden, the figure most responsible for Beatrice's death? Rappaccini? The rival scientist Baglioni? The supposedly adoring Giovanni? If the story is ambiguous about all this, what is the quality of that ambiguity? In other words is this just a game of assigning the guilt or can we identify a broad range of complicity in the destruction of innocence—parents who "want only the best" for their own children; small-minded professional competitors who gloat at the failure of the enemies; lovers who, in worshipping illusions, really love only themselves?

After a brief absence from NAAL, "Wakefield" has returned, and its presence here allows us to see Hawthorne in a very different light, as a pioneering writer about urban settings and the very real possibility of self-loss—not in an encounter with witches at midnight or sinister men of science but in a turn down a wrong block and a simple variation in the habits that pass for personality and a life. If the other stories look "back" to the New England Puritan past or to fantastical enclosures in a European never-never-land, "Wakefield" looks forward to Baudelaire, Sartre, Eliot, Beckett, and others who found much to fear in the distractions and mind-killing routines of the new urban wilderness.

Students will probably have an easier time with "The Birth-Mark," as it seems to play by all the rules and themes that became evident in "Rappaccini's Daughter"—the foolhardiness and depravity of seeking perfection or superhuman power; the fatality of mistaking infatuation and idolatry for love; the reduction, in one's own mind, of other human beings to objects to be manipulated, overhauled, or otherwise controlled.

Questions for discussion:
- In other stories, Hawthorne proves his skill at creating theatrical protagonists, figures distinguished by passion, obsession, brilliance. Why does he make Wakefield such a nobody? Wouldn't he be more compelling as a villainous tormentor, a cold manipulator of his own wife, and his own fate? Why not?
- What are the thematic connections between "The Minister's Black Veil" and "Young Goodman Brown?" Are we supposed to figure out, or really care, what "really" happened in the forest that night and in Hooper's past to cause these permanent transformations in their character?
- Think about self-knowledge as a theme in these stories. Which of these characters truly comes to know something about human nature and to know himself or herself in the process? Do any of them end up supposing that they "know" more about life or the human condition than they really do?

The Scarlet Letter

One of the rites of passage in an American education is writing a paper on *The Scarlet Letter*; the novel is so buried in amateur and professional analysis that it helps to remember what it was like to read the book for the very first time and to give students a chance to achieve some kind of direct and personal relationship with the text, especially before turning them loose on a writing assignment. This is a novel with great psychological intensity and complexity, and tethering through it with color motifs (red this, black that) and formal symmetries (three scaffold scenes, daylight, midnight, daylight, A's in the air, A's on breasts—maybe . . .) is a great way to lose track of what makes this book really interesting.

On "The Custom-House": as you move into the text, you might want to observe some peculiarities of this long introductory sketch—and you might decide to skip it altogether, if you sense that Hawthorne's portrait of the numbing routine of the now, as a contrast to the heightened drama of long ago, drains the curiosity of your young readers rather than raises it. If you do begin here, you might draw attention to the atmosphere of dream or hallucination that accompanies not only Hawthorne's discovery of the letter but also his entire memory of the customhouse itself. Also interesting are the moments in which Hawthorne blames others for his own "torpor" and his consequent difficulty in writing as well as the image patterns of this opening essay: the meals that he describes, the word portrait of the inspector, and Hawthorne's speculations about reconciling "the Actual and the Imaginary."

Consider the statement that Hawthorne makes early on: "To this extent and within these limits, an author, methinks, may be autobiographical, without violating either the reader's rights or his own." Is "The Custom-House" a revelation of its author—or another veil or evasion, like Hooper's black veil or Wakefield's private-joke sojourn in the next street?

The novel itself (or the "romance"—you could ask students to talk about what they think Hawthorne means by the difference as he lays it out in "Preface to *The House of the Seven Gables*") raises a lot of related questions. Think about the rituals and pageants of revelation in this book: Hester's first appearance in the prison door; the scarlet letter itself, embroidered beyond the point of ostentation; the three scenes on the scaffold; and Chapter XXIII, "The Revelation of the Scarlet Letter." Does Hawthorne's symbol, literally fastened to Hester's breast, allow him to bridge "the Actual and the Imaginary"? Compare Hawthorne's use of tangible symbol with Emerson's use of analogies. Is the scarlet letter also a way of seeing and of knowing, for Hawthorne's characters and for himself?

Questions for discussion:
- In Chapter II, Hawthorne writes of the women by the prison door (bottom of page 1379): "There was, moreover, a boldness and rotundity of speech among these matrons, as most of them seemed to be, that would startle us at the present day." If one of the themes of the novel is that the status and power of women has changed for the good over the intervening two hundred years, what is he implying in the above observation? How does this remark, and other portraits of women in the book, complicate our thinking about the status of women, then and now?
- The novel has a famous one-line paragraph: "The scarlet letter had not done its office." What does that line mean? Does the letter ever "do its office" with regard to the moral salvation or punishment of Hester Prynne?

- How do you read Dimmesdale's speech on the scaffold on Election Day, to the assembled multitudes, especially the paragraphs culminating with "Behold the one sinner of the world!"? At that moment, and on this final day of his life, how are Hester and Pearl figuring into his thinking?

- How does Hawthorne use Pearl, especially at the end of the book? He writes (page 1489) that her tears "were the pledge that she would grow up amid human joy and sorrow, nor for ever do battle with the world, but be a woman in it." What does that line signify? And how do we interpret the "moral" Hawthorne "presses" on his readers at the end: "Be true! Be true! Be true! Show freely to the world, if not your worst, yet some trait whereby the worst may be inferred!"

HENRY WADSWORTH LONGFELLOW

A couple of generations ago, Longfellow's reputation and popular audience were so robust that there could be no need to introduce him to any American or British roomful of marginally literate young people. In his lifetime his work outsold Tennyson, Browning, Arnold, all the remembered Victorians. In America the "fireside poet" phrase associated with him was a compliment then a phrase that acknowledged his extraordinary stature as a living American bard. His Brattle Street home was a place that tourists came to see, like the digs of a Hollywood celebrity, and at the turn of the twentieth century busts of Longfellow were standard front-hall décor in college and Carnegie libraries. Proficient in several languages and a skilled translator of Dante and many German lyrics, he was a true scholar as well as a world-famous artist. And with his strong regular features and grand beard, he also looked the part.

But by the second decade of the twentieth century, with the rise of English departments that had a special stake in obscurity, the "fireside" phrase became a gesture of condescension. A poet who tried to write for everyone—and succeeded—doesn't leave room for the intervention of scholastics. Insofar as the English-reading public still has "best loved poets," Longfellow counts as one of those, but what can we say about him in a classroom?

If the sweep and extraordinary ambitions of Longfellow's work are seen most easily in long poems like *Evangeline* and *The Song of Hiawatha* and the verse translation of *The Divine Comedy*, the NAAL selections give a sense of his range, in subject and also in voice. He wasn't "public" all the time; understanding the value of poetry as utterance overheard (as John Stuart Mill described it), as a quarrel with the self, as Yeats described it, Longfellow observes in ways that suggest several blended identities. He can seem as solitary as Frost or Bryant or Dickinson and as bardic or ambassadorial as Whitman, wise and knowing at one moment and deeply puzzled at the next. And in some of the works collected here, such voices come together as an evocative chorus.

Questions for discussion:

- Read "This Day Is Done" aloud—it doesn't take long to get through—and try to describe the mood, the psychological condition, that the poem seeks to create and address. If your students remember other poems about melancholy or "dejection" in the evening or at night—Gray's "Elegy Written in a Country Churchyard," Coleridge's "Dejection: An Ode," or the opening stanzas of Poe's "The Raven," pause to compare them. Does Longfellow directly or obliquely answer Coleridge's indulgence in "a grief without a pang?" Does he answer the nameless narrator of "The Raven," who maintains and deepens his melancholy by reading volumes of "forgotten lore?" What kind of "lore" does Longfellow prescribe for his own mood, and for ours?

- As a bard, a poet who like Virgil or Dante would express the humanity and experience of a nation or a people, Longfellow sometimes describes the Other from afar and sometimes imaginatively from within. With regard to race slavery he tries it both ways: there's a famous short poem called "The Slave's Dream," in which he enters the mind of a dying slave to tell us dreams of his former life as an African prince; "The Slave Singing at Midnight," on the other hand, gives us a slave who is not even seen but merely a voice in the dark. Longfellow keeps his distance here—with what tonal and thematic effect?

- A kindred question: "The Jewish Cemetery at Newport" can make a nice pairing with Emma Lazarus's "In the Jewish Synagogue at Newport," (Volume C of NAAL, page 518), a poem that speaks back to Longfellow in a spirit of respectful complication. Lazarus, as an American Jew and an "insider," speaks from inside the synagogue; Longfellow stays out under the sky. Why doesn't Longfellow go in? And how can you describe the intentions and themes of Longfellow's poem, compared to that of Lazarus?

- "The Cross of Snow" was written late in Longfellow's life, and it can be classified as an elegy, a public pronouncement about a private grief, a poem apparently inspired by the popularity of a recent spectacular painting by Frederic Church. Does this poem do what an elegy is supposed to? How do the final lines compare with the final lines of Bryant's "Thanatopsis," Poe's "Annabel Lee," or any of Bradstreet's elegies for her grandchildren?

JOHN GREENLEAF WHITTIER

Born in the same year as Longfellow and classified with him, then and now, as one of the Fireside Poets, Whittier shows a style conspicuously different from his friends, and students will pick up on those differences fairly easily. Working from the headnotes in NAAL, you might begin with some attention to what distinguished Whittier as a public figure. As a Quaker, he was committed to the virtues of a plain life and was also, from his youth, ardently against the institution of race slavery. Longfellow wrote earnestly and guilelessly for a vast and varied public; Whittier went farther in trying to emulate the warm austerity of ordinary New England life with language and meter. He was also a celebrant of unadorned family routine and ordinary folk—to the extent that modern readers, accustomed to crisis, headlong plotting, and jump-cut editing in their cultural fare, could find a long encounter with Whittier's famous, long, and patient "Snow-Bound" a cause for psychological cabin fever. One of the benefits of settling in briefly with these Whittier excerpts is that your dialogue could open into an exchange on the cadences and perceptions of private life, then and now, and whether we still have a capacity to settle in with others—some of them distinctly lacking in flash and theatricality—and pay a little gratifying attention.

Questions for discussion:
- Read aloud a stanza of "The Hunters of Men" and comment on the effects of the meter, these anapestic tetrameters, bouncy and reminiscent of ballads and light verse. Is this a light poem? How does it compare to other poems you have read so far, by other poets, on the subject of slavery? What does Whittier achieve by leaving off Bryant's sonorities and giving us a galloping ballad on this ongoing crisis?
- "Snow-Bound" is a poem about what? How does Whittier make this reminiscence a reverie rather than a nightmare? This was a very popular poem through most of the American nineteenth century and on into the twentieth, as industrial and urban life took hold and rapid communications came on in waves. How do you account for that popularity?
- Are poets like Whittier and Longfellow possible for us anymore? What cultural practices may have replaced them—and what do you think, personally, of that succession?

EDGAR ALLAN POE

You might find it useful to open with observations about the rediscovery, or reinvention, of Poe: his fade into obscurity in America for three decades after his death; his rediscovery and veneration by symbolist and imagist poets in France; his re-importation to America as an imaginative writer of real consequence rather than merely as a maestro of gothic entertainments or a show-off in romantic verse.

But did the French get it right? Later on in your classes on Poe, you might want to speculate on how and why Poe has become so influential in our popular culture, a forebear of mountains of gothic novels, slash-and-hack films, and gruesome television shows. Poe has changed *for* us, and he has changed *us*. The largest and most vexing questions might be how we should take him "seriously"—and what our efforts to do so say about our notions of seriousness in imaginative literature.

The unconscious, the world of dreams and the drift into sleep, informs Poe's work, and students may study this fixation in some of the poems, including "The Raven" and "The City in the Sea," and many of the short stories, including "Ligeia" and "The Fall of the House of Usher." But this is a subject that plays no great role in his famous essay "The Philosophy of

Composition," and students may wonder if this is a comprehensive and serious guide to reading Poe.

Questions for discussion:
- When Poe argues in "The Philosophy of Composition" that sheer emotional intensity is the be-all and end-all of a poem, does that fit with the experience of your students? They might cheer for the idea that poems should be brief—but do they agree that emotional excitement is the chief reason for verse? Do they think Poe means what he says—or could this be a posture as much as a work of literary theory?
- When Poe asserts that the ultimate subject for a poem is the death of a beautiful woman, is he "serious"? In "The Poetic Principle," when he says that "a poem deserves its title only inasmuch as it excites by elevating the soul" (page 1625), what do you think he means by "soul"? Does he mean something that the New England Puritans would have recognized? What happens when we read "Annabel Lee" in the context of Poe's statement in "The Philosophy of Composition" that beauty moves the soul best when the subject is sad and that, therefore, the death of a beautiful woman becomes the "soul" of poetry? Do we have to read "Annabel Lee" as a bouncy generic ballad? Or can we read it aloud in a way that expresses Poe's designs on our mood? Why does Poe need to kill off Annabel Lee to achieve the male speaker's maturity and poetic inspiration? And if the conversation heats up, you might ask for observations about how romantic male writers, as a group, constructed women as subjects in their poetry and fiction.
- How does our thinking about Poe's art alter when we turn to "The Imp of the Perverse," and to Poe's famous relish for put-ons and practical jokes? Students have a lot of experience with the way that comedy and horror, deadly seriousness and put-ons, mingle in popular gothic entertainments, with their habit of becoming reflexive and self-satirizing. What about here? Is there an element of the absurd about "The Raven" and is that absurdity possibly intentional?
- Can we read any of these stories allegorically, as we might read Hawthorne? Can we read these poems and stories as being fundamentally about the mind? What happens if we try reading "The Tell-Tale Heart" and "The Masque of the Red Death" this way—as allegories for mental states or emotions?
- "The Black Cat" and "The Tell-Tale Heart" make a handy pair, as they are both stories about a horror and a crime buried beneath the innocent-looking surfaces of an ordinary house. Read aloud the last paragraph of "The Tell-Tale Heart" first, and then try an oral approach to the final lines of "The Black Cat." Does a fresh experience with the crazy narrator of "Heart" carry over to what you hear in the voice of the other story? *Was* there a second cat?
- When students turn to "The Purloined Letter" and enter the familiar territory of the detective story, they might compare this narrative with Poe's tales of the supernatural. What are the different effects he

achieves in "The Purloined Letter"? How do Dupin's cleverness and rationality go together with his idea that "the material world abounds with very strict analogies to the immaterial"? Consider the statement in light of Emerson's use of the analogy in *Nature*. Compare Dupin's language with Poe's in "The Philosophy of Composition": is the character a double for his author?

ABRAHAM LINCOLN

You may find that a return to Lincoln's words as significant literature will be a refreshing experience. In American elementary and secondary classes, excerpts from these speeches have echoed so often that students may have tuned them out—and they probably haven't thought about them much as literary documents, crafted for a specific audience and historical moment. The Gettysburg Address and the Second Inaugural Address are revolutionary moments in discourse of American leaders: plain, brief, taut, and carefully cadenced, they were written to be read as well as heard—and were perfect for recitation by others, at a time when declamation was a standard subject in American schools.

Questions for discussion:
- You might point out that at Gettysburg, the featured speaker on the program was Edward Everett, a Boston Brahmin and famed orator who spoke for more than two hours before Lincoln rose on the platform. Lincoln knew something like that was going to happen: how does his speech respond to that immediate context?
- Comparing the two Lincoln Civil War speeches to the "House Divided" speech in 1858 can provoke some observations about how words can be shaped to be heard—or overheard. In "House Divided," what assumptions does Lincoln seem to be making about the thinking and the attention span of his audience, this gathering of weary politicians and reporters at the end of a convention?
- Have your students ever watched a political convention on the last day? What are the challenges for the person at the rostrum?
- Why are there so many rhetorical questions here and none in the two presidential speeches? How has Lincoln grown as a rhetorician and as a leader?
- During the Civil War, when newspapers, national weeklies and monthlies, and overloaded telegraph systems were so important to getting the news out and maintaining morale, what kind of speech would have been more effective—as front-page news and as an expression of national sentiment?

MARGARET FULLER

The Fuller selections in NAAL present a rich experience of the most important woman among the New England transcendentalists and one of the most interesting, independent American minds of the middle nineteenth century. "The Great Lawsuit," Fuller's long essay on the intellectual and social subjugation of women ranges widely, through contemporary literature, ancient mythology, philosophy, the arts, history, the realities of public and domestic life; it alludes to Shakespeare, Isabella, George Sand, the U.S. Constitution, Spenser's Britomart, a dreamed-up modern Miranda, Orpheus and Eurydice, Mosaic law, the French Revolution, Isis, Sita, Mary Wollstonecraft, mesmerism—it seems that nothing is left out. Are these comparisons and allusions random, stream of consciousness? In other words, is "The Great Lawsuit" an accretion rather than an organized essay? Or is there a sequence, and a cadence, to the way that these issues and allusions are raised and to the style that they are raised in?

"The Great Lawsuit" takes a while to warm up, and the opening paragraphs are long and ornate, to the extent that modern students may feel like tuning out before reaching the quick, sharp, imaginary exchanges and short incisive paragraphs that constitute the best-known parts of the essay. Especially in its lively "Miranda" passages, "The Great Lawsuit" is an excellent place to open questions regarding the development of a discourse that escapes certain male predispositions, about formal argument and engagement with experience. Fuller shines as a creator of dialogue, and her tighter, more economical paragraphs can make Emerson's symphonic sentences and grand generalizations seem overbearing. To put it another way, Fuller's style, as it gradually comes clear or breaks away from conventionality and formality in "The Great Lawsuit," may represent a very different spirit and style for addressing and persuading others and understanding life: there is a delight in give and take, in open-endedness, rather than in displays of overwhelming rhetorical force and the "settling" of big questions.

Questions for discussion:
- Fuller calls the essay "The Great Lawsuit"— but why? What were lawsuits like in the nineteenth-century Anglo-American legal system? Were clear, quick victories to be expected? Is there anything sardonic or playful about Fuller's title? In comparison to the way Emerson argues or pleads a case—for example, the opening paragraphs of "Self Reliance"—does Fuller's wit weaken hers or get in the way somehow? Does it change, or even satirize, the nature of argument itself, as that ritual has evolved over several centuries, under male-governance?
- Why is so much space given over in Fuller's essay to domestic relations, to husbands and wives, especially considering that Fuller was never married and eventually lived (and died) out beyond the pale, as far as Anglo-American matrimony was concerned? Is this section of the essay a gesture of accommodation? Is it subversive in some way, or Fabian (to borrow an adjective from decades later), in the way that it addresses the American domestic scene?

Summer on the Lakes

"Summer on the Lakes" shows us another side of Margaret Fuller—not the writer with a cause but the wandering observer, trying hard to be entirely open to new experience. The sequence at Niagara Falls, however, gives us an early encounter with a paradox that will grow only stronger for writers of this time and after. Thanks to steel and wood engravings and lithographs in albums and shops and also on the walls of American homes, the most famous spectacular sights on the North American continent are now "seen" by countless people long before they visit them in the flesh. At the edge of the cataract, Fuller is troubled by the fact that the vista before her looks a bit too much like the pictures, and her description of the setting tries hard for fresh details and angles.

Questions for discussion:
- There is much about flowers and small plants here, and limited vision: the Wake Robin and the May Apple (bottom of page 1661), and the falls "black as night" (top of page 1664). Why does Fuller spend so much time looking down at her feet or into the shadows, hereabouts, rather than up and out into bright sunshine?
- When Fuller journeys out to northern Illinois—not known now as an especially spectacular landscape—her enthusiasm for wide landscapes and high vantage points seems to rekindle. Why there, rather than along the Niagara River?

New to NAAL are a couple of avowedly political writings by Fuller—her spirited review of Douglass's *Narrative* and a commentary on the meaning of the Fourth of July—an essay that offers great opportunities with Douglass's views on the same subject (pages 2140–43). Fuller's reflections are brief but strongly aligned with the fundamental principles your student have seen in "The Great Lawsuit"—and also with principles espoused by her Concord friends, Emerson and Thoreau.

Questions for discussion:
- A crucial paragraph in "Fourth of July" seems to veer away from the expected path of the essay—public history and public obligations—to emphasize that "private lives, more than public measures must be the salvation of the country" (middle of page 1676). How does this observation connect to Emerson's emphasis on the solitary self in *Nature* and "Self Reliance" and to the Thoreau chapter "Solitude" in *Walden*?
- Fuller's review of Douglass, for all its praise, describes the *Narrative* as having "torrid energy and saccharine fullness" (bottom of page 1673) and pauses to chide Garrison's introductory remarks for their "usual over emphatic style." What do these observations suggest about Fuller's temperament? Do they dilute the praise of Douglass's book or have some other effect?

Cluster: Slavery, Race, and the Making of American Literature

From several perspectives, this is the most challenging cluster in the anthology. The opening selection, from Jefferson's *Notes on the State of Virginia*, is a passage that many of his admirers would prefer to avoid—and twentieth-century textbooks featuring his work commonly left it out. The five excerpts that follow Jefferson in this cluster, essays and speeches by David Walker, William Lloyd Garrison, Angelina Grimké, Sojourner Truth, and Martin Delany, can be read as rejoinders to the celebrated author of The Declaration of Independence, the Founder who put the phrase "all men are created equal" into the national imagination—whence it would enter, by slow, hard stages, into the national ethos.

In the context of a literature course, conversation about this set of writers can range much farther than collective disapproval of Jefferson's racism and hypocrisy. These moments in Jefferson's work can be read as indicating grave flaws in thinking and in character; but scores of major American writers and intellects, from Henry Adams, Mark Twain, and Edith Wharton through Hemingway, Eliot, Pound, Robert Lowell, and Ken Kesey, are liable to similar charges. A class of inquisitive students will want to do more than pay homage to contemporary ethics and decry, once again, race slavery as the grimmest dimension of American history. In this cluster we can observe very interesting contrasts in literary styles and in the fundamental idea of what constitutes an effective argument. As expository prose, Jefferson's commentary works in a different way from anything that comes after in the cluster, and students may be engaged strongly in a contemplation of tone, evidence, and paragraph structure.

Questions for discussion:
- Jefferson regarded himself as a man of science, and along with his achievements as a statesman he is remembered to this day for an array of interesting domestic inventions and gadgets and for his lifelong interest in the natural world. The opening paragraph of this excerpt is extraordinarily long, almost relentless. Why doesn't he pause or break up the prose, as he does in The Declaration of Independence? Do you see relentless "scientific" exposition or argumentation here or some other rhetorical strategy at work? Where, in your view, are Jefferson's grossest lapses in logic, observation, and basic knowledge of the world—and how is language used here in an attempt to maneuver past these weaknesses?
- Jefferson dismisses the work of Phillis Wheatley very brusquely, commenting that Wheatley was a powerfully religious writer but not a true poet. What reasons does he give for this summary judgment? Why doesn't he describe or challenge in any detail the merit of her work? How might Wheatley be an embarrassment to Jefferson's argument?
- In his discussion of African Americans and race slavery, Jefferson alludes to "the Creator"; Walker invokes Jehovah and "the Lord God of heaven"; citing Jefferson's words in The Declaration of Independence, Garrison quotes the famous phrase "endowed by their Creator" but closes with a capitalized, ferocious vow, "SO HELP ME GOD!" Describe the differences you sense in the way the Almighty is invoked by each writer.

- Ask your students to choose and read aloud one short passage by Garrison, Delany, and Sojourner Truth. What similarities do they hear among these authors with regard to style and sound? What are the tonal differences, and how would your students explain them?
- The shortest passage in the set is Sojourner Truth's complete speech at the Women's Rights Convention in Akron, Ohio, in 1851, and this speech is transcribed, as the speaker never learned to write. What does Sojourner Truth accomplish in this brief address, and what lessons can we learn here about the effectiveness of brevity?
- Grimké relies heavily on the New Testament to support her argument for abolition; Martin Delany, however, makes powerful use of a narrative from the Old Testament. What relationships do your students see between the tone and intention of these excerpts and their respective use of one Testament or the other?

HARRIET BEECHER STOWE

Uncle Tom's Cabin is a book that was, and is, "big" by any measure. Selling millions of copies in hundreds of editions and having a real effect on American social and moral thought, it's often known to today's students via myth and misconception. Students can feel some gratification in arriving at a text that, unlike *Moby-Dick* or *The Scarlet Letter*, really shook the world in its own time and achieved vast popular success—but they may want to know, right at the start of the conversation, what all the fuss was about, and why the doors of the canon have creaked open only lately to admit (after a long lapse) a book that was written for the millions and plays by so many of the rules of popular fiction.

If your students find this first encounter with Stowe intriguing, you might want to assure them that the entire work, which can look bulky on the shelf, especially with many added pages of editorial introducing and annotating, is actually a fast read, at least as fast as Dickens, and that one way of accounting for its vast success—even in the United Kingdom, where it actually did better than in the United States, against a legion of established and popular novelists—is that Stowe was uncannily skillful at mixing the action and melodrama with meditative chapters, some of which read like symposia on race slavery. The interludes of reasoned debate, back and forth, usually between genial white men and women, about the "Slavery Question," conceal a fire, however, that breaks out explosively in the final chapters of the novel.

Questions for discussion:
- Chapter I of *Uncle Tom's Cabin* opens with two white men in conversation, mixing business with a bit of front-porch moralizing. Read this chapter as a reader might have encountered it in 1851, as an installment of a serialized novel—in other words, with no foreknowledge of where it is going. After you've finished the chapter, look back at its title and comment on any undertones you might find there.

- *Uncle Tom's Cabin* can be read as a point of arrival in a long American quest to evolve a morality out of the Puritan heritage, the words of the chartering documents of the republic, the ethos of the Enlightenment, the values of transcendentalism. To put it simply, a suspense had been building: was America going to stand behind what it had been saying about the consequentiality of the individual life, the importance of direct experience and personally acquired wisdom, the equality of all human beings? On what does Stowe's moral fervor seem to be based? Latter-day Calvinism? Concord-style ethics? Franklinian rationalism and self-reliance? Some fusion of all of these?

- Why, over the years, has Tom been variously admired and vilified for his temperament? This can be a complex question: students may have personal and painful experiences with "Uncle Tom" as an epithet, to the extent that they may be surprised and bothered by the way that Stowe lauds him in this novel. Why this kind of character in the foreground, at this particular historical moment?

- If students have heard of Tom before, they may have heard of Simon Legree as the villain of the piece—and if they follow the cue of, say, *The King and I*, they may think of the novel as the agon of the final chapters between the stoic and saintly Tom and the self-hating, Satanic Legree. The other whites in the novel are remembered less well in the popular imagination, but Stowe spends a great deal of time developing them—more, actually, than she spends on developing Tom and his fellow slaves. Why all of this attention to these genteel whites, who carry no whips and do no violence themselves and who have elaborate and sometimes eloquent excuses for their various degrees of noninvolvement in the issue of race slavery? Ask a question like that, and you may reach an area of real importance in Stowe's novel: the book's sustained wrath about the supposedly good men and women who do nothing. Ask how the portraits of these complacent whites might have a special effect in creating the shock and suspense of the novel and in reaching Stowe's overwhelmingly white, middle-class, church-going northern audience where it lives.

- In Chapter XIII, "The Quaker Settlement," we have a vignette of a family on the north shore of the Ohio River, at the lower reach of the Underground Railroad. Eliza, who has escaped over the ice floes, listens to a conversation between Rachel and Ruth (pages 1746–48), and remains largely silent. We know from previous episodes that Eliza is quite articulate; why is she quiet at this point? What might Stowe's purposes be in unfolding the family conversation at such length?

- Technologically, socially, and aesthetically, how can we account for the huge appeal of this book? As students speculate about this, you may want to bring up the revolution in printing and in transportation that was taking place just before and during the publication of *Uncle Tom's Cabin*. Steam-powered presses and electrotype had suddenly raised page production, for newpapers and popular magazines, from around one thousand sheets per hour to tens of thousands; the web of railroads now allowed publishers to ship large quantities of printed books farther and cheaper than ever before—and suddenly the smash best seller, selling hundreds of thousands of copies in a few months, was a technological possibility. But students will want to speculate about the way that the novel works within and against the popular romantic or sentimental narrative, and they can draw on their own experience (with popular modern novels that they have read on their own) to look at the way that these representative chapters exploit and resist expectations.

FANNY FERN

As a comic writer in middle of the nineteenth century, and as a woman seeking to make her own way in the world while American political feminism was only beginning to take shape, Sara Willis Parton had to be quick, agile, and sharp. Satirizing social conventions and pieties can be easy—but to satirize and ingratiate at the same time requires skill. For several years, "Fanny Fern" had to rely on her wit and her charm to survive, and in reading her work now we can see genius in her unusual rhetorical style.

Questions for discussion:
- How would you describe the pace of a Fanny Fern narrative? Ask a student to read a few lines aloud and compare them to lines from some other prose stylist of the period, someone that the class has read recently—Emerson, perhaps, or Thoreau. There's a hectic, breathless quality to Fern in "Aunt Hetty on Matrimony" and "Hungry Husbands," an impression of someone talking very fast. What are the effects of sheer velocity on satire—and especially on how it might strike a reading audience?
- "Aunt Hetty" seems like a stock figure from Anglo-American comedy, the blunt older woman who speaks her mind in rambling monologues to relatives and friends. What can we imagine as the context in which Aunt Hetty speaks? Why does most of this monologue come at us as one huge paragraph? How does the sketch induce us to laugh *at* Aunt Hetty and her opinions or at the institution of marriage—or at both at the same time? What are the advantages of assigning these opinions to a quirky relative? Why doesn't Fern use a similar strategy in "Hungry Husbands?"
- "Barnum's Museum" gives us a glimpse of Fern's work as a reporter, of sorts. What rhetorical strategies do we see at play here, strategies that breathe life into what could easily be a dull narrative of exhibits in a gallery? How does the ostensible disorganization of the report contribute beneficially to the effect?
- In "Tom Pax," Fern assumes the voice of a complacent husband. What clue does the name "Pax" (Latin for "peace") provide about the character of the speaker? If students have read Fuller's "The Great Lawsuit," ask them to compare the personality of Pax to the made-up "sorrowful trader" in Fuller's essay, the overbearing husband who *thinks* that he does all the real thinking for his own family.

• In comparison to these other works, the *Ruth Hall* chapters tell a story more akin to a Dickens novel than to broad social satire. This is a story about a woman with children, struggling to survive. In looking at these excerpts, students might consider the adaptation of Fern's agile style to the demands of "serious" narrative. How might the pace of this narration, and the clarity and conciseness of the individual sentences here, help the story resist a descent into melodrama?

Harriet Jacobs

The six chapters from *Incidents in the Life of a Slave Girl* included in the anthology represent a coherent, integrated unit that conveys the power of Jacobs's narrative and shows her raising questions about slavery and particularly the experience of women in slavery. Chapters I and VII focus on family connections. Jacobs contrasts the powerful emotional bonds enslaved families felt for each other and the horrors of a legal system that did not recognize slave marriages or the primary bonds between parents and children. Chapters X and XIV explore what students might term Dr. Flint's sexual harassment of Linda and Jacobs's presentation of Linda's moral right to choose a lover. Throughout Jacobs's description of Linda's relationship with Mr. Sands, she addresses herself to white women readers and is concerned that they will identify with Linda as both a woman and, later, a mother and yet not judge her behavior by their own codes, which prescribed chastity. Jacobs implies that Linda felt she could achieve some measure of protection for children she might have with Sands, and so this proved to be in the short term; later, in part of the text not printed in NAAL, Sands marries and, under the guise of taking Linda's daughter Ellen to educate her, turns her into a house servant for his family. Yet she knows that she cannot shelter her child when it is born a girl: "slavery is terrible for men; but it is far more terrible for women." Explore with students differences between Douglass's *Narrative* and Jacobs's *Incidents*.

After an abortive attempt to run away, Linda hides in the garret of her grandmother's shed. Chapter XXI will raise many questions for students. The image of the loophole seems accurate to describe the garret in which she hides; she lives in a space that would not be visible to anyone who looked. It is as if she had "escaped" slavery by finding a "loophole" within the institution; has she "all but" escaped Dr. Flint by hiding for seven years in her grandmother's shed? If so, her "freedom" does her little good, and her children might have been better served had she escaped to the North. She compares herself to Robinson Crusoe; ask students to explore the accuracy of this comparison. Chapter XLI, "Free at Last," serves as an ending for Jacobs's narrative—her story "ends with freedom; not in the usual way, with marriage." Ask students to explore what freedom means for Linda and her children. "Free at Last" shows Linda still with no home of her own, and her daughter has not received the education she has wanted for her. The chapter hints at the lingering ravages of slavery and the deficits the newly freed persons experienced by virtue of being propertyless, uneducated, and separated from family members.

Questions for discussion:
- Without *Incidents*, and with only Douglass's account, would we know much about the sexual harassment and abuse of enslaved women?
- In Chapter XXI Jacobs uses the intriguing metaphor of the loophole; what does this mean?
- If escaping to the North would have better served her, and her children, why did she stay?
- Jacobs implies that she wants to remain near her children, even though for a long time they do not know she is there; does she remain a mother, except for the "loophole" that her children do not know where she is?

WILLIAM WELLS BROWN

As a recovered author and a new inclusion in NAAL, Brown might be easily situated alongside of Harriet Jacobs and Frederick Douglass in a set of slave narratives—but doing so could cause us to miss the uniqueness of Brown's project, his effort to bring personal experience into two genres, or possibly even three—factual memoir, narrative fiction, and something in between, a third-person omniscient recounting of his own life experiences. When you introduce Brown, it's worth pausing to consider with your class that particular historical and cultural moment in which he was writing: in the middle of the nineteenth century the American public was being addressed and exhorted from many directions, and in many voices, about race slavery, and autobiographies and novels enhanced each other and also competed with each other for attention. *Uncle Tom's Cabin* would prove a triumph for fiction in the cause of abolition—but at what cost to the credibility and the audience for factual memoir? In dealing with slavery as a national emergency, Brown experiments to find a genre and a voice worthy of the truth.

Questions for discussion:
- In the excerpt from Brown's *Narrative*, one standout quality is the attention paid to the details of ordinary commerce related to slavery in the South and West: the mundane selling of human beings here and there along a route; the trimming and polishing of older men for sale, like used cars with a quick paint job and a layer of wax. What are the effects, on an audience, of this kind of narrative? Does it undercut the horrors of this trade or somehow enhance them?
- Brown and Douglass both make use of poems by others in the course of telling their own stories. Why are these verses included? What are the effects of these breaks in the personal account?

HENRY DAVID THOREAU

In Thoreau's "Resistance to Civil Government" and "Slavery in Massachusetts" we see him as the prominent exception among his contemporaries to the pattern of evading confrontation with social and political issues of his day. And *Walden*, despite the premise of separation from society on which it opens, emphasizes the practical aspects of Transcendentalism. Ask students to locate Thoreau in a tradition of American writers from Bradstreet through Franklin who speak in a personal voice and address the common reader. How do the effects Thoreau achieves in "Resistance to Civil Government" or *Walden* differ from those Emerson creates in "Self-Reliance" or "Nature"? Ask students to compare and contrast "Nature" and *Walden* as literary works: how are they conceptually similar but technically different? Many who found it difficult to find logical discourse in "Nature" will perceive a narrative design in *Walden*. How does Thoreau manage a happy balance between logical and analogical thinking?

Walden

You will probably want to spend several class sessions on *Walden*. Here are some questions and issues that can be raised in sequence:

- Focusing on "Economy," ask students to address Thoreau's practical concerns. What, for Thoreau, is wrong with the daily life of his contemporaries? What were his motives for going to Walden? What led him to write the book? How does his version of writing in the first person compare with Hawthorne's in "The Custom-House"? Find evidence that he is making a pun on *I* and *eye*; recall Emerson's "transparent eyeball" in *Nature*. Are Thoreau's criticisms of his own society applicable to ours? How seriously are we to take his suggestion that students ought, quite literally, to build their own colleges? Compare Thoreau's list of materials for his house at Walden with Franklin's list of virtues in *The Autobiography*. Is there evidence in "Economy" that Thoreau is constructing an analogy, or is he writing a how-to book in the tradition of "The Way to Wealth"?

- In "Where I Lived and What I Lived For," students can consider again the creation of analogies in *Walden*, suggesting here that analogy becomes a method of introspection and religious meditation for Thoreau. Stanley Cavell in *The Senses of "Walden"* suggests that *Walden* is a scripture. You can review ways in which American writers before Thoreau achieved literary authority and what different relationships writers have to scripture, especially the Bible. Does Thoreau achieve literary authority by going back to what he sees as the very source of creation, in nature at Walden? Thoreau's experience at Walden becomes a record of his way of seeing the world; as it does for Emerson, the process of learning for Thoreau involves making the analogies he discovers as a result of going to the woods. In Thoreau's very ability to create the analogy he has the experience; Transcendentalism can thus be seen as the first American spiritual movement based on a theory of language. That theory is Emerson's as well as Thoreau's, but Thoreau is able to find the analogies he wants in the life he is living on an hourly, daily, and seasonal basis at the pond.

Crucial to considering *Walden* as scripture are the frequent references Thoreau makes to Eastern religious experience. He writes that every morning "I got up early and bathed in the pond; that was a religious exercise, and one of the best things I did." How can bathing in the pond be a religious exercise? (He seems to mean that it is a spiritual experience, not just part of his routine that he follows religiously.) Following his own inclination toward analogy, bathing in the pond metaphorically suggests his daily immersion in the meaning of the experience of the pond. To jump into it suggests, by means of analogy, his daily attempt to understand it. It cleanses, renews, wakes him up—provides a rippling effect by which he can reach Eastern enlightenment, "to reawaken and keep [himself] awake, not by mechanical aids, but by an infinite expectation of the dawn." Bathing in Walden becomes an interim "mechanical aid"; when he becomes able to keep himself awake without the pond, he won't need it anymore.

You can ask students, at this point, how Thoreau's meditation differs from Puritan meditation. Thoreau (like Franklin) is also focusing on a single mark or spot—but instead of looking for his theological or economic salvation, he is attempting to transcend the world of literal limits, what Emerson calls the relative world. Yet there is so much of the literal world in *Walden*. There is a sense in which the very rhythm of working in the physical world, finding an analogy in that work to spiritual life, and feeling—temporarily, at least—at one with the universe become cumulative for Thoreau. The process enables him to make successive leaps between relative and absolute worlds, to transcend the limits of material existence, truly to become eccentric (a word that he cites as particularly important at the end of *Walden*). Walden Pond becomes his eye (see the chapter "The Ponds").

Beginning with "Brute Neighbors," you can trace Thoreau's deep submergence into the character of Walden Pond as nature's "face." Then the last three chapters, "The Pond in Winter," "Spring," and "Conclusion," all build to Thoreau's description of the transcendent moment in which he has the experience of confronting absolute truths. In "The Pond in Winter," Thoreau makes the analogy between sounding the depths of a pond and "sounding" the depths of the human mind, as one might theoretically do by pursuing Eastern meditation techniques. Thoreau has no mantra but his pond; his "depth" of knowledge of the pond prepares him for an even deeper dive into his own imagination, his own consciousness.

"Spring" heralds new life at the pond and new light in the writer. Here he discovers that "the day is an epitome of the year"; the small scale of Walden Pond (and ultimately of *Walden* as book or scripture) is what makes it useful as an analogy. He concludes, at the end of "Spring," that "we need to witness our own limits transgressed, and some life pasturing freely where we never wander." Becoming eccentric, getting outside our own limits, trying to transcend the narrowness of our own experience, can give us the vision of larger life, of some life "pasturing freely where we never wander." The exploration of life by means of analogy possesses a spiritual dimension that logic does not.

But he leaves the pond because he has learned its lessons. When the person becomes enlightened, the vehicle of enlightenment is no longer necessary. The religious technique, or the poetic analogy, is viewed not as an end in itself, but as means to an end. The basic idea in *Walden*, then, is that of self-expression, Thoreau's attempt to find a way to make visible and concrete his sense of who he is. His greatest fear, as he expresses it in "Conclusion," is that his "expression may not be *extra-vagant* enough." It's hard to get students to be extravagant themselves, because it means encouraging them to "wander outside" the limits of everything they have learned as received knowledge, prescribed feelings, and "right" and "wrong" ways to think.

Civil Disobedience, Slavery in Massachusetts, and *A Plea for Captain John Brown*

NAAL 7 includes three overtly political short works by Thoreau, "Resistance to Civil Government" (the famous "civil disobedience" essay, so important to Gandhi and Martin Luther King), "Slavery in Massachusetts," and "A Plea for Captain John Brown." Spread out over a period of about fifteen years, these documents reached their audiences—very small and local ones, at first—as rhetorical heat was rising everywhere in American print culture, while abolitionism and resistance to it gathered strength and succession and civil war came on.

In discussing these works as a set, your class could look for fundamental conflicts here between Thoreau's celebration of eccentric individualism and his intention to espouse and advance a popular cause. Ending slavery and saving John Brown—or at least the reputation and memory of John Brown—would require the assent and assistance of a multitude, but Thoreau's temperament and rhetorical style are better remembered for provoking individual, *independent* thought, and for setting the self playfully and wistfully apart from everyone else. What are the stylistic strengths and weaknesses of these attempts to reach and sway a crowd of listeners or readers?

If your students show interest in this important question about Thoreau's essay into political arenas, you could explore it by means of the following specific questions:

- Ask a student to read, slowly and aloud, one especially provocative paragraph in the middle of "John Brown," the one that begins "This event advertises me that there is such a fact as death—the possibility of a man's dying" (top of page 2058). What is this paragraph doing in the middle of a speech about John Brown? What echoes do students hear from *Walden*, especially from Chapter 2 ("Where I Lived, and What I Lived For")? Where does the line "Let the dead bury their dead" come from, and what are the risks of using it in this new context?
- Compare the paragraph with the closing lines of "Slavery in Massachusetts": what deep, abiding urgencies inform Thoreau's political thinking as well as his dream of a good personal life? Are there echoes of Emerson here as well—and differences in tone? What would you describe as

Thoreau's attitude towards his own audience, comprised mostly of his Concord and Framingham neighbors?

- "Slavery in Massachusetts" dates from 1854, when the New England and Middle Atlantic press was full of abolitionist reasoning, homily, and polemic, and the aftershocks of *Uncle Tom's Cabin* were strong all over the nation. In such a context, how does Thoreau give his own speech a special character and sound?

- Ask another student to read the opening paragraph of "Resistance to Civil Government," and then open up questions comparing the voices of these two documents. Are there evasions or escape phrases in "Resistance" that don't turn up in either "Slavery in Massachusetts" or "John Brown?" Are there underlying differences in the urgency of these three works, and do those differences make themselves clear in the voice of each text?

FREDERICK DOUGLASS

NAAL now includes two selections from Douglass's work which have been scarce in anthologies: the second autobiography, *My Bondage and My Freedom* (1855), and Douglass's one sustained effort at narrative fiction, *The Heroic Slave*, a story about Madison Washington and the successful real-life rebellion that he led on a slave ship in 1841. You also have the complete *Narrative of the Life of Frederick Douglass*, and one of his commentaries on the Fourth of July. Therefore a class interested in Douglass and accounts of American race slavery can look carefully into the challenges of retelling, at ways in which factual experience, and personal experience, can be transformed and restyled, as the intended audience transforms as well as an author's perspectives on his or her own past.

Because Douglass wrote and spoke publicly with the support and encouragement of New England abolitionists, many of whom were strongly influenced by the values and literature of transcendentalism, a good start can be made by thinking about the *Narrative* as a complex response to that movement, that way of constructing identity. If your students have read samples of Emerson's and Thoreau's celebrations of the self, as sovereign and immune, somehow, from the brutalities of social life, then the opening of *Narrative* may stun them. It opens not with accounts of physical brutality but with slavery's assault on self-knowledge, self-affirmation: the obliteration of basic facts about personal history, facts that Emerson and Thoreau and Fuller could take for granted. When you do not know when you were born or how old you are, or who your father was, what are the psychological effects? How does that complicate the achievement of the self-knowledge that the Concord writers called for so vigorously?

Students may also want to make comparisons with regard to prose by moving in several directions: from the controlled formal heat of the *Narrative* to the rhetorical capework of Emerson at the start of "Self-Reliance" or the playfulness of self-confident Thoreau, "sure of his dinner" like one of Emerson's imaginary small boys. A comparison of Douglass with Jacobs is

more difficult. It is possible that after an encounter with Douglass's com-
posure, *Incidents* will seem overheated. If that is the impression, then attention could be paid to the very different predicaments that Douglass and
Jacobs faced, not only in bondage but also in freedom. When Douglass periodically celebrates his hard-won emancipation, is he talking about a condition that could be available to Jacobs or other black women, even when
liberated from servitude to white masters? How might gender influence and
differentiate the experience of these writers?

When Douglass returns to his personal history in *My Bondage and My Freedom*, he begins it with enhanced theatricality. We have more about the harsh
landscape and physical privations of slave life on the Eastern Shore, and he
moves more quickly into a painful account of life for families—for grand-
mothers, mothers, and small children. Why are the proportions changed here?
Do students sense an alteration in the temperament behind the new account?
In compressing some of the experiences of *Narrative* to take up less space in
a longer autobiography, what effects have been gained or sacrificed?

As a novel about an actual historical figure and real events, *The Heroic
Slave* steps even farther into charged and overtly emotional discourse; moreover, the company that this narrative must keep, on the shelves of abolitionist literature, is different from that of the autobiographical writings in
which he addresses and challenges transcendentalist optimism or complacency. In 1853 *Uncle Tom's Cabin* is an international sensation, and fiction
has proved a powerful weapon for bringing race slavery to the attention of
a vast public. But popular fiction can also be a distraction from recognizing
truth, an obstacle in winning attention—and Douglass's novella responds to
both opportunity and hindrance.

Questions for discussion:
- The opening chapter of *The Heroic Slave* includes a long soliloquy,
  overheard by a white man named Listwell (a name with an obvious
  symbolic value, "listen well"). Why begin the novel in this way, with a
  cadenza of rhetoric? Read aloud ten or twelve lines beginning with
  "When he saw my uplifted arm" (middle of page 2145). How are we
  supposed to hear these lines? As an experiment in realism? If some
  other objective is implicit here, what might it be?
- The most dramatic event in Madison Washington's career, the revolt he
  led on the *Creole*, is told not by himself or by an omniscient narrator;
  it unfolds in a conversation between two sailors. What are the advantages and drawbacks of keeping the event at such a distance?
- Choose three emotionally intense passages from Douglass's writings—
  one from the *Narrative,* one from *My Bondage and My Freedom* or
  "What to the Slave Is the Fourth of July"—a good choice from the latter would be the paragraph beginning "Would you have me argue that
  man is entitled to liberty?" (bottom of page 2142), and a paragraph of
  soliloquy or oratory from *The Heroic Slave.* On the basis of those selections, describe special and recurring characteristics of the voice of
  Frederick Douglass.

WALT WHITMAN

I often have very good luck teaching Whitman and Dickinson together as a pair of crucial figures in the making of modern American poetry—poles apart in some ways, kindred in others. Two great streams of American discourse rise here. As the headnotes observe, Whitman makes possible Hart Crane and later on plays a major inspirational role for the Beats, the Confessionals, and contemporary poets like Robert Pinsky, Cathy Song, Adrienne Rich, and various other masters of the open form. Robert Frost, Richard Wilbur, Robert Lowell, Louise Glück, John Ashbery, and a host of others owe a major debt to Dickinson—and there are many contemporary voices, including some of the poets I've just named, in which we can hear the echoes of both great sources.

Even so, as with Dickinson, the lineage from Whitman runs back in time as well as forward. Whitman can be looked at as a culmination of certain deep and basic American yearnings, not just in poetry but also in philosophical and devotional prose, running through Emerson, even through Jefferson and Franklin, and all the way to Winthrop. Some speculation along those lines could do much to situate Whitman's mind in the history of the American imagination, the boundless dream, the hunger for new beginnings.

Entering and appreciating the *craft* of Whitman's poetry, however, is a different sort a project. Some students will think it chaotic, a saturation in tides of exclamation and redundancy; others will wonder if all the rules and qualities which distinguish poetry from prose have been abandoned here and might think that all of this works on a poetics of personality, an overarching "Walt Whitman," asserting over and over that he can and will say whatever occurs to him in the instant of the writing. Again the comparison to Dickinson will be heady and also useful: here is a poet who sprawls, and there is a poet who seems to lock herself always in constrictive meters borrowed from Christian hymns. Can all of this be poetry, and poetry of the same historical moment?

Questions for discussion:
- If your students have read Emerson's "The Poet" and some of Emerson's poems, you might start with this: in their view, which of the two poets follows Emerson's guidelines more faithfully—Emerson or Whitman? What are the qualities of Whitman that might make him more Emersonian than Emerson himself? In the poems, what differences in temperament come out—and why might Emerson have been shocked when Whitman reprinted Emerson's letter of congratulation at the front of the first edition of *Leaves of Grass*?
- NAAL now includes a selection from Whitman's "Democratic Vistas," which can be read for guidance on Whitman's voice as well as his aspirations as a bard. Ask a student to read aloud, one of the emotionally charged and prophetic paragraphs—for example, the one beginning "Then still the thought returns" (bottom of page 2301), and then choose a passage from *Song of Myself* that picks up on similar sounds

and rhetorical devices. Could you versify such a paragraph, Whitman-style? With regard to democratic values, what justification can be offered for Whitman's long lines, his lack of rhyme, his abundant catalogs and enumerations? How have other modern American arts, besides poetry, expressed these values?

- "Out of the Cradle Endlessly Rocking" is an elegy, more or less, and elegy that takes an enormous chance in the middle, offering us the "words" of a couple of birds outside the window of a small boy. Does it work? If so, what are the elicited moods or suspensions of disbelief that make it work for you? If we stay with elegies, a formidable challenge for a poet of such buoyant optimism, what happens when we compare the two famous elegies about Abraham Lincoln? Do you prefer one over the other? When Whitman moves from darkness, in his poems, back into the light, by what process does he return to faith?

- What would you say is the conceptual unit of a Whitman poem? In other words, what does he seem to think are the qualities that make a line, a stanza, a poem? What is the effect of his long sets of repetitions? Is *Song of Myself*, like *Walden*, intended as a kind of secular scripture? If so, what are the traits of this poem that support those indications?

- "Trickle Drops" and other *Calamus* poems included in NAAL offer us Whitman on the subject of male sexuality. What connections can we see between these poems and Whitman's dream of America as it is and as it might be? In these poems, and in "Live Oak, with Moss," does Whitman stay with his avowed mission to "unscrew the doors from the door jambs"—or are there some "doors" that he leaves closed and locked?

HERMAN MELVILLE

A few days with Melville can be a high point in a survey course, provided that your students are comfortable about plunging into NAAL's well-chosen selections, especially the chapters from *Moby-Dick*. They may wonder whether these few pieces from such a thick volume can give them a sense of the whole text and having heard the rumors that this is a Big Hard Great American Novel, they may have their defenses up or come to class expecting that there is some profound overarching theme that pervades every sentence and phrase of every Melville narrative. They won't expect wit, humor, changefulness, exuberance, breezy vernacular American English, a host of engaging and brilliantly drawn characters—or any of the other qualities that make Melville delightful to read and not just a collection of cumbersome themes.

One of the virtues of *Moby-Dick* is that it really is about what it is supposed to be about—a voyage on a whaling ship—and you might want to tell your students that what they're not reading (the chapters that aren't in the anthology) includes more about the details and bric-a-brac of whaling, sailing, and cetology than most of them would ever want to know. You might start with some facts and speculations about life on one of these whalers—your Greenpeace convictions need not get in the way, as all this happened a long time ago when this dangerous, deadly work was regarded as vital. Take a moment to tell them how small these whaling ships were, how long they went out for, what kinds of crews they picked up (Melville's collection of cannibals, Calvinists, Indians, and seadogs from all over the world is not far from the truth), and what kinds of people would spend a year to three years or more of their lives in such an enterprise. This is life on the edge; and students can sometimes empathize with Ahab's drive to create firm conviction and sublime or monomaniacal purpose amid nothing, if they understand the work that these characters do and the company that they keep.

When you get around to symbols, you might want to begin with some discussion of what symbols are, not just what they signify about the thing symbolized but about the mind and mood of the individual who creates or gravitates to the symbol. In other words, if symbols can be interesting as provisional attempts to penetrate to truth, or express possibly transient perceptions, or seasons of the mind, then the act of reading becomes much less mechanical and deadening than a decoding of the whale or the whalebone leg or any of the gams. These are Ishmael's attempts to make sense of what he sees and what he has been through. And if students can keep that understanding in mind, that these are the creations of an eager human being, trying (perhaps with no permanent success at all) to understand the world and his place in it, then connections can be made on which students will be able to build their own.

"Bartleby," therefore, makes a very nice pairing with the *Moby-Dick* excerpts, both for its apparent oppositeness as a story (a confined, domestic, claustrophobic urban tale) and for its commonalities (its array of characters, its bizarre humor, its intense and possibly unsuccessful struggle to understand life and fellow human beings, its thorough grounding in actual experience). If you began *Moby-Dick* with a conversation about the realities of whaling and then begin "Bartleby" with some talk about mindless, dehumanizing, mind-wrecking work, students will have plenty to tell you. Bartleby is a human photocopying machine, and most students who have worked summer jobs will be quick to tell you that work this grim has not gone away with the mechanized office.

In your class you may have erstwhile roofers, corn detasselers, telemarketers, potato fryers, intelligent young people who spent months in front of a computer terminal or on an assembly line to pay for college. Ask them to speculate on what a life of such work would have done to them; also ask if they had the experience in those jobs of working with some other individual whom they could never figure out. It can be very hard, in the long routines of repetitive work, to really know the poet from the fool, the tragic figure from the true machine in human form. If students want to jump to full credence in the narrator's conclusion about Bartleby, that he was a sensitive soul brought to grief by his work in a dead-letter office, see if you can loosen that conclusion without driving them into what they might regard as frustrating ambiguity. Again, if this story is in some ways about the sad, funny quest to understand others and to understand the self, then it is certainly about much and not ambiguous at all about the predicament of the sensitive mind amid the demands of modern life.

Billy Budd, not published until thirty years after Melville's death, is a thrill to read, a posthumous treasure and a supremely crafted tale—so well crafted that students may run the risk of allowing the allegorical rumblings of the tale's first half to determine their reading of the story's ending. Again, you might want to spend some time establishing that Melville had done his homework regarding the predicament of England in the midst of the Napoleonic Wars: most of Europe was in the hands of the enemy, and survival depended on the Royal Navy—and in the navy, conditions were brutal and mutiny was a real possibility. It's important to make that clear, especially if students feel an urge to turn the tale into an allegorical chart and to assign stable values to each character: Billy as Adam or Christ or both; Claggart as Satan or one of his minions; and Vere—what of Vere? If they decide that Vere is Pilate they are no more than half right, which means that they deny themselves much of the modernity and human understanding in the story. Vere sits in Pilate's seat, to be sure; but he doesn't "wash his hands" of the case. Quite to the contrary, he insists that his drumhead court convene and judge Billy Budd by the strictest and harshest standards, even though a part of Vere (in our judgment the best part of Vere) cries out against doing so.

Students will want to know what's going on here. If you want to get into Hobbes and his constructions of both sovereignty and political identity, you can do so here; but if you fear that this will just muddy the issue, you might open the question of how we can willfully and consciously define ourselves—as students; as leaders; as professionals; as clear, firm, limited creatures of one sort or another, acting to the end on contractual and statutory obligations—and almost believe that this public or social "us" is the real us.

Questions for discussion:
- To what extent might this narrator be using Bartleby as an evasion, a way of not looking squarely at the emptiness of the narrator's own life?
- Did Vere convince himself of what he convinced the court?

CLUSTER: NATIVE AMERICANS: REMOVAL AND RESISTANCE

NAAL gathers together several short or excerpted documents from a complex and grim chapter of American history, the tangle of treaties, usurpations, wars, "removals" and outright massacres that drastically reduced the Native American presence in lands east of the Mississippi River.

What insights can we try for in a course in literary history? From these samples of a vast and varied written record, one important dimension we can glimpse is a clash of languages and styles, differences in sound and attributed eloquence that had, and continue to have, an impact on how these various documents are received. Elsewhere in this guide I've offered a suggestion, picked up from other writers, that one insidious way to reduce the importance of a people is to treat them as quaint or archaic, to relegate their culture and life to the past. With regard to Native Americans the romantic and sentimental tradition followed this pattern frequently, preferring to elegize over the Last Mohican or the vanished glories rather than engage with the indigenous peoples who were still very much on the scene. Translation can be treacherous craft: by rendering the words of the living chief into ancient-sounding idioms, you make him a figure in a museum. Black Hawk, in a strict sense, cannot speak for himself: he sounds like one of Fenimore Cooper's vanishing Delawares; the Cherokee writers, however, have learned American English, and they use it with power—and they not only sound different; to a white American reading audience, they would seem, as fellow human beings, uncomfortably real and familiar.

Questions for discussion:
- Read aloud a paragraph from the life of Black Hawk and a paragraph from the speech of Petalesharo, looking for difference in the strategy of the translation. What subtle differences do you hear in these voices, and what effect to they have on how you imagine each speaker?
- The famous "Cherokee Memorials" were written in English, to "the Public"—in other words, to a white American audience concentrated on the East Coast. This is a moral and a legal argument: what cherished documents and values, among that white audience, does the "Memorial of the Cherokee Citizens, November 5, 1829" appeal to, and why?
- Writing from Concord, a place from which the Indians were long gone, Emerson writes to President Martin Van Buren about the impending Cherokee removal. Where in this letter does Emerson sound as heated and intense as he does in his major essays—and where does he sound remarkably mild? What explanation can we give for this variance in his rhetoric here?

Elizabeth Drew Stoddard

If you're teaching Stoddard in a welter of other fiction from the age of realism or in a historical sequence of nineteenth-century narratives about love, money, and middle-class life, you can find much in "Lemorne *versus* Huell" to make this story stand out—but to do so, it might be a good idea to begin by enjoying its literary roots and echoes. Students who remember "sophomore survey" experience with British literature, or even a good high-school AP English course, will pick up the vibe or spot some of the clichés: an independent young woman of modest means comes to a big city to live for a while with an eccentric, abrasive, but likeable aunt; a lawsuit among relatives, really a chancery case, smolders in the background; romance breaks out unexpectedly and awkwardly with a mysterious man, possibly an adversary; and our heroine has choices to make and mysteries to solve. Should she stand up to the aunt for the sake of love? Can she know, for certain, whether the handsome, urbane suitor is really as indifferent to the matter of money as he declares and not a fortune hunter? The dramatic situations and the repartee may suggest a lot of famous ancestors and contemporaries: Austen, Dickens, Thackeray, Henry James, or even Hawthorne.

The fun, and the purpose, of situating the story in this way would lie in recognizing how Stoddard puts her own spin on familiar plot devices and tropes. If Margaret's interactions recall, for example, Elizabeth Bennett with Lady Catherine in *Pride and Prejudice* or Esther Summerson and Lady Deadlock in *Bleak House*, the interpersonal chemistry in Stoddard's story seems quite different and in some ways richer. Margaret is as feisty as her rich and formidable Aunt Eliza; the two of them speak candidly to each other, even to the borders of outright insult—and they seem to like each other as well as to respect each other as players of a rough, affectionate, intimate game. Margaret's social background may be plain, like her taste in clothes, but in conversation her allusions are urbane and highly literate, playful, without sounding pretentious. Students may enjoy a conversation about this story, and especially about Stoddard's skill in breathing new life into old literary ideas.

Questions for discussion:

- Where does the story end up? Margaret wakes up in the middle of the night with a stunning recognition—"*My husband is a scoundrel*"—but what do we hear in that utterance? Shock and disappointment? A tinge of satisfaction, or even of pride? What do we know about Margaret at this point, and how does that prior experience affect the way we might hear her final words?
- Take a long look at some of the fast-moving conversations between Margaret and her auntor between Margaret and Edward Uxbridge. Are these plausible exchanges between human beings? Do you get the feeling, here and there, that the characters are talking about something other than the subject at hand? If some of these conversations seem like competitions, what are those competitions about?
- There is a considerable amount of wit and humor in this story; but is it clear, from the outset, that this tale will have funny moments and comic dimensions? What are the early signals as to the mood of "Lemorne Versus Huell?" Where is the comedy at its richest?

FRANCES E. W. HARPER

With Harper, we encounter a minority author facing challenges that arose for many American writers who sought to write passionately about personal ordeals and social injustice—at a cultural moment when romanticism, gothicism, and sentimentality were thriving in the print media and visual arts, and melodrama was in ascendancy on the Anglo-American stage. To put the problem bluntly: how can a terrible truth be told, with the stylistic intensity that such truth requires, when all around you hyperbole and stylistic extravagance are threatening to exhaust the English language? How, for instance, can a true slave narrative, told in graphic detail, compete for attention in a flood of sensational made-up tales of villainy, torment, narrow escape, and heroic demise?

These questions aren't rhetorical, and they aren't antique: your students will probably know of many modern situations in which spectacular Hollywood "special effects" and outlandish adventure stories have numbed a generation to real-life catastrophe, unfolding in the streets of the world. The NAAL selections from Harper's work attest to her understanding that in the

American cultural arenas of her time, fact and fable were blending together, and readers of national and regional journals were ingesting literary brews so highly spiced that discrimination among truth, partial truth, and outright fantasy was often difficult. Ascending to national prominence just before the outbreak of the Civil War, and boasting a wartime circulation of well over one hundred thousand copies, *Harper's Weekly* made a habit of publishing bathetic short stories of love and loss in the same pages and columns as reportage from the battlefields. And for all its benefit to the abolitionist cause in the North, Harriet Beecher Stowe's *Uncle Tom's Cabin* deepened a popular taste for stories of fictional African Americans—over and above factual accounts of the travails of actual people.

Questions for discussion:
- Published soon after *Uncle Tom's Cabin,* Harper's "Eliza Harris" retells and comments on one famous passage in Stowe's novel, the harrowing escape of the slave Eliza from the South to the North, across the treacherous ice of the Ohio River. Why would Harper write a poem about this fictional character? What dimensions or implications of Eliza's escape does Harper develop? What importance can be ascribed to this project, to an African American poet offering a poem of tribute to the imaginative creation of a white American novelist?
- In this array of poems by Harper there are several which develop the meter and structure of English ballads and hymns. In what circumstances does this meter seem especially appropriate and effective. What themes of Harper are intensified by her use of these forms? What are the risks of using them?
- If you compare the poems with one another and also with the prose selections, you will see that Harper experiments with various levels of rhetoric. Describe these language choices in specific passages, and comment on the effectiveness of each choice.
- In American literary histories, Harper's "The Two Offers" is often cited as the first short story published by an African American writer. The NAAL commentary on the story observes that the racial identity of the characters is never mentioned and never clearly suggested. Why not? How might this decision reflect the predicament of being a "first" example in an important American literary genre?

EMILY DICKINSON

NAAL supplies you with enough of Dickinson's poems to keep you going for many class sessions—and those sessions can be highlights of your semester, provided that you and your students can find several kinds of access into this complex, contradictory, and fascinating material. The general strategy I'll suggest here unfolds in the following stages:

- First, acquiring comfort with the sound of Dickinson. It's enormously important that students find and practice ways of reading these poems, aloud at first and then privately, so that the thumpety-thump of her strict meters and rhyme schemes doesn't occlude their encounter with how she dances within those self-imposed constrictions.

- Second, recognizing how many different Emily Dickinsons are here. In the teaching of poetry, and especially of nineteenth-century British and American "public" poetry up to this point, one explicit or implicit subtext is coherence of theme and temperament, the implication that one or two Bryant or Longfellow poems, well chosen, can provide a moral and psychological map for dozens or hundreds, or that you can follow a Whitman into the darkness of disbelief with full confidence that sooner or later he will bring you back into the sunlight. Dickinson presents us with a modern human being, an artist with a full range of moods and flashes of insight and joy and terror that do not "add up," much as our own agglomerations of thought and feeling might not add up. A comfort with contradiction and dramatic contrast is important to a reading of Emily Dickinson.

- Third, Dickinson in her time: Sewall's enormous biography takes note of the national magazines and newspapers and books that flowed into the Dickinson house, demonstrating that this legendary recluse of Main Street was thoroughly connected to the politics and intellectual ferment that was underway a hundred miles east in Boston and Cambridge, down the Connecticut River in Hartford and New Haven, and farther away in the cities of the mid-Atlantic. One good introductory vector to follow is the complex relationship to the Emerson circle and the Boston Brahmins that followed, the spirit of transcendental optimism. As was true with Hawthorne, it would be a major mistake to construe Dickinson as some kind of white-knuckled refuser of that joy, a diehard Calvinist in temperament if not in faith. There are moments of ecstasy here that can rival the transparent eyeball on Concord Common or Thoreau at dawn. Where does Dickinson sound like close kin to these transcendentalists—and where does she turn against that buoyancy?

- Fourth, an interest that might seem idiosyncratic: an exploration for the Dickinson *place,* the natural and human landscape in which these poems unfold. Every major poet in NAAL up to now has been situated (by himself or herself or by a legion of critics thereafter) in a physical and social context. Bradstreet in her family home or standing by the ruins of it; Wheatley in that strange perilous comfort of Boston domestic servitude; Bryant out in his woods; Longfellow in his graveyards and colonial byways; Whitman in the bustle of New York, and so on. Where is Emily Dickinson? The last time I visited her bedroom in the family house in Amherst, the college had one of her famous white dresses on display—on a mannequin without a head attached. One of our jobs, as teachers, is to avoid presenting a headless Emily Dickinson. We need to see her *seeing,* and some attention to the town and the landscape that take shape over the course of her poems helps us understand why she became such an inspiration to Robert Frost, Robert Lowell, Richard Wilbur, Sylvia Plath, and a host of other strong poets of the following century.

Because the first objective—hearing the poetry in these poems—is easy enough to work on without obtrusive instructions here, we can think about the second matter, the multiplicity of voices and moods in these thousands of poems. Thomas Wentworth Higginson famously suggested some categories for sorting out Dickinson's themes and recurring interests, and these categories have endured, inflected though they might be with certain Gilded Age inhibitions. Those categories were "life," "love," "nature," "time," and "eternity." Modifying or updating them slightly, to countenance the fact that some of Dickinson's thinking—or aspirations or terrors—seem more modern or modernist than Higginson might have liked, we can experiment in class with reading poems in groups, so that students can recognize recurring themes and important variations on those themes:

Life: 112; 236; 320; 339; 372; 1773
Sexuality, desire, and love: 39; 225; 269; 409
The natural world: 207; 359; 656; 1096
Imagination, social adversity, and the despoliations of time: 112; 409; 479; 519; 598; 620; 764, 1263
Mortality and eternity: 112; 124; 202; 207; 236; 339; 448; 479; 591; 1773

After you have looked at poems in some of these groupings, you might see if you can provoke some questions about sorting Dickinson out in this way. Don't some of these poems fit into more than one of these lists? Are there poems here that fit under the general heading but nonetheless seem radically different from the others in that group? Where do we see Dickinson returning to the same dreams or motifs almost obsessively, seeking out their challenge, or even their pain, again and again? How does one poem in a set illuminate others?

Additional Questions for discussion:
- The guide's notes for Whitman suggest that you could look at Whitman and Dickinson as opposites in several ways—the prosody and word choices that each poet prefers, and also the idea of who the poet is, whom he or she is speaking to or for, and where a poem or a set or cycle of poems needs to go. All right—what about similarities between Whitman and Dickinson? Can you find Dickinson poems that seem Whitmanesque in mood or theme? In rhetorical daring? What do they have in common?
- Read aloud one of Dickinson's most famous poems, 479 [Because I could not stop for Death], at the beginning of a class session, and then return to it periodically after visits to other Dickinson poems—about time, traveling, nature, death, burial, joy. Try poem 448 [I died for Beauty]; 656 [I started Early]; 591 [I heard a Fly buzz]; and others that students suggest—and after each of these other poems, consider how each sheds light on the mood, the psychological fixations, fears, or yearnings, the volatile balance of belief and disbelief that might be at the heart of 479.

- What if we read this same poem as about a real landscape? If we look at an old map for the route that a carriage would take from the Dickinson house to the local cemetery where many of the Dickinson family were buried, we see that we might pass sights that the speaker sees out her window—a school, open fields—and at the cemetery itself there is a house "in the ground" right across from the Dickinson gravesite—what they used to call a receiving tomb, a winter shelter for coffins when the ground was too deeply frozen to dig a new grave. What are the gains or complications of thinking about these journeys as taking place in an actual, local landscape? Can we think of Dickinson as a nature poet like Bryant or even Whitman, and also as a poet of great, dark and universal imaginings?

Rebecca Harding Davis

Davis's story "Life in the Iron-Mills" can allow you to end your course by making thematic connections with earlier writers and introducing your students to an early work of literary realism. Ask students to compare the atmosphere in Davis's mill with Melville's "The Paradise of Bachelors and the Tartarus of Maids" and to compare Davis's nightmarish descriptions with Poe's. Students who have read some Dickens in earlier courses (especially works like *Hard Times, Bleak House,* and *A Tale of Two Cities*) will hear a familiar ring to Davis's grim opening panorama and should join a discussion of how realist and romantic motives can intertwine.

They may also want to compare Hugh Wolfe's creation of the korl woman with women characters created by Irving, Poe, and Hawthorne and to think about the korl woman's special hunger in light of Dickinson's own poems about yearning. There are also similarities to note between the bondage of Davis's mill workers and Douglass's portrait of race slavery. Comparing the very last lines of Walden ("Only that day dawns to which we are awake. There is more day to dawn. The sun is but a morning star") to the closing of "Life in the Iron-Mills" ("its groping arm points through the broken cloud to the far East, where, in the flickering, nebulous crimson, God has set the promise of the Dawn") can provoke a far-reaching discussion of hope in nineteenth-century American literature: what that hope consists of and what assumptions it is founded on.

CHAPTER 9

Teaching Notes for Authors and Works: Volume C, American Literature 1865–1914

Realism and Its Variants: Regionalism, Local Color, and Naturalism

The problems of realism and the genre of narrative fiction dominate the concerns of post–Civil War writers. The meaning of the term *realism* is complicated by the fact that, as the period introduction in *NAAL* suggests, there were "other realists" and there were critical categories that seem somehow both related and different: regionalism, local color writing, and naturalism (which at the turn of the century was often termed "new realism"). Furthermore, this is the period for which we have the richest array of surviving Native American texts; how do these texts intersect with critical categories such as realism or regionalism?

One standard approach to teaching the period is to begin with Twain and James and then touch on those "others." One difficulty with this approach is that American authors (like Davis) began writing in a realistic mode decades before Twain and James published their major works. If we begin teaching the period not with Twain, but with the realistic literary works that were published in the 1860s and 1870s, we can give students a better sense of the evolution of American literary realism, which began as a mode of perception and a way of thinking about American life. It achieved the stature of "theory" only when William Dean Howells (and James) wrote so many editorial columns (and prefaces) in an attempt to define the American "art of fiction."

In American fiction, the realistic mode may have its origins with Stowe and some of her contemporaries, including Davis. Literary historians also see signs of realism in Thorpe. To understand the evolution of American realism, students need to see what happens to these early strains, and what happens is that a group of writers—mostly women—develop the genre of regionalism, represented in NAAL by Jewett, Chopin, Freeman, Chesnutt, possibly Oskison, and Zitkala Ša. In conveying features of the earlier literary tradition, you might want to teach Jewett and Chesnutt before Twain, even though all of the particular regionalist texts anthologized in NAAL were published after *Adventures of Huckleberry Finn.*

What all of the writers in realistic modes share is a commitment to referential narrative. Despite the evidence of invention, the reader expects to meet characters in the fiction who resemble ordinary people in ordinary circumstances, and who often meet unhappy ends. (The pattern of the unhappy ending is much less prevalent in regionalism, however.) The realists develop these characters by the use of ordinary speech in dialogue, and plot and character development become intertwined. Some writers make use of orthographic changes to convey particular speech rhythms and other elements of dialect peculiar to regional life. They all set their fictions in places that actually exist, or might easily have actual prototypes; and they are interested in recent or contemporary life, not in history or legend. Setting can become conspicuous as an element of theme in local color and regionalist fiction. And the realists rely on a first- or third-person-limited point of view to convey the sensibility of a central character or, in the case of the local color writers, the altered perception of the outside observer as he or she witnesses the scene.

Realism and Native American Literature

The anthologized selections from Native American oratory, songs, legends, fictions, and autobiographical memoirs in one sense belong to a variety of different genres; but they also comment in interesting ways on the intentions and strategies of literary realism.

As the headnotes observe, Native American literature during this period represents an "encounter" between traditional Native American oratory and the new demands of the practices of Euro-American culture, namely the occasions at which Indians used both oratory and writing to try to make beneficial treaties, to achieve their land claims, or to adapt their own practices to meet the demands of the whites. Thus the body of Native American literature represented in this period indeed records an acute consciousness of of white American life and ways of saying. Setting is everything in some of these narratives; land becomes the fundamental source of conflict as well as the source of metaphor, spirituality, and identity for large groups of native peoples. Furthermore, read together and interwoven with Euro-American texts, the Native American materials all imply the existence of and looming threat by an outside observer (sometimes equipped with Hotchkiss guns), who, alas, is also the narrator of a conflicting story of events and the narrator who controls not only the guns but also the language of legal discourse.

Once students explore the suitability of terms like *realism* and *regionalism* for Native American texts, they may find them inappropriate; but the terms may have served the function of pedagogical bridge to an enlarged appreciation for Native American literature taught, inevitably in a survey course, as part of literature in the United States. To make connections between the anthologized Native American texts and the much more familiar concept of realism—as well as to understand crucial distinctions between the two—encourage students to view realism as a literary effect as much as, if not more than, a genre or a defined body of narrative strategies.

Then even the Ghost Dance narrative—which is told by a variety of narrators in a variety of genres, including Wovoka and his transcribers, Eastman, and tribal songmakers—may be viewed as a collectively told "text" of Native American realism, despite its origins in a vision and its survival in songs and legends. This collectively told narrative also serves as a useful corrective to the theory of realism as articulated by James, which focuses on a single stationary observer and his particular perspective from "the house of fiction" (or what he calls "the posted presence of the watcher, . . . the consciousness of the artist" in his preface to the New York edition of *The Portrait of a Lady*). The collectively told narrative of the Ghost Dance and its aftermath, Wounded Knee, can be viewed from several perspectives at once in Native American literature. The realist observer becomes apparent to the reader, "appears" to the reader (as if reader response to Native American texts involved forming a Wovoka-like vision of his or her own), as a collective, or even "tribal," grouping of observations that confirm each other. These observations share a theme and referentiality (the focus is on the gulch in which the women and children were massacred and buried in snow), emerge from more than one "watcher," are confirmed by more than one pair of eyes, and above all provide a counternarrative to the absence of this story in Euro-American "realism" of the period.

The particular mode of realism that seems to assume the closest kinship to the perspective from which the body of Native American literature is spoken or written is that of regionalism.

While it is certainly true that traditional Native American literature must be viewed as central to itself and not even part of "American literature," American literary history (and canon revision politics) led to the revision of anthologies of "American literature" in the late twentieth century to "include" Native American materials and literary scholarship about these materials. From the perspective of such anthologies (as NAAL), both regionalism and Native American literature are noncanonical, marginal representations of American life; both cannot separate setting from the development of character; and both foreground the contrasting perception of persons on the margins of American life in the nineteenth century with those who own the land and the property, who make (and break with impunity) the laws, and who consign certain persons to separate lands, or separate spheres or regions.

WALT WHITMAN AND EMILY DICKINSON

See notes in Chapter 8 (pp. 154–55, 160–63).

MARÍA AMPARO RUIZ DE BURTON

About Ruiz de Burton, the headnote is almost apologetic, observing that "her work accepts many racial stereotypes even while arguing against others" and seeing those contradictions as a sign of "the difficulty of articulating an ethos completely free of derogatory assumptions about racial or ethnic 'others.' " As an early figure in Mexican American literature, Ruiz de Burton is certainly not Sandra Cisneros. Published more than a hundred and twenty years ago, *The Squatter and the Don*, very much a work of its own time, would probably flunk any test for political and social values commonplace in the early twenty-first century. Recovering Ruiz de Burton and representing her in an important anthology like NAAL should be regarded as an intellectual and aesthetic challenge for all of us, not as a gesture; to keep her work with us in any meaningful way, our reading of the text must find more of interest there than grounds for a good retrospective scolding or drab origins of a tradition that got much better later on.

Luckily, Ruiz de Burton's own special project, and the literary forebears she favors, are strongly visible in the excerpt, and a discussion of "The Don in His Broad Acres" can center on the "broad" panorama that she offers of life in the region around San Diego. Charles Dickens is invoked outright in the opening line of the chapter, and you could start by asking why, and what the effects are of such an invocation. Most of your students will remember *Great Expectations, A Tale of Two Cities,* or *Oliver Twist* from high school or other college courses or reading for pleasure. When Dickens writes a novel on a grand scale, touring through a wide range of places, social classes, and spectacular conflicts, how does he handle characterization? Out beyond his protagonists, when and why does he make use of stereotype and caricature? What are the advantages and drawbacks of such a strategy? Taking a step back from Dickens to consider other nineteenth- and twentieth-century narratives with epic ambitions—works by Scott, Tolstoy, Frank Norris, George Eliot, and Charles Reade or modern novels and films on a grand scale, like *Lonesome Dove, Lawrence of Arabia,* the ponderous novels of James A. Michener or Tom Clancy or Tolkien's trilogy *The Lord of the Rings*—when and where does a "flattening" of characters take place and with what effects, what benefits? Moving back into *The Squatter and the Don,* you could focus on the two longest monologues of Don Mariano in his conversation with Matthews and Miller, the paragraphs that begin "You are too good business men (bottom of page 96) and "The water is the sea now" (middle of page 97). How are we to read these avalanches of fact and summation? As plausible words from a human being speaking intimately to other men? Or has another purpose taken hold? Can your students think of other situations, in literature or drama or film, in which verisimilitude is foregone, for a while, in service of some larger purpose?

Mark Twain

Huckleberry Finn

Why read *Huckleberry Finn* again? It's likely that most of your students have read the novel at least once before, in a high school English course, in a history course, or on their own; and if they haven't, they have probably seen some of the many films of the story. However, the chances are good that they haven't considered the novel from the perspectives you are developing in your own course: the evolution of an American vernacular, the imaginative transformation of the North American landscape, the Romantic and Realist traditions, themes of individuality and escape, the sources of wisdom and conscience in this culture, and imaginative fiction's address to race slavery and the predicament of minorities and women. *Huckleberry Finn* can be reread from any or all of these perspectives; but it is probably a good idea to avoid too much zeal in imposing one reading at the expense of all others. The reasons are perhaps obvious; since the early twentieth century, the novel has weathered one systematic interpretation after another: disturbed Freudian dream, New Deal hymn to the Common People, Symbolist poem, formalist masterpiece, radical (or reactionary) political tract . . . the alternatives stack up high, and few of them have had any effect on the popularity and image that this novel enjoys with a worldwide audience. The problem is complicated by the fact that many readers (including perhaps many of your students) feel that this novel is *theirs*, a freewheeling tale told by an ordinary boy, improvising his way through a world presented as it really was—and a story that is, or should be, out beyond the systems and evaluations of modern academe.

If you sense that your class is uneasy about being urged into some overly systematic reading of *Huckleberry Finn*, then it might be a good idea to present the novel, and Twain, as requiring us to do a different kind of close reading than we do on a highly crafted work like *The Scarlet Letter* or a short story by Melville or Poe. "Fenimore Cooper's Literary Offenses" can work well as an hors d'oeuvre before the plunge into *Huckleberry Finn*. Twain's commentary on Cooper and on Romantic fiction is still fresh and funny (especially if your group has experience with Cooper); and this essay is as close as we can come to a forthright statement by Twain about the Realism that he supposedly championed. We can see in this comic piece that Twain's "realism" is reactive, a rejection of the extravagances and illusions of Romantic narrative, and that Twain's mode defines itself by what it isn't at least as much as by what it is. *Huckleberry Finn* can be read many ways, of course; one such way, which follows naturally from a look into "Fenimore Cooper's Literary Offenses," is as a book about the impact of Romantic and sentimental fiction, drama, poetry, and illustration on the Mississippi River world in which Huck and Jim try to survive.

But the first order of business, and perhaps the most important objective in rereading the novel as part of an American literature survey, is to help students find ways to engage with literary works that suggest or demonstrate genius and that may please them deeply but that from some perspectives may be formally flawed. To clear the air, it might be worth drifting through the novel's early chapters to look at the evidence of false starts and abandoned intentions. This book did begin as a potboiler, as *The Adventures of Huckleberry Finn, Tom Sawyer's Comrade*, and it seems also to have begun as a detective story. If we look at the bric-a-brac in the floating house (Chapter IX), which Huck catalogs at such length, and at all the details that are provided in regard to the faking of his own death, we see some of the remains of the plot that Twain eventually abandoned. However, if we ignore those detective-story relics and try to describe the novel's plot as a flight to freedom and as the quest to free Huck's friend Jim, then we have major problems explaining why the two of them continue to flee southward, after missing the confluence with the Ohio River and the route into free territory. And as for formal symmetry and perfection: though you may hesitate to give Ernest Hemingway any last word about American literature, you might toss into the conversation his famous remark that after Chapter XXX—when Jim is trapped at the Phelps farm—the rest of the novel is "cheating." The ending of the book has been debated for fifty years; and students should know that however they feel comfortable reading it (or ignoring it), their views can find validation somewhere in the welter of published criticism.

Another unsettled controversy also requires some attention: the question of how the book is to be read as a commentary on racism and the appropriateness of including in the canon, as required reading on thousands of syllabi, a novel that uses the word *nigger* freely and dozens of times. A strong and time-honored case can be made that *Huck* is very much about racism, about a culture that instills and enforces dehumanization and prejudice, an ideology that can be escaped only for brief interludes when the human social world fades away and something more natural and innocent can flourish. A good case can also be made that if this were the intended theme of the novel, then Twain did not stay with it faithfully: the other Tom and Huck narratives that Twain wrote thereafter fail to show much interest in social justice for African Americans or in Jim as a rounded and interesting character. If students reach an impasse in settling, in some general way, the rightness of listing this novel as an American classic and a must-read for students of all races in all contexts, then see if they want to make distinctions among contexts. When and where would they feel comfortable teaching the novel? To what kind of class? In what sort of historical moment?

As you move into the novel, here are some suggestions for developing a different sort of close reading, a close reading suitable for a work in which high art might be quite different from highly polished formality.

- The opening page can be read carefully, attending to Huck's language and to Twain's strategy in getting the novel going. Huck claims no literary authority; his idea of a story apparently seems to be the simple and unadorned telling of actual events, moving from one incident to the next, without the embellishment of elaborate commentary or even subordinate clauses. Compare the beginning of *Huckleberry Finn* to the opening paragraphs of *The Scarlet Letter*, and students will see why

Hemingway felt that the modern novel begins right here. But if the language and the teller have grown simpler in some ways, the narrative, in a broader sense, has grown more complex, more reflexive, more aware of the paradoxes of writing and reading novels. To introduce himself, Huck refers us back to Twain, who "told the truth, mainly" about two boys who do not exist; but then again, "Mark Twain" does not exist either, does he? Is there a playful address to "truth" and to "realism" here, by a writer who is supposed to be a master of the mode? Is realistic fiction a hopeless contradiction in terms? If such questions are asked in an appropriately light hearted way, students may be more willing to enter the novel as, in some senses at least, an epistemological funhouse, a meditation on how illusions and ordinary life get intertwined—in ordinary life as well as in narrative fiction.

- When Tom Sawyer shows up in the novel and Huck acquiesces to being a member of Tom's gang, we see how make-believe, borrowed from Romantic fiction, pervades childhood in this world; soon afterward we will encounter plenty of situations in which adults show themselves susceptible to the same disease. The deeper realism of the novel grows especially clear hereafter, for the nature of the real, of genuine emotion, moral action, and social behavior, all come into vigorous and sustained question. Here and afterward, you can raise questions about Tom's influence on Huck, when Tom is on the scene and when he isn't. Tom, we should remember, is several years younger: do students find Huck's compliance and his occasional admiration, plausible in a fourteen-year-old boy? Does Huck end the novel as morally grown up as we might like him to be?

- As you move past the point in the novel at which Twain put aside the manuscript (Chapter XVI, where the steamboat runs over the raft), it's worth stopping to observe what intentions have been abandoned or outgrown and what has happened not only to the plot but to the characters. Jim, for example, has become much more interesting as a moral presence in the work, Huck's "sound heart" has finally brought him to a full recognition of his friend's humanity and dignity, the Ohio River has been missed somehow, and the novel has cut itself loose from nearly every expectation with which a reader might have begun it. *Huckleberry Finn* is often classified as picaresque, as a way of addressing this escape from conventions and from its own opening; but are we witnessing here not just the liberation of one white boy's mind but also of American narrative fiction? The novel may seem loose, but it should not seem strange: students have read works like *The Catcher in the Rye*, *One Flew Over the Cuckoo's Nest*, *Their Eyes Were Watching God*, and *The Bell Jar*, all of which may owe something to the "breakout" of Twain's novel from prevailing habits of literary form. Ask students to talk about what has been gained and lost in this act of escape.

- The Grangerford-Shepherdson feud is based on actual violence that Twain knew about as a young man growing up along the Mississippi. But these chapters about the Grangerford household, their values, pretensions, and impact on their own children, can bring a lot of interesting commentary out of a class, especially now, when the papers are full of senseless mayhem based on family and pseudo-family affiliations and contorted ideas of honor and macho behavior. You can have a good deal of fun with Huck's description of Emmeline's poems and "crayons"—Huck tries comically and poignantly hard to be respectful of her morbid work, but his similes betray his real reactions. It's a bravura piece of narrative description; but beneath the comedy, beneath this struggle between common sense and supposedly genteel aesthetics, there are hints of a tragedy, a young girl destroyed by the sickness of the family values around her and the sickness of the sentimentality being shipped into this home from the "sivilized" world.

- As the duke and the dauphin usurp the raft, some students may wonder if the "cheating" hasn't begun already, in other words, if Twain isn't making Huck and Jim into "extras" in a tale of con artists and fools. It would be worth spending some time, therefore, on the duke-dauphin chapters as a unit in the novel, to observe their overall pattern and the effect on Huck's thinking. The initial scams of the two con men may seem relatively innocuous: if the Pokeville camp meeting is so ignorant and foolish as to believe a wild tale about pirates from the Indian Ocean, perhaps they deserve to be gulled; and the Bricksville we see (the site of the Boggs shooting and the Royal Nonesuch) seems so meanspirited, lazy, and cowardly that we may cheer when the three visitors (for Huck is now an accomplice) fleece them with a bad stage show. But after this, the tone darkens, and Huck's involvement with the duke and the dauphin becomes morally perilous. When and why does he decide to take a stand against them? Does he do it on principle? Is he moved by a pretty face? By his "sound heart?" Or by a touch of that sentimentality or degraded romanticism that have overwhelmed Tom Sawyer and Emmeline Grangerford? You may expect some lively debate over questions of this kind.

- The Phelps farm chapters, with Jim incarcerated and tormented and Huck and Tom playing children's games with the life and liberty of a grown man, need to be looked at carefully rather than passed over as padding or an awkward coda to a narrative that really came to an end somewhere before this point. Students will want to speculate on Huck's moral situation and psychological development, on the "realism" of his fall back into being Tom's sidekick, on the plausibility of his apparent failure to generalize from the various lessons that Jim and his river adventure have taught him, and on the thematic value of this final sequence. Is the last paragraph of the novel optimistic? Indeterminate? A foretaste of the pessimism that, according to some critics, overtook Twain in the final decades of his career?

Roughing It and *Letters from the Earth*

The excerpts from *Roughing It* and *Letters from the Earth* give us one glimpse of Mark Twain from near the beginning and another from near the end of a career that spanned more than forty years, carrying him from small-town newspaper work, riverboat piloting, stand-up comedy, and misadventures in the Wild West to heights of international fame, to wealth and gentility and a notorious bankruptcy; and ultimately to the status of lonely sage. This was a career of amazing adventure and variation—so much so that his admirers have argued for generations about what values, what dimensions of his temperament or his politics, constitute the Mark Twain that we should remember best. The Lake Tahoe chapter of *Roughing It*, a naïve celebration of majestic nature and also of the spectacle of its destruction, comes from a travel book that was intended to sell tens of thousands of copies door to door. But the late writings gathered and published as *Letters from the Earth*, appearing decades after the death of Sam Clemens, come from manuscripts that he kept private.

Of special relevance to these two works is what happened to Sam Clemens in between. Certainly the American frontier "closed," taking with it the illusion of limitless landscapes, available for anyone's appreciation, exploitation—or outright destruction; the ongoing revolutions in natural history, geology, microbiology, and astronomy brought home to Clemens's generation, as never before, Pascal's old speculation that mankind drifts between one abyss and another, the infinitely large and the infinitely small. The bookshelves are full of scholastic arguments about whether Mark Twain, in his final years, became an atheist, an antitheist, or some new, mysterious, modern variety of believer.

Rather than tangle your students in questions of that size—questions that require a great deal of reading to answer well—you might ask about *uncertainty* as a recurring and evolving theme in Mark Twain's work throughout his lifetime, and his use of laughter to float us away, like Huck's raft, into uncharted moral territory:

- After accidentally setting the forest ablaze on the shore of Lake Tahoe, Sam and his companion climb into the boat and compare the spectacles: the fire itself and the reflection of the fire on the clear surface of the water. Mark Twain seems to be celebrating illusions here as an alternative to truth and also critiquing that notion. Where do we see similar themes emerging in *Huckleberry Finn*? When Huck describes a sunrise on the Mississippi River in Chapter XIX, how does the boy blend illusion and truth in his telling? When we turn to "Letters from the Earth," where do we find a critique of human imagining—and what is the spirit of that satire?
- For the letter from the angel to the Buffalo coal merchant, describe a "safe" interpretation of the satire—and also a not-so-safe interpretation. In other words, how might the humor here be read as essentially innocuous, with regard to religious faith, and how might it be read as harmful? In this sketch and elsewhere in Mark Twain's work, what cues do you find as to whether to gravitate toward belief or toward heresy?

BRET HARTE

During Harte's prime years as a writer—the ten years after the end of the Civil War—he produced short stories about life in the mountains and gold-fields that reflect an important transitional period in the creation of the literary West. Raised in an educated family from the East, Harte brings a full portfolio of cultural experience to the wilds, and playfully and earnestly he experiments with applying those allusions, metaphors, and tropes to the description of people and situations that are often "off the map," fundamentally different from the experiences of his audience.

Harte can also be enjoyed as an American writer in the midst of a contest between romanticism and realism: a well-established tradition of sentimental fiction, with high feeling and outbreaks of nobility and valor, and a rising imperative to tell the truth about new places and new varieties of American social life. "The Luck of Roaring Camp" skirts pretty close to all-out sentimentality yet steers clear of that abyss; "Miggles" is a portrait of human beings who veer irretrievably off main roads of cultural practice and conduct yet remain recognizably human and empathetic nonetheless; "Tennessee's Partner" is the kind of story that some of your students might recognize as an ancestor of novels by Larry McMurtry, narratives that celebrate varieties of friendship and fidelity, even of love, that follow none of the playbooks of civilization and achieve a strange nobility of their own.

Questions for discussion:
- To begin with style and rhetorical strategy: ask students to run an eye over these stories again, looking for peculiar or glaring comparisons or metaphors—"a Raphael face," "Romulus and Remus," the "Arethusa, Seventy-Four" "Caliban and Miranda," "Memnon," and so on. What is Harte up to here? Showing off? Do these allusions add any interesting dimensions to the narrative? If so, how?
- "Miggles" might be the oddest story of the set, as there's no clear plot to it, other than an unplanned visit to a woman who has made a strange and private decision and has either lost her way because of it—or found her way. Read the complete paragraph on page (middle of page 339) in which Miggles relates crucial details of her past, beginning with "It was along time before I could get the hang of things. . . ." What are the implications of her voice trailing off, and why do we see her, at the end of this paragraph, "completely in shadow"?
- Harte's stories, and many tales of the West written after his time, often feature deep, wordless bonds between people who choose to live apart, in a vast landscape. Rarely do the people in these relationships explain them well—or at all. What is the thematic effect of that reticence or silence?

HENRY ADAMS

Whether or not Adams read Du Bois, for pedagogical purposes we can see the excerpts from *The Education* as thematic variations on the Du Boisean theme of "double consciousness." Like Du Bois, who summarizes nineteenth-century black thinking in 1903, Adams writes as one born in 1838 yet wanting "to play the game of the twentieth" century. *The Education* is another book in the tradition of Franklin's *Autobiography* but interesting because of the new directions Adams goes in.

As it happened, he never got to the point of playing the game at all—he lost himself in the study of it, watching the errors of the players—but this is the only interest in the story, which otherwise has no moral and little incident. It is a story of education—seventy years of it—the practical value of which remains to the end in doubt.

The development of self-reliance in the American writer and thinker leads Adams to write that "every one must bear his own universe." Unlike Franklin, Adams does not become a politician but rather finds literary symbols that, as the headnote to Adams in NAAL asserts, make *The Education* to many readers "the one indispensable text for students seeking to understand the period between the Civil War and World War I." For Chapter XXV, "The Dynamo and the Virgin," presages modern life in the symbols that express the split between technology and spirituality. Adams writes clearly; students could easily prepare a summary of the argument of this chapter. In class, you can continue to focus on Adams's early modernist ideas: what happens to human energies—symbolized by the force and power of the Virgin and of ancient fertility goddesses—in an age and in a country that replaces human with technological power, and is it possible to state, "with the least possible comment, such facts as seemed sure" and to "fix for a familiar moment a necessary sequence of human movement"?

AMBROSE BIERCE

The very word "Chickamauga" would have called up a lot of associations for magazine readers in 1889, when Bierce published the story—as a powerful ironist, Bierce thought carefully about the expectations and cultural experience of his audience, and he seemed to take pleasure in turning conventions and assumptions upside down. As writers who plunged into the subject of the Civil War, a subject that had been nearly drowned in bulky histories and memoirs, and in romantic and sentimental overtelling, and who found ways to make that subject surprising and achingly fresh and real, Bierce and Stephen Crane make a remarkable pair.

Because your students may have run into Crane's *The Red Badge of Courage* in middle school or high school, you could ask whether they were reminded of that novel while reading "Chickamauga" and suggest that they mention moments that seem especially reminiscent of *Red Badge*. There's also a chance that your class will include one or two Civil War buffs, who may want to talk about actual moments in that history which ring true—or don't—with Bierce's account of the confusion and hell of life behind the lines. For example, at Gettysburg, below Culp's Hill on the northeast edge of the Union line, there was a place called Spangler's Spring, where wounded and exhausted soldiers from both sides staggered or crept for a bit of fresh water and a moment of truce. Chickamauga was for a while a rout for the Union forces until General George Thomas rallied his division and stopped it; and in the chaos, experiences like the ones Bierce imagines may have unfolded.

Questions for discussion:
- The first paragraph of "Chickamauga" opens in a way that might remind students of chapter openings in *Red Badge*—in other words, with a stunning lack of specific reference to place or time or era. Why does Bierce do that? What body of knowledge, in his audience, can he take for granted? How does he exploit that knowledge or work against it?
- Like Crane and other American writers at the end of the nineteenth century, Bierce was aware of developments in the visual arts, new ways of seeing and representing the world. Take a close look at the paragraph that begins "The fire beyond the belt of woods" (bottom of page 369) and comment on what kind of art this seems like? Do your students have experience with French Impressionism, the landscapes of Monet, Pissarro, Sisley, Cassatt, or Hassam? Talk about the use of detail here and also the use of a certain blurriness. If they find this to be an effective strategy, why do they feel it is?
- The story ends with a small boy looking carefully at the mutilated corpse of one soldier. Again, the moment might recall a scene in *Red Badge,* in which Henry Fleming, fleeing the battle, encounters his first dead man, a young man like himself, sprawled against a tree, with eyes wide open. Why end here? What has this story been about?

NATIVE AMERICAN CHANTS AND SONGS

The best strategy for approaching these transcribed oral works might be to read them in a broad context rather than isolate them from each other or as a group away from the other materials in NAAL. In many cultures, chants and songs have done similar important kinds of cultural work: they can encourage resolve, peace of mind, a sense of group identity, connection with the past and with the divine. They also can provide solace or other sorts of escape from the verbal and psychological turmoil of ordinary life and the moment of order and consolation that can come from saying and hearing the same things again and again.

Questions for discussion:
- What, then, are the resemblances between some of these chants and nineteenth-century poetry by white Americans?
- Are some New England poets seeking these same values?
- When Du Bois turns to the "chants and songs" of African Americans as a focus for his meditations on being black in a predominantly white America, does he search for qualities similar to ones in these Native American texts?

NATIVE AMERICAN ORATORY

In his discussion of Native American oratory, Andrew Wiget (*Native American Literature* [1985]) observes that "from the first centuries of white settlement in America, the oratorical ability of Native Americans, their artful talent for persuasion, was noted by Europeans," and he cites Jefferson's *Notes on the State of Virginia* as offering the "moment of highest praise."

Cochise

Cochise's speech makes a plea to retain "a part of my own country, where I and my little band can live." As the headnote observes, this is an example of oratory addressed to white listeners, and its theme is land. You can make the speech live for readers in a couple of ways.

First, ask students to recall (and reread) the Pima Stories of the Beginning of the World, for the opening sentence of Cochise's speech makes an indirect reference to the emergence myth of creation of some Southwest Indians, a myth in which humans crawl out from a hole in the ground: "This for a very long time has been the home of my people; they came from the darkness, few in numbers and feeble." It's important that students catch this reference, what Euro-Americans would call a literary allusion, but what for Cochise links the spiritual origins of his people with their present predicament (and the occasion for his oratory). It also provides evidence for the headnote's observation that for Native Americans there were no fixed distinctions between the spiritual and the secular.

In light of Cochise's allusion to the emergence myth of the Pimas and the Apaches (locate for students the reference at the end of the Pima "Story of the Flood" to the origins of the Apaches as "the first ones that talked"), you might want to note that Native American literature itself "emerges" with such power during the years 1830–90, when the Indians themselves were losing their battles with the whites. And yet the emergence myth implies the cyclical destruction and reemergence of Native peoples as well as their migrations. Perhaps the new "emergence" of Native American literature in the larger canon of American literature through the contest for space or literary "territory" in anthologies represents the triumph, or at least the persistence, of Native American cultures, despite several acts of destruction by the world maker.

Second, trace with students the numerous and pervasive references to land in the speech and all of the different ways in which Cochise configures the meaning of land to his people. Variously, land becomes imaged as "these mountains about us," "home," and "our country," and the Apaches are portrayed as integral to that landscape, as, early in the speech, Cochise compares the way his people "covered the whole country" to the way "clouds cover the mountains." The rhetorical occasion for the speech, namely to arrive at a treaty that would yield "a part of my own country," establishes its form, in the sense that Cochise defines himself and his people as quite a "part" of the country. In formal terms, the speech becomes synecdoche: he speaks for all, and the terms in which he speaks establishes an identity between people and their land. To take away the land kills the people who are "part" of that land; if the people have been reduced in numbers, then they can survive on "part" of that land, but they must be on that land. Like the deer that flee the hunter in a later image from the speech, the Apaches exist only on the land that has been their home.

Charlot

This speech addressed to Charlot's fellow Flathead Indians lives up to its description in the headnote as "a powerful critique of the white people's ways." Contrast with students the tone and language of Charlot's speech with Cochise's; focus on the evocation of shame in the speech and discuss the way racism attempts to obliterate emotions of shame; compare this with Apess's "An Indian's Looking-Glass for the White Man," another indictment of white treatment of native peoples. Ask students if the rhetorical stance of the speaker reminds them of any historical works in Euro-American literature—for instance, Paine's "Thoughts on the Present State of American Affairs" from *Common Sense*, or especially Jefferson's Declaration of Independence. Students might compare the rhetorical construction of King George III in Jefferson's Declaration with Charlot's rhetorical construction of "the white man" in the centennial year of the United States. What are the advantages of using "he," suggesting an individual rather than a government or a general population, throughout the speech? Charlot's speech conveys an expectation of being overheard. Students can consider and compare closely the rhetorical strategy of these documents. How does Charlot center and portray the predicament? A cause has to be made clear: a source of oppression has to be identified, coalesced. How does Charlot accomplish that task? Constructing the Other in each of these political statements designed simultaneously to arouse enmity against "King George," "the white man," and "man" and support for the cause of the oppressed also increases students' awareness of the use of rhetorical devices as part of the process by which writing becomes a form of political action that Native American speakers, perhaps because of their tradition of oral practice and the extent of their own grievances, were quite skillful in employing.

HENRY JAMES

In the cluster on realism and naturalism, the excerpt from James's "The Art of Fiction" gives us a sense that James sided with William Dean Howells, in a general way, with regard to keeping faith with truth and representing life as we (or some of us, anyway) actually find it. In that famous essay he writes, "The only reason for the existence of a novel is that it does attempt to represent life." But unlike Howells, who asserts a reality that is referential and shared, James places greater emphasis on the *inner* reality, on "life" as mediated through the mind. He insists on "the power to guess the unseen from the seen, to trace the implication of things, to judge the whole piece by the pattern" and also contends that "Experience is never limited, and it is never complete; it is an immense sensibility, a kind of huge spiderweb of the finest silken threads suspended in the chamber of consciousness, and catching every airborne particle in its tissue" (bottom of page 918).

And for many younger readers, there's the paradox: if Howells is correct in affirming that the reader is the ultimate arbiter of a fiction's realism and that "the only test of a novel's truth is his own knowledge of life," then you can expect your students to have trouble seeing Henry James as a genuine realist. James's London, his Paris, his Florence, his New York, are cities that often seem hermetically cleansed of ordinary folk, of coal smoke and rubbish, of the poor, and even of the middle classes that Howells and George Eliot favored. Moreover, his narratives often ignore the ordinary "experience" of solving everyday problems: finding a decent apartment, balancing a checkbook, or catching a train—the daily stuff that other realists found to be deeply embedded not just in our schedules and negotiations but in ourselves. One great challenge in teaching James, then, is encourage students to delight in the psychological complexity of the relationships that James creates so meticulously, even in the short fiction.

Daisy Miller

As one of James's earlier successes, *Daisy Miller* provides a good place to start with this author. We have the lineaments here of a familiar story, a tale of young love, misunderstanding, death, remorse, all in evocative and (for that time) exotic European settings. James is drawing on tropes from the sentimental tradition and working to make them his own.

You might want to historicize the story briefly before plunging into the text: after the Civil War, Americans with money and leisure began to pour into the Europe that they had read about in histories, art books, and romantic poems. Steamships, a railroad network, and an apparently durable peace (after the upheavals of 1848 in France, Italy, and elsewhere) made the Old World seem accessible and safe. Disease, however, was still a serious threat, in those decades before Pasteur's discoveries took hold and before any sort of effective treatment evolved for malaria or other destructive ailments that thrived in warm climates. The "little Protestant cemetery" in Rome, and also the one in Florence, contain many graves of British and American travelers who never imagined they would be staying so long.

Questions for discussion:
- To keep the pattern of class conversation fresh, why not start with the final paragraphs of the story, beginning with "Winterbourne almost immediately left Rome" (middle of page 429), and reading down to the end. What do you think of this as an ending for a story about star-crossed love and the death of a lovely and promising young woman? How is James varying the conventions here, with regard to what the "leading man" is supposed to learn from an experience like this?
- The names of some of the characters are suggestive–Winterbourne, Daisy, Costello. What shading do those names give to the tale? Do they enhance the realism in some ways? Do they turn the story into a fable? Do they belong in a work of realistic fiction?

- James is often mentioned as one of the pioneers of cosmopolitan fiction, narratives about people who live and think in international ways, escaping from the supposed parochialism of national identity. Does this story offer any cautions about that frame of mind, about the possible dangers of forgetting where one comes from and forgetting the prevailing values and temperament of one's own place?

The Real Thing

This story makes a nice transition to the enigmas of "The Figure in the Carpet," for "The Real Thing" can be read as a wry meditation on the consequences of the pursuit of truth—or at least the kind of "truth" that an working artist (literary or otherwise) can come to prefer over the actualities under his nose. In some ways this fable plays off one of the oldest in the Western canon, the Aesop fable of the farmer and the mountebank: in that brief story, an audience prefers the entertainer's imitation of a squealing pig to a country farmer's noise under his cloak—a noise which turns out to be "the real thing." We also have a first-person narrator here who does not come off as admirable and likeable—an artist who exploits and distorts and misunderstands. For readers, that's an experience that proves handy in thinking about deceived, deluded, or possibly depraved first-person narrators in other works of Henry James.

Another historical note: with the mechanization of printing in the middle of the nineteenth century and the development of new technologies for transferring images to paper, illustrations became a big-time feature in magazines and newspapers. Work for artists (good and not so good alike) boomed in the big cities—but along with those opportunities came new obligations. To illustrate words on a page means harmonizing with the intentions of verbal texts and the tastes of authors and editors as well as reading audiences.

Questions for discussion:
- We have two pairs of people to (literally) look at, as themselves and as the artist prefers to see and draw them: Major and Mrs. Monarch, and Mrs. Churm and Oronte. If you're moving on to this story after *Daisy Miller*, stay with the names for a moment. If this is a story about the manufacture of artificial "real things," why use names like these?
- How "real" are the Monarchs, outside the realm of the studio? In other words, is there something inherently artificial about their actual life? If your students have had previous encounters with deluded, threadbare aristocrats in plays by Chekhov, or down-at-the-heels "masters of deportment" in novels by Dickens, they might want to talk about this anomaly: that the "real world" might be full of people who are really playacting.
- What is your final view of this narrator? Is he a dedicated artist? An opportunistic hack? In his pursuit of a kind of truth, has he become irretrievably aesthetic? Reread the passage (top of page 435) beginning

"A painter's models put on—or put off—anything he likes," continuing down to "We only thought we might be more like *some* characters." What's strange about this passage? What are the cues here about the real situation of the Monarchs that our narrator doesn't see or prefers not to see?

The Beast in the Jungle

One way of situating James firmly in his era is to look at his efforts as an ironist and the mordant ironies at the heart of this story: first John Marcher misses his destiny by looking for it too keenly; and second (and worse), his "destiny," because of that narcissism and fixated vigilance, is to be a man to whom nothing really happened, a man who lost his one great chance for love and fulfillment. Because irony is an enormous presence in works of Hardy, Gissing, Wilde, Conrad, and Mark Twain, it's worth looking hard at this story for James's special variations on this powerful trend.

Questions for discussion:
- James uses a first-person narrator in some of his famous short works, including "The Figure in the Carpet" and *The Turn of the Screw*. Why use a third-person limited narrator for "The Beast in the Jungle?" We see the world over Marcher's shoulder. How then do we know what he doesn't seem to see—what May Bartram is thinking and feeling?
- May Bartram keeps her silence until the very end of her life, thereby dooming not only Marcher's hopes for happiness but her own as well. Why does she do that? Is this plausible? Have we lost this ability to wait so stoically for others to perceive—or did we ever have it? James's characters are often astoundingly mum about big secrets, waiting, to the point of immolation, for others to figure them out. Why does he bring us into the company of such people, keenly watching and waiting for one another to catch on?
- The beast is Marcher's metaphor for his fate—he believe in it, a menacing Other that waits to spring as soon as he turns his back. There are a lot of monstrous alternative selves in fiction at the end of the nineteenth century: the hideous portrait of Dorian Gray, Jekyll's nocturnal Mr. Hyde, and Marcher's very "unsettled" feeling about the nature of reality makes it difficult for him to go along with social forms. And so he lives with his "figure" of the beast as the hypothesis by which he understands his life. When the beast springs, in a sense, he will be able to live; until then he can't consider marriage. The beast becomes his disfiguring quality—he calls it "a hump on one's back"—and Spencer Brydon's other personality, from an unlived life, in James's "The Jolly Corner." How do we account for this literary fashion, and what is James's special contribution to it?
- On page 457, Marcher says to May, "What saves us, you know, is that we answer so completely to so usual an appearance: that of the man and woman whose friendship has become such a daily habit—or almost—as to be at last indispensable." What is packed into this sentence,

indicating what Marcher sees about himself and life, and what he doesn't see?

The Figure in the Carpet

It's a good idea to come at this story as the last in an opening encounter with Henry James, for "The Figure in the Carpet" is one of the most reflexive and slyly playful of any that he wrote. There are a lot of arguments about its tone and intention; my own "take" is that it's an ironic comedy, written when James, as "The Master," might have been wondering about the wisdom, or even the basic sanity, of investing so much intelligence and life in imaginative literature—as a writer or as a connoisseur. Are we supposed to sympathize with our narrator? Are we to imagine Vereker as the Great Genius who left a "stupendous" insight in his fiction, concealed for (almost) no one else to see—or should we enjoy him as a great practical joker, pulling so many legs at once?

Questions for discussion:
- When Gwendolyn discovers (or claims to discover), the figure in the carpet, the grand scheme and deep meaning of Vereker's work, why doesn't she tell the narrator? What do her motives seem to be?
- Read carefully the conversation that begins on page (top of page 482), with "Don't you think you ought—just a trifle—to assist the critic?" Describe it as a human interaction. Is Hugh Vereker leading and helping the narrator? Teasing and misleading him? What motives can we infer from his spoken words?
- Over the course of his career, James created a number of protagonists who never seem to catch on to the truth around them or to the truth about themselves. Sometimes those narrators tell the story themselves—and even when they do so, recounting everything in their own words, they might not "get it." What personality and values do you see emerging in the narrator of "The Figure in the Carpet"?
- Of Drayton Deane, the narrator speaks with contempt, condescending to Deane's lack of literary insight and finesse. How does the conversation on page 497, confirm or alter our impression of Deane and of the narrator himself?
- What do you think is the "figure in the carpet" of "The Figure in the Carpet"? That James's work is also a great complex shape with a profound meaning at the center? That the quest for deep meanings in imaginative works is inherently absurd?
- Compared to other James stories, how plausible is this one—a quest, extending so many years, for the deep meaning of an array of fiction by one esoteric and aloof "master"? What body of experience with James's work, or with the study of literature in classrooms, do you need to have in order to enjoy this story?

Sarah Winnemucca

These excerpts from *Life Among the Piutes* could be described as lyrical as well as autobiographical and morally engaged. Winnemucca offers us a fabric of reminiscence, of wisdom from her elders (including extensive quotations), and long moments when she seems to swing away from any sort of linear narrative to reflect on the human condition. To engage with these excerpts, students will need to lay aside any preoccupations with form and locate passages where Winnemucca's voice rings out with special clarity.

It's worth remembering that the Paiutes and Utes (a related group) had recently been subjected to some excoriating descriptions by white American writers, including Mark Twain, whose account in his best-selling book of adventures in the West, *Roughing It* (1872) was especially nasty, and apparently not based on any real firsthand experience with these peoples. Slandering the tribes of the Intermountain West was safe and easy for white authors writing to white audiences back East, at a moment when the "Great American Desert," previously thought to be little more than a picturesque wasteland, was penetrable by railroads and found to be full of mineral wealth. Indigenous people had to be persuaded or forced out of the way, and popular literature was playing its part. This was the context in which Sarah Winnemucca told her story.

Questions for discussion:
- Read aloud a couple of passages of general reminiscence; for example the passage beginning "Our boys are introduced to manhood by their hunting of deer" (bottom of page 508). Are such passages writing "back" to any predispositions or assumptions in Winnemucca's overwhelmingly white audience? Where do you see indications that this need to respond is on Winnemucca's mind?
- The most polemical paragraph in these excerpts is the one beginning "Oh, for shame!" (middle of page 511). Compare the logic here to strong moments in Equiano or Frederick Douglass. What similarities do you see? Why does Winnemucca "hang fire" until this point in Chapter VIII of her book?
- At the opening of Chapter II there are two paragraphs about the raising of children. Read them aloud and think about the larger literary context, the legacy of the New England transcendentalists. Do you find echoes of that legacy in the way Winnemucca summarizes the moral and spiritual life of her people?

Joel Chandler Harris

Harris was a prolific and popular writer, and deep into the twentieth century his dialect stories offered an idyllic memory of life in the Old South: of peaceful race relations among white and African Americans, where philosophical old "uncles" like Remus dispensed wisdom in the ancient folk way, with fables—and aspired to nothing more than that social role. Harris's work was scorned during the height of the civil rights movement in the sixties, as a kind of minstrelsy, a white man enriching himself by dressing up to enter-tain in rhetorical blackface.

But we can complicate our thinking about Harris and make observa-tions about some larger issues with regard to race and imaginative writ-ing in America. Harris uses heavy dialect that is not his own—and so does Charles Chesnutt, and Mark Twain, and Harriet Beecher Stowe, and later on, William Faulkner, Eudora Welty, Ralph Ellison, Richard Wright. A good discussion can center on the art of dialect, and also on the ethics of its use.

Questions for discussion:

- To start with a firm look at the text: choose a passage from an Uncle Remus monologue and compare it to a passage in Chesnutt's "The Goophered Grapevine" and also to a passage in *Huckleberry Finn*—for example, the passage in Chapter 15 (page 159), where Jim, in a heavy dialect, upbraids Huck for his deception. Writing dialect is a craft—you can go too far, and also not far enough, in representing a voice. Look carefully at the way that words are inflected to create a sound. In your view, who does it better, and why?
- What are the ethical complications of writing in dialect? Does the race of the author matter? Should it? Are there specific context within a nar-rative when it's called for, and others where it would come off as racist caricature? Or does "who's reading," and where and when, matter as much to this question as "who's writing"?

EMMA LAZARUS

Of the Lazarus selections in NAAL, "The New Colossus" will ring a bell with your students, thanks to lessons they had about the Statue of Liberty back in elementary school. "In the Jewish Synagogue at Newport" may give you more to talk about, however, as the poem is a direct response to the famous Longfellow poem in Volume B. Lazarus's rejoinder to Longfel-low is thoughtful and complex, not a simple refusal of his perspective: in their form and rhetoric, her lines echo the earlier poem, paying a kind of tribute to it, even as they politely alter or correct the theme.

Questions for discussion:

- Richard Rodriguez has often observed that one of the favorite strate-gies, intentional or not, for marginalizing a minority group is to relegate it to the past, to speak of that people as essentially extinct. Are any live "Hebrews" perceived in Longfellow's poem? When Lazarus says, "Now as we gaze, in this new world of light, / Upon this relic of the days of old"—who is the "we"?
- The final two stanzas of the poem seem to drift out to the graveyard, to join Longfellow in his elegiac stance. The poets stand in the same place—but in this ending, what are the differences in tone?

SARAH ORNE JEWETT

In the traditional presentation of late nineteenth-century American fiction, Jewett and Freeman are often grouped with the local color writers, and regionalism becomes a descriptive term for the entire group. A closer look at American literary history reveals that regionalism and local color writing developed as distinct but parallel genres and that regionalism was the first of the late nineteenth-century fictional genres to emerge. Stowe published "The Pearl of Orr's Island," the work that influenced Jewett's own development, five years before Twain's "The Notorious Jumping Frog of Calaveras County," and during the same decade that Hawthorne and Melville were publishing their most significant work (the 1850s), Alice Cary, Rose Terry Cooke (not anthologized here), and Stowe herself were establishing regionalism as a genre. By the time Jewett published "Deephaven" (1877), she already had a regionalist tradition to write within; and although by the chronology of birth order she and her work appear to follow Twain and James, the publication of "Deephaven" precedes that of *Adventures of Huckleberry Finn*, *The Rise of Silas Lapham*, and *The Portrait of a Lady*.

KATE CHOPIN

In a sense *The Awakening* is a story about rebellion of a quiet sort, a coming of awareness that compels a young person to seek complete escape from a social world that can never seem other than a deathtrap. Margaret Fuller heads for Italy and revolution; Huck lights out for the territory; Ishmael "quietly take[s] to the ship," and Thoreau moves a mile out of Concord for a couple of years, to try a life of partial solitude. Edna's rebellion, however, leads to self-destruction, to drowning ambiguously in the Gulf—rather than a longer, slower drowning on shore.

In Chopin's quest to present Edna's entrapment, despair, and (possible) suicide from her own point of view—a journey that leads through illicit sex and eventually into a deeper sort of solitude in which sexuality seems to be transcended or left behind—she uses the technique of shifting the narrative center. Often we see Belle Isle through her eyes, feeling her inchoate resentment and lassitude; at other times, however, we see and hear interactions that she cannot, and students will want to talk about Chopin's decisions with regard to point of view: when and why she stays with Edna, and when and why she leaves the side of her protagonist.

Around Edna, Chopin creates an environment that seems uncannily real in the fact that the oppression cannot be neatly sorted out. Edna's uncomprehending and dismissive husband is obviously a big part of the problem. But so is the young, seductive, and (finally) weak Robert, whom Edna may never come to see clearly, and there is the cadence of life on Belle Isle, and even the climate, with its hot days and humidity and the host of excuses for taking no action. The real world we negotiate can indeed seem like a muddle, and tidy dominion over it might be an illusion favored by romantic fiction and lesser imaginations.

One other matter to bear in mind as you move into this work—it's quite possible that some of your students will not like Edna at all, will resent the fact that she often seems to stop short, with a headache or a spell of faintness, rather than push through, like favorite heroines in British and American fiction, to some satisfying avowal or anagnorisis. Elizabeth Bennet and Jane Eyre come to see themselves clearly and to speak their mind; James's women protagonists almost always achieve a firm, life-changing breakthrough in their own self-awareness; even Scarlett O'Hara, down to her last carrot (in the movie, anyway) gives up on being a coquette and eventually speaks rousing defiance to the skies. There's no moment like this for Edna, and some of your students will want to know why there isn't.

Questions for discussion:
- That's a good question to start with: why Chopin does not allow Edna to rise up at any point and speak her own mind completely and clearly, to anyone else, or even to herself. Could this be the very heart of the oppression that she experiences, an oppression so complete as to deny the victim a full sense of her own predicament? Choose two or three moments where Edna seems on the verge of that kind of recognition or utterance and discuss how these moments work in the novel.
- What about the array of men in Edna's life—Pontellier, her father, Doctor Mandelet, Robert? None of these people are villains in a classic sense, are they? If not, what kind of evil might they represent, individually or together in a nasty arrangement of fate? In literary naturalism, what evolution are you seeing in the nature of evil, and the kind of damage it wreaks on others?
- Read closely one scene in the novel, the closing scene of Chapter XXIII (bottom of page 588) in which Edna and Léonce have dinner with Edna's father and Doctor Mandelet. In this scene, each of the four characters tells a story that reveals a great deal about the teller's character. What do we discern through each narrative? Edna tells a romantic story of two lovers who paddle away one night and never come back. Why is it Edna's story, among them all, that most engages the imagination of her audience?

MARY E. WILKINS FREEMAN

Like Jewett, Freeman wrote in the genre of regionalism, and also like Jewett, Freeman places women's lives and regional vision at the center of her stories. Freeman's "A New England Nun" makes a useful companion story to Jewett's "A White Heron." Ask your students to evaluate the motivations and final choices of Louisa Ellis and Jewett's Sylvy. Freeman focuses on Louisa Ellis's experience, and she portrays her male character, Joe Dagget, fairly sympathetically. "A New England Nun" presents Louisa Ellis's vision and decision not to marry as valid and normal, but Freeman doesn't earn the reader's sympathy for her female character at Joe Dagget's expense. She portrays Joe as well meaning and honorable, if typical of his time and place (many young men left New England to make their fortunes elsewhere in the years following the

Civil War). Some critics have called Louisa sexually repressed. A lively discussion will follow if you ask your students whether they agree.

"The Revolt of 'Mother' " earns Freeman a place in the humorist tradition, with a difference. Once again, she includes "Father's" perspective in her story of "Mother's" revolt and suggests "Father's" ability to enlarge his own capacity for empathy. Unlike writers of the Southwest humorist school, for whom local color implied acceptance of off-color jokes about women, Freeman does not elevate Sarah Penn by caricaturing Adoniram and making him the object of ridicule. Like Jewett's "A White Heron," "The Revolt of 'Mother' " may be read as Freeman's response to local color writing. From the opening line of the story, what Sarah Penn seems to want most of all is to engage her husband as her audience and to find acceptance for her own voice. Revolt may be too strong a word to describe Sarah Penn's attempt to make herself heard; she remains within the family structure, even if she has managed to redefine its terms; Nanny's impending marriage, not Sarah's own frustration, moves her to act.

Freeman contributes to the development of regionalism by collapsing narrator and female protagonist. Ask students to consider the absence of narrators in Freeman's stories and to contrast this with the reliance on narrators by her contemporaries, most notably Jewett and James. Where Jewett makes it possible for a reader to empathize with a regional character and to imagine that character speaking in his or her own voice, Freeman actually stands back from her own regional canvas, allowing her characters' voices, not a narrator's perspective, to create their own stories. Unlike Jewett, Freeman does not dramatize a shift in the center of perception, from, say, the ornithologist of "A White Heron" to the nine-year-old rural child; instead, Freeman writes from a position where such a shift has already occurred. She frames her stories carefully—Louisa Ellis's window and the Penns's barn door carefully limit the world she depicts—but within that frame, she creates a fictional territory in which characters can articulate the perspective of marginal women as central. The tight form of her fiction both fences out and fences in; she writes as if regionalism both opened up and protected that small space within which late nineteenth-century women were free to express their vision.

ANNA JULIA COOPER

As a new selection for NAAL, Cooper's "Woman versus the Indian" runs rather long, and if your course has already engaged with Equiano, Harriet Jacobs, Sojourner Truth, and Frederick Douglass, you might be tempted to skip over this less famous essay on human rights and the status and potentiality of American women. But think twice: Cooper's contribution to the African American prose tradition is experimentation and refreshment with regard to style and rhetorical strategy. With poise and confidence, she lays claim to a different and broader legacy of public discourse, and she also makes a dramatic break with certain tropes in a century of argument for the equal treatment of America's races and genders.

Questions for discussion:

- To engage with "Woman versus the Indian" as a document in a literary history, you might focus first on some astounding variances in Cooper's voice and the organization of her argument as she moves deeper into the subject. Compare a couple of passages: the very long and oratorical section on pages 648–49 beginning "The American woman of to-day not only gives tone directly to her immediate world" and the outbreak of short paragraphs on page 654, beginning with the curt "I think so" set off by itself. Sometimes Cooper inundates us with words, like Emerson in a high heat; at other times she seems to adapt Margaret Fuller's strategy of hit-and-run, offering observations that surprise for their concision. What relationship do you see between these respective styles and the particular phase of the argument?

- On page 654, in a long and very heated paragraph beginning with "One of the most singular facts about the unwritten history of this country," Cooper launches into a roundhouse attack on white Southerners. What's happening here? Is Cooper transgressing her own message of mutual respect and tolerance? Is there any playfulness in this caricature or any sense that she is pausing to give white Southerners a dose of their own medicine? Can you think of outbreaks in Emerson or Thoreau that compare with this?

- Though Cooper, at the end of the chapter, comes around to an invocation of the Almighty and the Christian tradition as the ultimate ground for social equality and mutual respect among the races, nearer the middle of the essay she puts special emphasis (bottom of page 653) on "teaching GOOD MANNERS," as if that were a better and more reliable basis for change than Scripture. Why might Cooper try such a shift in argumentative strategy, at this point in our cultural history?

BOOKER T. WASHINGTON

The Washington materials give us a real opportunity to talk about the construction of an American identity, of an autobiography, and of a text that converses with other important documents in our cultural history. Writing at the very end of the nineteenth century, Washington was deeply aware of the historical and literary moment in which he was working: Franklin, Jacobs, Douglass, Whitman, Ulysses S. Grant, and many other autobiographers had already done much to establish the pace, subject matter, and general configurations of an American life set down on paper. Your students have probably engaged with some of these forebears (or competitors) in the craft and art of American-style autobiography.

You might focus on the opening pages of *Up from Slavery* and the way it continues and departs from traditions developed by Douglass; you might spend some time with much later passages in Washington's book that describe the mature leader's daily schedules, work routines, and conceptions of success, recreation, and personal contentment, and compare these to procedures and values laid out by Franklin or Thoreau.

Questions for Discussion:

- Where do your students see suggestions that Washington is echoing or resisting moments or assumptions that we associate with the contemporary writers he was "competing" with?
- Does Washington conceive of his audience as similar, somehow, to Franklin's?
- Does Washington present themes and tones in *Up from Slavery* that might account for why his book, which was hailed as a classic for decades, has fallen into eclipse in more recent years?
- In what spirit does Washington distinguish his own upbringing from middle-class conceptions of childhood?
- When Washington talks about his strategies as a public speaker, what assumptions might be indicated about the complexities of maintaining personal integrity and Emersonian-style honesty while also striving (as Washington affirms that he does) to please an audience so thoroughly that not one listener would ever leave the hall?

Charles W. Chesnutt

It would be a mistake to present Chesnutt as merely another local colorist in a heyday of such writers, an African American working faithfully in the mode and fashion pioneered and dominated by white authors. His situation is in some ways more complex, and his handling of it is worthy of our attention—not because he needs to be redeemed but because the way he approaches his situation can help us recognize the breadth and depth of what he achieves.

In several ways, Chesnutt's situation was supremely paradoxical, as black writer of mixed race, narrating black experience in a context already well supplied with narratives of black experience, written by white people. Moreover, the situation of African Americans in the United States had obviously changed much in the preceding thirty-year period—to the extent that the perceptions, personal histories, and identities of this minority had never been more scattered and diverse. Chesnutt was a realist by conviction—but in which direction did "the real" lie: back in the rural South and the plantation life? Or as far from it as one could flee? There were also profound ironies having to do with his situation as an artist, working in a mode in which the flashy counterfeit could often strike a reading audience as more "true" than the true article.

Chesnutt, accordingly, speaks in a chorus of voices, and he violates expectations, not just in terms of plotting but in terms of the realist mode itself. The motive may be to return his readers to a condition of wonder, of the rapt attention that can come with seeing things freshly or for the first time. Like Twain, like James, like Wharton, Chesnutt will throw plausibility out the window at times in pursuit of a more important or larger sort of "realism." His frame-tale narrators (as in "The Goophered Grapevine") don't serve merely to give Chesnutt himself some safe distance, or to socially remove himself, from the story he tells; the strategy allows us to approach, in stages, something unfamiliar, where (as your students might say) all bets are off—an American reality where the conventional, white, turn-of-the-century audience would find very little that was familiar to it and where, in a sense, anything could happen.

It's probably a good idea to engage with "Grapevine" and "The Wife of His Youth" before attempting "The Passing of Grandison," as the tone and viewpoint of that story will puzzle some of your students and possibly trigger some anger. "The Wife of His Youth" is a story with a safer sort of twist, somewhat like an O. Henry tale, except the twist has the resonance that a plot twist might have in a Hawthorne romance. An old woman wanders by chance into the life of a man who believes, to his core, that he has left his old life and his old self behind and has achieved full amalgamation into sophisticated urban life, or at least into this new African American gentility, where Tennyson's poems have replaced the spirituals that Du Bois lauds in The Souls of Black Folk.

Questions for discussion:

- Is Liza's return the return of Ryder's soul? Is the transformation that simple? What will happen next, after the last page of this narrative?
- Does Chesnutt seem to be offering some forecast here, about the future of his people? Or does he puzzle over that future, as Hawthorne seems to when he engages with present-day New England?

"The Passing of Grandison" can be taught as a tale that throws us into several dilemmas at once. There is an aura of farce here, centering on a subject that might seem anything but farcical to an American author of black ancestry. A superficial and complacent white Southerner, the indolent Dick Owens, struggles to impress and woo the blond, judgmental, and also indolent woman of his dreams (straight out of Central Casting) by sending a trusted family slave north to freedom, a slave who seems to have no interest in running away. A sit-com emerges; some of your students will recall Twain sketches that work with similarly elaborate conceits. Grandison *seems* to be out of Central Casting too, but therein lie the twists of the story: in plot and also in perspective and theme.

Questions for discussion:

- After being led to the Canadian border and virtually hijacked across it, Grandison, after months of privation, finds his way home again, like a faithful abandoned pet—but why? What does the end of the story reveal about Grandison that has not been grasped by his owners and has not been conveyed by the omniscient narrator?
- This turns out to be a tale of heroism, one man's quest to rescue a family from bondage—a quest that unfolds without the soliloquies or avowals of noble purpose that we see in Chapter III of Uncle Tom's Cabin or Part I of Douglass's The Heroic Slave. Why does Chesnutt

deny Grandison such a voice about his own intentions? What traditions and trends is Chesnutt working with—and also against?

Charles Alexander Eastman (Ohiyesa)

In Chapter VI of *From the Deep Woods to Civilization* (not in NAAL 7), Eastman writes about the difficulty that Native American parents endure, as their children are sent away to government boarding schools: "I was of course wholly in sympathy with the policy of education for the Indian children, yet by no means hardened to the exhibition of natural feeling." Later on, in the chapter included in NAAL 7, however, he seems to speak from an oddly marginal position: "I scarcely knew at the time, but gradually learned afterward, that the Sioux had many grievances and causes for profound discontent, which lay back of and were more or less closely related to the Ghost Dance craze and the prevailing restlessness and excitement" (middle of page 719). Eastman speaks the Sioux language but with power vested in him by the U.S. government, and he thus sometimes seems alienated from the Sioux point of view.

For the larger narrative of the story of the Ghost Dance religion and the Wounded Knee massacre, Eastman's narrative offers a powerful eyewitness account of impending conflict and of the aftermath and consequences of the massacre. You might ask students to trace references to the "new religion" that has been proclaimed at about the same time as Eastman's arrival at Pine Ridge. Then have them examine Eastman's narrative for evidence that might explain the resistance of white settlers to the Ghost Dance religion.

Questions for Discussion:
- Read carefully Eastman's account of the Ghost Dance War itself (pages 721–22). While not an eyewitness to the massacre, Eastman presents himself as an "ear witness," hearing the sound of the Hotchkiss guns. How does this oblique account parallel his relationship to the Sioux people?
- What Eastman sees of the wounded and dead when he visits the battlefield tests his assimilationism but does not ultimately change his course of action: "All this was a severe ordeal for one who had so lately put all his faith in the Christian love and lofty ideals of the white man" (bottom of page 723), he writes—and sets his day of marriage to a white woman for the following June. Compare Eastman's words and actions with those of William Apess, in "An Indian's Looking-Glass for the White Man" sixty years earlier. How do the terms of the discourse differ?

Pauline Hopkins

Representative of the general character of *Contending Forces,* the excerpts in NAAL seem to be from two different novels—to the extent that there's a danger here: students who are thrown off by Chapters III and IV may not make it to the impassioned and vividly represented debate of "the American Colored League" later on in Chapters XIII and XIV, which offer an extraordinary tour through various positions on the "Negro Question" at the turn of the twentieth century. Hopkins works in two very different modes in this single novel—stock romance and also a variety of realism in which contemporary political and moral viewpoints eclipse matters of plot and characterization. This might not be a coherent book, but there's no question about its ambitions or its urgency.

Questions for discussion:
- *Contending Forces* begins on familiar ground: a happy, contented patrician family, overthrown by a flat-out villain recognizable as such to everyone except the victims; a scurrilous henchman given a taste of his own medicine and vowing revenge; an innocent child deprived of comfort and social standing and forced to take his chances in the cold world beyond his Edenic youth. In these opening chapters, does Hopkins succeed in developing anything original within this framework? If she has important matters to explore later on, why begin with this?
- If students have read selections from *Uncle Tom's Cabin*, ask them how these two novels can be compared as amalgams of melodramatic fiction and other aspirations?
- Look carefully at the words of three speakers in Chapters XIII and XIV. Why does Hopkins arrange the speakers in this sequence? Why does Luke Sawyer get the "last" word in this debate, and what are the complications of his position?

HAMLIN GARLAND

Garland's "Under the Lion's Paw" usefully contrasts with Freeman's "The Revolt of 'Mother.'" Although Stephen Council initially helps Haskins get a good start, Garland focuses on the futility of Haskins's labor, and the concluding scene creates a tableau similar in effect to the end of Bret Harte's "The Outcasts of Poker Flat." Haskins is "under the lion's paw," and Butler (and Garland) leave him "seated dumbly on the sunny pile of sheaves, his head sunk into his hands." The reader views Haskins—like Mother Shipton, Piney Woods, and ultimately Oakhurst as well—from the outside. Contrast the poverty of the homeless characters in "Under the Lion's Paw" with the inadequately housed Sarah and Nanny Penn in Freeman's "The Revolt of 'Mother.'" Garland bases the power of his story on its portrait of the bleakness of poverty; Freeman bases hers on her protagonists' awareness of their own strengths.

ABRAHAM CAHAN

New to NAAL, Cahan's "The Imported Bridegroom" offers wonderful possibilities for discussion of fiction's role, and responsibility, in representing the American immigrant experience—and in classrooms where first-generation Americans are confidently in attendance, a conversation about

Cahan can have special poignance. If you are lucky enough to have such students working with you, you may have heard from them already about the complexities they face in deciding who they are (as opposed, sometimes, to who their parents want them to be) and about how they are navigating these riptides of new knowledge and belief and doubt that roil a modern American campus. Like Shaya on his first visits to the Astor Library, an innocent boy stunned and moved by the sheer wealth of books around him and heretofore unimaginable possibilities for learning and growth, good students from traditional families often face a protracted crisis, a recognition that if they follow these new opportunities, and their own desires, they could stray uncomfortably or even irretrievably far from the world and values in which they grew up. In public lectures, the contemporary Mexican American essayist Richard Rodriguez often says that "When you come to America, America can give you everything—but you will lose your children." From one hundred years before Rodriguez, this is a story about that kind of gain and loss.

All of which is to say that a class on "The Imported Bridegroom" could easily evolve into a collective inquiry into the nature of the American self, a conversation that might exhilarate some of your students and, possibly, trouble others in the room. How far you go in such directions, if you decide to sail on these headings at all, will depend on levels of mutuality that only you can gauge. It would be shame, however, to lose sight of the delicate craftsmanship of Cahan's text, the balancing he works for in writing to his immediate community—American or American*izing* Jews from Eastern Europe—and also in trying to reach a much broader range of readers, in a quest to introduce and humanize these strange-talking immigrants, who on so many levels are so easy to misunderstand.

Two key questions, then, which require some time to work through: how can we describe the tone of Cahan's story? And how and where do we see him reaching out to each of these very different audiences? In "The Imported Bridegroom" we have the makings of a situation comedy: a mismatched good-hearted young people, forced together at first, who develop a deep relationship and an alliance of sorts against the elders who set them up and now regret doing so; a clumsy and obtuse father who nonetheless means well, gruff in demeanor but also putty in a daughter's hand; and a daughter whose major failing, in her father's eyes, is that she has become, in obstreperous and inevitable ways, an thoroughly American girl, precisely because he has raised her in America. Even so, woven into this comedy are passages of great poignancy. Asriel's trip "home" to Poland is a failure in many ways. He is welcomed in his old village, yet he is also a stranger, an outsider; and when he visits the local cemetery, the resting place of his own parents and looks at "this piebald medley of mounds, stones, boards, and all sorts of waste" (middle of page 779), he feels the mordant possibility of his own dissolution, the prospect that in leaving all this behind, he has become prosperous but has also become nothing.

Questions for discussion:

- Cahan obviously knows these people and this economic and social predicament firsthand, but how would we describe his voice, his implicit relationship to the characters in this story? How is his voice differentiated from the voices of his characters? Does he sound like a dweller in this neighborhood? A knowledgeable visitor from somewhere else?

- These characters, recent immigrants most of them, might be expected to speak in heavily accented English or in Yiddish or Russian or some mix of these and other languages. But in Cahan's tale they speak without accents, without a salting of non-English words and expressions—in other words, without any of the dialect that turns up in stories from this period by Harris, Hart Crane, and Chesnutt. If we listen closely however, we can hear a syntactic twist here and there, the reversals and up-and-down swings that suggest speech in this ethnic community. Why might Cahan handle the speech of his characters in this way?

- Whom is Cahan writing to and for and with what intention? Is his presentation of life on the Lower East Side charged with the same intentions as Chesnutt's "The Wife of His Youth" or Garland's "Under the Lion's Paw?" What is gained and what is sacrificed with such stylization?

- What is gained and risked by telling a story of love, reticence, misunderstanding, and youthful rebellion against tradition—in other words, one of the oldest stories in the world?

CHARLOTTE PERKINS GILMAN

Like Chopin's *The Awakening*, "The Yellow Wall-paper" shows us a woman caught in materially and financially "comfortable" but lethal domestic circumstances, a woman who, like Edna, struggles for some kind of self-discovery and affirmation in a context that seems perfect not only for keeping her confined but also for confounding her ability to think clearly about herself. If Gilman can be classified, in a general way, with the literary naturalists, then we should take care to see her as a writer who did not use irony as a substitute for moral engagement. Moral indignation radiates in Gilman's prose and poems, and the convergence of anger and craft does much to set her apart, even in her time.

Before starting in: with regard to the new story in this set, "Turned," it's worth observing a dramatic change in the population that provided domestic service, working as maids and cooks, nursemaids and gardeners, between the time of this narrative and now. Around the turn of the twentieth century, middle-class homes across the country were sustained by immigrant "girls" from Ireland, Sweden, Norway, Italy, and elsewhere in Europe. Some of these women were the ancestors of your students—or maybe even your own great-grandmother! In other words, Gilman gives us all a glance back to a moment with uncanny parallels to our own, when a new wave of immigrants, coming to America from different point on the compass, is filling these roles in the workforce, as a way of joining American economic and social life.

Questions for discussion:

- Because "The Yellow Wall-paper" is a story about confinement, madness, and fate, what happens if we compare this story to Poe's "The Fall of the House of Usher" and Henry James's "The Beast in the Jungle?" Does "The Yellow Wall-paper" rate as a horror story? If so, can you make a case that for modern readers Gilman's story is the most frightening of these three?

- Obviously much of what happens in "The Yellow Wall-paper" is interior, hallucinatory. Even so, can we see this narrative as an experiment in realism? Is it better to read "Why I Wrote 'The Yellow Wall-paper'?" before or after engaging with the story—or not at all?

- At the ending of "Turned," we find ourselves at a moment reminiscent of the ending of Chesnutt's "The Wife of His Youth." How can we compare these endings as points of moral arrival? What would you say is the intent of each story, as a vignette of contemporary life?

- When Gilman turns to poetry, she remains true to her politics and her polemical temperament. How do those intentions and emotions influence her poems, for better or worse?

EDITH WHARTON

The two Wharton selections, "The Other Two" and "Roman Fever," offer an interesting contrast: "The Other Two" can be read as a domestic comedy, at least at the outset, while there's plenty of melodrama in "Roman Fever," as well as a nod back to "Daisy Miller." Wharton, for a while, regarded herself as a disciple of Henry James, and their friendship and correspondence spanned many years. If your students are coming to Wharton after James, they may enjoy the elements of resemblance but also Wharton's achievement of her own voice and of moral perspectives that are rarely simple. What brings these two stories together, setting them apart from the James selections? Like James, Wharton focuses frequently on the leisured classes, people with the cultural comforts, genteel education, energy and resources to concentrate on the connoisseurship of human relationships, complex motives, and the intricacies of consciousness. Unlike James, however, Wharton's social elite can seem haunted, lost—and not because of some denouement but really from the outset. In the fashionable life of New York and the Continent there's a hollowness that these people often struggle to ignore and avoid, and Wharton is sometimes wry, and sometimes achingly direct, in bringing it into view.

One more suggestion before diving in: it might be worth pointing out that a century ago, divorce was fairly rare and a matter for whispered conversation behind the back, and a "divorcée" was often regarded as somehow tainted or dangerous, regardless of her culpability or innocence in the failure of a marriage. Because it's a good bet that the parents of some of your students are divorced, these students might be puzzled by all this business with raised eyebrows and innuendo. Wharton is writing about a different social era and getting that clear at the start could help the conversation.

Questions for discussion:

- "The Other Two" is told from the point of view of Waythorn, a man of early middle age, a comfortable businessman. How does Wharton's choice of language suggest his temperament? Read the first full paragraph of the story (bottom of page 830) and the long passage on the bottom of page 837 beginning with "He realized suddenly that he knew little of Haskett's past." What do the word choices in these passages suggest about Waythorn's imagination, the way he evaluates others and the world?

- When Waythorn is seated during "luncheon" a couple of chairs away from Varick (page 835), we hear a great deal about the details of "good living," fundamentals of gourmet and sybaritic indulgence from a century ago. James rarely offers such details—why does Wharton do so here?

- The story ends with Waythorn accepting a cup of tea with a laugh, in the company of his wife and her two previous husbands. A happy ending? If there is a deep problem of some sort here, what values or kinds of conduct have been responsible for creating it?

- If your students have read *Daisy Miller* they will be eager to look at this as a "remix," a return to crucial scenes and settings in James's tale of a young woman undone by a visit to ancient Roman ruins after dark, transgressing rules of class conduct and also risking her health. We are a full generation later, and "Roman fever" is a thing of the past—or is it? Our protagonists, these two matrons, are self-described "old lovers of Rome." What have they done with their lives?

- When you read the long paragraph on page 845 beginning with "Well, perhaps I wasn't," what words and phrases stand out as peculiar? "Exquisite?" "Specimen?" "Estimable pair?" "Irreproachable, exemplary?" What kinds of attitudes and values do these words suggest, and what happens later on to challenge those attitudes?

- The story ends rather melodramatically, with a secret crime coming out, and years of buried resentment rising into view. Where does the story end up? Who wins? What do you make of the final line?

IDA B. WELLS-BARNETT

For good reason, Wells-Barnett relies heavily on transcribed newspaper reports about Robert Charles and the New Orleans police and justice system, as well as on letters from people who knew firsthand about Robert Charles; the published journalism provides the most solid documentation available to her as she tries to tell the whole story. Before they plunge into a reading, however, your students might be encouraged to keep an eye out for Wells-Barnett herself, and not get lost in all this material by others: in a course in literary history, your class will want to discern the temperament of the writer, the moments where we can sense her presence, as a center of intelligence and indignation.

Questions for discussion:
- Toward the end of the selection, Wells-Barnett centers on the worldly effects that Robert Charles left behind, especially the published materials in his room. What does she find there, and why does she accord it so much importance?
- Beginning with "Captain Day started for Charles' room" (top of page 859), Wells moves into mordant sarcasm, always a difficult undertaking on the printed page. How does that tone come clear? What are the cues that we are not supposed to take this paragraph "straight?" Does the context, the many paragraphs preceding this one, do most of the work of establishing the voice? Are there rhetorical strategies in the paragraph itself that provide a sufficient cue as to how to hear it?

Sui Sin Far

Like other writers who sought to represent the immigrant experience at the turn of the twentieth century, Sui Sin Far faced a complex challenge, and your students may enjoy "In the Land of the Free" much more if the group takes some time, at the outset, to sort that challenge out. Far is in a classic predicament for an American writer, "ethnic" or not: as a naturalized American citizen with full command of the English language and the culture of the West, Far is both *inside* the experience of new arrivals and *outside*; the people she writes about in this story are familiar to her and also estranged—much like the literary audience that she is writing for. Like Hemingway a generation after in *For Whom the Bell Tolls*, Far translates the Cantonese dialogue of Hom Hing and Lae Choo into an English with a King James Bible feel to it, and that remarkable strategy can form a good basis for a set of discussion questions:

Questions for discussion:
- Beyond the implication that Cantonese has different structures and formalities from American English, what are the aesthetic or thematic effects of offering the dialogue in this way? What literary and cultural experience might Far be hoping to evoke in her audience—an audience of middle-class and predominantly white Americans? If the Book of Exodus, or other books of the Old or New Testament come to mind, what thematic light might those associations cast on how we read this story of modern wanderers?
- Is Far thinking of these new Chinese immigrants as a "them" or an "us?" In other words, how would you describe the empathy or the distance that you sense in this story?
- In part III of the story, the lawyer James Clancy is introduced in a peculiar way, first as a "young man," then as a "young lawyer," and then as Clancy, presumably a white young lawyer of Irish descent. Why does Far cadence the exposition in this way? What might it imply about the

evolving awareness of Hom Hing, about the situation he is in, and Clancy's identity and motives?

- As a Chinese American, does Sui Sin Far have a special literary and cultural license to write stories like this? What are the ethical risks of trying for this kind of perspective?

MARY AUSTIN

Like others who followed her in writing the American West—a tradition that includes John Steinbeck and Larry McMurtry—Austin writes of encounters with wanderers and social outcasts, people who go their own way. In those moments of encounter, conventional social practices and values seem contingent. And like Sui Sin Far, Austin takes up the task of speaking for people who in a sense cannot speak for themselves, people with no access to print, people with the kind of life and temperament that excludes them from the written word, and even from listeners, other than lone and patient listeners like Austin herself.

At the outset, it's worth pointing out that Austin may have a personal stake in telling this story, that she herself was a wanderer and something of a loner. The headnote makes that clear, and an opening look into "The Walking Woman" can be a browse for clues that this writer, this teller, has something else in mind than the collecting of peculiar human specimens from the desert Southwest.

Questions for discussion:
- To pull students into a conversation about the style of the story, focus on the elaborate metaphor on page 889: "It was one of those days when the genius of talk flows as smoothly as the rivers of mirage through the blue hot desert morning." This is the most ostentatious metaphor in the tale, and it stands out. What is the effect? What does it imply about the mind of this storyteller? Would more metaphors of this sort enhance the tale? Or would they quite possibly spoil the effect?
- The emotional climax of the story is probably the set of paragraphs that begins "The wind was stopped and all the earth smelled of dust" on the bottom of page 891. Two narratives here are intertwined: the Walking Woman's account of making love with Filon, and the moment of deep, almost wordless mutual understanding between the Walking Woman and the narrator. What about the clauses beginning with "but no; as often as I have thought of it," clauses that seem to hesitate or to modulate the experience? Why does the storyteller move in this direction?
- On the bottom of page 892, the short paragraph beginning "At least one of us is wrong" seems, at a glance, like a moral to a fable. Yet what are the ambiguities that are embedded in the line "But the way we live establishes so many things of much more importance"? Do these ambiguities seem contrived? Or are they connected to larger recognitions about how modern life is constructed?

W. E. B. DU BOIS

The moral and political problems, and the problems of personal and cultural identity, raised so eloquently by Du Bois in these selections can fuel plenty of discussion—about race, politics, and painful continuing differences between professed national values and actual social practice. You may not, however, have to make an either/or decision as you plan your classes in regard to teaching this from aesthetic or political perspectives. Du Bois was an uncommonly skillful writer, and a fully respectful reading of *The Souls of Black Folk* should take note of his sense of pace, his analogies and extended metaphors, and his expert understanding of when to make use of the rhetoric of the pulpit and when not to, when to reach into the cultural experience of an educated audience and when to turn to the details of ordinary life as experienced by African Americans after the Civil War.

You might select an especially strong passage—strong not just in the complexity of its content but also in the energy of its prose—and work backward, toward the beginning of the chapter, to observe how Du Bois prepares the way for a rhetorical adventure of this sort. The beginning with "The history of the American Negro is the history of this strife—this longing to obtain self-conscious manhood, to merge his double self into a better and truer self" and the one following it (top of page 897) can provide such a starting point. What are the connections—both logical and intuitive—between these paragraphs and the song selection that opens the chapter and the personal memories that come soon after it? If the long conceit about the "mountain path to Canaan" returns the reader to the familiar imaginative territory of the Calvinist and evangelical traditions, how has Du Bois prepared us to accept this old (and perhaps time-worn) analogy as something relevant and fresh? How would students describe an overall strategy of *The Souls of Black Folk*, the discernment, in the lines of supposedly simple African American spirituals, of complex ideas of selfhood and self-fulfillment? Is this a writerly tour de force, a display of wit, mental agility, and (perhaps) late Victorian sentimentality by one author working in a mainstream tradition? Or does Du Bois make this venture into cultural anthropology ring true and convince us of the deep wisdom within the ordinary and the plain?

The necessary two-ness of Washington and the "double consciousness" that Du Bois expresses allow students to see the emergence of real stress points in the concept of a referential, universal, or reliable reality. While it would not be accurate to say that the double consciousness of American blacks and of American women led to ways of thinking that would produce modernism, it was one aspect of the social environment that made and continues to make central concepts of modernism seem relevant to American experience. While neither a naturalist nor a modernist, Du Bois can be interpreted as a transition thinker—someone who observed the social forces at work in his own moment, who wrote to move common people, and who located his vision within the increasing sense that reality and identity might not be inherited or mysterious but rather, like myth, invented.

Cluster: Realism and Naturalism

New to NAAL in this edition, the cluster on realism and naturalism provides a foray into the first genuine theorizing of American fiction and its aesthetic and cultural missions. This is a gathering of commentary by working novelists who were in the midst of practicing these modes as well as defining and defending them. As students move from James and Howells through Norris and Dreiser, the big rifts in thinking will come clear: though naturalism is very often summarized as an offshoot of realism, there are differences so great as to make these movements seem opposite to one another rather than kin.

But before plunging into an exercise of charting these contrasts and conflicts on a blackboard, it's worth reading two or three of these excerpts first as *literary* texts, reading for qualities that one might look for in the imaginative fiction by this set of authors: temperament, voice, overt and unspoken assumptions about literature as an art or a social apparatus. When those qualities are observed, ideological differences become clearer—as well as differences in the fervor with which these different views are offered.

Try asking a student to read aloud one or two paragraphs from Howells's "Novel-Writing and Novel-Reading," to catch the pervasive gentility and collegiality here—not the middle-class complacency of which Howells is often and wrongly accused (he was, in fact, more ardent and persistent and courageous in advocating for social justice than either Norris or London or any other major naturalist except perhaps Dreiser) but rather the breadth of taste here and the open embrace he extends, welcoming many different sorts of approaches to representing the human condition under the general banner of realism.

Howells was also a pragmatist, a bit like Henry James's famous brother William: understanding that the strongest constituency of novel readers in the United States of his day were intelligent women from the middle and upper classes, Howells advocated a fiction that would reach them directly, complicating their thinking about moral and social issues and empowering them as a cultural force.

After a sampling of Howells, ask another student to try the Norris selections, which might sound bolder and more theatrical as rhetoric. Norris was a writer who liked blunt and roundhouse perceptions about art as well as human nature, and that confrontational and sensationalist temperament can come through in these paragraphs.

Questions for discussion:
- Does Norris "mean it" when he argues that literary naturalism is not a variant of realism but really a newer kind of romanticism? What is the reasoning behind this declaration—and what do you think of that reasoning? If Howells is writing for a broad audience of magazine readers, or for his constituency of women from the new middle class, people with aspirations to culture and taste as well as moral improvement,

whom do Frank Norris and and Theodore Dreiser seem to be writing to and for?

- If naturalism, as Norris describes it, is virtually coerced into romantic configurations because of certain doctrines about human nature and human possibility, at what point can fiction of this sort become *aesthetic*—in other words, an exercise in color or sensation or spectacle for their own sake rather than for conveying some sort of moral engagement with the human condition? If a question like this provokes a confused silence, ask your group to ponder what overtly naturalistic films that they have seen—Scorsese's *The Departed* or *Taxi Driver*, for example, or *Reservoir Dogs* or other films by Quentin Tarantino—are really "about," if they are about anything at all. If we are supposed to care about Carrie Meeber in *Sister Carrie* or Maggie in *Maggie: A Girl of the Streets*, are there novels and films of a similar style that induce a moral numbness or a sense that no exploration of human nature is taking place?

- If the second question provokes a lively debate about the various intentions and effects of literary naturalism, you might close in tighter on differences among the avowed realists, especially James and Howells. Howells takes chances in his description of the focus and subject matter for realistic fiction (you might want to point out that in his prose he often doesn't play by his own rules!). James is more evasive in talking about issues such as social class and what he means by "truth to life." Why does he do that, and where do we see a similar abstractness or evasiveness operating in his short fiction?

Frank Norris

Like Stephen Crane, Frank Norris died young, and as we read their work more than a century after, we have to wonder not only about the effects (for good or ill) of the literary naturalism that caught them up in their youth but also about what might have happened had they had lived longer. Would they have moved beyond some of those doctrines? Would they have also outgrown their bouts of infatuation with irony and condescension, a trouble seen often in writers before they reach full maturity? No way of knowing, of course, and so the Norris legacy is in some respects a lesson in naturalism as an aesthetic practice rather than a moral inquiry. He tells of people with limited intelligence and worldly prospects, people in desperate situations, blindly and vainly struggling, sometimes, against the realities of their own predicament—and very often compounding their own misery and that of others around them. But there's a border, ineffable perhaps but nonetheless important, between courageous and graphic mimesis and sensationalist voyeurism—between "telling it like it is" and telling it for thrills. In our multiplexes the no-holds-barred documentaries and devastating tales of mayhem and war play right next to the films featuring gore for the sheer hell of it. As your students look at this recovered story by Norris, in some ways a crude draft of material that went into *McTeague*, they will want to argue about what's going on here, the degree of this author's moral engagement with his chosen subject.

Questions for discussion:

- What are the major situational ironies in this story? How do they compare to the ironies in Stephen Crane's *Maggie,* also a story of women brutalized and trapped in the worst neighborhoods of an American metropolis?
- When Trina and "Missis Ryer" get into a protracted argument, and then a fight, about which of them has the more brutal husband, what is the tone? What emotional reactions are elicited, and how?
- Calling his story a *"fantasie,"* Norris includes little asides in his narration that seem to play off against a tradition of romantic folktales. Read for example the long paragraph beginning "The Ryers' home (or let us say, the house in which the Ryers ate and slept)" (middle of page 932) or the short paragraph beginning "When eleven o'clock had struck" (top of page 934). What observations and comparisons stand out for you in these passages, and what do they convey about the narrator's relationship to the story he tells?

THEODORE DREISER

If you're coming at Dreiser after a pause with the cluster on realism and naturalism, or after an experience with Kate Chopin, Jack London, or Stephen Crane, you have a good basis for trying a comparison of naturalistic writers in action, which will allow you to sense the variations in their enthusiasms and literary style. Like Crane, Dreiser is a devotee of irony. But more like Chopin than either Norris or Crane, Dreiser allows his women protagonists a measure of self-awareness and empowerment as they struggle for some kind of hold in an oblivious and treacherous social and sexual environment.

What you have here is an opening sample of a sprawling novel, the work on which Dreiser's reputation as a naturalistic writer is most firmly based. We get Carrie Meeber into Chicago from her small-town upbringing, and we get her to the near edges of what could be trouble, with jobs, money, and men. One of the best ways to engage with these two chapters is to center on style, on Dreiser's presentation of himself as a narrator, the kind of omniscience he takes up to tell this story of a character who could never tell the story of herself.

Questions for discussion:

- For starters, you might focus on the third paragraph of Chapter I, a paragraph fairly certain to rub some of your students very much the wrong way. Dreiser writes here like a minor god, knowing all about the ways of the city and the fate of young women who leave home to try their luck in such places. What is the effect for your students? Are they reassured to find themselves in the hands of a narrator so supremely knowing and confident of his own knowledge? Do they find these interventions obtrusive? There are also moments in Crane and Norris where the narration pauses for broad perspectives and grand overviews. If we compare such moments, what differences in tone and strategy do we see?

- Staying with Dreiser as a stylist: as an experiment, ask your students to choose a long paragraph from either chapter and try deleting at least half a dozen adjectives and adverbs from the passage without injuring the sense or the effect? Can they do it? What are the advantages and drawbacks of Dreiser's laying on the modifiers so thickly?
- At the opening of Chapter I, this omniscient narrator tells us, flat out, that Carrie "was possessed of a mind rudimentary in its power of observation and analysis. Self-interest in her was high, but not strong." Compare the description of "the man" in Jack London's "To Build a Fire," especially the one in the early paragraph (pages 1057–58) in which it is announced that "The trouble with him was that he was without imagination. He was quick and alert in the things of life, but only in the things, and not in the significances." Would James or Howells take interest in characters like these? With regard to storytelling and holding the attention of intelligent readers—readers presumably more imaginative and observant than either of these two—what are the consequences of centering on such people and of defining their limitations so bluntly and right at the start?

STEPHEN CRANE

As one of the showcased authors in any broad discussion of American literary naturalism, Crane can represent the special power of the mode as well as its limitations. When it was picked up from French and British writers by an energetic crop of young men in the United States, the practice on our own shores became almost euphoric. Here at last was a way of explaining everything that mattered about human nature and destiny: name and describe the heredity and the environmental circumstances of each character, and you have that individual revealed to the core. With social Darwinism and early and inept forms of eugenics grabbing headlines and commanding attention in scholastic circles, literary naturalism was a way for the artist to join in, to raise or assist in a rebellion against romantic and Victorian constructions of personality and prospects and also, along the way, to indulge in certain popular prejudices.

American naturalism, especially as practiced by young male authors, was also fueled by irony. Younger writers of any mode or moment often prefer an ironic perspective, as it can fill in for a tempered and forthright moral position. It's a sad fact that of the liveliest and most gifted American naturalists, Theodore Dreiser was the only one to live beyond his thirties. Whether the others would have outgrown, over time, their fascination with doctrine and dark ironies is a mystery that can never be solved.

With a diminished belief in the possibilities of the human spirit, in the prospects for escaping the trap of one's own blood and upbringing, problems also arose with regard to plot, for if your protagonist is inherently incapable of doing much at all about the predicaments in which he or she is raised, then extraordinary things have to happen to that character to keep things moving along.

Having set that background, however, it's worth looking at Crane's brief life to observe that as a young man facing the very real prospect of death at an early age, he had a special right to the naturalistic outlook and temperament. The Crane selections in NAAL allow students to see the variety of forces against which the protagonist in the Crane universe must fight. "The Open Boat" is a good place to begin, as it provides an easily understood panorama of the forces of nature against which the characters are pitted: the vast blind power of the sea, the varieties of weakness in the human body and mind. It's worth emphasizing, at the start, that "The Open Boat" was based on firsthand experience, and that Crane here might be seen as meditating on insights he achieved almost at the cost of his own life. In his twenties, dying of tuberculosis, he wrote many narratives in which destruction lurks just around the corner, ready to spring on the fortunes of human conflict or some simple and basic misunderstanding of the perils all around.

New to NAAL, Crane's novella *Maggie: A Girl of the Streets* is a gritty, updated variation on a theme that your students will recognize, especially if they have encountered Foster's *The Coquette* in Volume A. Once again we have a parable of a young woman undone and killed by her own innocence, by false promises offered to her in a culture of hypocritical and exploitive males.

Questions for discussion:
- If your students recognize the ancestry of Maggie, Jimmie, Pete, and others in this narrative, a good conversation can center on the differences here: the lack of intelligence and charm in the family or the seducers; the lack of eloquence, of anagnorisis or any kind of tragic self-understanding, in Maggie herself. Why does Crane deny his readers that kind of closure?
- Does the culminating irony of the tale, the drunken mother's weepy "fergiveness," have any moral implications?
- How would you describe the authorial perspective in *Maggie?* In other words, what stake does Stephen Crane seem to have in the archetypal story he offers here?

JOHN M. OSKISON

"The Problem of Old Harjo" may be discussed both as a Native American text and as regionalist fiction, and the two readings complement each other. To see how it relates to other Native American works anthologized in the 1865–1914 period of NAAL, begin by comparing Miss Evans with Charles Eastman's wife-to-be, Elaine Goodale. For Miss Evans is the prototype of the young, white, well-meaning, and often female Christian missionary to the Indians. Unlike the more experienced and less idealistic Mrs. Rowell, who expresses racism in her attitude toward "the old and bigamous" among the Creek Indian population (stating that "the country guarantees [Harjo's] idle existence" even though the truth is that he is materially solvent on his farm), Miss Evans is capable of seeing Harjo's situation as he sees it himself and withholds moral judgment. Harjo mutely questions her. and she questions Mrs. Rowell, then her old pastor in New York, even implicitly church doctrine when she is tempted to say to him, " 'Stop worrying about your soul; you'll get to Heaven as surely as any of us.' " Yet the "problem of old Harjo" becomes Miss Evans's problem, and although the story seems unresolved at the end, since the problem remains insoluble, her "solution" (if not "solvent") is to recognize that circumstances have somehow tied her to this particular mission station, to this particular "impossible convert." Tied to Harjo "until death came to one of them," does Miss Evans become in effect yet another "wife" to the bigamist? Even if not, Oskison is nevertheless suggesting that the real agenda of the Christian missionaries is to suppress Creek culture in the young until the old men die off. What is this agenda but a continuation of the Ghost Dance War in another form?

Readers familiar with Native American literature may recognize Harjo as a figuration of the trickster archetype, which they may have encountered in the Native American Trickster Tales in NAAL: a transformative character who represents the dilemmas of change—change for the old Creek but also change necessarily in the Christians, if anyone is to achieve genuine salvation. The story's apparent lack of resolution—"And meanwhile, what?"—not only conveys the disruptive effect of the trickster figure but also the process of highlighting trouble in the prevailing moral order. Old Harjo brings into relief the basic contradiction inherent in the encounter between the Christian missionaries and some Native Americans, which perhaps might be summed up in Mrs. Rowell's (long) wait for the "old bigamists" to die out. Yet as the story's ending attests, Harjo's powers include tenacity, and he engages Miss Evans in a temporal "problem" for which the only solution would be genuine change in the moral order of things. She becomes his "wife" to the extent that the trickster figure who appears in some Native American legends may represent sexuality and desire, and her wish to assure him of salvation is humorous within a Native American tradition, for the trickster (as students may recall from the Pima "Story of Creation") is already Coyote, the divinely powerful child born when the moon became a mother. So Coyote is another version of the Messiah of the Ghost Dance religion in the sense that, in a "trickster" mode, Coyote—or here, Harjo— becomes incarnate to point up moral failings in the creation.

Read from the perspective of regionalism, the story's portrait of the relationship between Harjo and Miss Evans becomes an exercise in empathic exchange. Miss Evans is capable of moving into Harjo's moral and affectional universe because she is able to look with, not at, the "problem" Harjo presents. At the same time, her sympathy for him works implicitly to challenge the moral, political, and religious control Mrs. Rowell represents. Although Oskison's story may not on initial reading appear to be as sophisticated as Chesnutt's "The Goophered Grapevine," both involve powerless and disenfranchised persons (old Harjo and Uncle Julius) creating a situation that will force whites to reveal their own moral limitations. In both stories, it is the cunning of the powerless that sets up the "looking glass" to white society; in posing his "problem" week after week in the church, Harjo is indeed expressing his cunning, for has Miss Evans converted him or has he converted her?

As a fictional representation of Apess's critique, "The Problem of Old Harjo" has much in common with the work of Chesnutt and other nineteenth-century regionalists. Or, to put it another way, regionalist writers invented the white characters (like Miss Evans) capable of responding to figures like Harjo, whether we view him as a Native American trickster or as a "realistic" problem occasioned by the encounter of cultures, in this story represented by the conflict between the Christian missionary and the "old and bigamous" Creek.

JAMES WELDON JOHNSON

In the array of widely read African American authors, Johnson has slipped in and out of attention over the last few decades, in part because the title of his most famous book, *The Autobiography of an Ex-Coloured Man*, seems both wry and guileless. With light skin and an uncommon education, Johnson had an uncommon opportunity to select and shape his own adult identity, and the decision he reaches in *Autobiography* (page 1038), that "I would change my name, raise a moustache, and let the world take me for what it would," has been seen by some readers, over the years, as a refusal to align himself overtly and steadily with any collective quest for black identity. The perspective that Johnson upholds in his prose, and even in his poetry, is one that your students may recognize as eerily American, however—a perspective that enjoys and also suffers from the condition of being on the edges, never entirely caught up in any group or condition and never really belonging either. Thoreau a mile out of Concord, Whitman and Dickinson oscillating between camaraderie and supreme loneliness, Nick Carraway and Ellison's Invisible Man—there's a long list of writers and protagonists in this general condition, and your students may want to expand it as you develop a context for reading Johnson.

Questions for discussion:
- The most compelling sequence in the excerpt is Johnson's eyewitness account of a lynching. On the middle of page 1037, beginning with "The Southern whites are in many respects a great people," he attempts a summation and a judgment that may surprise some members of your class. How would you describe the motives and the spirit of this completion for the episode?
- Johnson provides a memoir of a long conversation in a railroad car (pages 1025–27) in which a white Texan, a Jew from the North, and several others along with himself discuss race and prejudice and the future. Does it matter that this conversation takes place on the road, on a journey? Thinking back to Crèvecoeur, Thoreau, and Whitman on the open road, and others who comment on America while on the move, discuss the advantages and peculiarities of offering social and cultural overviews from that condition.
- Like Du Bois around the same time, Johnson gives special attention to the tradition and power of the "Negro spiritual." Why does he do so?

What does he find there, and in what ways is the spiritual tradition open or closed to him?

PAUL LAURENCE DUNBAR

In his short life, Dunbar was a prolific poet who worked in many forms and voices, and the new NAAL selections show us some of that surprising variety. Like Chesnutt, James Weldon Johnson, Pauline Hopkins, and Ida Wells-Barnett, Dunbar joined a complex project, to establish an African American literary voice at the turn of the twentieth century, a voice that could speak to a predominantly white reading public in styles that it understood and respected while also affirming a distinct contribution, a sound and a sensibility that came from elsewhere, from a body of experience beyond the Anglo-Saxon world. In these selections we see Dunbar writing elegies in a style that Tennyson or one of the British poet laureates would have recognized and commended, a style more conventional and conservative than Whitman's great elegies, "Out of the Cradle" and "When Lilacs Last in the Dooryard Bloom'd." We also see him rhyming in dialect, representing a rhetorical style and sound that you wouldn't have heard around the campuses and literary clubs of 1900. How do these poems complement each other, to give us a sense of a complete Paul Laurence Dunbar?

Questions for discussion:
- The preacher who speaks in "An Ante-Bellum Sermon" takes care to say, "I will pause right hyeah to say, / Dat I 'm still a-preachin' ancient, / I ain't talkin' 'bout to-day." Why does the preacher say that? Is Dunbar, writing as this bygone preacher, in a similar predicament?
- "Sympathy" has become famous for supplying, in its last line, the title of Maya Angelou's famous autobiography. Read the poem carefully and describe the tone of that conclusion.
- In a tour through a good poet, individual poems can illuminate one another, and works stand out more because of a background of other verse, a landscape in which we can see them better. The elegy for Fredrick Douglass and the elegy for Harriet Beecher Stowe praise these writers for plain and forthright speech, for moral courage in what they published. With that context in mind, what tone and implications can we find in Dunbar's "We Wear the Mask"?

JACK LONDON

Jack London's "To Build a Fire" is a standard in English courses as early as the eighth grade, and some of your students will probably have keen memories of its graphic description of the stages of freezing to death in the Yukon wilderness. If you are approaching these stories in the context of literary naturalism, however, you will have many new things to talk about: for example, the subtlety or self-evidence of themes in these tales and the open question of whether these stories inherently advance the loosely Darwinist doctrines that gave literary naturalism its force around the turn of the twentieth century.

The NAAL has enhanced the London selections with three additional stories that move farther out from the direct experiences and ethos of a white American author, who is after all still a white male no matter how many miles he has logged on land or sea. "The Mexican" eventually settles into the consciousness of the young, tough Felipe Rivera, raised in the villages and the streets and dedicated to revolution, a martyr to the core; "The House of Pride" is about a prudish, white second-generation patrician missionary living on Oahu; and "Mauki" (the biggest imaginative stretch) tries to look at life and colonial enterprise from inside the mind of a South Pacific cannibal and headhunter. As you look at this group of ambitious stories, two large-scale questions may arise and collide: first, how can Jack London presume to know such people so thoroughly? And second, if a writer like London doesn't try to tell the story of Felipe and Mauki—then who will? Literary naturalism might have been simplistic about human nature, reductive in its thinking about the fundamental motives of the self; but the mode could also be ambitious, and naturalistic writers like London took chances farther out of range than many artists in our own time.

If you feel that the habits and limitations of American literary naturalism might wear thin as a subject, especially after a sojourn with Norris, Chopin, and Dreiser, you could escape the "-isms," at least for a while, and speculate on why this kind of narrative, compelling and memorable and powerful as it is, has become the stuff of popular fiction while supposedly serious fiction has turned in other directions? If Henry James, as a consummate realist, held that literature should be (in his words) "a celebration of life," then what of narratives like "To Build a Fire" and "Mauki"?

Questions for discussion:
- How is "The Mexican" a tour de force—in other words, a demonstration of special prowess by Jack London? In this one story he presents the inner workings of a Mexican revolutionary group and of Los Angeles prizefighting at the turn of the century as well as the psychological response of Felipe to these and other settings. In moving us through these worlds, how convincing is London?
- We don't get the "back story" on Felipe until "The Mexican" is well underway—in Part II. Why does London delay so long in telling us all this about the boy?
- In the middle and later twentieth century, London's work was often accused of taking racist shortcuts with regard to characterization, resorting to stereotypes. Some of these come up in conversations in "The House of Pride," for example on the bottom of page 1088 in the exchange beginning "You are pure New England stock." Does London's use of stereotyping seem appropriate to you in some contexts, but not in others? Why or why not?
- Choose a long paragraph of exposition from a Jack London story and compare it to an expository paragraph from Norris, Dreiser, or Stephen Crane. Do all the literary naturalists sound alike? What distinctions can we make among these voices?

ZITKALA ŠA

Zitkala Ša's three autobiographical essays invite comparison with other autobiographies by women writers. Students may find it interesting to read Rowlandson's *Narrative* in which the author describes her capture by the Wampanoag Indians against Zitkala Ša's narrative of "capture" by the "palefaces." Suggest that Zitkala Ša's account of her removal from the reservation and attempted assimilation into white culture provides a twist on the Indian captivity narrative of the colonial period. It's also interesting to think about Zitkala Ša as a Native American Daisy Miller.

Although Zitkala Ša's work does not, strictly speaking, belong to the genre of regionalism—it is autobiography, not fiction—nevertheless, there are elements of fictional form, especially in "Impressions of an Indian Childhood." She uses images—learning the "art of beadwork" or the cropped and "shingled hair"—that characterize both her own life and the larger plight of other Native Americans. "Impressions of an Indian Childhood" also possesses an aesthetic distance that students might associate with fiction. At the end of the third selection, "An Indian Teacher among Indians," Zitkala Ša herself acknowledges that "as I look back upon the recent past, I see it from a distance, as a whole." Perhaps the reason for this distance is that, at least in "Impressions of an Indian Childhood," she writes about a developing child whose path of development as a Sioux becomes so pinched off that the older child and adult narrator cannot even repair the discontinuity.

She also writes in English about events that took place when "I knew but one language, and that was my mother's native tongue." The act of rendering her Sioux childhood into English creates its own fiction, for she writes about herself at a time in her life before speaking and writing in English was even imaginable. Like the regionalists, Zitkala Ša depicts a female-centered universe and her own refusal to be silenced, and she triumphs on behalf of the disenfranchised "squaw" when she writes of winning the oratory contest, although Zitkala Ša's estrangement from her own mother only deepens as she proceeds with her autobiography. She loses her connection with the world of nature, becoming a "cold bare pole . . . planted in a strange earth."

CORRIDOS

In a very interesting moment of transition in the popular music of the United States, these *corridos* are appearing in NAAL for the first time. The music of Mexico and Central and South America used to be quite distinct from the "Top 40" sound blasting out of North American stereos; now, however, ranchero music can be heard on FM stations as far north as Chicago and Indianapolis; the "Latin Grammys" draw a massive and multicultural American audience; on college campuses Salsa dance nights are commonplace; and hemispheric superstars like Shakira and Juanes can pack the largest venues with fans from many different ethnicities and social classes. Arrangements borrowed from Latin America are commonplace in "mainstream" pop, and songs that merge sounds and languages of north and south will be well familiar to your students.

Because these are English translations of brief Spanish songs, a good discussion might center on this material as a wellspring of the above developments, and as a tradition with kin in other realms of North America.

Questions for discussion:

- Where have your students encountered contemporary examples of the *corrido* tradition? Have they encountered it in "indie" rock? In recent folk music or in folk artists that their parents still play around the house? Does the tradition continue in recognizable form?
- The headnotes make clear that the *corrido* is associated not only with a sound and an ethnic group but also with specific geographical regions and sites. Extend that thinking a little: does *where* you hear a particular song have an effect, for you, on what it is and how to think about it? What happens to a *corrido* song, or any song of commemoration or protest, as it moves from place to place, and from time to time?
- As music travels the airwaves of the world, it does so in very different forms, and with different implications. Though supposedly independent or "alternative" artists can turn out to be branded products of global corporations (packaged "hippie" groups manufactured by major record labels go back to the middle sixties), the "democracy of the Internet" allows new music to be uploaded from practically anywhere. As your students search for authentic sounds and voices in an amazing cacophony of products and choices, how do they sort things out?

WOVOKA

For Wovoka's vision (as well as the entire range of Ghost Dance/Wounded Knee narratives included in NAAL), offered here in two versions as "The Messiah Letters," the headnote is as important as the text to the classroom reception. Spend time going over the details of the Ghost Dance religion and the subsequent massacre at Wounded Knee. Explore with students the statement from the period introduction that "armed action against the settlers and U.S. troops had failed. Many American Indians turned to spiritual action as a means of bringing about desired ends. From this impulse arose what has been called the Ghost Dance religion." The implication here is that some northern Plains Indians knew that they could no longer defend themselves in battle and, therefore, turned to spirituality to save themselves and give themselves hope. Read the two "Messiah Letters" carefully with students and identify specific aspects of the letters that link them with Native American traditions and with Christianity. Ask students why Euro-Americans seem to have had such difficulty imagining the concept of religious freedom for Indians. Recall Apess's "An Indian's Looking-Glass for the White Man" and apply his strategy of eliciting shame in his white Christian readers to the white settlers' resistance to the practice of a Christian-inspired religion by a few defeated bands of Indians.

Cluster: Debates over "Americanization"

As a goal or a process, "Americanization" remains an open-ended debate, as heated now as it was a hundred years ago. And as was true at the turn of the last century, the debate encompasses many perspectives, self-interests, anxieties, and values. Then as now, there was fear about the fate of democratic institutions under multicultural pressure, about terrorism and its possible importation, and about a polyglot nation of languages and cultures so separate and diverse as to end the possibility of imagining the United States as "united" in any fundamental way. And also, then as now, the debate was inflected by science and pseudoscience, by true and mythologized history, and by the reality and the prospect of international or intercultural war. Shadowing all the editorials, manifestos, historical narratives, and personal memoirs was another issue that has not been diminished by the passage of time or the revolution in communications technology: who the effectual public really was and how to reach them.

The excerpts we have here are short and varied. Some of them are impassioned complaints, like Martí's and Chesnutt's; others, like Roosevelt's *The Strenuous Life,* include aggressive interpretations of national and cultural history. Remarkable among this set are the pages from Jane Addams's *Twenty Years at Hull-House,* pages full of personal experience, narrated with modesty and emotional poise, encouraging readers to build outward from fact to their own conclusions.

Questions for discussion:
- The biography of Theodore Roosevelt allows us to see clearly the personal stake he had in the values he espoused as American ideals and the qualities he looked for in the history of the United States. He was severely nearsighted, a problem that wasn't diagnosed until he was well into his childhood, and as a boy he was regarded as a "weakling." With very hard work (and very good eyeglasses) he built himself up into a robust young man, and kept up his interest in horsemanship, hunting, arduous travel, and outdoor life until nearly the end. Using Roosevelt as a point of departure, how can we interpolate the personal dimension of these other texts? In Chesnutt's review, where is Chesnutt? Is Martí's text a generic call for political freedom, or does Martí come clear, as an individual personality, in that text as well? Where does that personal dimension strengthen the text and where might it undercut the credibility?
- Helen Hunt Jackson refers in passing to Gaius Marius lamenting at the ruins of Carthage (middle of page 1160). What are the implications of that allusion? What kind of an audience is she reaching for, and why?
- Anna Julia Cooper takes Howells to task for his portrait of African American parishioners and church practices in a short work that has nearly dropped out of sight now, *An Imperative Duty.* Her objection to this caricature opens a much larger question about authors and literary works that have stayed at the center of attention in American literary

history, "classics" that include racial and ethnic stereotypes. With regard to other works that your class might know—*Huckleberry Finn*, "The Waste Land," *The House of Mirth*, the poetry of Pound and Stevens, how much should this issue figure in our thinking? A few years ago, there was a much-publicized face-off between the African American poet Ishmael Reed and two African American women novelists, Toni Morrison and Alice Walker, over their portrayal of black men in their fiction. Some of your students will probably have direct experience with episodes of *South Park, The Simpsons, Borat,* or other comedy shows or films where racial and ethnic stereotyping is obvious, but where the shows seem to get away with it. Thinking about all those writers, works, and controversies, we can ask does our culture grant a "license to caricature" to some authors or cultural contexts, but not to others? If so, what do the ground rules seem to be, and what might that situation suggest about the current state of "Americanization" as a process and a subject for debate?

CHAPTER 10

Teaching Notes for Authors and Works: Volume D, American Literature 1914–1945

In moving forward to the Moderns, you probably face at least three different questions right away:

- How and why did these writers see the world differently from writers in earlier periods and centuries—what we might call a thematic approach to understanding modernism?
- How and why did they choose their images and their narrative and poetic forms?
- How might their gender, ethnicity, or class have influenced their writing—how did pluralism, both within American culture and as it derives from international influence (particularly by Joyce, Woolf, and Yeats), emerge as a determining factor and a consequence of modern literature?

Selections from Native American and African American writers allow students to explore these questions, and you can also perceive continuing colonial attitudes (in both white and minority writers) that manifest themselves in racial segregation and discrimination.

BLACK ELK AND JOHN NEIHARDT

Make use of the NAAL headnote, especially the fact that Black Elk could neither read nor write and spoke little English when he told John Neihardt the story of his great vision and talk about the context within which Black Elk Speaks was created: Black Elk telling his story to his son, Ben Black Elk, who then translated it into English for Black Elk's "adopted" son, John Neihardt, while Neihardt's daughter, Enid, wrote it all down and other Sioux elders contributed their memories of events. Then, later, Neihardt worked from his daughter's transcriptions to produce *Black Elk Speaks*. Discuss differences between Neihardt's work and the work of early twentieth-century social scientists who often paid Native American informants to tell their stories. Neihardt was himself a poet; in agreeing to tell his story to Neihardt, holy man Black Elk was recognizing a kindred spirit.

Even so, there had to be limits to that kinship, and the long account called "The Great Vision" requires some careful preliminary discussion if we are going to engage with it effectively in an American literature course. We have to decide, at least tentatively, what we are reading or listening to or overhearing: this is a personal experience (spiritual, religious, psychological, carefully allegorical, or some combination of them all) related across a considerable cultural and linguistic divide to a white listener who constructs a written, printed narrative that is subsequently collected into a literary anthology and read by ourselves. A lot of transformations are involved here— so many, in fact, that recovering the original intention and texture of Black Elk's narrative, and its cultural and historical moment, may be impossible for nearly everyone except an expert in the Sioux peoples of the last century. Still, we can value the way in which this narrative extends and enriches our collective sense both of the nature and possibilities of North American storytelling and of the individual self.

Black Elk Speaks records only the first twenty-seven years of Black Elk's life, ending with the Battle of Wounded Knee. Neihardt ends *Black Elk Speaks* with an image of drifted snow in "one long grave" at Wounded Knee. Although Black Elk himself lived another fifty-nine years, Neihardt closes his text with what some readers have described as Black Elk's spiritual death and the end of tribal independence; for as Black Elk himself states, after the end of Sioux freedom, he and his people become simply "prisoners of war while we are waiting here."

Black Elk Speaks, therefore, shapes the form of Black Elk's story as Neihardt works to create the full effect of Sioux tragedy in his white readers, just as Black Elk himself was capable of feeling in himself the pain of the people. The act of the bicultural collaborator creates empathy in the modern reader. The act of teaching *Black Elk Speaks* likewise places the instructor in the position of bicultural translator, using the classroom and discussion of the text as a way to complete the circle between the American undergraduate student and the text that writes Black Elk's name in our canon of collective attempts to define the American identity.

Questions for discussion:
- In opening discussion on the excerpts from this work, you can begin by asking students questions that will help them explore the interesting narrative form. To the question "Who is speaking?" they may answer, Black Elk. Fine—but who is narrating? Black Elk or John Neihardt?
- How do the circumstances of this composition (a transcription of a first-hand account) affect students' perception of authorship of the work?

- Though your students will have some familiarity with the cultural importance of the Vision Quest among native peoples of the western Plains, can they speculate about how the pronoun I is used in Black Elk's account and what that pronoun signifies?
- When he presents himself as one chosen to receive special wisdom from the Six Grandfathers (most of us have only four), how are these nameless teachers and their young pupil described to us? Why don't all of his grandfathers have names?
- Is this a "spiritual" education in the European or New England sense of the word? Are power and wisdom achieved through creating or discovering "identity" as a thing apart?
- When Black Elk becomes "the spotted eagle floating" and then moves to the bay horse and finds himself "painted red all over," are these self-aggrandizing representations? Why might there be so much emphasis on "the earth," the ground, in Black Elk's vision?

WILLA CATHER

My Ántonia is one of the quickest long "reads" in NAAL, and your students will breeze through it—and perhaps feel uneasy about enjoying it, worrying that they must have missed something, especially if you're coming at this work chronologically, through thickets of modernist difficulty. At the bottom of anthologized pages of Pound, Eliot, Amy Lowell, Stevens, and other "high modernists" the footnotes abound; with Cather they are hardly necessary, and in the context of the early twenties, when this novel took hold, a lot of "serious" literature was demonstrating its seriousness by not being accessible on the first try.

It's an easy out, therefore, to situate *My Ántonia* on another shelf, as a guileless continuation of a realist tradition that rolls back through Sarah Orne Jewett and William Dean Howells and forward through one of Cather's popular contemporaries, Laura Ingalls Wilder, or as a mix of realism and literary naturalism that might include Hamlin Garland, Ole Rolvaag, Sinclair Lewis, and so on, perhaps all the way up to Larry McMurtry. Though these are comfortable, plausible games of classification, there is a major drawback: situating Cather in this way eclipses the possibility that this is a writer who understood the broader literary and cultural contexts of her time, that her work responds—not flamboyantly, perhaps, but deeply—to some of the same tides and provocations that inform the high modernism that was taking shape in London, Paris, and New York. In other words, we can enrich our reading of Willa Cather if we can see her as key figure in the creation of a modernist pastoral, a mode that countenanced everything that Pound and Eliot saw and spoke of, but presented those moods and perceptions on the American Great Plains rather than in the context of the city.

Questions for discussion:
- This book is about Ántonia Shimerda, a young immigrant girl who grows up in Nebraska, experiencing love, hardship, and aging.

Nonetheless, for long stretches she seems to fade into the background, and a great deal of attention is paid to prairie dogs, wolves, harsh winters, and the lives of others in a couple of Nebraska settlements. Why does the narrative sometimes seem to lose track of her? How does her periodic disappearance from view affect the mood and the emerging themes of the story?

- Cather tells the story through the words and eyes of Jim Burden. Why does she adopt that strategy rather than tell of Ántonia and her world with an omniscient narrator, as Crane narrates *Maggie,* as Chopin narrates *The Awakening,* and as Dreiser narrates *Sister Carrie?*
- Read aloud the long paragraph that opens with "If I loitered on the playground after school" (page 1280) and the paragraph that begins with "These were the distractions I had to choose from" (bottom of page 1296). If we took these passages out of their respective chapters and thought of them as prose poems, what poets might they recall, and why?
- As the novel closes, Ántonia is seen in a series of glimpses over the years, and then she fades out of view. Why don't we get a big ending, a death scene, a final meeting in the sunset? Read the last paragraph of the novel aloud and compare it to the final page of Fitzgerald's *The Great Gatsby.* What similarities and differences do you see, in tone and theme, as these narrators think about the past and the future?

AMY LOWELL

When situated in a sequence including Masters and Robinson, the Lowell excerpts can seem very different, in their ambitions and accessibility, than they might if we read them in conjunction with H. D. and Ezra Pound, who come soon after. Is Amy Lowell an easy impressionistic Edwardian or a difficult modernist? Some critics feel that Lowell is too sentimental to be a great poet; others believe that these emotional dimensions are no problem at all and even a strength. Whatever the verdict among your students, including Lowell's voice in your syllabus will make room for early discussions of female mythological characters that will inform much poetry by women and men in the twentieth century (in "The Captured Goddess" and "Venus Transiens") and will introduce what Baym calls "appreciations of female beauty" in poems by women. Indeed, a few of the poems included here—"Venus Transiens" and "Madonna of the Evening Flowers"—may be considered love poems to specific women or to women in general.

Questions for discussion:
- Is Lowell's "imagism" best regarded now as a movement in its own right or as a transition to something else?
- What are the special strengths and limitations of the imagist strategy in poetry?
- If "sentimental" is an accusation against Lowell, are we mistakenly accepting the devaluation of the very concept of the sentimental and its legitimate role in poetry?

Gertrude Stein

The Stein entries are going to be a train wreck for students who approach them with their close-reading methodologies fully engaged and hot from deep-meaning searches that they may have conducted with various realists and modernists that have come before in your course. In reading Stein, they don't get it; and some students can become anxious or angry or (worse) quietly demoralized, like those visitors to the Cabaret Voltaire in Zurich, where dadaism had its birth in the midst of World War I, who couldn't figure out what was going on because they tried too hard to decode the words and action on the stage. Actually, the problem with Stein in this particular context can be just as bad or worse—because, enshrined in an anthology, discourse that might otherwise beguile or pleasantly dislocate becomes academic text that must be sounded and understood or else all is lost!

Perhaps a way to grow comfortable with Stein, and to get much further in reading these selections, is to back up a bit and converse about those many sorts of cultural experiences in which things don't make sense but that you can enjoy anyway and not worry about "getting it"—because from somewhere you get the message that getting it isn't the point at all. Your students listen to plenty of music and see plenty of video and film that, in a strict sense, they can't decode or fathom and would feel absurd trying to do so. The pictures don't fit the words; the words are sometimes nonsense. An approach like this tends to make Stein seem a contingent writer, responding to and in a sense resisting certain mainstream Western habits of prose and poetry (and the perhaps artificial categorical differences between the two), but understanding first what Stein is *not* doing is an effective way of opening a discussion of what she accomplishes as new American writing.

Questions for discussion:
- Why is it that they (the characters)—or rather we (our society)—can accept uncertainty and even complete mystification in some art or entertainment experiences but not in others?
- Can we take pleasure in adventures such as this, adventures into prose and poetry that seem to escape the usual chore of making sense and being clear?
- When your students have gone home after a day of classes, barraged by tomes of deadly earnest, highly rhetorical argumentative prose— showing us this and telling us that and proving to us something else— can a yearning arise for an escape into a freer sort of writing, where meanings (in a Victorian or standard modern sense) are less important than the intellectual and psychological refreshment of getting lost?

Cluster: World War I and Its Aftermath

Modern Americans commonly forget that this was the first overseas war that killed hundreds of thousands of men in the U.S. Army and Navy, and literally millions of British and French and German soldiers on the Western Front alone. The battle around Verdun wiped out nearly a million *poilus*

(French infantry); a monument in Ypres, to British losses near that devastated Belgian town, lists over fifty thousand names—roughly the total number of dead in the dozen years of the Vietnam war—and these are the names of only the missing in this one battle. If you wander the aisles of cathedrals in northern France—Amiens, Chartres, Reims—you will see small and austere monuments with the simple words "To the Memory of One Million Dead of the British Empire," and the roads along the Somme River are still lined with Commonwealth cemeteries, thousands and thousands of graves, meticulously maintained.

As you can imagine, the literary and artistic outpouring about this catastrophe was enormous, and because this was also a crisis about the value of a civilization that could fall into such mayhem, the response went in many directions.

One good way to open the excerpts in NAAL is to look at them as experiments in finding American voices capable of engaging with this terrible moment. Some of these writers, like Alan Seeger, follow in a strongly British tradition, sounding like the famous English poet of the war's early years, Rupert Brooke, who exemplified the Oxbridge ideal of a stiff upper lip, poised understatement, and dignified intensity under the most terrible circumstances. The prep schools and the Princeton University that produced Seeger and Wyeth were places of high Anglophilia in the early years of the century, and Seeger carries that tradition into his verse. Wyeth doesn't. John Reed is also an aristocrat but from the West; Hemingway was a middle-class school dropout from the Chicago suburbs; Cummings was a true "Harvard man," descended from a line Boston Unitarians; Gertrude Stein, the ghost writer of *The Autobiography of Alice B. Toklas,* who was in Paris for most of the war, had a Jewish heritage, received a Radcliffe education and completed advanced work in science and medicine, and had a steady income from family investments. Wyeth ended up in some of the worst action on the front; Fauset wrote not about her own experiences but about fictional characters inspired by the actual lives of men she knew. In each case a different perspective, background, and relationship to the war; in each case a different way of writing about it.

Questions for discussion:
- Because the *Alice B. Toklas* excerpt could exasperate some students, it might be a good place to begin. "Toklas" (Stein) writes of the war experience as a series of nearly disconnected memories, often in sentences that seem disconnected in their grammar and punctuation. Read aloud the tree paragraphs describing the front, beginning with "Soon we came to the battle-fields" (top of page 1386) and including the aesthetic meditation on camouflage. What is striking, surprising, or possibly unconscionable about this voice and perspective? Does it open up a psychological reality about the experience of war?
- Compare the Princetonians, Seeger and Wyeth, without feeling that you have to achieve a preference of one over the other. Compare their poems as ways of engaging with war personally and psychologically.

In what circumstances might you want one sort of poem—or the other?

- John Reed is writing from home, about the war from the home perspective. Describe the pace and language of his commentary. What is the implied audience? What would you say is the real subject of this essay?
- Like some of his poems, the excerpt from Cummings's autobiographical *The Enormous Room* works through jumps and disconnections. Time and sequence often seem to be muddled or forgotten. Why?
- Fauset gives us a glimpse of life behind the lines, in a staging area before the actual entry into the trenches and the battle. What are the ironies that organize these paragraphs, and what suspense do they create in the overall fabric of the story?

Robert Frost

Like Cather, Frost retains elements of realism, and like her, he portrays moments in which his speaker's perception changes as central to his poetry. Several class periods can be spent on individual poems and representative poems by other twentieth-century poets through the fulcrum of an analysis of Frost. You can prepare for a discussion of "The Oven Bird" by reading "Nothing Gold Can Stay," with its allusion to Eden and human mortality. "The Oven Bird" deserves an important place in our discussion, because Frost's other poems, his essay "The Figure a Poem Makes," many other works of literature by modern writers, and even the concept of modernism itself seem contained and articulated in the poem's last two lines: "The question that he frames in all but words / Is what to make of a diminished thing." The bird and the poet ask questions that express the central modernist theme: How do we confront a world in which reality is subject to agreement or lacks referentiality altogether? How do we express the experience of fragmentation in personal and political life? How do we live with the increasing awareness of our own mortality—whether we face the prospect of human death (as the speaker does in "Home Burial," "After Apple-Picking," or "'Out, Out—'"), the death or absence of God (as Frost considers in "Desert Places" and "Design"), or mere disappointment at our own powerlessness (as in "Stopping by Woods on a Snowy Evening")?

In regard to "The Oven Bird," ask students to hear contrasting ways of intoning the last two lines. You might read the lines first with emphasis on the phrase "diminished thing," so that the pessimism in Frost and in his conception of modern life receives most of our attention. But read them again, emphasizing the infinitive "to make," and the poem seems to reverse its own despair, to create the possibility that creative activity can ease the face of the lessening, the "diminishing," of modern perception.

Other works offer this positive response to the bird's question. In "The Figure a Poem Makes," Frost defines the act of writing poetry as "not necessarily a great clarification" but at least "a momentary stay against confusion." Students who have studied the Volume A and B material may see

Frost's solution to his own metaphysical problem as one more variable than Edward Taylor's attempt to sustain a metaphor through the length of one of his Preparatory Meditations to arrive at the language of salvation. Frost emphasizes, though, that he wants to be just as surprised by the poem as is the reader. And his description of the thought process that a poem records applies to our own endeavors in the classroom as well—whenever we try to engage students first and then teach them how to order their engaged perception. Frost contrasts scholars, who get their knowledge "with conscientious thoroughness along projected lines of logic," with poets, who get theirs "cavalierly and as it happens in and out of books," and most students prefer to identify with the poets. Frost might, indeed, be describing an American epistemology, as it works best with students: "They stick to nothing deliberately, but let what will stick to them like burrs where they walk in the fields."

No study of Frost, at any class level, is complete without close analysis of the great poems "Birches" and "Directive." Students at any level profit from line-by-line discussion of "Directive," particularly in contrast with the earlier poem "After Apple-Picking." In this poem, the speaker's troubled sleep results from his realization of the imperfection of human power to "save" fallen apples (or fallen worlds) or to fully complete any task as someone with godlike power (or any "heroic" human being before the modernist era) might have been able to do. "Directive" transcends those limitations, offers a specific path to take ("if you'll let a guide direct you / Who only has at heart your getting lost") and arrives at a vision of spiritual regeneration unparalleled in any of Frost's other poems: "Here are your waters and your watering place. / Drink and be whole again beyond confusion."

Questions for discussion:
- How does Frost embody both American Dream and American nightmare?
- How does his poetry, as he writes in "Two Tramps in Mud Time," allow him to "unite / My avocation and my vocation / As my two eyes make one in sight"? How do Frost's images suggest that, long after the apparent decline of transcendentalism, the analogical thinking of Emerson and Thoreau would become a permanent part of the American imagination?

SUSAN GLASPELL

Encountered alone, this dramatized version of Glaspell's famous short story "A Jury of Her Peers" may seem like an ordinary script for a half-hour TV detective drama. And time and subsequent imitation of Glaspell have not been kind to the play's gothic atmosphere: today's students who come to us loaded with latter-day New England horror stories about brutality, madness, and revenge in old farmhouses far off the main roads will not at first find much of interest here. As social observation, however, the play regains interest if it is situated with other imaginative literature about the crisis facing countless women through much of the nineteenth and twentieth centuries, a crisis of isolation, of thwarted creativity, of marriages founded on a lack of understanding or love. Gilman's "The Yellow Wall-paper," Chopin's *The Awakening*, Frost's "Home Burial," Anderson's *Wines-burg, Ohio* stories—if some of these are opened along with *Trifles*, students will be encouraged to see the predicament of these women as a recurring important theme rather than an excuse for a mild dark drama. Then they can think about modern analogues—novels by Stephen King, films by Hitchcock and his many imitators, rural-nightmare shows on network tele-vision.

Question for discussion:

- Have changes in literary and dramatic style and tastes enhanced our ability to present such daunting predicaments? Or do those changes somehow impede that attention?

SHERWOOD ANDERSON

If students have been reading chronologically through NAAL, they will be ready to see Anderson as writing in the fresh wake of realism, of natu-ralism, and of the regionalist and local colorist traditions. These are tradi-tions that he both respects and resists in achieving an individual voice. Anderson wants to know where it all begins—to focus on a particular house in a particular street—and to try to figure out, by examining origins, who he is and who we are. Anderson's life before he declared himself a writer illus-trates a classic theme in nineteenth-century fiction by white male writers; ask your students to recall Irving's "Rip Van Winkle" or Twain's *Huckleberry Finn*. Like the characters in that earlier fiction, Anderson also seems to have suffered a form of amnesia, sudden disappearance, or inexplicable depar-ture, one day, from his life with his wife and his job at the paint firm. In leav-ing his life in Ohio so abruptly, Anderson expressed the incompatibility of living conventionally and also writing an American book. Winesburg, Ohio, though fiction, emerges from an autobiographical impulse, and the reporter in that work, George Willard, experiences the young writer's conflict. Later in life, Anderson would write a memoir titled *A Story Teller's Story,* which tells the story of Anderson himself still within the eggshell, before his "hatching" as a storyteller.

Several related themes characterize the anthologized stories from *Wines-burg.* Anderson portrays conflict between inner emotions and outward behavior; Alice Hindman and Elmer Cowley share this conflict although they express it differently. Sexual repression and displaced aggression enter American fiction in *Winesburg*, and each of the anthologized stories shares this theme. In Elizabeth Willard, sexual repression and repressed identity become interconnected, and in "Adventure," Anderson hints at "the grow-ing modern idea of a woman's owning herself and giving and taking for her own ends in life," although his own fiction explores the stunting of women's lives, not their "modern" alternatives. Writing itself becomes the American passion for George Willard; the "queerness" that interests Anderson in some of his characters (Elmer Cowley and Mook in " 'Queer' ") suggests an

American illness caused by inarticulate inner lives that the fiction writer might be able to "cure."

At the end of "Rip Van Winkle," Rip takes his place as the "chronicler" or storyteller of the village and thus moves from margin to center in his position in the town. Anderson's portrait of the American storyteller—in his character George Willard and in the events of his own life—addresses the marginality of the white male writer. Anderson's marginality is central to his vision; despite his portrait of the way American life has twisted and thwarted individual development, he chooses to portray it from without, not envision recreating it from within. Like Huck Finn, George Willard escapes Winesburg and, in the process, becomes capable of telling a story.

Question for discussion:
- How does Anderson's departure from Ohio define his role as a writer?

WALLACE STEVENS

Poems such as Frost's "The Oven Bird" and "Desert Places" allow students to experience modernist feeling; Stevens translates the central thematic concern of modern writers into an intellectual framework. We can begin by reading "Of Modern Poetry" line by line and make connections between the idea of "finding / What will suffice" and making something "of a diminished thing." This poem links modernist thought to World War I, breaks with the realists' "script," and ends with actions that appear referential ("a man skating, a woman dancing, a woman / Combing") but can be understood only as manifestations of what is spoken "In the delicatest ear of the mind," not as semantic symbols.

Students' greatest difficulties in reading Stevens are in how to move beyond the apparently referential quality of his language and to learn to read it as dynamic forms of abstract ideas. "Anecdote of the Jar" works well to analyze closely. This poem forces students to push beyond the referential features of the language, for its meaning resides not in the jar but in its placement and in the larger design the poem creates and imposes. But that larger design is an arbitrary creation of the poet, not the manifestation of divine presence in the universe. We can work through other Stevens poems that illustrate the poet's power to make his world's design. "Thirteen Ways of Looking at a Blackbird" can help students see the problem of perception in a modern world in which there is no shared reality. In "The Idea of Order at Key West," the woman makes order out of the diminished thing by singing, thereby becoming "the self / That was her song, for she was the maker." And "The Emperor of Ice-Cream" proposes as the modernist's reality a world that lets "the lamp affix its beam" to show, as "The Snow Man" states, "Nothing that is not there and the nothing that is." Ask students how the idea that nothing is there—except what the imagination invents—becomes a manifestation of American self-reliance. For Stevens, all forms of order are created by human perception; nature itself reflects human values only as we project our image onto the natural world.

Stevens responds to the oven bird's question in the first line of "A High-Toned Old Christian Woman": "Poetry is the supreme fiction." Mary Loeffelholz directs the reader's attention to two repeated activities in Stevens's poems: (1) looking at things and (2) playing musical instruments or singing. Ask students to identify poems in which these activities appear (for the first, see in particular "The Snow Man," "The Emperor of Ice-Cream," "Thirteen Ways of Looking at a Blackbird," "Study of Two Pears," and "The Plain Sense of Things"; for the second, see in particular "A High-Toned Old Christian Woman," "Peter Quince at the Clavier," "The Idea of Order at Key West," "Of Modern Poetry," and "Asides on the Oboe"), and explore the parallels between making music or singing and writing poetry, on the one hand, and perceiving or observing and giving existence to reality, on the other. These parallel activities replace the Christian God, create new gods or mythological forms, and allow us to devise our own supreme fiction. The new mythology or fiction, for whom the poet is both creator and secular priest, explains the presence of so much continually unexpected imagery in Stevens. Furthermore, Stevens's own poetry provides an answer to the woman's musings in "Sunday Morning."

In "Sunday Morning," Stevens creates a dialogue between a woman and a narrator, or a dialogue of one that shows the woman thinking within her own mind, and he alters the meaning of Christianity. The poem transforms the religious connotations of Sunday into those of a human-centered "day of the sun," in which, since we live in an "island solitude, unsponsored, free," we invent as our supreme fiction, our god or our explanation for the way the universe works, the very mortality that is the only "imperishable bliss" we know. Stevens proposes making ritual of the diminished thing, creating fellowship "of men that perish and of summer morn," and seeing "casual flocks of pigeons" not as "homeward bound" but rather as nature's "ambiguous undulations." Nature has no message for us, but in the act of writing (and reading) poetry, we can create our own order, one that becomes more beautiful because it is the projection of "man's rage for order" and, therefore, as fragile as human life. "Death is the mother of beauty" for Stevens because it intensifies the act of "arranging, deepening, enchanting night" (in "The Idea of Order at Key West"), the act of taking momentary "dominion" (in "Anecdote of the Jar"), or the "old chaos of the sun." Poetry serves Stevens (from his book of collected lectures *The Necessary Angel*) as a "means of redemption." Project human mortality onto this world and make art out of the moment of sinking "Downward to darkness, on extended wings," create a "jovial hullabaloo among the spheres."

The images of the sun that form the focus for the woman's meditations in "Sunday Morning" also provide Stevens's central image in other poems. Build class discussion around a group of these poems and examine the way Stevens builds his real image of what the supreme fiction might look like on the sun itself. Give students time to work through the experience of Stevens's concept of the supreme fiction. For many, reading Stevens will seem like heresy, a fundamental challenge to their own religious practice. Allow them to compare notes on their various perceptions of Stevens's work.

Use class discussion as an exemplum of modernist thought; a class of any size may approach "Thirteen Ways of Looking at Stevens," or "a visibility of thought, / In which hundreds of eyes, in one mind, see at once."

Question for discussion:
- What should we make of a world in which there is not external order?

MINA LOY

Mina Loy is remembered as a true adventurer, roving far and shattering social and aesthetic rules along the way. During various phases of her adventure she associated with Stein, Picasso, Wyndham Lewis, and any number of cutting-edge modernists; her temperament, her ardor about taking these experiments and enthusiasms literally on the road throughout so much of her life, sets her apart from peers who remained in salons and studios and comfortable "bohemian" neighborhoods. Because your students may feel a special pull to this tale of adventure, an experience with these three poems, when set in a broader landscape of modernist verse, can center on the disquiet here, the indications of a mind and a heart deeply uneasy about remaining anywhere, in any moral or emotional perspective or aesthetic formulation.

Questions for discussion:
- "Parturition" is one of the first poems we have from any English-speaking writer about the physical and psychological actualities of giving birth. After sampling the voice at the start with some reading aloud, turn to the closing lines with their tone of wry repose and acceptance: "The next morning / Each woman-of-the-people" through "Of which she is sublimely unaware." How does the speaker arrive at this state of mind, this attitude toward herself, toward women, toward the human condition? Over the course of the poem, what right has she earned to arrive here?
- As the notes indicate, "Brancusi's Golden Bird" is homage to a set of famous modernist sculptures (see page C2). What aesthetic similarities do you see when you compare the sculpture to the poem about it? Where do you see indications that Loy is attempting to do with words what Brancusi is doing with bronze?
- "Lunar Baedeker," as the title poem of one of Loy's important collections, carries a good deal of thematic weight: it's normal and customary for critics and general readers to take a cue from a poem selected in this way and to probe it for guidance about fundamental intentions in the book where it is highlighted. After reading the other Loy poems, what do you see in "Lunar Baedeker" that provides this kind of guidance to reading and understanding her work?

WILLIAM CARLOS WILLIAMS

How does Williams answer the question "what to make of a diminished thing"? We can begin with "A Sort of a Song," which directs its reader to write a poem about the thing. Make nothing of it but the thing itself.

Because there may not be meaning, so don't insist on it. And we can talk about characteristics of Williams's poems, trying to elicit, in discussion, some of the central features of imagism: exactness, precision, compression, common speech, free verse. "The Red Wheelbarrow," "The Widow's Lament in Springtime," and "Portrait of a Lady" work well for this discussion. We can analyze "Spring and All" closely, suggesting that the process Williams describes becomes, in part, analogous to the creation of a poetic image. Some students have difficulty understanding the concept of the image; and in teaching Williams, you might take time to talk about the eidetic faculty— what happens in the mind when we read a visual description. "Portrait of a Lady," read aloud with appropriate emphasis ("Agh!"), can help them "hear" another kind of image.

You can then talk about some themes in both Williams and Frost; students may suggest that, despite his objectivity, Williams's poems lack the pessimism of some of Frost's. Critics also often compare Williams with Whitman. Ask students to discuss this connection. Several modern poets try to write longer poems, perhaps with the epic form in mind.

Questions for discussion:

- Look at love and death in the poems—and how they strip those themes of sentimentality. What happens to Williams's view of human life in poems such as "Death," "The Dead Baby," and "Landscape with the Fall of Icarus"?
- How does Williams's use of poetic technique develop his themes?

Ezra Pound

Read a few Pound poems to see how he uses the image: "In a Station of the Metro" and "The River-Merchant's Wife: A Letter" work well, although students sometimes have difficulty actually seeing Pound's image in the first poem. Does the poem's second line work only if one sees a contrast between the faces and the black bough? Does Pound assume light-skinned faces? "To Whistler, American," "A Pact," and "The Rest" are easily accessible to students. "Hugh Selwyn Mauberley" and *The Cantos* will present problems for some students.

Questions for discussion:

- Considering the complexity of the classical allusions in "Hugh Selwyn Mauberley" and *The Cantos*, does Pound's dictum to "make it new" succeed?
- Because "In a Station of the Metro" is an adaptation from the haiku tradition, you could bring in a few examples of translated Japanese haikus and compare them to Pound's experiment. The haiku, as a form of poetry, is centuries old; how then is "Metro" an example of making poetry new?
- Read aloud stanzas of three or four different Pound poems, including a selection from *The Cantos*. Is there a distinct Pound voice immanent in these various poems? How would you describe it?

CLUSTER: MODERNIST MANIFESTOS

Reading and talking about literary manifestos requires a shift in the kind of attention we pay—and also perhaps a measure of healthy and good-natured resistance. Since the end of the nineteenth century, with those first boilovers of Montmartre outrage, the manifesto author is commonly "in your face," and this confrontational style has been around so long that the heated language and extravagant demands can seem cartoonish or self-parodic. Actually, the element of self-parody goes back to fringe groups like the Hydropaths, the Incoherents, and the Bon Bockers in the Paris of the 1880s: the Hydropaths claimed to despise water and to drink only absinthe and wine; the Incoherents insisted that everyone should stop making sense; the Bon Bockers took their cue from a painting by Manet of a complacent fat man sitting and doing nothing, just drinking a beer. Alfred Jarry, a notorious absinthe abuser and ether sniffer, went so far as to declare that the laws of physics should be tossed out. Compared to all that, the declarations in Wordsworth's and Coleridge's "Preface" to *Lyrical Ballads* 1798 kickoff to the manifesto era seem mild and scholastic to a fault. Not even Marinetti could top the wild men of the *fin de siècle*. For wonderful books on the subject of these vast refusals, have a look at Greil Marcus's *Lipstick Traces: A Secret History of the Twentieth Century* (1990) and Phillip Dennis Cate and Mary Shaw's *The Spirit of Montmartre: Cabarets, Humor, and the Avant-Garde, 1875–1905* (1996).

Anyone who roves through manifestos about literature and art—and there are reams of such documents—soon begins to see a pattern to the demands. Something needs to be cleaned up, scoured of ornamentation, mannerism, decadence; life needs to be looked at with fresh eyes, in new ways; life has changed and art needs to change with it or lead it; simplicity and power have to be discovered or brought back. Sometimes these declarations are couched politely in the art itself. The opening of Robert Frost's "The Pasture"—I'm going out to clean the pasture spring; / I'll only stop to rake the leaves away / (And wait to watch the water clear, I may)"—is about as close as Frost came to a modernist manifesto. Frost used the poem as the first in several collections of his work, and in its poised and concise statement of purpose it's not all that different from Ezra Pound's manifesto. Sometimes the art plays by the rules that the manifesto lays out and sometimes not.

How to read such discourse, in the heat of the moment or long after? The twentieth century was an age of great showbiz as well as an age of ambitious and brilliant art, and part of the challenge of negotiating these documents is discerning when we are in the presence of bombastic vaudeville and when something more serious is going on. In any case, when a writer pushes, the reader at some point must push back. This was a theme to consider in learning to read Emerson, and it's worth remembering as we launch into these polemics.

Questions for discussion:
- Marinetti and Pound number the items in their manifestos like a list of nonnegotiable demands. It's well known that when Marinetti took his

futurism lectures and tirades on the road, he was often greeted by polite and warm applause, but there were also times when he was confronted and heckled for not having the courage of his own convictions. That history brings us into confrontation with a basic question—does Marinetti mean everything he says here, like item 10, about destroying "the museums, libraries, academies of every kind"? Look through the array of line items in Marinetti and Pound and ask what is really intended by each. Dramatic gesture? Fundamental change of culture and consciousness?

- Mina Loy makes flamboyant use of typography in her "Feminist Manifesto," a strategy that came back in radical documents that circulated on college campuses and "hippie" neighborhoods in the 1960s. What is the thematic and tonal effect of these visual cues and flourishes? What voice do you hear, in this document, and how does it compare to Pound's?

- Compared to these others, Willa Cather's commentary seems quieter and more aligned with a tradition of civil discussion. Read aloud the paragraph beginning "If the novel is a form of imaginative art" (top of page 1509) and consider the relationship of each sentence to the next. Are there propositions here that can be questioned? Are there ideas and assumptions here that are specific to Cather's moment but perhaps not to our own?

- The excerpt from Williams's "Spring and All" shows us simple sentences and short paragraphs. But what are the challenges of reading these paragraphs? Do they connect logically or intuitively? Do these paragraphs enact the revolution that they call for? If so, how?

- Langston Hughes expends more language, but is he more difficult? What social and political urgencies might require Hughes to work for absolute clarity and coherence here—in contrast to how Loy and Williams write about art?

H. D.

Several strategies for reading H. D. may enlist student interest. Using Nina Baym's comments about imagism as a guide, trace H. D.'s formal uses of the image in her poetry, and compare her work with that of Amy Lowell, Williams, and Pound. Alternatively, move ahead to other women poets whose work reflects H. D.'s influence. For example, Susan Gubar (in "The Echoing Spell in H. D.'s Trilogy," in *Shakespeare's Sisters* [1979]) suggests comparing H. D.'s use of the seashell image to Moore's "To a Snail." (See also Moore's poem "The Paper Nautilus.") The last stanzas of "The Walls Do Not Fall" are clearly echoed later in Rich's poem "Diving into the Wreck." Even further, Gubar suggests that to really understand H. D., we need to move beyond discussions of imagism and modernism (and psychoanalysis) and explore "H. D.'s sense of herself as a woman writing about female confinement, specifically the woman writer's entrapment within male literary conventions, as well as her search for images of female divinity and prophecy."

Reading H. D. as a feminist modernist and a poet who is trying to express her discomfort with male-defined representations of women and of history may provide students with another approach to her poetry.

Because H. D. has been fully appreciated only by recent feminist critics who write about modernism, you or your students may find useful Susan Stanford Friedman's critical biography *Psyche Reborn: The Emergence of H. D.* (1981), in which she traces H. D.'s development as a feminist modernist and in particular her interest in a woman-centered mythmaking. From "Leda" to "Helen" to the goddesses Isis/Aset and Astarte in "The Walls Do Not Fall," students will at least find the female figures to counterbalance the presence of the All-father and Osiris. H. D.'s closing lines of that long poem ("we are voyagers, discoverers / of the not-known, / the unrecorded") have particular resonance for women in a modernist world.

MARIANNE MOORE

In *Naked and Fiery Forms: Modern American Poetry by Women* (1976), Suzanne Juhasz describes Moore as "the leading American woman poet" of her generation but not the "leading American poet" and comments on the contrast between Pound, who "does not have to deny his masculine experience, because it is all of mankind," and Moore, who makes "a neat division between 'woman' and 'poet,' with art and artistry belonging to the domain of the latter." Juhasz's framework is useful for reading modern American women poets; she suggests that the second generation (in which she includes Muriel Rukeyser, Elizabeth Bishop, and Gwendolyn Brooks) continued to separate "woman" and "poet" but that writers at mid-century (Denise Levertov, Sylvia Plath, and Anne Sexton) begin to function as both "woman" and "poet."

Teaching Moore following Juhasz's framework will help contextualize both Moore's avoidance of women's experience in her poetry and the increasing attention poets later in the century pay to women's experience. Indeed, students will find it difficult if not impossible to locate any gendered experience in Moore. She writes either with a gender-neutral first person (in "Poetry" and "In Distrust of Merits,") or about generic "man" (as in "A Grave" and "What Are Years?"). Only nature is feminized (as in "The Paper Nautilus").

Editor Mary Loeffelholz comments in her headnote that in Moore "the reader almost never finds the conventional poetic allusions that invoke a great tradition and assert the present poet's place in it." In Juhasz's framework, this is because women of Moore's generation could not find or present themselves as part of a great tradition. What Moore does do, like many of her contemporaries, is reinvent poetry for herself or find a new form for what she thinks poetry should be. Locate and discuss Moore's statements on the act and art of poetry. Analyze in such a discussion "To a Snail." What happens to poetic language when there is an "absence of feet"? Also analyze closely the frequently anthologized "Poetry." Often students have difficulty understanding why a poet like Moore would write with such passion about the nature of poetry itself. Build on previous discussions of the image to help them find the contrast, in the poem's middle stanzas, between the discursive statements Moore makes ("we / do not admire what / we cannot understand" and "all these phenomena are important") and her use of images drawn from precise observation of the animal world, such as in the poem "The Paper Nautilus." What does she mean in trying to create "imaginary gardens with real toads in them"?

Ask students to locate rhyme in "The Mind Is an Enchanting Thing." Most will not have discovered rhyme (as students, in reading Frost, do not immediately perceive rhyme in "After Apple-Picking"). What is the effect of the use of rhyme?

Which poems illustrate Moore's response to the modern way of seeing the world? Discuss her views of war as an "inward" struggle in "In Distrust of Merits." How does her image of the world as an "orphans' home" comment on the modernist themes of her contemporaries? Ask students to extend Moore's discussions—of enslaver and enslaved and our being "not competent to make our vows" about not hating—to our own contemporary social and global conflicts, to the resurgence of nationalism in the world, and to the significance of "I inwardly did nothing" in the context of bias incidents and hate speech on college campuses and in U.S. society as a whole.

RAYMOND CHANDLER

In the 1930s, as varieties of modernism continued to be refined and to mutate in salons of Bloomsbury and seminar rooms in New York, and as latter-day realists and literary naturalists found validation in the frightening realities of the Great Depression and the bloody rise of Fascism, Nazism, and Stalinism, other writers went in different or idiosyncratic directions and won sizable audiences among intelligent American readers in so doing. Chandler is a wellspring of a popular tradition that your students will recognize from "film noir" festivals or recent action flicks that try to exploit and parody at the same time. Transmogrified into the context of a literary anthology, his work undergoes an epistemological change, and students might enjoy a conversation about that: how what we look for in a story depends on where we find it.

Chandler gives us the stuff that clichés will soon be made of: tough-talking private detectives with gut-instinct ethics trying to survive in a Los Angeles of glitter and sleaze; jittery, beautiful, dangerous women with money, concealed weapons, and Something to Hide; cops who enforce the law in their own charming way; fedoras, double-breasted suits, nightmarish streetscapes—it's all here, and your students will know it from a stack of DVD films by directors as long ago as Michael Curtiz and as recent as Quentin Tarantino.

But as a literary experiment in theme and style, *what* exactly is this? Is Chandler bringing an unprecedented dose of realism or literary naturalism to the well-established genre of the detective story, pulling Sherlock Holmes out of his tweeds and his book-lined study and plunging him into seedy bars and LA back alleys? Or is something else going on, an elaborate gesture in stylization, in varieties of romanticism, rather than a venture into social and psychological truth?

One effective way to open Chandler is to concentrate for a few minutes on style, especially on his use of metaphor. Parodies of hard-boiled detective fiction often focus on elaborate similes, dishing them out for laughs. How does the early master of this technique use it not to break the mood but rather to achieve intensity?

Questions for discussion:

- Look over the opening five pages of "Red Wind" and choose three or four stand-out similes or metaphors, lines like "when he came up with it he looked as guilty as if he'd kicked his grandmother" (bottom of page 1541) or "Her voice lacked the edgy twang of a beer-parlor frill. It had a soft light sound, like spring rain" (middle of page 1546). Ask your students about the effect of this kind of descriptive language and the pace at which it is inserted into the narrative. What would be the effect of Chandler-delivered lines like these more frequently—one on every page or one in every paragraph?

- Ask a couple of students to read a page of dialogue aloud, back and forth, as if these were lines in a play or a film script. What voice inflections occur to them as they read these lines, and why? Do we have plausible dialogue here? If it's not so plausible, are the distortions a part of the fun?

- Students will know a lot about stories and films that owe a debt to Raymond Chandler. What can they say about his contribution to popular culture? What are the pleasures and the effects of this genre of fiction? What are we doing, imaginatively, when we read it or watch it?

T. S. ELIOT

"The Love Song of J. Alfred Prufrock" works well to read closely with students. Find images in the poem that serve as Eliot's "objective correlative" for Prufrock's particular emotions and for the state of feeling in the modern world (as Eliot saw it). *The Waste Land* raises a problem students have with modernism generally: that so many twentieth-century poets make extensive use of classical allusions or interweave references to Renaissance painters or quote writers in languages other than English. Berating students for not having a classical education doesn't help them much. Discuss the poem in context with "Tradition and the Individual Talent," in which Eliot defends his own method and describes the good poet as the one who is able to "develop or procure the consciousness of the past."

Although Eliot presents a "waste land" as his variation on the "diminished thing" that symbolizes human personality and culture in the modern world, his answer to the oven bird's question is not to make something (entirely) new or to show Stevens's snow man confronting "the nothing that is not there" and inventing a "supreme fiction" but rather to surrender the individual personality of the poet. The poem becomes a medium that expresses the essential history of the culture. Eliot writes in his essay that "Impressions and experiences which are important for the man may take no place in the poetry, and those which become important in the poetry may play quite a negligible part in the man, the personality." He combines traditions from mythology and legend, anthropology (with references to vegetation myths and fertility rites), classical literature and culture (including Shakespeare and Wagner), the Tarot, and comparative religious cultures, and he juxtaposes these traditions with images of isolation, fragmentation, uncertainty, and waste, hoping to use "these fragments" to "shore against" the ruins that are Eliot's variation on Frost's "diminished thing."

Question for discussion:
• How does Eliot depersonalize the poet in *The Waste Land*?

Eugene O'Neill

Long Day's Journey into Night demonstrates that one of the strong features of twentieth-century American literature is the continuation of what O'Neill's Edmund calls late in the play "faithful realism." But O'Neill's realism differs from that of the late nineteenth-century writers even as it seems to extend some of their concerns. In fact, O'Neill's play sometimes seems a compendium or a spectrum of American ideas that long precede the late nineteenth century, for he presents the Tyrones both as deeply conditioned by their past and as characters who face in their daily life (in this classically unified one-day's play) the fragmentation that is one symptom or consequence of the modernist sensibility.

Mary's descent into the madness of morphine addiction becomes the play's emblem, and although O'Neill is writing, in part, about his own mother here, he is also sensitive to Mary's position as woman in the American family and in American history. As the play unfolds the history of Mary's medical treatment and of her husband's attitudes toward her condition, students will make connections between Mary Tyrone and both Edna Pontellier and the narrator of "The Yellow Wall-paper." O'Neill suggests that modern life is more difficult for women than for men: Mary might have played the piano but married instead, thereby depriving herself of the coherence of vocation. In marriage, and especially in marriage to the peripatetic James Tyrone (rootlessness itself becomes a modern condition), she cuts herself off from having woman friends with whom she might ease her loneliness (O'Neill adds early scandal to the fact of marriage as a way of doubly cutting Mary off from other women). And in choosing to ease her loneliness by following Tyrone on his tours, she is forced to reject even the traditional solace of making a home for her children, so that the series of choices becomes irreversible, and her need for something to ease her emotional pain and to dull her perception of her own meaninglessness increases.

Within the family structure, Mary also suffers the anachronism (in the twentieth century) of not being able to move beyond the scrutiny of external forces that seem to control her. When she tells her husband, "You really must not watch me all the time, James. I mean, it makes me self-conscious," she is experiencing the radical emotion that led the deist Founding Fathers to revolution in the 1770s. But, unlike the deists, who experienced a fundamental shift in worldview when they accepted the idea that God might not be watching them all the time and fought for self-determination from the system of divinely ordained British monarchy, Mary Tyrone is only made "self-conscious" by Tyrone's scrutiny.

She suffers self-consciousness and is not inspired by it. She is not self-conscious in a way that leads other modernists to insight; she is only increasingly made aware of her own worthlessness. O'Neill underscores that worthlessness by presenting the role of wife as one based on constant humiliation and defined by Tyrone's need to feel he has made "good bargains" in life—he makes others pay the price he won't pay.

Throughout the play, O'Neill presents Mary as someone living in a kind of dream state (especially as she becomes more and more detached by the effects of taking morphine) that might have made sense for Rip Van Winkle but, protracted into the twentieth century, simply compounds her sense of disorientation and alienation. She says at one point, early in the play, "None of us can help the things life has done to us. They're done before you realize it, and once they're done they make you do other things until at last everything comes between you and what you'd like to be, and you've lost your true self forever" (top of page 1632). For students who have studied Irving, the language Mary uses here will seem reminiscent of Rip's "identity crisis" when he returns to the village after his twenty-year sleep. Later in the play, thinking aloud to the hired woman, Cathleen, Mary ties that disorientation to the death of what students might see as her own American Dream. She says, about the fog, "It hides you from the world and the world from you. You feel that everything has changed, and nothing is what it seemed to be. No one can find or touch you any more" (top of page 1648). Her language clearly echoes Irving's here, but it also conveys the isolation of American self-reliance carried to its historical extreme and epitomized in the role of twenty-century American wife and mother—Mary must be self-reliant to survive and must do so in a world devoid of human context other than her own family. She asks the play's central question: "What is it I'm looking for? I know it's something I lost" (bottom of page 1683).

Her son Edmund, the autobiographical voice for O'Neill himself, is the only character who understands his mother's drug addiction as the play progresses and who suffers the consequences of trying to articulate the kind of pain she feels. In Edmund's statements, students who have read twentieth-century European literature will hear connections to Camus and Beckett. Edmund also feels the absence of home; and referring to his nebulous, nameless lack of power to control his life, he says, "They never come back! Everything is in the bag! It's all a frame-up! We're all fall guys and suckers and we can't beat the game!" (bottom of page 1638). Later he calls himself "a stranger who never lives at home" (middle of page 1684). Like Mary, he would like to "be alone with myself in another world where truth is untrue and life can hide from itself" (top of page 1663), but he chooses poetry rather than morphine to ease his own pain, and then must confront his own failure as a poet. In a scene with his father, Edmund says, "I just stammered. That's the best I'll ever do. I mean, if I live. Well, it will be faithful realism, at least. Stammering is the native eloquence of us fog people!" (middle of page 1674). In depicting Edmund's "stammering," O'Neill underscores both the need to express modern consciousness and the difficulty of finding the words for it. Other twentieth-century writers will take some comfort in making the attempt; Edmund's "faithful realism" prevents him from idealizing his "stammering." In brother Jamie's cynicism ("The truth is there is no cure") and father James's despair ("A waste!, a drunken hulk, done with and finished!"), O'Neill completes his portrait of the disintegration of the American psyche and American family life and yet presents that portrait within the conventions of literary realism.

CLAUDE McKAY

McKay is a strong inclusion in any survey of modern American literature, especially if the course is intended to look into complex relationships between form and content in verse. McKay's form choices may come as a surprise, for the notion still seems to run deep (not only among students but also among critics and teachers) that "free verse" or at least unrhymed, loosely metered verse signifies honesty, spontaneity, and emotional intensity whereas sonnets, rhymed couplets, and other traditional patterns all suggest accommodation to social practices, conventional beliefs, and ordinary values. McKay is a passionate writer and a political radical, and he writes sonnets, uses rime royal, and frequently employs forms reminiscent of Pope, Wheatley, and Longfellow.

Questions for discussion:
- Does the compression and control of McKay's narrative form diminish the strength and intention of his work? Or does confinement, in some way, seem to increase its poignancy?
- Does McKay's demonstration of such narrative expertise, in what has been predominantly a white European literary practice, parallel or support some purpose that can be found in the content of these verses?

ZORA NEALE HURSTON

Hurston worked as an anthropologist as well as a writer and wrote "The Eatonville Anthology" after graduating from Barnard College and returning to her birthplace in Eatonville, Florida, to transcribe the folktales and folkways she remembered from childhood. Like her later *Mules and Men* (1935), both the "Anthology" and the essay "How It Feels to Be Colored Me" explore origins of consciousness—both collective and individual—that Hurston transforms into mythology, her attempt to explain the creation of the universe, to understand why the world is the way it is. Mythology does not overpower Hurston's fiction; rather, it empowers her use of folk history. Ask students to locate suggestions of mythology in "The Eatonville Anthology";

see, in particular, the opening of Section XIV: "Once 'way back yonder before the stars fell all the animals used to talk just like people."

Question for discussion:

- Are there important differences between Hurston's handling of talking-animal folktales and the way Harris told them in the previous century?

The Gilded Six-Bits

Like most of the African American women writers represented in NAAL, Hurston was a risk taker—so much so that her reputation has gone through some dramatic swings in the past forty years. In this story she steers very close, perhaps dangerously so, to certain stereotypes that have been widely exploited over the years. Students who have followed recent controversies about BET and the Def Jam comedy forms will already be aware of the complexities of telling this kind of tale: how it is interpreted can depend very much on who is reading it and in what context.

Question for discussion:

- Where are the stereotypes in "The Gilded Six-Bits"?
- Is Hurston playing along with them? Subverting them? Correcting them?
- What kind of audience is this story implicitly intended for and in what kind of political and moral context?
- Does the story take unexpected turns—not in plotting but in tone?
- In what ways does Hurston distinguish her own voice, her own perspective, from that of Missy May and Joe Banks?

NELLA LARSEN

Like Larsen's protagonist Helga Crane, *Quicksand* itself is fast-moving and restless, and your students may have responses at the ready in regard to its pace and its surprising leaps among settings and social classes. Larsen plunges her heroine into many different arenas where African American identity is being prescribed, reinvented, and liberated or where it has failed to find its own way: a repressive school in the South, the Black Belt in Chicago where Richard Wright situated *Native Son*, upscale communities within the vibrant culture of Harlem in the twenties, then Copenhagen and a personal experience a bit like Josephine Baker's in Paris, then Harlem again, and finally a marriage and an exile into the rural South, where the novel reaches its eerie end.

Students may find this journey dizzying and headlong and may be inclined to explain it away as reflective of Larsen's own life. To suggest that there is control here, and direction, and a stylistic roving here to parallel the leaps around the map, you might ask them what novels or stories *Quicksand* reminds them of—as a narrative of growing up, a story of a young independent woman trying to find her way, a story of being a stranger in every community you encounter, of being driven by a nameless yearning. The answers may lead back into NAAL if you're reading *Quicksand* as part of a sequence in the anthology: students may recall Edna's predicament in *The Awakening*, moments in Chesnutt's "The Wife of His Youth," and episodes and narrative strategies in Hart Crane, Garland, Cather, and other American naturalistic authors. Larsen's is a literate book, in uneasy conversation with an American literary tradition, predominantly white, which, like Helga Crane, Larsen has to achieve some mix of accommodation and individuality in relation to. In a sense, the conflict here—a stylistic and thematic conflict—may prove more interesting than the plot and the major character herself. Is Larsen's portrait of Helga reminiscent of Edna Pontellier? You might note how often Helga feels faint or physically ill at moments of crisis relating to herself, her hopes, her feeling of entrapment, and compare those moments to ones in which Edna is overcome by fever or heat or fatigue just when she seems to be on the cusp of an important recognition. The conversation may range outward from the reading list in the course and encompass other novels and stories that students often have in common. What about other literary characters of the twenties? Fitzgerald's Nick Carraway in *The Great Gatsby* or the people in "Winter Dreams" or Carrie Meeber in Dreiser's *Sister Carrie,* who also drifts into Chicago and is swept away by happenstance and luck, or Isabel Archer in *The Portrait of a Lady*? It's likely that your students will have encountered many stories about young people driven by a deep dissatisfaction with their own circumstances and by yearnings that are a mix of the superficial and the spiritual, the material and the profound. *Quicksand* is a story in dialogue with those other stories, affirming that the African American experience both is, and is not, a story that modern readers will find familiar and classifiable as a tale of the American Dream—of making it and of being accepted, of coming home.

Once the kinship of *Quicksand* has been glimpsed, you and your students may want to engage tough questions regarding Helga's appeal as a protagonist. Is she likeable? How much empathy are we supposed to feel with her? Some of your students may find her too headstrong, too fast and passionate and abrupt and self-centered in her choices, perhaps an African American forebear of the Scarlet O'Hara that Margaret Mitchell would create about ten years later. Difficult, hard-to-love heroines take hold in American letters around the end of the nineteenth century: Dreiser's Carrie, Wharton's Lily Bart, Henry James's Fleda Vetch, Frederic's Celia Madden, Norris's Trina Sieppe, and closer to Larsen's time, Fitzgerald's Daisy Buchanan and Nicole Diver. So unpleasant leading women are familiar in American letters—but what are the risks of assigning these difficult qualities to a mulatto protagonist?

If students feel empathy with Helga—and it's likely that they will—then some attention can be paid to her story as potentially tragic—what missed opportunities and strategic or moral mistakes lead her into her final disaster? Are her crucial decisions foolish ones—quitting the school in Naxos, turning down the marriage proposal of Axel Olson, losing or turning away from other bright and well-heeled suitors back in America? When Olson paints her portrait, and Helga sees there "some disgusting sensual creature with her features," has Olson revealed a kind of truth that Helga does not want to face? Or has Helga encountered and been repelled by a deep-lying European assumption about the "real" nature of African American women? When in a kind of spell Helga marries the Reverend Pleasant Brown and passes away from us in a long giddy sleep of empty rural life and endless childbearing, is Larsen dealing out retribution like the ending of a Greek tragedy? Is this the ending you were expecting? What are the implications and dangers of portraying a "down-home" resolution as a kind of disaster, perhaps a fate worse than death for such a heroine? You may find that in the closing pages, many of your students were poised for Helga's death, a suicide like Edna's or a succumbing to disease, to provide a tidy close to this wandering tale. They may be irked by what they encounter instead. Why doesn't Larsen end the story with Helga's death? What unfinished struggles are suggested by the ending we do get, with Helga returning to a species of physical if not psychological health as Mrs. Brown and bearing her fifth child?

E. E. CUMMINGS

Consider what it would mean to ask whether Cummings is a "serious" poet. Describe the ways in which he experiments with language in poems such as "anyone lived in a pretty how town" or "my father moved through dooms of love" and consider their effects. Ask students to read "Buffalo Bill's" or " 'next to of course god america i" out loud and discuss what happens to poetry that is meant to be read, not spoken. Locate modern themes in Cummings; place him in context with Frost (compare "pity this busy monster, manunkind" with Frost's "Departmental").

JEAN TOOMER

Discuss "Georgia Dusk" as a variation on Emerson's call for an American poet a century earlier. What, for Toomer, will be the characteristics of that "genius of the South"? And what will be the literary tradition for that "singer"? Locate Toomer in the context of other black writers or writers about black experience in NAAL, for example, Harris and Chesnutt. What does it mean, in Toomer, to make "folk-songs from soul sounds"?

Analyze "Fern," first from the narrator's point of view and then focusing on Fern herself. What is happening within the speaker as he imaginatively recreates Fern? What is the literary analogue in Toomer for Du Bois's "double consciousness"? How does Toomer evoke "the souls of black folk" in this excerpt from *Cane*? Place Fern herself in the context of other works by American male writers, such as Poe's "Ligeia" or Anderson's "Mother." Toomer gives Fern a moment of speech when she asks, "Doesn't it make you mad?" and then his narrator interprets what she means. Does he give her a voice? Consider the last sentence in "Fern": "Her name, against the chance that you might happen down that way, is Fernie May Rosen." What, in this sentence, gives the reader more clues to Fern's identity than Toomer's earlier idealization of her? Is there any "real" Fern beneath Toomer's portrait of her as his narrator's muse? Note Toomer's reference to the black woman who "once saw the mother of Christ and drew her in charcoal on the court-house wall." The allusion is one piece of evidence to suggest that black women, as well as men, have tried to record their visions; they have been artists as well as inspirations for art.

F. Scott Fitzgerald

Students who have read *The Great Gatsby* will sense that in some ways "Winter Dreams" is a compact version of Fitzgerald's most famous novel and that obsessions and mixed emotions that characterize Nick Carraway are also present here, in Dexter Green and the nameless narrator, who often sounds like Nick in his uncanny mix of adulation and contempt for what he sees in the world of the rich and the glamorous. To start the conversation a bit enigmatically and get the students to look at Fitzgerald from fresh per-spectives, you could put two famous epigrams on the board. One from Nietzsche:

In the end one loves one's desire, not the thing desired.

and one from Oscar Wilde:

There are only two tragedies in life: one is not getting what one wants, and the other is getting it.

Some students will recall moments in *The Great Gatsby* that resonate strongly with "Winter Dreams"—the moments where Nick imagines Gatsby acquiring Daisy after so much longing and feels regret and a measure of dis-appointment that the quest is now over. Nick himself, as the narrator of *Gatsby*, has similar moments with Jordan Baker: his desire for her rises when she moves out of his reach. All of which can lead up to a more com-plex conversation about the narrator of "Winter Dreams" and his unsteady empathy with Dexter Green. There are moments when this narrator seems superior to and dismissive of this Black Bear Lake world of golf and fash-ion and money and a bit contemptuous of young Dexter for falling for it. At other times, however, the narration seems as breathlessly credulous as Dex-ter does. Or else it seems to present a strange commingling of the two sen-timents, the wonder and the contempt.

"Babylon Revisited" comes from an array of stories about men and women who have made it, people who have lived beyond the year or two of glory that Gatsby achieved before he died, perhaps mercifully, in his own West Egg swimming pool. These are stories of people who move unhappily through glorious locales: the Riviera and Paris, the comfortable private places in midtown Manhattan, the exclusive resorts of Switzerland. An opening topic for your class: discuss the differences between this kind of story and the modern trash novel, the kind sold in drugstores or beach-supply shops, about the woes of being a supermodel, a Hollywood sex sym-bol, a magnate in fashion or the perfume trade. If students hesitate, you might grab a paragraph or two and suggest the difference: no matter how dissipated or dislikeable the Fitzgerald protagonist or how unsympathetic— or voyeuristic—we might feel toward the general situation that the story offers us, there are gorgeously phrased moments of insight about human nature, the mingled emotions of going back and coming home, the internal conflicts of wanting and not wanting in the same instant. As flush times and bad times come and go, Fitzgerald's reputation will have to rely on his prose to carry him through, and with the sound and pace and agility of his prose your discussion can begin and end.

Questions for discussion:

- After the class probes the truth of these epigrams, you might test them on the values of Dexter and the narrator of "Winter Dreams." Does Dexter love Judy Jones? Is the fascination with her or with a life and a social class that she represents? If she had not been out of reach or mercurial in Dexter's adolescence and young manhood, would he have pursued her as hotly?
- In his emotional turmoil at the end of the story, what is going on? Is Dexter's regret for lost time and lost opportunity, for a life with Judy that he never had, entirely an experience of pain? Or do you sense a pleasure lurking somewhere in his nostalgia, a final superiority—of himself over Judy or of men over "women" as the upper classes in the early twentieth century had constructed women, as lovely and ephemeral acquisitions?
- Ask a student to read aloud the paragraph that begins section II of "Winter Dreams," searching for the tone of it. What do your students hear in these lines? Something like the uneasy voice of Nick at the opening or closing of *The Great Gatsby*?
- Why does Fitzgerald favor the predicament of the hero on the edge of the glamorous life, looking at it with these conflicting emotions, suffering from and in an odd way delighting in his exile?
- When Dexter says, at the very end of "Winter Dreams," "That thing will come back no more," does he believe that wholeheartedly?
- Has Dexter stopped looking for the glamorous and impossible dream? Will he ever be capable of loving a woman for what she is, not what she represents as a status symbol?
- Are Fitzgerald's narratives unique because they tell stories of growing up? Or is it that the major characters in them never quite grow up as much as they tell themselves they have?

WILLIAM FAULKNER

As students begin to read *As I Lay Dying* they experience fragmentation and dislocation. After assigning only the first five or ten monologues, you could spend much of the first class period allowing them to discuss the expectations they bring to a novel as readers and how *As I Lay Dying* disrupts those expectations. The initial confusion they feel as a result of Faulkner's disparate narrative sections and points of view can help them understand modernism as a challenge to their ways of seeing the world. If allowed to express their own disorientation, they begin to use Faulkner's novel as an exploration of ways of knowing (epistemology) as well as of ways of being (ontology) in a disordered universe.

We begin with a preliminary discussion of the book's title in light of earlier thematic discussions of modernism. What does the reader expect, given this title? And how does the novel, from its opening sections, thwart those expectations? Who is the "I" of the title? Just Addie Bundren? What or who else does that first-person point of view include? And how does the past tense of the title create a preliminary absurdity before the reader begins the novel? In eliciting students' initial confusion about the opening sections, try to give them the experience of posing Faulkner's own questions as he lets his characters speak. What do they know as they read, and how do they know it? You might closely read Darl's opening section. Where does Faulkner "locate" the reader? Part of what "lies dying" for readers new to Faulkner is any reliance on the author as someone who will facilitate knowing. Faulkner shows readers only what his characters know, not what readers may feel the need to know.

As students proceed through the novel (over the span of an additional two or three class periods), you can spend class time describing what Faulkner is doing. A class might want to consider novelistic conventions—character development, plot, use of a narrator, chronology, narrative form—and assess the extent to which Faulkner uses or rejects traditional elements of the novel. In the collective act of description, students make numerous statements about *As I Lay Dying*: they note the number of narrators (fifteen by the novel's end) and sections (fifty-nine separate monologues); they distinguish among the narrative voices by making descriptive observations: Darl has, by far, the most sections; some central characters—Jewel and Addie—have only one monologue; monologues by Darl, Jewel, Dewey Dell, Anse, Vardaman, Cash, and Addie create a nexus of family dynamics; other characters—Cora, Tull, Peabody, Samson, Whitfield, Armstid, MacGowan, Moseley—express a wide range of possible social responses to the Bundrens. These descriptive statements may make some students feel that they have "figured out" the novel, and you may observe that their attempts to "solve" the novel may be premature and may actually be covering over their uneasiness as readers, lest they become lost in a work without omniscient authority.

They also establish collective understandings about the characters in the novel that become shared facts and that serve as a prelude to interpretation. The attempt to bury Addie becomes the family members' ostensible reason for the journey to Jefferson, which provides Faulkner with his novel's narrative structure; but most of the Bundrens also have other reasons for the trip. Cash wants the free ride back to Tull's, where he is supposed to work on his barn, and he dreams of a "talking machine." Vardaman remembers something in a store window (the toy train) that Santa wouldn't have sold to town boys. Anse wants to get some new teeth. Dewey Dell hopes to buy a drug-induced abortion. Darl twice narrates events at which he could not have been present and in other sections appears to "know" things that others have not told him (he knows Dewey Dell is pregnant and that Anse is not Jewel's father). Among all of Addie's survivors, Jewel seems best able to feel the depths of his connection to his mother, to mourn her death, and to achieve emotional resolution. (At the end of Cora's section just preceding Addie's monologue, Addie tells Cora that Jewel "is my cross and he will be my salvation. He will save me from the water and from the fire," and indeed, Jewel first saves Addie's coffin in the ford and later from the fire Darl has set to Gillespie's barn.)

The group effort to figure out what can be known in reading the novel becomes a pedagogical analogue to the Bundrens' own journey. The parallel tensions of burying Addie (for the Bundrens) and figuring out what is happening in the novel (for the members of the class) comment on the act of modernist reading: without the storyteller/guide of traditional narrative, the task of arriving at an understanding of Faulkner's text (analogous to bringing the coffin to Jefferson) places much of the burden of creation on the act of reading itself.

As a result of description, students move toward interpretation. The elements of form they observe lead to their perceptions of character. For example, they note the repetition in the form of the images Jewel and Vardaman create as a way of grieving for Addie: "Jewel's mother is a horse" and "My mother is a fish." Then they can ask, which image works best to help the character resolve grief? In responding to the question, they explore the relationship between image and feeling, between word and meaning, between the novel as a form and the attempt to order the fragments of human consciousness.

Central to exploring Faulkner's search for theme, meaning, and order is Addie's single monologue, placed off-center in the novel in the second half, long after Addie has died and the Bundrens have begun their journey to Jefferson. To what extent does Addie exist in the novel? Although she gives the other characters their ostensible reason for action, she herself does not act. Neither does she speak, except to acknowledge Cash as he builds her coffin. Her monologue in the novel may appear to give her a voice, but her death has already silenced her and prevents her from making her genuine presence known. She exists for others as their own projected need. Interestingly, what occupies her thinking in her monologue is the uselessness of words. Discuss Addie's various statements about words: "words dont ever fit even what they are trying to say at"; a word is "just a shape to fill a lack"; a name is a "word as a shape, a vessel . . . a significant shape profoundly without life like an empty door frame"; words are "just sounds" that people have "for what they never had and cannot have until they forget the words." In the narrative structure of Faulkner's novel, Addie is herself "just a shape to fill a lack."

The visual image of the coffin that appears in Tull's third monologue typographically disrupts, once again, the reader's expectations; for although Faulkner has violated readers' expectations of linearity and wholeness in narrating As I Lay Dying, he at least uses words. With the visual image of the coffin, followed later by Addie's description of words, Faulkner creates a series of concentric visual images or shapes that serve both to contain his novel's meaning and to express the limits of narrative form. In Faulkner's thinking, each of the following is associatively synonymous: the visual figure of the coffin, the name Addie, the narrative form he has chosen for the book (it is spatial, a world laid out by compass and rule), and the book itself. *As I Lay Dying* effectively becomes Addie's coffin, a fiction in which she is silenced by the title. And like her family in Jefferson cemetery, she might be listening to the other fifty-eight monologues, but she'll "be hard to talk to."

As I Lay Dying can have a profound effect on students who are themselves struggling to emerge from silence and to explore the world's order and form, to discover whether it has any or whether they must join the human collective task of making form and meaning. Students may empathize with Addie's silence and may find it reflected in Vardaman's obsession with his mother as a fish or in Cash's inability to speak except to focus on the coffin's construction or need for balance. *As I Lay Dying* demonstrates the novelist's own struggle to emerge from silence, and students may believe that it is only partly successful or that Faulkner is saying that it is possible to achieve only partial success.

In evaluating the relationship between the construction of form—as a coffin or a novel—and of meaning, ask students to think about Darl. Is he crazy? If so, what makes him crazy? Interestingly, Darl has by far the least difficulty with silence; he can speak for others as well as for himself. Is he a mere scapegoat at the novel's end? Do the other members of his family believe he "knows too much"? Or has he failed in some basic way to create a form for what he knows? Darl is the only character who cannot make a connection between himself and some concrete object. He has no coffin, horse, fish, abortion, or reason to go to town. Students may find it difficult to believe that Darl "goes crazy" at the end of the novel, in part because, in many of his monologues, he closely resembles a traditional omniscient narrator, one whose own identity does not intrude. Who then is Darl? If he cannot express his connection in terms of an image, a form—coffin or novel—his knowledge and creativity become destructive. Darl simply cannot "be contained" in a form; therefore, as Cash realizes at novel's end, "this world is not his world; this life his life." In Darl's failure to achieve a form for human consciousness, Faulkner implies his own struggle for meaning. What to make of a diminished thing?—make something of it, find a word to fill the lack, write a novel that will reconcile human need for form with the formlessness of human consciousness. Cash's briefest monologue locates *As I Lay Dying* in the progression of Faulkner's career as a novelist: "It wasn't on a balance. I told them that if they wanted it to tote and ride on a balance, they would have to." *As I Lay Dying* rides precariously, a book about silent knowing necessarily told in words. Expecting to be told, students emerge from *As I Lay Dying* with the uneasy knowledge that words no longer—for the modernist—carry ultimate authority. As Addie expresses it, "the high dead words in time seemed to lose even the significance of their dead sound." Perhaps literary authority itself is at least a part of what "lies dying" in Faulkner's modern fictional universe.

Hart Crane

Crane can be hard to engage with in a quick-moving survey course. His prosody varies; as a visionary poet and a twentieth-century bard, he takes on immense subjects; his verse presents a first-time reader with a bewildering range of moods and temperaments; and the story of his short, tumultuous life can shadow the poetry so much that the verse can become subordinate to the biography, mere exhibits in an investigation of the man. If you want students to appreciate, on the fly, Crane's ambitions as a poet and the variety of voices that he mastered, the best way to begin might be to take two extended stanzas from two different parts of *The Bridge* and examine them closely and comparatively. Whitman tried to embrace all of American experience, but his prosody did not show this kind of variety.

Questions for discussion:

- Why are there so many different stanza structures and types of language in *The Bridge*? What effect does this variety have on the poem as a whole?
- Are the different voices in the poem in some ways a kind of incantation, calling up not just different historical moments, but different eras in the history of the American imagination?
- What do students think of Crane's experiment, not just in seeing but in creating one long poem in such a variety of styles?

Ernest Hemingway and Thomas Wolfe

Hemingway and Wolfe are near neighbors in NAAL, and there is much to be gained in looking at them together if one of your objectives is to help students increase their awareness of the variety of literary styles that were applied to modern experience. Students can see here a spectacular contrast, opposite ways of refreshing American narrative catching the feel of contemporary life: Hemingway the minimalist, the stoic, the great doubter of emotional and intellectual display, and Wolfe, the ecstatic describer, the lover of adjectives and unending periodic sentences, the believer in saying. Judging by the post-1945 prose fiction that is included in NAAL and other canon-making anthologies, Hemingway seems to have won the face-off: Vonnegut, Carver, Beattie, Silko, and many other contemporary writers show his influence. If students need some coaxing to engage in these speculative questions, you might ask them to compare the closing paragraphs of "The Lost Boy" and "The Snows of Kilimanjaro." They are both elegiac in a sense, both about loss, death, and the problem of understanding the meaning of one human life. But the tonal and thematic differences will be strongly apparent, and contrasting the passages can open up a broad discussion about saying, and not saying, as literary and artistic values.

Questions for discussion:

- Why did Hemingway's style prevail over Wolfe and have a greater influence in post-1945 American fiction?

- What was it about modern experience that made minimalism an appropriate response—perhaps more so than Wolfe's ebullience?

STERLING BROWN

Brown chooses the principle of contrast between white man and black man as his subject in "Mister Samuel and Sam" and "Master and Man." In these poems, the differences between white and black are settled by the common denominators of death and harvest time, and yet as the poems appear to resolve differences, they also end by highlighting the inequalities within those common denominators (both Samuel and Sam may die, but the harvest is more bounteous for the Master than for the Man). Other poems (such as "He Was a Man") also derive their form from the principle of contrast, but the holding back of detail in early stanzas typical of a ballad about the life of a man yields to more detail, and the ballad's "story" turns out to be the progress by which this "man" is reduced to not a man in the eyes of white people. The promise of unfolding in the ballad form is negated (and demonstrated by the poem's consistent use of negatives—"It wasn't about," "Didn't catch him," "It didn't come off")—by the poem's ultimate irony, that it's impossible to write a story of a man's life when he isn't viewed as a man. Thus the title's assertion ("He Was a Man") becomes the poem's primary message. "Break of Day" continues the ballad/blues form and a variation on the same theme: "Man in full" becomes "Long past due" by the poem's end.

LANGSTON HUGHES

Before the Harlem Renaissance writers of the 1920s (Hurston, Toomer, Sterling Brown, Hughes, and Cullen are all associated with this period), most black writing took the form either of the slave narrative of the middle nineteenth century or of "racial uplift" literature or polemical writing characteristic of the turn of the twentieth century (and represented in NAAL by Washington and Du Bois). While most African American writers wrote for white audiences, Hughes may be the first African American writer to view his white reader's interest, and his role as speaking voice, as a form of encounter not unlike those early encounters between Europeans and Native peoples during the period of exploration and colonization. You can begin teaching Hughes with "Visitors to the Black Belt" and discussing the two-sided perspective this poem gives about Harlem. More than an exercise in language ("*Across* the railroad tracks" versus "*here* / On this side of the tracks"), the poem ends with a simple question and answer that resonates with the problem of postcolonialism. "Who're you, outsider? / Ask me who am I." In these lines, the poet teaches the reader, by means of the expected question, how to ask the speaker who he or she is rather than to assume he or she already knows. If the outsider learns to know his or her place as outside, then the person on the inside ("To me it's *here* / In Harlem") has room to define himself. So Hughes is pleading with his white audience not to draw conclusions about black life without asking him, without allowing him, to define its reality and meaning and—in other poems (such as "I, Too," "Madam's Calling Cards," and "Freedom [1]")—what it means to be an American.

The other side of the experience of encounter involves the responsibility it places on the poet. Echoing Whitman in "I, Too" and self-conscious about both calling for a black American poet and responding to that quasi-Emersonian call in "Note on Commercial Theatre," Hughes responds very simply: "I reckon it'll be / Me myself! / Yes, it'll be me." From the perspective of literature of encounter, if Hughes can imagine a white readership "encountering" black experience and black art with genuine interest (perhaps for the first time on a large scale during the Harlem Renaissance), then he has the responsibility to make certain that experience and that art don't become "colonized," commercialized ("You've taken my blues and gone—"). The person who recognizes that colonization is taking place must struggle against it, especially by resisting being appropriated in a white someone else's image. Thus Hughes moves beyond Brown, whose poetry stresses contrast and counterpoint, to include contradiction and the two-way experience of encounter.

Students will also find in Hughes's work an appreciation for black women's struggles and an attempt to represent women's experiences. In one of his greatest poems, "Mother to Son," he also connects his own answer for the modernist question to a woman's voice and a woman's experience. If you read this poem closely with students, you might focus on the contrast between the mother's description of the stairway itself and the image she arrives at ("Life for me ain't been no crystal stair") as a controlling metaphor for her vision. The poem shows the mother arriving at modernist order in the chaos of "sometimes goin' in the dark" by making this particular image. Ask students to consider the numerous connotations of the image of the "crystal stair" as well as the way Hughes is experimenting with levels of diction, in effect raising the level of diction in this phrase. Raising the level of diction and "racial uplift" become ground notes in his work; see, for example, "Genius Child," in which Hughes moves beyond protest to a transcendent belief in the "genius" of black life ("*Kill him*—and let his soul run wild!").

And in the Alberta K. Johnson poems (here represented by "Madam and Her Madam" and "Madam's Calling Cards"), Hughes demonstrates the complexity of the relationship between black woman and white woman. When Alberta responds to her Madam's profession of love by saying "I'll be dogged / If I love you," Hughes is making a simple statement of fact: if relationship with the Madam means that Alberta Johnson has to work even harder, she will indeed be "dogged," for it will kill her, and indeed, Alberta must stop short of "loving" the woman she works for if she is to love herself at all. And that she does love herself is clear in "Madam's Calling Cards": "I hankered to see / My name in print." Both like and unlike other characters from this period, Alberta Johnson wants to be an American but doesn't consider herself an immigrant: "There's nothing foreign / To my pedigree."

KAY BOYLE

As an O. Henry Prize winner, "The White Horses of Vienna" is a useful example of topical mainstream fiction from the thirties, when the Depression and the rising threat of another world war were causing uncertainty in American literary circles. National and international emergencies can embarrass aesthetic experiment, and the complex sonorities of modernism rang false in the ears of many people who saw trouble coming and felt the imperative to reach and warn multitudes. Realism and naturalism flared into brightness again; fables with transparent meanings seemed, to some artists, a classic and better path to try, under those circumstances, than another excursion into obscurity. Boyle's story isn't a hard one to read or decode; in fact the simplicity of the style, the austerity of the plot, and the clarity of the themes here might give some students a feeling that they have dropped down into an easier league, especially if they have grappling lately with high modernists. One good way to open up this narrative is to situate it, to compare the style and the form to work by Cather or Hemingway or Porter if you have been reading them as well; or to take a longer view, recognizing a mood and a strategy that runs back to the wellspring of American short fiction, the fabulist and allegorical work of Nathaniel Hawthorne. If your course covers a lot of ground, a turn in that direction can heighten an awareness of distant echoes that your students may be picking up in Kay Boyle.

Questions for discussion:
- The doctor, the doctor's wife, the mayor and the apothecary, and the soldiers who visit the little house: in this story most of the people have no names. Only for the "young doctor" does Boyle give a last name, Heine—and more often than not he is referred to without recourse to it. What is the effect of this quirk in the telling? Where have you seen it before, and what might the advantages and disadvantages be of withholding this commonplace information?
- Have you read any stories before in which a small but intense drama unfolds in a place apart from ordinary social life, from cities and towns? Think of works in the American tradition where a removed or lonely natural setting is the context for a drama between a husband and a wife, or two lovers, or a couple of rivals, or some combination of this sort. What does the setting accomplish? With the Nazi takeover of Germany and Austria unfolding in spectacular fashion in populous cities, why tell a story situated in a cabin in the picturesque hills?
- A couple of fables are woven into this story—the young doctor's account of the maharaja, the white stallion, and the groom and the allegorical story that the doctor tells with his puppets. What thematic weight are these fables intended to carry, and how well do they carry it?
- Since 1935, when this story was written, the history of Nazi Germany and the Second World War has been told in thousands of narratives and photographs and films—in every possible medium of communication and art. Viewed in that context, how has Boyle's story held up over time?

COUNTEE CULLEN

He rhymes, he scans, he sounds Shakespearean here, like Keats or Tennyson or Dickinson there—it's not surprising that Cullen's achievement, in his brief life, should have gone through a phase of dismissal after his death. When critics call, as they periodically do, for rough and flamboyant authenticity, such "Phi Beta Kappa verse" can look contrived, a performance to please a wrong audience. To read Cullen that way is to miss the intensity of his struggle within and against a tradition, to master it, join it, and resist it all at the same time. If that description suggests an irrational or paradoxical drive, then it is also human and rich—and because of those conflicts you might consider reading Cullen in light of other conflicted American masters, like Bradstreet and Dickinson, both of whom seem to resound in the NAAL selections. You could start with the last two quatrains of "Uncle Jim," quatrains that your students might guess were straight out of Dickinson if they came upon them in another context. You could move from here to the ending of "Incident" and again ask how the poem is and is not a contemplation in the Dickinson manner. If students sense that Cullen is in a "lover's quarrel" with a literary tradition that both schools him and excludes him, and if they have some experience with canonical British writers, you might try "Yet Do I Marvel" as a poem that pushes back, as it were, against the sonnet tradition of Shakespeare and Milton. Look at the grammar and syntax here: they seem defiantly unmodern at times and far from an African American vernacular.

Questions for discussion:
- Where are the similarities between Cullen and Dickinson the closest in "Uncle Jim"?
- What do your students think about the final lines, which veer away from Dickinson's world and look to a different tradition: an African American and family source of wisdom?
- In regard to Cullen's references to Tantalus and Sisyphus—allusions typical of English verse more than three hundred years ago—do they belong in a poem from the Harlem Renaissance? What is Cullen doing? What opposite or conflicted motives might cause him to speak from the heart in such a voice?

RICHARD WRIGHT

Since "The Man Who Was Almost a Man" was published within a year of his great novel *Native Son*, we can look for similarities in theme and in the motivation of characters. This is a story of a crisis brought on by desperation and sudden bizarre circumstance, a crisis that could change or ruin a young man's life forever. In some ways the story reads like a prologue to *Native Son*: set in the Deep South, the tale ends with a potentially dangerous protagonist, in isolation, heading off into the darkness of his fate—perhaps to a place like Chicago.

Questions for discussion:

- Discuss what "being a man" means to Dave Saunders. Why does the gun represent manhood to him?
- Does a black boy in the 1930s South automatically get "to be a man like anybody else" or does he have to make that happen?
- Why does Dave Saunders want the power to "kill anybody, black or white"?
- How does Dave Saunders move beyond Washington's views of black identity in *Up from Slavery*?
- Is Dave another heroic fugitive, like Douglass? Does he have a destination at the end of the story?

CARLOS BULOSAN

Bulosan writes about cultural and psychological predicaments and, in a sense, from within a literary predicament as well. In telling of ordinary people from traditional cultures adjusting to life in America and being changed so much by that experience as to be unable to go home again imaginatively or psychologically, he offers a prose style strongly reminiscent of Hemingway, especially when Hemingway is writing about country people, Italian soldiers, untutored Spanish peasants, Native Americans, or others from beyond his own upbringing and social class. Bulosan, like Hemingway, emphasizes a distance between the teller and the people told about.

Questions for discussion:

- Does Bulosan's simple style enhance a sense of empathy and understanding with his characters?
- How does Bulosan establish authorial distance from his characters?
- Does Bulosan's style help us understand Bulosan's relationship to his own heritage or heritages—Filipino and American?

CHAPTER 11

Teaching Notes for Authors and Works: Volume E, American Literature since 1945

Stanley Kunitz

Kunitz is a good place to begin when surveying poetry since 1945, as he brings many classic American voices forward, blended and transformed, as he builds a body of verse with amazing range of subject and sound.

Questions for discussion:
- If students hear Whitman in the cadences and language of "Father and Son" and "The Wellfleet Whale," where do these and other poems turn in new directions or break away from that Whitman voice?
- If "After the Last Dynasty," in its austerity and echoes of a classical Chinese tradition, ends with a paradox and a question, what is the sequence of perceptions that arrive there?
- Are incongruous literary artifacts in evidence here—Stevens perhaps, or William Carlos Williams?
- When Kunitz ventures imaginatively and physically into the heart of New England—to fish, to walk the beach, commune with a dying whale—what does he take with him that is old and new, familiar and out of place?
- Where does "The Wellfleet Whale" echo Whitman's "Out of the Cradle Endlessly Rocking," and where and how does Kunitz's poem break away?

Eudora Welty

"Petrified Man," like many of Welty's great stories about small town southern life, is a comic marvel but a challenging narrative. As students become happily lost in the blather of the beauty shop, they may miss the fact that there is a plot here and a meditation on the entanglements of truth, human nature, and the arts of telling. The story is almost entirely dialogue, and Welty gives us very few cues as to where we are or what to think of these people, other than the cues they give about themselves. Discuss the relationship that emerges for us between Leota and Mrs. Fletcher. Also, you might want to discuss at some point the undercurrent of violence in "Petrified Man."

Questions for discussion:

- Does Mrs. Pike exist? At what point do our suspicions begin to rise?
- How does Leota's story show her attempt to gain control over her own life? Is she successful?
- Who is Billy Boy?
- Why is Leota taking care of him?
- And why does Welty give him the last word, the cliché comeback, "If you're so smart, why ain't you rich?"

INTRODUCING STUDENTS TO CONTEMPORARY AMERICAN DRAMA

An introductory course in American literature, especially in twentieth-century or contemporary literature, offers students a unique opening into the experience and meaning of drama as an American literary form. American writers have certainly produced great plays before the contemporary period; and drama served a vital function for Americans as early as Tyler's *The Contrast*, when delighted audiences flocked to view Jonathan's comic rendition of what an "American" in 1787 might look like. Few of your students, however, will have thought much about the uses of drama in their own lives.

One way of beginning is simply to ask students to talk about drama in general. What do they associate with drama? Almost all of them will have read Shakespeare in high school; they may have learned, as a result, that drama belongs to an elitist category of literary forms. Are any students willing to challenge that impression? Others may recall acting in less serious high school plays: comedies, musicals, or plays written especially for high school acting. A few may have written and/or acted in original plays as children or may have parents who participated in community theater groups. Others may associate a family trip to New York City to view a Broadway play as some initiation rite into adult life and culture. Some may associate drama with television situation comedies. Even with this limited range of responses to the experience of drama in their lives, you can begin to explore the variety of functions drama serves. What are some of the differences between literature that one reads, often alone in a room, and a play that may be "taking place" before the viewer's eyes, as that viewer sits in a group with others? Is a play "shown" or "told" when the performers stage it? What kinds of effects does the stage play make possible? And what does it mean to dramatize?

Contemporary drama may elicit students' ability to engage in the reading process more readily than contemporary American poetry, which often seems deliberately to distance the reader with its private meanings, idio-syncratic uses of language and imagery, and sense of barriers between speaking voice and reader of the text. Drama, however, seems to require a viewer; a play creates audience in the process of making character, situa-tion, scene, and dramatic effect; the student, in the act of reading, becomes a collaborator in creating a visual image of the scene.

The plays included in Volumes D and E of *NAAL*, by their very choice of subject matter and realistic treatment, may particularly elicit the student's capacity to become engaged, to become created or re-created as audience. When O'Neill explored American family life in *Long Day's Journey into Night*, he did not exhaust our increasing fascination for the function and fate of the American family. Perhaps the crisis in family life for late-twentieth-century Americans brought on the crisis of consciousness that earlier in the century we associate with World War I and the question of the death or absence of God or design in the modern world. Family life provides a central focus in the work of Williams and Miller. If the American family is dead or absent, who or what "mirrors" an American identity that contin-ues to evolve?

TENNESSEE WILLIAMS

The loss of "Belle Reve" seems to establish the tarnished American Dream as one of Williams's central themes in *A Streetcar Named Desire*. Some students may see Blanche DuBois as a conventional symbol for the loss of that dream: as an unmarried, aging belle, she worries about her clothes, her appearance, and her ability to attract men and uses alcohol to ease her loneliness. But is the loss of desirability, or desire itself, the play's subject? Does Blanche want to find an object for her desire or to be a desired object?

Williams might have made desire itself a symbol; instead, throughout the play, he focuses on explicit sexuality. What particular scenes define desire as sexual in the play? Ask students to discuss in particular the relationship between Stanley and Stella. Their attraction for each other is sexual, and most students will equate sexuality with heterosexuality and, as it is pre-sented in this play, with a hierarchy of physical dominance (the men in the play, especially Stanley, use physical abuse as part of sexual power; see Stan-ley's comment to Blanche, " 'Oh! So you want some roughhouse!' ").

But this play revolves around that moment in Blanche's past when she married a "young boy" who tried to find "help" in Blanche for his homosex-uality. When she discovers him with "an older man who had been his friend for years" and that day tells him how much he disgusts her, he blows his head off. For most students, presuming that heterosexuality is "normal" and homosexuality "deviant," this moment will establish Blanche's tragedy as a conventional one—she has loved young and lost—and the moment in which homosexuality enters the play will quickly recede. Raise the possi-bility that from this moment on, Blanche's sexual identity becomes ambigu-ous, despite the fact that Williams has made her a woman in the play, and suggest also that although Stanley and Stella both seem secure in their gender identities, their very insistence on continuing to reaffirm their sexual relationship by means of violence—thereby asserting Stanley's "manhood" and Stella's "womanliness"—begins to raise the question of the origins of gender determination as well.

What would it mean to say that Blanche's sexual identity becomes ambiguous in the play? Near the end she tells Mitch, "I don't want realism. I want magic! . . . I don't tell truth, I tell what *ought* to be truth" (top of page 2236). What are Blanche's props for her "magic"? Ask someone to study her array of furs, costumes, jewelry, and perfume in the play; she wears all of the trappings of gendered femininity, like the legendary Mae West (the statuette Mitch wins for Blanche at the amusement park). But her success in establishing her appearance depends on her avoiding the sun and even electric light. Without the costumes, who would Blanche be? What would it mean to call her a "woman"? And who are her consistent objects of desire? Williams is exploring the way female identity is made, not born.

Ask students to think about Stanley's response to Blanche. What motivates Stanley to rape her? What does she represent that makes him want to humiliate her? Blanche sees Stanley—with his phallic "genius"—as subhuman; Stanley sees Blanche as undermining his control over Stella ("You remember the way that it was? Them nights we had together? God, honey, it's gonna be sweet when we can make noise in the night the way that we used to and get the colored lights going with nobody's sister behind the curtains to hear us!" [top of page 2232]). But Stanley is also acting out of a variation on homophobia—or is homophobia a variation on misogyny? Stanley hates Blanche because she insists on wearing women's costumes and yet refuses to define herself as degenerate or to excuse her sister for her submission to Stanley. In raping Blanche, he is raping the wearing of women's costumes, the flaunting of sexuality by women (or by men who refuse to be "phallic"). No wonder that Stella tells Eunice, "I couldn't believe her story and go on living with Stanley." The sexual "stories" Blanche and Stanley tell totally contradict each other. Blanche exhibits desire without violence; Stanley achieves his through violence and humiliation.

Ask students to talk about Stella's grief at the end of the play: "What have I done to my sister?" How has she betrayed Blanche? Has she also betrayed herself? In what version of sexual desire does the "truth" lie? The play ends with Stanley and Stella, having eliminated Blanche from their world, returning to their hierarchical heterosexual roles: Stella weeps in luxurious abandon, Stanley unbuttons her blouse. Is this desire? Or a more destructive lie than Blanche's "magic"?

JOHN CHEEVER

Cheever makes an excellent foil for Tennessee Williams, and he offers a demonstration of how postwar American literature has brought us a proliferation not only of regional works but of different possibilities regarding the presentation of temperament. Rightly or otherwise, Williams has become associated with hot climates, hot passions, overt sexuality, and spectacular (if not always eloquent) breakdown scenes in which primordial desire and deep pain are exhibited and confessed. Cheever's associations are in some ways the opposite: his landscape, physically and psychologically, is often the suburban landscape of southern Connecticut and Westchester County, New York—upscale neighborhoods two hours or less by train or car from New York City, landscapes in which urban comforts blend (sometimes attractively, sometimes grotesquely) with a real or contrived pastoral setting and in which people may try to balance and sustain their inner lives in part by keeping their lawns, houses, and outward personalities well tended.

The classic Cheever breakdown, so strongly contrasted with Williams's, is of a sort he associated with prep-schooled, Ivy League-trained professional men and their façade-conserving wives: a sudden wave of anomie, of deracination, an unexplained compulsion to take on or persist in some bizarre or self-destructive activity or to quietly tear the fabric of the artificial life that surrounds them and their families. Students can work back and forth between Cheever and Williams, strengthening their own powers to compare and discuss works in light of one another and musing on how deep the class differences and regional differences still run in contemporary America.

Question for discussion:
- Does even madness have its local rules, its cultural shape, its regional identity?

BERNARD MALAMUD

"The Magic Barrel" also works well with A *Streetcar Named Desire*, because there are similarities between the works that help students formulate their questions. Salzman's idea of Paradise is to find a good woman for Leo, the rabbinical student, and to keep Leo away from his own daughter, Stella, a "fallen woman." (Is Williams's Stella also "fallen"?) When Leo falls in love with Stella's picture and arranges to meet her at the end of the story, Malamud depicts their meeting in "fallen" terms: Stella is dressed like a streetwalker, Leo runs forward "with flowers outthrust" (or as if he and Salzman had exchanged places, and Leo is now a cupid or the FTD florist's winged messenger bearing flowers), and Salzman, convinced that there is no good man, chants prayers for the dead. But Leo pictures in Stella "his own redemption," and Malamud suggests that although Leo becomes less than a rabbi by the end of the story, he becomes consequently more of a man, more of a human being. Simply loving, in this story, does recreate Paradise because it makes it possible, once again, for Leo to love God—and even to create God in a human image. In Malamud's terms, Leo's love for the fallen Stella makes him a good man, and although Salzman mourns, the story has a happy ending. Less is more for Leo. As he becomes the "diminished thing" in Salzman's eyes, he is more capable of human love. In short, this is a parable, and students will enjoy speculating on Malamud's connections to some of the oldest kinds of storytelling in the Western tradition.

Ralph Ellison

Students by this point in your course will have much to say about the use and abuse of symbolism—to draw them into the power of *Invisible Man* and to encourage them to read the entire novel, it's worth pausing to see how Chapter I works both as an allegory and as a splendid piece of realistic narrative. Compare Ellison's protagonist with Dave Saunders in Wright's "The Man Who Was Almost a Man." The two might seem incomparable in educational background and social possibilities; discuss how they may be set up against different barriers.

Questions for discussion:
- In the Prologue to *Invisible Man* the older protagonist writes, in retrospect, "responsibility rests upon recognition, and recognition is a form of agreement." How is this observation relevant to his experiences as a young man in Chapter I?
- How does the boy's attempt to deliver the speech he himself has written comment on the literary tradition of American black writers?
- What are the symbolic and real obstacles he must overcome in trying to find his voice and to express his point of view?
- What might it take for the white men at the smoker to "recognize" and "accept" the invisible man? Is the white woman in a better position than the black boy? Does either have power in the world of the back room?
- Are we on familiar ground here in other ways with a narrator on the edge of the experience witnessing drastic action by others who, in a sense, act and are sacrificed for him?
- Is there anything of Nick Carraway in Ellison's teller?

Saul Bellow

One of a handful of American Nobel Prize-winners, Bellow has a reputation for being dauntingly intellectual: in a Bellow story, one ordinary-looking man, not especially successful or even known, walking down one New York street on one ordinary day will open up as a cosmos, an inner world where Conrad, Marx, Hegel, Henry James, Condorcet, and a mob of other thinkers and public and private personalities will riot and conjoin in amazing thought patterns. The worst and saddest mistake to make in reading Bellow, or in presenting him to a college class, is to take cadenzas of this kind as some sort of showing off, for usually the opposite is true: throughout his career, Bellow wrote good-natured, human satires about the seductions of the intellect, how we hunger to know so much, and how little good it does in handling the streets of modern America or the big questions about the human condition. At the end of his most celebrated novel, *Herzog*, a compulsive professorial letter writer, arguer, and last-word seeker decides to just shut up and not even tell his cleaning lady what to do; other Bellow heroes resort ultimately to one sort of silence or another, yet rarely is it a silence of defeat or of contempt for other human beings. James's old adage, that literature is a celebration of life, is strong throughout the Bellow canon.

The Adventures of Augie March is in some ways an attempt to refresh and modernize the picaresque novel, a mode that flourished in England in the eighteenth century and that was epitomized, in American literature, by *Adventures of Huckleberry Finn.* These loosely plotted narratives offer a different sort of suspense: will the protagonist or the teller of the story (frequently they are one and the same) succeed in constructing a coherent identity out of a hodgepodge of experience—personal adventures and mischief, encounters with others, and a jumbled and miscellaneous cultural legacy—and achieve some manner of wisdom? The voice of a memorable picaresque narrator is often a blending.

To help students get a feel for Bellow's rhetorical style and for the plot or "suspense" in Augie's memoir, ask them to read a couple of paragraphs aloud, with special sensitivity to the voice they hear on the page, to peculiarities in the structure of sentences, and to surprising allusions and juxtapositions. What are the effects, for example, of referring to Heraclitus in the second sentence of a personal account and to a grandmother's overfed "wind-breaking" poodle on the same page? Of mixing *Tom Brown's School Days,* a Victorian Anglo-Saxon popular novel and something of a classic, with outbursts of Yiddish and secondhand accounts of an old lady getting a set of false teeth?

Questions for discussion:
- If Augie sounds like he lives in many imaginative and cultural worlds at once, does that quality suggest other American narrators that your students have encountered—Huck Finn, Nick Carraway, Ralph Ellison's Invisible Man, Chief Bromden in *One Flew Over the Cuckoo's Nest*?
- If Augie is having trouble sorting out who he is, and which traditions he should take to heart, what about his brother Simon, who seems to be loading up on British novels and details of American history?
- Is Augie ingratiating as a narrator? Is he funny?
- *Augie March* is a thick book—one of Bellow's longest—and the opening chapter of any novel needs to give a busy modern reader a good reason to continue. What do your students see here that might move them forward—or away?

ARTHUR MILLER

Death of a Salesman gives American family life itself the power to create character—almost as if the play were about the inability of any playwright to invent roles he or she has not already played or watched in the tragedy of family life. The family is both the play and the playwright. And in this play, the family prescribes certain roles for each of the four main characters that they continue to reenact in the process of discovering what they are. Students, following Linda's cue, will focus on Willy Loman himself: "Attention must be finally paid to such a person." Neither of his sons is able understand why he has so much trouble communicating with them. Unlike Mary Tyrone or Blanche DuBois, Linda Loman has no identity of her own. Miller implies that Linda has kept her husband from going to Alaska and "conquering the world." Miller leaves the interpretation of his character's intentions out in the open, which will provide some profound class discussion material.

Questions for discussion:
- Why doesn't Loman accomplish anything?
- Why does he have such trouble genuinely talking to his sons?
- Is *Death of a Salesman* realistic in its portrait of Linda?
- What was Linda's role in Loman's decline?
- Does Linda see inadequacies in her husband that he was unable to recognize in himself?
- Does Linda never criticize Loman or want to defend Biff against his father?
- Who raised these children, anyway?
- Is the role of the American father as provider a myth without basis in fact? Who does "provide" in this play? And what is Miller indicting? Capitalism? Family life in general? American fatherhood?

JACK KEROUAC

Your students may find Kerouac easy to read but difficult to talk about, for a variety of reasons. Some members of your class are likely to know his work and legend already, for *On the Road* has shown considerable staying power as a wish-dream, for younger readers, of escape, cultural rebellion, and freewheeling adventure in wide-open American spaces. To some readers, Kerouac's appeal lies in the powerful impression that he evades the taint of the classroom, all the apparatus of scholastic literary analysis. There's no plot here, no clear exposition of themes; the chapters in *Big Sur* seem to peter out or halt abruptly rather than conclude in some shapely way; characters flicker in and out of focus; settings seem to change like jump-cuts in a music video. The paradox will probably be there in the room with you: you and your students are trying to find a way to talk coherently about a text that refuses conventional notions of coherence, a work that tries hard to be thoroughly out of school.

To get a good conversation going, it might be well to take a few steps back and talk about a broader cultural context: the mythology of California and the Beat legacy; the lure of the "beatnik," "hippie," "bohemian" life; the succession of famous American stories that celebrate the open road, the meandering sea voyage, the trek into uncharted territory, as an American rite of passage. When the group has likened *Big Sur* to other works they know—including films, plays, television shows about wandering, spiritual voyaging, haphazard self-discovery—you could ask about an irony or a nemesis that seems to arise here and there in these excerpts: the process by which today's escape or fresh idea becomes tomorrow's fad and fashion. *Big Sur* was published several years after *Dharma Bums* and *On the Road,* and at times the narrator seems to chafe at the prospect that "beatniks" and watered-down Zen Buddhism have caught on with a multitude and that the struggle now is to stay, like Huck, "ahead of the rest." Monsanto's (Ferlinghetti's) City Lights Bookshop is already a tourist landmark and groupies are breaking the windows at home, and like the footsore hitchhiker along Highway 101, the narrator finds himself exhausted and aimless and stranded in a flow of tourists, looking for a world that he helped to make known.

Questions for discussion:

- Students will have encountered "Zen" in many surprising places in contemporary culture. There are Zen potato chips, Zen spas and health clubs, Zen decorating hints and self-help books and exercise videos, most of which have little or nothing to do with Bodhi Dharma and the spiritual practices that came to Japan from China in the Middle Ages. Plastic statues of the Buddha preside over hot tubs in Las Vegas casino hotels and over swimming pools at Maui resorts. Your students can probably think of many other examples. How do those uses resemble or differ from the way that this narrator and his friends make use of Zen or allude to Buddhist and Taoist texts and practices? When this narrator and his friends talk about Zen and Buddhism, how are those practices invoked? How much impact does Zen study and spirituality seem to have on the way these characters think and conduct their lives?
- There are some long monologues embedded in the text of *Big Sur.* Why are these monologues included? How can we describe the human dynamics in which they occur? In other words, what are the indications that the speaker intends to be listened to—and that the hearer is supposed to be listening? In what kinds of social or intimate situations are monologues of this sort welcomed or tolerated in our own lives?
- As an experiment to understand the aesthetics of the Beats, ask your students to compare the sound and pace of a long passage in *Big Sur* to a dozen lines from Allen Ginsberg's "Sunflower Sutra" or "A Supermarket in California." How would they describe and account for the similarities that they hear?

Kurt Vonnegut

If *Slaughterhouse Five* is a novel, it is also an account of an author trying to *write* a novel based on horrific firsthand experience. By a bizarre twist of fate, Vonnegut, as an American POW, was imprisoned in one of the few safe places in a beautiful German city that the Germans believed would never be attacked from the air—and as a result he was one of the few survivors of a coordinated air assault that burned the historic center and killed tens of thousands in a single night. There are a lot of stories about the Second World War, by people who saw the catastrophe up close; *Slaughterhouse Five* is unusual in that it situates those horrors within the landscape of life after the war, the return of routine, the onset of forgetfulness—where memory is eroded and transformed to the point that the truth itself becomes charged with dream. The novel is also striking as an inquiry into "reality" and into realism and surrealism as literary values and as states of mind. Are some experiences too grotesque or bizarre to be sorted into paragraphs on the printed page, in a memoir or any other sort of writing? Vonnegut's prose will appeal to some readers and possibly exasperate others, and a sampling of the book should probably begin with the form and style of what we find here.

Questions for discussion:

- Even a glance through the selection will bring home the fact that Vonnegut likes one-liners, quick isolated observations or comments that suggest stand-up comedy or private journal entries. Read several of these in the context of longer paragraphs that come before and after. What tone do you pick up on here? Are these offered as insights? As refusals to consider too deeply?

- There are several digressions here, including observations on the Children's Crusade of the early thirteenth century, accounts from the Old Testament, and memoirs of situation-comedy life in upstate New York. Why are these digressions in the narrative?

- The phrase "So it goes" pops up at several points in the selection—for example, at the end of the paragraph on the middle of page 2464 beginning "And on the other side of the field . . ." and at the end of the shorter paragraph on the bottom of page 2465 beginning "The veteran decided to take his care into the basement." What are the implications, thematic and psychological, of this repeated phrase, in context and overall?

Grace Paley

A conversation about Paley can range far: into modern writers and American politics, the status of women in urban cultural and professional contexts, the transformations and development of realist motives as they interconnect in various ways with ideas associated with modernism and postmodernism. If you are uneasy about classifying Paley in one clutch or another of contemporary writers (and she resists classification), you might enter this tale as a story about storytelling—not a self-indulgent or self-promoting exercise about individual genius or the supposed magic of fiction but about writers and intended audiences, about whether any mode of narration can achieve simple and profound truth, and about whether all this making of fiction really serves any purpose in a world grown so complex, changeful, and forgetful of the struggles and the rich inner life of the private self. Some of your students have probably been wondering about such issues all term, and Paley can bring those concerns eloquently into the open.

It's a disarming tale that students will probably like very much, as it respects and celebrates creative intentions that in other circumstances are scorned or condescended to: pleasing people whom you love, sharing the heartfelt perception with a father or mother, respecting the life and thoughts of fairly ordinary human beings—people who may not belong in art films but who nonetheless are capable of powerful insight. There is a kinship evident here not only among Paley, Malamud, and Bellow, but also between Paley and American writers at least as far back as Rebecca Harding Davis, and students will help you speculate on those relationships.

CLUSTER: POSTMODERN MANIFESTOS

Collected from various corners of the literary world in the past half century, these excerpts can be fun and advantageous to read as a group, especially if one of your objectives is to empower your students to develop as independent, truculent readers, bringing sharp-eyed curiosity to their explorations rather than subjugating themselves to the pronouncements of the famous and the wise. In the instructional notes on the modernist manifestos, I suggested that this form goes back a long way, at least as far as Wordsworth and Coleridge, and that there are old patterns that later writers, ardent as they may be to "make things new," find it hard to avoid. One recurring proposition is that the status quo, whatever it is, is saddled by outmoded styles and stale mannerisms and needs a good cleaning-out in order for the artist to do a better job of representing things as they are; another is that times have changed in deep ways, that cultural experience now is enormously different from what it was the day before yesterday, and that forms and aesthetic values have to be overhauled in order for art to keep up.

So—between modern and postmodern, what are the changes in the cultural predicament, changes that writers feel they have to address in prose explications, calls to arms, or sidebars? Many of these cultural shifts and earthquakes are countenanced in the excerpts here, and in the headnotes to the cluster; even so, in reading through this set you may notice a few other contingencies lurking in the background, unacknowledged.

First, there's the continued erosion of boundaries between public and private speech. Frost published his own mild but firm statements of poetic duty in essays, and in brief epigraphic poems like "The Pasture"; Pound put his polemics in one literary review after another; and in the heyday of American modernism, journals like the *Partisan Review* were full of combative rhetoric about the condition and obligations of the arts. But Hunter Thompson's observations on the postmodern condition come at him, and at us, in a cloud of drug-fueled hallucinations, intensified by the surrealism of nightlife in Las Vegas; Elizabeth Bishop, writing to Robert Lowell about Lowell's violation of privacy and decency in *The Dolphin*, thought she was writing a private letter—but true to the spins and jumps and involutions of the postmodern condition, her private communication became a public document, widely published words on which Bishop and her poems can be pinned down, by critics, like specimens of butterflies.

Another major change that literary artists, by and large, would rather not talk about is the absorption of many of them into tenured positions at colleges and universities. The Professor of Philosophy and the Writer in Permanent Residence may assume a demeanor and a voice that might not come naturally to a writer who has to earn his or her keep every month in some other way, and the "intemperately mild" disposition for which William Gass accuses (and also congratulates) himself might be a function of economic comfort and assured status as much as a clear-eyed address to the way we live now, as authors and readers. Charles Olson, enacting ferocity and uncompromising rebellion on the printed page, wrote less often about the fact that he was also a college president, *ex officio* a creature of compromise and negotiation; as an African American woman seeking a place at table still dominated by white men, Audre Lorde had a very different personal mission, and different urgencies, when she wrote that poetry, for her, was "Not a Luxury."

All of which is to say that your students should be encouraged to voyage bravely into this miscellany, sorting out the courage and the complacency, and deciding for themselves which pronouncements have held up well as an access into the postmodern mind.

Questions for discussion:

- Sukenick deals in vast generalizations. Choose two or three of these broad statements and look at them carefully for factual accuracy and for implications. Which ones work for you as trenchant observations about the cultural past and present? Which ones might not, and why?
- In the course of his essay, William Gass makes several passing comments about science, mathematics, and logic; yet he doesn't say much about matters on the mind of other writers in this set. Read the paragraph that begins "There is a fundamental contradiction in our medium" (bottom of page 2469) and discuss its subject and mood, as well as its relationship to contemporary culture.
- Have a look at Gass's sentences about this, beginning with "He will avoid recording consciousness since consciousness is private" (middle of page 2491) and then glance at the excerpt from *Fear and Loathing in Las Vegas*. Compare Gass and Hunter Thompson on the place and propriety of "consciousness" in fictional, and fictionalized, narrative.
- Frank O'Hara writes (middle of page 2496) that "only Whitman and [Hart] Crane and [William Carlos] Williams, of the American poets, are better than the movies." That cuts out a lot of American poets, living and dead. Do you think O'Hara is being serious in this manifesto for "personism?" In what spirit should we read it?
- As observed above, Bishop's private letter to Robert Lowell, a letter between old friends, has been turned by publication into a standard document in the reading of her own work. Where should we go to look for "manifestos" in an author's published and unpublished work? Do authors actually play by the rules that they lay out, in "overheard" writing like this or in essays and speeches that they offer to the wider world?

JAMES BALDWIN

"Going to Meet the Man" is an imaginative leap as well as a political risk: an African American writer exploring, from the inside, the mind of a Southern white racist. Furthermore, brutal as he is, Jesse is not portrayed without a measure of sympathy: Baldwin presents him as the victim of an upbringing in a deep, inescapable culture of race hatred, culminating in a lynching that, for all the talk around him and from him about the nonhumanity of black people, terrifies him and awakens in him a human empathy that he seems to be spending the rest of his life trying to suppress. The small-town world that Baldwin creates is rich and intense, and sexuality, racist dogmas, direct firsthand experience, and deep, almost wordless, anxiety and guilt seem to contend in the consciousness of this protagonist. Nonetheless, we now read in an era when writers and directors are regularly chided for straying too far from home territory and for presuming to imagine the psychological life of someone from the other gender or from a different race or culture.

Questions for discussion:
- Does Baldwin succeed at this difficult and dangerous artistic feat?
- Is a bold act of understanding like this, published in the very midst of the civil rights struggle of the 1960s, an important political or moral act or a gesture that resonates beyond the usual reach of imaginative fiction?

FLANNERY O'CONNOR

In "Good Country People," Mrs. Hopewell says, "'Everybody is different. . . . It takes all kinds to make the world,'" but she doesn't really mean it. She would prefer that all the world, and especially her daughter, be "good country people" like herself. As unlikely as it might have seemed, Hulga has chosen as a love object a person who both infantilizes her and tries to idealize her—someone whose psychological connection with her resembles her mother's own.

Questions for discussion:
- What would it mean for Hulga to take her mother as her model? Contrast the two sets of mothers and daughters depicted in the story. What are Hulga's "crimes"?
- What makes her unforgivably "different" to her mother? What is Hulga looking for in Manley Pointer? What does she find?
- Look at the mother-child imagery of Pointer's "seduction." What do Manley and Mrs. Hopewell have in common?
- What is the story's final betrayal?
- Is it possible for Hulga to escape being her mother's daughter?

URSULA K. LE GUIN

Students who have been moving through the fiction chronologically, worrying over the symbolic dimensions or pretensions of various writers before this point, may panic when they get to this story, so it's a very good idea to try to relax them and suggest that "Schrödinger's Cat" may be a tale about not knowing rather than a story with all sorts of concealed profundities. Le Guin is writing about a paradox that shadows the life not only of the writer interested in science, science fiction, and fantasy but of any sentient person who tries to understand worldly experience: that there are powerful and seductive theories out there that are imaginatively almost ungraspable or that threaten to overthrow or render absurd any attempt to make sense of our own situation. The story is in some ways about quantum physics, a body of thought that most of us outside that discipline do not understand at any level beyond the superficial. The story is about that puzzlement, about what can happen to our imaginative life when we try to grasp the principles of uncertainty, of the inherent instability or contingency of what (for several centuries) we had taken (again, perhaps without much real understanding) as the fixed laws by which the universe operates.

Nonetheless, this story (as well as the other Le Guin selection, "She Unnames Them") seems lighthearted, playful: this is not a portentous allegory but something like a giddy hallucination or reverie of a sort that an informed modern consciousness might undergo in a hypnogogic state or a daydream. You might ask students to toy with and analyze the first long paragraph. What is the tone? What kinds of expectations are set up in this moment? What kinds of expectations and readerly habits do we need to drop to move on into the story? If students seem tense, draw them into a recognition that they deal with surrealism, crazy visual situations, and narrative discontinuities all the time: in rock videos and in big-budget films that they queue up to see on summer weekends. If they can surrender their interpretive anxieties in those situations, then why not here? The answer, of course, is that when a narrative moves into a classroom or an anthology, it becomes a "text," and what would beguile and amuse before becomes threatening now. That's an idea very much worth developing in regard to Le Guin and many other texts that you have been encountering this semester.

Donald Barthelme

Before you launch into Barthelme, it might be a good idea to encourage students not to feel frustrated if they don't get it, don't see some special significance in "The Balloon" or sense that the narrator has a palpable emotional stake in the telling of the story. The voice here is classic Barthelme, and times change.

Barthleme's heyday was during the period of happenings, put-ons, and general resistance against notions that logic, literary and artistic conventions, official analyses and histories, and other attempts to guide cultural conduct or individual thought were really worth anyone's time. In the history of the modern short story, overtly engaged tellers are a strong tradition, running back to Wharton. In the narratives of Fitzgerald, Ellison, Malamud, Bellow, Baldwin, Paley, and others, we can imagine the narrator as passionately engaged in an act of remembrance, a variant of Coleridge's Ancient Mariner, telling the tale because he or she is compelled to do so. Against this tradition of passionate engagement, Vonnegut and Barthelme offer resistance, and in that sometimes overheated context, the drably objective voice of "The Balloon" could seem radical or refreshing. There is a tradition behind that too: some of your students may recall Mersault in Camus's *The Stranger* or the voice in Samuel Beckett's *Malloy* or some of the postwar essays and plays of Jean-Paul Sartre. As in those earlier texts, the mood of Barthelme's tale is unsettling not because of what happens (which is not much) but the matter-of-fact way in which those events are received and remembered.

Your students may want to know right away what you think the balloon signifies or argue the matter among themselves—but it might be well to duck that question for a while and attend first to the style of this narrative. If you have been suggesting that hearing a work, apprehending a tone, is very important to opening its meaning, this is a good place to try out that principle. Ask a student to read a bit of "The Balloon" aloud, giving it the tone that he or she thinks is appropriate. Ask other students if they agree with the reading and to try their hand at a sentence or two. If you hear lassitude or melancholy evolving in that succession of readings, ask where it's coming from, where in the words on the page. Focus on the verbs in one of those longer paragraphs. Compare the paragraph you chose to a passage of similar length from Bellow, Baldwin, Le Guin, Fitzgerald, or some other author whose verbs can dance and buzz on the page. One of the oldest rules in creative writing workshops is to try for interesting verb choices—yet Barthelme favors variants of is and was, passive expressions, verbs with little or no vividness or action. You can spread out from here into speculations about this story as a commentary on contemporary everyday urban life and the possibility that cities and city habits can condition us to take everything as only a minor variant on the routine. Oh. Look. A giant balloon. Uh huh. What else is new? A massive, mysterious thing appears over midtown, and the reportage from this narrator is even duller than a weekend local newscast or a talk show on a Sunday afternoon. Predictable interpretive arguments break out and fill hours and pages, and to no avail. The last words of "The Balloon" are "awaiting some other time of unhappiness, some time, perhaps, when we are angry with one another."

Questions for discussion:
- What kinds of verb choices does Barthelme favor? Why would he choose such verbs?
- Is this story about a balloon at all? Or about habits of response, the way that overworked or overwhelmed people respond ritualistically to anything new?
- How does Barthelme parody the arguments that jam our printed pages and daily lives—arguments even perhaps about the meaning of short stories like this?
- Does this narrator sound as if he would be capable of any emotion as strong as anger?
- What, if anything, might it take, to bring his energy levels up, cause him to speak and act as if he cared about what he was seeing and doing?

Toni Morrison

You may find that your students have previous experience with Morrison, because *Sula* and *Song of Solomon* have become regulars in advanced high school courses and freshman English sections. It is likely, however, that they haven't previously read a work as concise as this by Morrison. Since at least the 1980s, her work has defied easy categorization; so rather than begin with possible connections between this story and American Realism and Natural-ism, you might ask what other narratives *Recitatif* reminds them of—other works by Morrison or works by other fiction writers, dramatists, or screen-writers. The tale has many kin in contemporary American literature after all, it is a story of two women, formerly childhood friends, who meet by chance and struggle to rediscover some key memories, evade some other ones, and find grounds for intimacy and empathy despite the effects of time and personal experience. There are stories and films in profusion that cover such ground, but rarely in this way and with the themes that Morrison emphasizes here.

Twyla and Roberta don't struggle to impose meaning on life, but rather to find meaning within their personal experience, to accept and engage with the realities that have overwhelmed them since childhood and to discover, as Twyla puts it, "How to believe what had to be believed." Circumstances change and they change again: the late sixties culture gives way to the mate-rialism of the seventies and eighties, and each of these people is carried along and to some extent transformed.

Can students see any connection between that general theme and Twyla's emphasis on food and her interest in matching up "the right people with the right food"? Why does she stay at the demonstration, carrying her sign, even when the disorder of the group has made her own placard meaningless? Words seem to fail her, and cultural correlatives (like Jimi Hendrix) keep changing, and people not only shift social classes but shift values and atti-tudes along with those classes. But is this a pessimistic story? Or do iden-tity and friendship show themselves as transcendent somehow undamaged in their essence by change? And why is the story called *Recitatif*, which, as the headnote observes, is a narrative that is sung in a free-form way? Is there a suggestion, implicit in this title, that the music of experience is more important than wordy, prosy explications?

John Updike

Updike will be well known to you not only for his best-selling novels and respected short stories but also for his enormous literacy and accomplish-ments as a critic of art, film, poetry, fiction, and American culture. The chal-lenge in teaching one short work by him lies in conveying the range of cultural experience that can make itself felt within a fairly conventional-looking tale of middle-class trouble. To show how this story might stand apart from a legion of tales about "middleness," separations, divorce, and the failure of love, why not start from the beginning and end and work toward the middle? Turn to the last paragraphs and talk a little about the risks inherent in closing a story with a question like "Why?"

If your students have read Wharton's "Souls Belated," ask them to review that story with an ear for the words that are used there in tense, important conversations—and then to speculate on ways in which American realists, bygone and contemporary, understand language as central to the fabric of reality.

Questions for discussion:
- Can a story about a middle-class family bear the weight of a question like that?
- What does the young boy mean by that question, and what does his father hear in it?
- This is a breakthrough moment, but a breakthrough from what kind of confinements?
- Turn to the opening pages, then, and look at two passages: one of descriptive narrative and one of human speech. What kinds of details does Updike pack into his opening paragraph, and why? What kinds of language—what vocabularies—are Joan and Richard using when they speak to each other? What are the effects of those word choices?
- If this is a couple encumbered, and perhaps undone, by the bric-a-brac of ordinary routine, acquisitions, and professional aspirations, are they encumbered also by a baggage of English words?

PHILIP ROTH

As is true in many of his novels and stories, Roth mixes broad comedy with a serious moral and identity crisis in "Defender of the Faith." The historical context is crucial to understanding what is at stake here, and you might want to spend some time describing the odd season between VE Day (the surrender of Nazi Germany) and VJ Day (the surrender of Japan). Millions of American troops, in Europe, in the Pacific, and at home, were expecting an all-out assault on the Japanese mainland, and redeployments and high anxiety were everywhere. There was also significant tension between combat veterans and new recruits—the men who had seen battle and those who had passed through four years of war in relative safety.

Questions for discussion:
- Within a war context, how is the story like a situation comedy?
- What are the somber issues that lurk within it?
- Why name the protagonist Marx?
- In the middle of the twentieth century, what "Marxes" did the American public know, and love, and fear? What do these mixed associations suggest about the sergeant's evolving impression of his own identity, as an American, a soldier, and a Jew?
- What are the risks of portraying Grossbart as an operator and a cheat? What ethnic stereotypes does Roth use here, perhaps dangerously?
- What are possible reactions from within Roth's own ethnic group, and from non-Jewish American readers?
- What similarities do you see between his predicament and that of Captain Vere in Herman Melville's *Billy Budd*?
- How is this story interesting as a crisis in the formation of an American Jewish identity, an identity complicated by Nazism, the Holocaust,

and the experience of service in the U.S. Army overseas and coming home again? As members of other American minority groups enter military service and experience combat, are similar stories possible now, about the unfinished process of becoming American?

AMIRI BARAKA

In the fifties and sixties, Baraka's relationship with experimental writers was complex, and *Dutchman* might be read as a commentary on that unpredictable mix of intimacy, exploitation, and hostility that, as a black artist among white artists and literary camp followers, he experienced firsthand. However, some of the continuing power of the play is that it looks at more dimensions of urban and interracial experience than just the literary. Quick, false pretenses of mutual understanding, racial stereotyping, hostility lurking just below the relative quiet and businesslike onrush of New York life—they are all here, and they suggest strong connections to the tradition of literary naturalism. Baraka is a poet as well as a dramatist, and his personal artistic rebellion is an informed and thoughtful one. Have students read a few selections of Ginsberg's *Howl*, or other high-intensity poetry from the Beats, and see if there isn't a resemblance there—a resemblance that can help locate *Dutchman* in a particular period of American letters and set it apart from the work of Baraka's contemporaries.

Question for discussion:
- To engage with this play, students might want to start with its cadenza passage, the long burst of eloquence from Clay just before Lula stabs him and the others in the subway car throw his body off the train. Is this mere street-talk brutality or does the language and cadence of Clay's rage have its literary kin and comparisons?

N. SCOTT MOMADAY

In the selections from *The Way to Rainy Mountain*, Momaday interweaves a Kiowa past to which he is connected by his bicultural memory, family, and tradition and a Native American literary future (or "renaissance," in the terms of critics) that re-creates in words a culture that exists only "tenuously," in memory. It proves to be Stanford-educated Momaday's thorough acculturation in what his nineteenth-century predecessors would have called "white" or "government" education as well as his command of the English language that makes both possible at once: the preservation of the past and a vision of a future for Native Americans. Unlike most of the Native American texts included in NAAL, Momaday's is not transcribed from a non-English language or from an oral performance—although he collects Kiowa tales and myths, with his father as translator—and he is writing simultaneously to native peoples and Euro-Americans. He is also writing for himself and for others like himself who want to hold on to a Native American heritage. This can include students, even white students, in the American literature classroom.

In some ways, *The Way to Rainy Mountain* becomes a "final exam" of the new Native American materials in NAAL, a way of testing students' knowledge and integration of their earlier readings. For understanding the form of the work requires at least some acquaintance with American Indian myths and history. The work begins with Momaday's contemporary rendition of the Kiowa myth of creation—an emergence myth, like that of the Pima "Story of the Creation" included in Volume A. Momaday traces the migration of the Kiowas and the legends they make, such as the legend of Tai-me, and their relation to other gods in the sky; he gives his grandmother, Aho, a position of reverence and a godlike voice from Kiowa history; he relates the development and loss of the Sun Dance ritual, what his grandmother remembers as "deicide"; he works through (with his father's help in translation) a series of Kiowa myths, counterpointed (or as if in encounter with) other voices—a voice of family and cultural history and a third personal voice of reflections on his place in the schemes of history and myth; and he ends with a poem, "Rainy Mountain Cemetery," which conveys his own vision.

The Native American poet in the late 1960s has been to the mountain, an Indian Moses, and has brought back his vision of "the early sun," on the mountain that "burns and shines," in an image of a new dawn approaching "upon the shadow that your name defines"—an unmarked dark stone that must serve as the marker for the beautiful woman buried in an unmarked grave near his grandmother's house, for all of the unmarked dead Kiowas, for the end of Kiowa culture itself. It is as if, for Momaday, the end of the Sun Dance ritual—like the end of the Ghost Dance religion (both of which occurred in 1890)—required a new vision a century later, and the Native American poet writes a version of the Messiah Letter, one that combines myth, song, and rituals of ceremonial prayer.

GERALD VIZENOR

Written with humor and reserve, Vizenor's story is in some ways about words and about living in two different cultures, in which the relationship between language and identity is entirely different. Vizenor portrays reservation life as a world of near silence, where words are spoken rather than written or read and where utterance has great importance and sometimes mystical power. To go into the outside world, however, is to enter a gale of talk and print, where people "talk and talk" like the blond anthropology student and where everything is analyzed verbally. Even the "sovereign tribal blank books" sold by mail order from an abandoned car transmogrify once they enter the white world: schooled in Samuel Beckett and the supposed eloquence of empty pages, professors do critiques of the books and teach them in California classrooms.

The comedy here is broad, but it may touch on an abiding predicament of being a Native American and a writer, a member of a group that understands the power of silences and not saying and the practitioner of an art that believes in saying endlessly. The paradox is real: language itself, any language, can get in the way of true expression and the culturally based inner life. Students will know the stereotype of the silent Indian all too well; he appears in forms ranging from Tonto through Kesey's Chief Bromden. This story can open some new perspectives, not only on cultures that favor reticence and silence but also on the transcultural problems inherent in seeking always to penetrate the unsayable with torrents of words.

CHARLES WRIGHT

As a poet, Wright loves to mix it up, blending in one poem a wide range of experiences, memories, and knowledge. Students may enjoy talking about the apparent miscellany of subjects and allusions in "Poem Half in the Manner of Li Ho" and "North American Bear" and consider whether they have encountered any other poets who bring such incongruities together: a Tennessee boyhood, ancient Egyptian and Chinese literature, modern history, Greek mythology. You might look at the closing verses of each stanza in "North American Bear," and compare these to closing lines in poems by Stevens and Lowell. Some of these lines are apparently unfathomable, disappearances into a mist; which leaves some room for open discussion on interpretation.

Questions for discussion:
- Does Wright's style of bringing incongruities together work?
- What does Wright suggest about a modern consciousness, a modern education? Does he seem pretentious?
- What does Wright like to do at the very ends of stanzas? What do such closings suggest about Wright's temperament, recurring themes, and idea of a poem?

MARY OLIVER

Because Oliver is very much a New England pastoral poet, it makes sense to encourage students to read her with other such poets in mind. The long, rich tradition of Anglo-American pastoral poetry can actually be a burden for the individual modern artist, if the quest is to achieve an original voice among so many other writers, living and dead, working in similar modes. Students who are comfortable with the overt control and polish of Frost, Wilbur, and Bishop may be disconcerted by the apparent freedom and spontaneity of Oliver's lines. If the objective is to distinguish Oliver's voice, you might begin with "The Black Snake" as a rewrite of or response to William Stafford's famous short elegy "Traveling through the Dark," which takes similar risks with a similar situation: an animal found dead along a highway, a poet trying to bear witness without descending into bathos or forced consolations. In some ways, Oliver goes further with her contemplation than Stafford does, saying things that he left unsaid. In "In Blackwater Woods" she opens a pastoral poem with prosody adapted from William Carlos Williams—not a poet known for conspicuous spirituality or for general truths garnered or glimpsed from observations of nature.

Questions for discussion:
- Does Oliver's pattern, of venturing into the unsayable, continue in her other poems?
- How does Oliver use the Williams Carlos Williams voice for her own purposes?

LUCILLE CLIFTON

Short poems in open forms by a minority poet—the temptation might be strong to read Clifton for racial and political themes, subordinating the depth and resonance of her voice and the broad poetic heritage she draws upon. There is anger here, and also grief, and pride, and stoic affirmations of life—but these poems also show wit and outbreaks of lightheartedness and here and there a touch of mystical insight suggesting other sources and traditions than those of the west.

Questions for discussion:
- If you start with "the mississippi river empties into the gulf", you can sense a complex, conflicted voice, aspiring at one moment to sound and signify like a prophet or a haiku poet—and in other lines calling those same moods and ambitions into question. Why does the first line of this poem begin with an uncapitalized "and," and why does that same line end with "and so forth," almost like a shrug? At what other places in the poem do the mood and the theme seem to change, and what is the overall effect?
- How would you describe Clifton's choices and strategies for ending her poems? Read the last three or four lines of several of these poems, and comment on where, emotionally and thematically, they seem to arrive.
- When all of the Clifton poems in NAAL are read together in a single sitting, what light do they shed on each other? How do they contribute to an overall impression of this poet—and how, in turn, does that overall impression help you read and hear individual poems in the set?

RUDOLFO A. ANAYA

Elsewhere in this guide I have cautioned against conversations which group American minority writers only with other "ethnic" writers, for that kind of attention can degrade unintentionally into ghettoizing. Anaya writes from a tradition that extends in many directions. There is a cinematic quality to his construction and arrangement of scenes, and from that perspective he is very much a writer of now, in and for a culture where the video screens light up rooms in penthouses and barrio tenements alike. But Anaya's style of writing also shows its connections to earlier generations of American writers who have written about dramatic and extreme situations among the poor—writers like Ernest Hemingway, John Steinbeck, Willa Cather, and Jack London.

Questions for discussion:
- "Magical realism" has become a popular mode in fiction and film—a heady mix of hard-edged authenticity and auras of the surreal, our

outright flights into fantasy. The young boy at the center of *Bless Me, Ultima* lives in two worlds at once, the world he sees around him and the one that he imagines. How do these worlds mix or collide in this story and with what results?

- A killing, a mob, a sick and misunderstood man, a voice of sanity, another killing nonetheless: Anaya takes us into familiar ground, with regard to the plot that unfolds here. How does he defamiliarize all this, and make it new?

- The chapter ends with an italicized passage that reads like a poem or a personal reverie. How does this ending connect, psychologically and thematically, to what unfolds earlier?

Thomas Pynchon

The short story "Entropy" includes some classic Pynchon themes and strategies: the high-intensity anxiety about nearly everything in human experience, from worldly human foibles to frightening laws of physics and uncrackable conundrums in epistemology. We also have the fast-moving, sometimes eloquent, but essentially flat characters orating and tearing about in the foreground: if asked for analogues, and encouraged to be free-wheeling, some of your students will suggest similarities with the Simpsons, other dark-toned comics by Matt Groening and Berke Breathed, and some of the more bizarre Hollywood dystopic comedies. Pynchon has been around long enough and has been popular enough to have had his admirers and imitators in television and film.

Questions for discussion:

- After students recognize that Pynchon operates on certain wavelengths familiar to them from popular culture, you might ask what he adapts from conventions of narrative and what he resists. For instance, it's a commonplace assumption that good stories run on characterization, that personages presented to us should be compelling somehow, or complex, and that what they do and how they fare should matter to the reader. Is that true for this Pynchon story? If it doesn't play by the conventional rules, then what does it do instead to hold the reader's attention?

- To approach the question from a different side: it's often (and rather gloomily) observed that Henry Adams's law of acceleration has proved true for human culture, that sheer speed and change have caused us to blur distinctions that used to be respected and that motion and metamorphosis have taken the place of substance in art, in letters, in the self. Is that a Pynchon theme? In other words, does this tale seem to be a symptom of such a problem, a commentary on that problem, or somehow both?

Raymond Carver

The headnote points out that when Carver died in 1988, his work was widely admired and imitated in academic circles, but since critical attention has focused on Carver as a refuser of many narrative conventions and a practitioner of a "stripped down" minimalist sort of realism, students may wonder what is going on here beyond a gesture of resistance against other kinds of fiction that were in favor in the seventies when Carver began to publish his collections. Your class is not likely to be interested in a transient and parochial dispute, and the challenge may be to open up "Cathedral" as a story that does take chances and that affirms the validity of engaging with the world imaginatively.

Since Carver is usually classified as a latter-day realist, students may be reluctant to see any symbolic dimensions to the key action in the story: the rediscovery of the majesty of a cathedral, not by seeing but by moving the hands and feeling. A little nudging of the story to bring out those dimensions will open up the possibility that even a work as austere as this can resonate in this way and can be about the recovery of the capacity for wonder, even in times of disbelief. The magic, if we can call it that, may lie in how we perceive and how we refresh our own ways of examining the world.

CHARLES SIMIC

If Simic's verse is characterized by short, flat, declarative sentences and by opening stanzas that seem dead set against overtly poetic effects, then students may want to look for and discuss moments where these poems seem to shift suddenly in pace, language, and theme. Simic is an intensely well-read poet, and like many postwar writers, his verse rings with the sounds and experiments of the other great writers of his era.

Questions for discussion:
- Where does Simic suddenly introduce a haunting memory or frightening personal experience, and to what effect?
- When he moves to a moment that seems gothic, lurid, or surreal, how has the poem earned our willingness to go there with him, to sense or accept a connection between the ordinary, the diurnal, and the concealed?
- Where might the reader hear touches of Lowell here, or Bishop, or Plath, or Ginsberg, or other poets associated with the confessionals, the Beats, and other schools of verse from the last fifty years of the twentieth century?

TONI CADE BAMBARA

You can expect that your students will come to Bambara with other African American writers and stories in mind: there's a good chance that some of them will have read James Baldwin's "Sonny's Blues," Toni Morrison's *Sula*, Zora Neale Hurston's *Their Eyes Were Watching God*, or other works favored in high school classes and entry-level college courses as glimpses into modern African American experience and experimental literary forms. An opening question, therefore, about the form of "Medley" could bring out generalizations (half-remembered from some other context) about resemblances between this tale and the forms and improvisations of modern jazz. An observation like that can be helpful, but it can also beg some important questions having to do with the realist tradition and certain basic expectations and practices in storytelling. To be absolutely true to life as we know it, true to the meanderings, cadences, and interludes of ordinary experience can be to tell no "story" at all. Analogues from the world of music may not answer the question: does "Medley" go anywhere or say anything?

If students find that problem interesting, then a good way to proceed might be to start with a specific, limited passage and work outward. "Medley" is in some ways a story about telling stories, and there are several moments when Sweet Pea, our narrator, muses on the talents of other people as tellers of tales and of the worth of any story, told badly or well. The paragraphs about Hector as a "bad storyteller," omitting and blurring the details of his reminiscences from the funeral business, offer much to talk about, especially if some attention is paid to Hector as "an absolute artist on windows," clearing the dirt away so that something, however mundane, can be seen clearly, as if for the first time. To what extent is that the experience of reading "Medley"?

Question for discussion:

- If some readers find the pace and direction of the story puzzling or exasperating, are they missing what the story is really about—the commingling of a lot of different experiences (emotional, aesthetic, mundane) in one consciousness and the way that these apparently miscellaneous experiences create one identity and voice?

MAXINE HONG KINGSTON

Kingston's "Trippers and Askers" can work exceptionally well in your class, if you are opening questions about how to create a distinct voice and a coherent identity out of the vast array of experiences in modern American culture. Kingston's thinking about this problem is anything but reductive: she recognizes that the contemporary artist, whatever his or her ethnicity and cultural preferences, constantly engages with high art and pop, the classic and the transient, the subtle and the banal. Wittman may be a Chinese American, but he lives in a vibrant city, and its changefulness, color, and life appeal to him deeply. His problem—funny and perhaps tragic in the same moment—is finding a way to speak, to love, and to be within a culture that both inundates him and marginalizes him.

The headnote points out a Joycean quality in the narration, reflecting the mélange of vocabularies and experiences with which Wittman tries to speak to himself and to create himself as an artist and as a lover: you might ask your students whether this wide-ranging, all-mixing vernacular suggests personal chaos or the possibility of some kind of resolution, a composite and resilient identity well suited to life and writing in a composite and quick-changing American landscape.

Questions for Discussion:

- One good place to start might be with the title of the chapter—a phrase from Whitman's *Song of Myself*—and with the resonant pun in Wittman's name: is he a latter-day Walt Whitman also seeking to weave a song of himself out of everything he has seen and experienced as an American? What are the risks to this would-be bard?
- Part of the suspense in this story lies here, in the risk that Wittman faces of becoming nothing as a result of his trying to say and encompass everything. Is this a noble artistic quest? A mad one? An act of artistic courage? Of cowardice?

ROBERT PINSKY

The headnote for Pinsky suggests relationships between his work and poetry of Bishop and Williams; but what students may find most striking—and initially daunting—about Pinsky's work is his vast range of associations and allusions, his apparent faith (a bit like Bellow's) that everything is connected somehow to everything else and that finding and relishing those connections is a source of consolation and hope. A contemplation of an ordinary imported shirt will take you, imaginatively, to the other side of the world, to moments in American history, to other American and British poets—and from George Herbert to "a Black / Lady in South Carolina." Students can enjoy a ride with Pinsky if they first can see that his leaps and allusions are not pretentious, not proffered to make students feel ignorant and small and to give professors something to footnote. These poems celebrate the act of thinking and the motions of the informed, experienced mind. A good way to proceed, therefore, might be to ask students to read passages from the long poem "At Pleasure Bay" aloud and with a bit of feeling, not stopping to worry about "Ibo dryads" or "the Soviet northernmost settlements" but thinking instead about a poetry that tries to cross boundaries of culture, time, and private experience.

Questions for discussion:

- A poem like this finds its subject and its metaphors everywhere, as if the speaker were a bard for the whole human race. Does the poem succeed?
- Does Pinsky take us places, imaginatively and intellectually, where other contemporary poets fear to go?

BILLY COLLINS

Because Collins began a term as poet laureate of the United States in 2001, students may want to know what the fuss is about—in other words, what distinguishes his work, and why he would be chosen from thousands of living American poets. Since newspaper reviews of Collins often use the word "accessible" to describe his verse, you could have a freewheeling discussion about accessibility as a virtue or a weakness in contemporary art and why it is that some critics use the term as a pejorative. Collins favors familiar words and opening situations, and his poems often begin with lines that suggest oral discourse rather than laboriously crafted verse. To discover where the poems change and complicate, students could do some core sampling, reading the first stanza and a stanza that comes much later in one of the longer poems ("Tuesday, June 4, 1991" and "Osso Buco" would work well for this) and speculate on the process by which the poem gets from here to there. Logic? Free association? Some complex intuitive process?

Questions for discussion:
- When you encounter poems like these in a tour through contemporary verse, a tour that involves many forays into the opaque, are you suspicious or disappointed when you read verse that you can understand, more or less, on the first or second reading?
- Compared to Rich or Graham or other contemporary poets, how does Collins dramatize the motions of the mind?
- If the language is not complex, and if the metaphors are easy to crack, is there a psychological complexity here that is worth our attention? How might we describe that?

MAX APPLE

"Bridging" comes from an errant subgenre of postmodern fiction, narratives that focus on the experience of being a hard-core fan of professional baseball. These novels, stories, and films stand out for reasons other than the subject they share: there's a strain of sentimentality here that seems to run counter to the anticorporate politics and inchoate cynicism that turn up so often in postmodern American writing. After the late sixties, as huge contracts, player strikes, drug scandals, and the sudden, frequent departure of beloved "home town" teams to far-away cities and fancier stadiums only confirmed Major League Baseball as an incorporated, ruthless entertainment enterprise, much of the box-seat enthusiasm among writer-fans shifted over to nostalgia. Baby-boom authors began to tell of bygone times "when it was still a game" and to proffer memories of Joe DiMaggio, Mickey Mantle, Whitey Ford, Hank Aaron, and other players of their own youth to generations that had seen these people only in occasional black-and-white photographs and film clips. Ray Kinsella, Donald Barthelme, Roger Angell, Don DeLillo, and many others have taken this track at one time or another. Psychologically and culturally, this might be an interesting phenomenon— adventures in vicarious masculinity and youth, for an aging generation of authors haunted by something—possibly the prospect of their own ineffectuality, or the rising futility of remembering in a fast-changing world, or even the futility of prose.

Questions for discussion:
- The introductory notes for "Bridging" tell us that the story is "obviously autobiographical" and that Jessica and Sam, the daughters in the narrative, are "as real as they can be." If that is so, what can we say are the author's personal objectives in writing this tale of family life?

- Ask a student to read aloud the paragraph on the top of page 2933, beginning "We both think about what might have been" and comment about it as a summary of an archetypal moment in fiction about domestic life, a close call with a love affair. Looking at the comparisons here and the implicit stage directions, discuss how effectively the moment is handled, and why it is here at all.
- "Bridging" is organized around oppositions, most obviously the father's masculine delight in baseball versus the daughters' rights of passage into Girl Scouts and young womanhood. Are there other symmetrical oppositions here to structure the story? How well do they work?

Gloria Anzaldúa

NAAL offers Anzaldúa in several roles—as polemical poet, writer of personal reminiscence, and editorialist on the problems of literary, linguistic, racial, and sexual identity. In "La conciencia de la mestiza" the personal alienation moves through layer after layer of complexity: the essay offers little hope that anyone in her predicament can shake off these constraining special traits and dive happily into some available group identity. Students may be puzzled by these sustained refusals and want to debate the importance of any single characteristic as a source of specialness or exile.

Questions for discussion:
- The essay moves back and forth between English and varieties of New World Spanish: what is suggested psychologically by these different voices in what purports to be nonfiction prose, a perspective from one writer?
- The end of the essay may draw attention as yet another invocation of nature and the earth as a source of redemption, consolation, welcome. Where have we seen this before?
- How does Anzaldúa arrive here, compared to how Thoreau arrives where he does in the final pages of *Walden*? And to how Whitman arrives where he does at the close of Whitman's "Out of the Cradle"?
- "How to Tame a Wild Tongue" offers sharp observations about the freedom and cross-pollination of Spanish in North America. How does that modern history compare to the history of American English, as celebrated by Whitman and Twain?

Sam Shepard

Ah, it's a jungle out there—or in the case of *True West*, it's a desert, with predatory coyote packs ready to pounce in the dark. Sam Shepard and David Mamet are currently the pillars of a tough-guy school of playwriting, featuring desperate men, blunt harsh language, and struggles for power, money, sexual dominance, the dynamics of a baboon troop in a postmodern and supposedly civilized setting. Because there are many recent films which explore (or exploit) similar themes—by Martin Scorsese, Clint Eastwood, Tommy Lee Jones, and Shepard and Mamet as well—your students may feel that they are on familiar ground here, and part of the challenge of teaching *True West* is de-familiarizing the play, discovering its variations from this pop culture mode.

If you have been doing a chronological course and have spent some time with literary naturalism at the turn of the twentieth century, you may have another initial point of reference, and possibly a stronger one, than the contemporary context. Literary historians like to arrange modes and movements and to assign them beginning dates and endings; but if your students remember an experience with Norris, Crane, Dreiser, Jack London, or other "golden age" American naturalists, you could begin by asking them about naturalism's return and the tonal and thematic kinship of Shepard and Mamet to work from a century ago.

But like the insistent stage directions for *True West*, the play's adornments of hard-core authenticity could be a deception or an enigmatic map for finding a different kind of "truth"—a psychological wilderness within one man's mind. Part of the fun of teaching the play, in other words, comes from raising the question of whether Lee and Saul and the returning mother are "really" there at all or only the figments of Austin's lonely and troubled imagination.

Questions for discussion:
- Beginning with Shepard's elaborate stage directions: observing that directors of plays commonly hate to be told by playwrights exactly what to do, what are the risks that Shepard is taking here, and why does he take them? Why does he take so much care about these details? Are there elements here that seem to slip out of the realm of absolute realism? What might they suggest to an audience?
- Read carefully the meticulous description of Lee and of Saul Kimmer in the list of characters, and try to imagine them exactly as Shepard describes them. If you were staging the play or making a film of it, what would such a "look" convey—not just about the fashion taste of these two characters, but the reality or surreality that we should see in them?
- In plays by Shepard and Mamet, longer speeches are sparse; and when they turn up, they focus our attention. Have a look Austin's lines (or soliloquy, perhaps) in Scene 8 (bottom of page 2291, beginning "I do, Lee. I really do. There's nothin' down here for me." How should they be understood? As a commentary on the loss of the "real" West to suburbia and domestication? An insight into Austin's grip on reality? Both?
- Why does the play end with a freeze-frame—in other words, with the brothers poised in a confrontation, rather than with some kind of resolution?
- Going back at least as far as the dramas of Eugene O'Neill, central characters have gained depth or complexity, in their presentation, from the context of family members. Over the course of *True West*, we learn that Austin's father and the mother are mentally unbalanced, that Lee is a misanthrope, a compulsive thief, and a liar, and possibly psychopathic. What might the implications be about Austin's sanity, especially as he sits in that room, trying to force his imagination to work?

Louise Glück

If Glück is read in a clear context, as a poet establishing one voice self-consciously amid a chorus of postmodern American verse and within a well-established and academically sanctioned poetry tradition, your students will probably have much better luck with her work than if she is read alone or in a scattering of American poets from the late nineteenth century into the late twentieth. Glück writes very much in the wake of other writers—Dickinson, Williams, Plath, and Lowell—but at the same time her strategy of not saying, of closing a poem with a mysterious and personal image or an emotion only partially expressed, achieves importance as a kind of resistance, as a rejoinder to the Lowell-Plath way of closing poems with a kind of crushing finality. To be mystical, Glück leaves things open-ended: hers is a kind of agnostic mysticism. Students may want to talk not only about the contextual specialness of her vision in comparison to contemporaries (Wilbur, Dickey, and Rich would work well for contrasts) but also about whether they find this kind of indeterminate spirituality convincing and sufficient as poetic discourse. In other words, Glück can be a very good mirror to the reading self, as it considers what it requires from contemporary poetry.

Alice Walker

Walker's depiction of her mother-daughter bond differs considerably from O'Connor's. While Mrs. Hopewell defines herself and her daughter by listening to the voices of conventional "good country people," the mother who narrates "Everyday Use" listens to her own inner voice and creates her own values.

Questions for discussion:
- How are Dee and Maggie different?
- What explains Dee's decision to rename herself Wangero?
- How do the quilt's values change for her and what do they mean to Maggie and the narrator?
- What does Walker mean by valuing "everyday use," even though the quilts may be, as Dee claims, priceless?

Annie Dillard

Pilgrim at Tinker Creek was a sensation when it came out more than thirty years ago, around the time of the first Earth Day and the vigorous adoption, especially on college campuses, of environmentalism as a serious cause. Tinker Creek is a place that's hard to find on anything but very detailed USCGS maps of Virginia; like Thoreau, who moved a mere mile out of Concord to look closely at life in and around a modest lake that no one had paid much attention to before, Dillard pays visits to this fairly typical Blue Ridge Mountain stream, not far from her home in Radford, to see things that usually go unnoticed—and in the NAAL selection she demonstrates her terrific eye for detail.

But Dillard also keeps an eye trained on an imaginative past, on the legacy of American nature writing that empowers her own work and also haunts it. Robert Frost famously observed that his poetry was "a lover's quarrel with the world"; Dillard can be opened as a lover's quarrel with Thoreau, Emerson, John Muir, Aldo Leopold, Frost, and other writers, most of them male, who continue to hold attention for powerful (and inevitably masculine) ways of seeing. If you're coming at Dillard after Emerson and Thoreau, you're in luck; if you're coming at her with Margaret Fuller and Emily Dickinson freshly in mind, you're in *more* luck—for Dillard, in this chapter, shows us her contribution to an alternative poetics that Fuller and Dickinson helped to pioneer: a complex and open-ended "quarrel" with the world as found.

Questions for discussion:

- One recourse—perhaps an obligation, really—of a contemporary writer writing about the natural environment is to bring something new to the experience: not just to see new places and details but also to bring fresh knowledge to the encounter. Read aloud the paragraph beginning "I walked home in a shivering daze" (top of page 3021). What do you find here, as mustered knowledge, that would not have been available to Emerson or Thoreau or Fuller, and what do these newer perceptions accomplish?

- The paragraphs about von Senden's accomplishments with cataract surgery and recovered sight, could be read as a rejoinder to Emerson's famous paragraphs in *Nature* about becoming a "transparent eyeball." Earlier, Dillard says "This looking business is risky." If this chapter is in some ways a dialogue with Emerson and the Transcendentalists, what are the differences in Dillard's thinking about "seeing?"

- There are "dark" sequences in this chapter, accounts of being outside as the light fades, and Dillard's mood grows darker as well. When Thoreau writes about the woods at night, where does he situate himself? Does Emerson show any interest in the natural world after sunset? What does Dillard accomplish here, by taking the observations and tone of her chapter in this direction?

ANN BEATTIE

Beattie's "Weekend" alludes to the film of the same name by Jean-Luc Godard, and what violence takes place in this New Yorker story takes place only in the language and as disjunction. Houseplants play a significant role in this story (the contemporary writer's concession to the loss of the external green world?), and Lenore projects and simultaneously contains her own violent fantasies when Beattie writes about her that she "will not offer to hack shoots off her plant for these girls." Otherwise, nothing happens in this story; Lenore, the "simple" character, asks Beattie's quintessential contemporary question, "Why do I let what go on?" Ask students how they interpret Lenore's statement that she is "simple." What does it mean to be simple in contemporary life? "It is true; she likes simple things." Yet Lenore's life and Beattie's "Weekend" are more complex than that. Does the word "simple" for Lenore allow her to defend against noticing the full extent of the lack of communication between her and George? "Weekend" presents a simple world of women, in which women are out of place; all of George's guests are "girls," and living with George without being married offers Lenore only the illusion of choice.

George joins a large list of contemporary characters who drink their way through their fictions, and as George drinks, Beattie shifts to passive voice: "another bottle has been opened." The point of the sentence seems to be that no one knows who has opened the bottle; agency unknown reflects the postmodern dysfunction.

Questions for discussion:

- How do students respond to Lenore's last action in the story, as she moves next to George on the couch?
- Beattie writes that Lenore leans her head on George's shoulder "as if he could protect her from the awful things he has wished into being." Lenore ends by giving George credit for wishing the existence of "awful things" in the world. Is this what Beattie means by "simple"? Does Lenore stay with George because she can attribute to him the agony of not being in touch?
- Because Lenore can listen to him teach that "there can be too much communication between people" and, therefore, not have to look too closely at herself, does "simple" mean attributing the state of the contemporary world to some other, human, agency, rather than focusing more clearly on the unknown agency of the passive voice?

DAVID MAMET

Students will find Mamet familiar territory for a number of reasons. Several of his plays and screenplays have been made into successful films, which have been available on video and DVD for years. *House of Games, Glengarry Glen Ross, The Verdict,* and others were box-office successes—to the extent that the Mamet style of hard-boiled language, laconic conversation, and unprincipled, ruthless action have been widely imitated in Hollywood films and television dramas. The proliferation of Mamet imitations, in fact, may cause students to wonder what is special about Mamet.

If you have been doing a chronological survey of the nineteenth century, then your students will recall the heyday of literary naturalism, and they will have no trouble seeing a relationship between Mamet's work and selections from Dreiser and Stephen Crane. You may want to have a freewheeling conversation about whether the usual dates assigned to naturalism (c. 1890–c. 1920) make sense at all, if naturalism went to the movies and entered pop literature and culture rather than gave way to other literary movements. You can also return to the dilemma raised by Norris: that a naturalistic narrative or drama isn't a breakthrough from art into truth but a mode that is stylized in a variety of different ways.

Have two students read, with some conviction, a page or two of dialogue from this play and see if they hear the odd cadences of a classic Mamet exchange—the repetitions, the little rituals that sometimes make his supposedly realistic characters seem to speak like creatures from some other planet. This will lead into broader speculations about whether the literary arts can ever, in any mode, represent things as they really are and human behavior as we really know it.

You can open some long-lasting perceptions if you come at this Mamet play comparatively—as a colder, more cynical reprise of Miller's *Death of a Salesman* or as a modernization of the themes in *Babbitt* or even *The Great Gatsby*. If you are feeling daring at this point in the course, you might ask about recent films that students have seen, films that seem somehow to borrow Mamet-type characters, speech patterns, and situations. You may hear about a number of films that you haven't seen, haven't heard of, or simply don't want to see: *Clerks, Chasing Amy, Pulp Fiction, Blue Velvet, The Comfort of Strangers*, and others that, as the students describe them, might astound you. But the conversation will be worthwhile if students become more aware of modern cross-pollination between the supposedly separate worlds of art and popular culture.

Yusef Komunyakaa

There is a unique voice here, and if you're doing a quick tour through contemporary writers at the end of the semester, Komunyakaa provides good reason to hit the brakes and look at these recent poems as *poems*, ambitious adventures with the English language and the accumulated and miscellaneous culture of the West. The danger in a fast flip through the later pages of any thick anthology, as I have said before, is that you'll come away with an impression of an array of contemporary representative "types"—personalities and ethnicities rather than conscientious artists who try to show us something new. With regard to Komunyakaa, it's important to read the entire set, as these selections provide a good introductory encounter with his reach: how much personal and collective experience he tries to bring to bear, the claim he lays to a poetic and cultural heritage extending far beyond his own region and immediate experience, and his courage in mixing it up.

Questions for discussion:
- Catullus, laudanum, Ariadne, and Son House blues—these are incongruous allusions: ancient Rome, nineteenth-century hallucinogenics, Greek mythology, and the Delta blues tradition. In what spirit, and with what effect, are they brought together in "When Dusk Weighs Daybreak"?
- What are the challenges of writing about the Vietnam Memorial, and how does Komunyakaa find his way through them, achieving a fresh perspective and a convincing voice as he looks at the names on the wall?
- There are very personal poems in this set, including "My Father's Love Letters," "Facing It," and "Nude Interrogation." Compare the tone, the

balance of "confession" and reserve that you find in these poems, and also compare this group, for the same qualities, to personal or confessional poems you may have encountered by Plath, Roethke, Robert Lowell, or Adrienne Rich.

Leslie Marmon Silko

At that point early in "Lullaby" at which Ayah does not want to think about her dead son, she thinks instead "about the weaving and the way her mother had done it." Craft defends against sorrow, for Ayah, and for Silko, who weaves the loss of Pueblo culture into Ayah's lullaby at the end of the story. Yet the promise passed down from generation to generation of Pueblo children from their mothers has been broken: "We are together always / There never was a time / when this was not so." Ask students to explore thematic similarities between Silko's story and others in Volume E of NAAL. Like Walker and Beattie, Silko also portrays the family in dissolution; however, Ayah has lost her children to the Bureau of Indian Affairs and to cultural assimilation with white people. It is not possible for her to reclaim them or to restore her sense of family. The loss of the possibility of family affects the relationship between Ayah and Chato, and Chato and many other Native American men in "Lullaby" turn to alcohol to numb their despair. Ayah does not drink; her experience makes the men afraid of her and to look at her "like she was a spider crawling slowly across the room."

Questions for discussion:
- Compare Ayah with the mother in Zitkala Ša's "Impressions of an Indian Childhood" and compare Zitkala Ša's portrait of the removal of Sioux children from their reservations with Silko's almost a hundred years later. What similarities and differences do they see?
- Ask students to examine the problems in the mother-daughter relationship that Walker portrays in "Everyday Use" when Dee also "emigrates" to another culture. How is this relationship different from the one in "Lullaby"?

Art Spiegelman

Including a set of panels from *Maus* is a bold new move by NAAL and sure to be controversial, as many readers and teachers may see this decision as a move away from firm dedication to literature as a medium of printed words. Ever since the waning decades of the nineteenth century, however, when chromolithography put vividly colored high-register images on the walls of ordinary American homes and new printing processes brought photographs into newspapers, magazines, and books, words and pictures have competed for our attention, often on the same page. We are a culture that looks and watches as well as reads, and we now have so much to take in and so much to forget.

Why would an American Jew create a long "comic book" about one of the most horrible chapters in the history of the twentieth century? Perhaps because *Maus* isn't about the Holocaust alone but also about telling and understanding and remembering. A dying generation must have its story told to, and by, a younger one; and in reaching that new generation, raised on television and movies and mounds of comic books, no holds are barred. There may be other considerations as well: sometimes mere words can seem to take too long to describe what needs to be recollected and told, and for those who listen and try to visualize, time and empathy are in short supply.

Questions for discussion:
- Because this is a graphic novel, we can start by just looking at it, as a visual experience, before moving into the narrative. Why are the images so stark and austere? Hundreds of graphic novels are in color: the technology is easy and there for the exploiting. Why these stiff figures, and black and white?
- In the opening panels of the excerpt, Spiegelman, as the son, comes on his father in the midst of a domestic spat and offers us a scene that is almost out of a sit-com: an old couple quarreling with each other about old and banal matters, threatening to break up when there's no real chance that they will do so or that any of this will change. What are the advantages and risks of including a scene like this?
- This selection from *Maus* focuses on the kind of story that might fade into the background in accounts of the Holocaust, a story about hiding in basements and barns, about taking chances in the streets of cities and villages. From the ordeal of the East European Jews there are tens of thousands of such stories. How might this kind of presentation resist the forgetfulness of history?

Julia Alvarez

As a writer of modern American prose, Alvarez is lively and unique. It's a testament to her skill that her work echoes and extends several important traditions. It's fairly easy to situate a narrative like ¡Yo! alongside Sui Sin Far, Abraham Cahan, and other authors who present the experience of immigrants, and the early, hard, and bewildering years of life in an American big city. But Alvarez's experimentation with style, her skill in creating, economically on the page, a voice that can strike the ear as distinct and rich with cultural experience, also recalls Mark Twain's *Adventures of Huckleberry Finn*. Breaking away from the convention of inflecting every word to represent an accent and a colloquial sound, Twain could flavor an entire paragraph by inserting an idiom only here and there, a touch of dialect. A good way to begin with Alvarez is to observe how she practices a similar art.

Questions for discussion:
- Ask a student to read aloud the second paragraph of the selection beginning with "I guess for each one in the family." If you hear a hesitation or two in the course of the reading, ask about these ripples, these variations from the conventional flow of American English. What

might they suggest about how this speaker sounds and about the depth of her immersion in this second language (English) and in American culture.

- The story of playing a bear and scaring the children into better behavior is the stuff of broad comedy. What are the effects of that story in making these people seem familiar to us and also, perhaps, setting them apart?
- Not long after, the chapter grows a bit darker: a gun hidden in the closet, the threat of raids and brutality by Trujillo's security police; and after the move to New York, the dangers of being shipped back to the dangers in the old home. How would you describe the overall tone of this chapter and the thematic consequences of commingling the light and the dark?

JORIE GRAHAM

Graham's long poem "The Dream of the Unified Field" offers an intense tour through Graham's major themes and her strategies as a poet. But because Graham's longer poems are adventures in intuitive connection, moving among personal experiences, cultural history, and many geographic locations, care should be taken when transforming her work into a classroom text. "The Dream of the Unified Field" is a labyrinth, an adventure in the labyrinth of the mind—and we need to assure students that getting lost is part of the experience of reading it. Students might feel a bit easier about making this journey if they have recently discussed some other long poems in NAAL, several of which echo here: Eliot's *Waste Land*, Lowell's "The Quaker Graveyard," Levertov's "September 1961," Wilbur's "The Mind-Reader," and Rich's "Snapshots of a Daughter-in-Law."

Questions for discussion:
- Compared to one or more of the aforementioned texts, how does Graham's poem move from one thought or memory to the next?
- The poem is in seven sections: what can we say about the breaks? Are the sections thematically or stylistically distinct?
- An intensely personal poem at many points, "Unified Field" ends with a long quotation—with additions and imaginative leaps—from the diary of Columbus, a document of encounter and conquest like those in the opening sections of NAAL. What is this doing here?
- Has this entire poem been about discovery, about wonder and concealed riches? Can we describe the relationship of this ending to the main body of the poem? We have "snow . . . coming down harder" in the opening lines, "downdrafts of snow" in the middle of part 2, a "midwinter afternoon" in part 5, and "blinding snow" at the very end?
- Should we consider the poem as woven together visually, like a vast painting?
- Are there other motifs and connections that draw it together? What kind of dominion does Graham achieve, here and in the other

representative poems, over her wide range of personal experience and literary and cultural education?

JOY HARJO

The first inclination of the class may be to talk about Harjo's prosody as a continuation or modernization of Native American songs and chants of the sort represented in Volumes A and B. This is a starting point, but you may want to help students see that there is a broad and paradoxical literacy behind and within Harjo's poems and that these poems, though private in their demeanor, speak to a varied audience. She is writing contemporary poetry in English; and like Kingston, Bambara, and others, she seeks to achieve a voice reflecting the totality of her experience as an American of mixed racial and cultural heritage.

Some questions to get the conversation moving can center on the variety in Harjo's prosody: do these variations reflect shifts in mood, subject, and voice? There is considerable emphasis on sound—as an effect but also as a subject. Talk, radio noise, church voices, sudden silences—all are accorded special eloquence and spirituality.

Question for discussion:
- Does a pattern of hopes and beliefs emerge among these poems? Or do they read as a preamble to a spiritual breakthrough rather than as a breakthrough in themselves?

RITA DOVE

The headnote for Dove suggests connections to the early work of Bishop, a poet known for meticulousness, craft, and an unsettling mix of detachment and passionate engagement in regard to her subjects. Students might want to compare "Banneker" to others works in which a poet imagines a figure from history—for instance, Kinnell on St. Francis, Sexton on Plath, Lowell on Jonathan Edwards, or Harper on Charlie Parker.

Questions for discussion:
- Ask your students to describe Dove's emotional presence in her own poems, especially in the endings of those poems.
- Why does she break the "Adolescence" reminiscence into several parts, rather than embrace the whole experience in one wide, passionate poem as Whitman or Ginsberg might?
- When she writes about Benjamin Banneker, what is her stake in that act of imagination?
- Why does she emphasize the mundane in Banneker's life rather than the Banneker one might find in the college history books?

ALBERTO RÍOS AND LORNA DEE CERVANTES

As Hispanic American writers, Ríos and Cervantes draw attention to the specialness of their cultural heritage—and one challenge in reading them,

especially at the end of an academic term, is not only recognizg the importance of that heritage but also seeing their work as interesting in ways that
extend in several directions. If you decide to read them together, you may
need to make clear that the intention is not to ghettoize, but to compare
experiments in form: Ríos is represented here by long poems that favor four-
stress and five-stress lines; Cervantes's poems seem quicker in their sound
and movement from one perception to the next. But Cervantes's "Visions of
Mexico While at a Writing Symposium in Port Townsend, Washington"
expands in ways that recall Whitman. Ask students to describe the overall
difference in the voice of these two poets—and to talk about moments when
each poet seems to rebel against his or her own patterns.

Question for discussion:
* Another rich subject for speculative conversation: the details from ordinary life that these poets focus on. Ask students to compile a quick list
of mundane objects and experiences that turn up in the work of these
poets and then to discuss what might be intended by these observations. An affirmation of a kind of citizenship, or commonality, with others within or beyond a minority community? A commentary on the
preoccupations of everyday life? A suggestion that something special
lurks just beneath the surface of the ordinary? Once you have gathered
a set of such speculations from your students, you might look for rever-
berations of other American poetic voices in the works of Ríos and Cervantes. Whom do they seem to have read and valued, and whom do
they reflect and quarrel with in their own verse?

AMY TAN

Because of her heritage and her favored subjects as a writer, Amy Tan can
be thought about as continuing and enriching a tradition extending back to
Sui Sin Far, the woman author who first wrote vividly about the Chinese-
American experience in the American West. If your class has read the Far
selections in NAAL, they will immediately feel the differences in how Tan
connects to the stories she tells. Far prefers the third-person voice, the bod-
iless and ostensibly impartial observer; Tan tells of Chinatown and these
families as a full participant in the action, and one of the obvious contemporary "American" dimensions to this excerpt is her sometimes playful,
sometimes rueful self-portrait as a rebel and a victim. In assuming that role
and tone she joins a big and raucous chorus of twentieth- and twenty-first-
century voices: Saul Bellow, Philip Roth, Julia Alvarez, Allen Ginsberg,
James Baldwin—the list goes on and on.

The mother's voice in heavy dialect, old-world, insistent, judgmental;
the daughter's voice colloquial, "like us," variously affectionate and
exasperated—to some of your students, this kind of pairing will probably
suggest another Asian-American woman voice that they know well: Margaret Cho, who also grew up in San Francisco, thriving in and fighting with
her own Korean heritage, and struggling—hilariously, in her stand-up comedy routines—to be herself rather than fit into any of an array of available

stereotypes. Students may want to contrast the poise and witty restraint of Amy Tan's voice to the sometimes outrageous anecdotes of Margaret Cho, as they each negotiate a personal and a family past.

Questions for discussion:

- There is a story within this story (pages 3159–61) that veers very close to cliché: the agonies of piano lessons, the anxieties and humiliations of recitals, and the demanding parent. How familiar is this kind of tale to your students—from other stories they have read or from personal experience? How does Tan breathe life into this classic (or trite) sequence from an American childhood?

- How do you read the final paragraph of the story, the account of the discovery that "Pleading Child" and "Perfectly Contented" are "two halves of the same song?" Does a line like that seem to whisper that the great crises are all resolved or that some deep wisdom has been apprehended? Has it? If not, how might we read these final lines, as another glimpse into the mind of the narrator?

Sandra Cisneros

Born and raised in a large family in Chicago, and with American academic training, Cisneros writes in English for an English-speaking audience, about a way of life that is in some ways between worlds: the experience of growing up Hispanic in various places in North America. She commonly writes from deep within that world, within the consciousness of her protagonist, whose sensory experiences and quick cultural and psychological responses and clauses can convey (at the outset) a sense that she does not really understand her own cultural situation. Cleofilas is a young woman in a small town—in Mexico, somewhere close to the Texas border, and she has lived her life in two "villages of gossips," small towns defined by disappointment: dull, low-paying jobs, exploitive, overbearing men, and the constrictions of a daily experience in which everyone's business is known by everyone else. How, then, does Cisneros's story become a document in the cultural history of the United States? We can put that large issue before a class at the outset and ask other, more manageable questions to get a grip on it.

Questions for discussion:

- One of the interesting quirks of the American realist tradition is that major works of fiction within it often focus on the ill effects of absorbing the wrong kind of fiction—romantic and sentimental fiction. *Huckleberry Finn* has much to suggest about the pernicious consequences of reading Walter Scott and Alexander Dumas; Henry James's Isabel Archer, heroine of his great novel *The Portrait of a Lady*, is impeded in her adventures in love and marriage because her expectations have been distorted by novels that she has read; William Dean Howells, in many ways the consummate American realist, often attacks sentimental fiction as a source of illusions and trouble. How does "Woman Hollering Creek" join that tradition? How are *telanovelas* influencing the hopes and expectations of people in this town?

- At the end of the story, Cleofilas is crossing the bridge over the arroyo. Has she changed? Will she change? What are her prospects as the narrative leaves her?

- In recent years there have been outbreaks of controversy relating to the works of Toni Morrison and Alice Walker with regard to their negative portrayal of men from their own communities. Is Cisneros liable to a similar charge here? How might you defend her on this issue?

- The essayist Richard Rodriguez often observes, wryly, that one erroneous cultural habit in the United States is to organize its own thinking into "east and west," rather than north and south—farther south than the Rio Grande. Extending this observation to Cisneros, what can we say about this story as an act of American cultural inclusion?

LOUISE ERDRICH

Erdrich is one of the most widely respected contemporary Native American writers; and the short story "Fleur" is packed with incident: violence, natural catastrophe, tense confrontations, and, at the center, a woman of mystery. So much is going on here that a reader can drift into an assumption that "Fleur" is an unspooling of personal experience, raw narration, whose only source—for event, character, and form—is Chippewa life in northern Minnesota. Part of the challenge of teaching Erdrich, therefore, is to encourage your students to see how highly literate a writer Erdrich is, "literate" not just in Native American lore, history, and contemporary experience but in techniques of modern American fiction, the predominantly white traditions of telling. Cather is here, and Faulkner, and O'Connor, and Hemingway, and many others as well—but to discuss Erdrich's implicit conversation with such other writers is not to present her work as ancillary to this tradition.

NAAL now includes several poems by Erdrich, and by reading them in company with "Fleur" your students can gain a stronger sense of the moods and perspectives that this writer favors. As a poet of the northern woods and prairies, she shows us natural and human experience mediated by cold air and reduced autumn and winter light. If there are outbreaks of anger here, they seem tempered by wind, snow, and a sense of long ages and passing time.

Questions for discussion:
- In looking into Erdrich's originality and understanding how her voice, by building on other voices, becomes her own, you might look at the long card game in the middle of the story, which can seem an extended calm. What is this episode doing there? What suspense does it create? What mysteries does it raise? What does it suggest about life in this place and the consolations and frustrations of living this way as woman or man?

- What about the final section of the story, the last paragraph block, which, like some closings in the tales of Joseph Conrad, seems to suggest that truth disappears under a cloud and that no amount of imagining or telling can ever recover it? If that's so, then what is the place of a story like this in the modern Native American tradition, and what does Erdrich's dialogue with her predominantly white audience accomplish?

- In the poem "Dear John Wayne," Erdrich follows a pattern seen in other Native American writers, directly addressing the legend or the ghost of a "cowboy" from popular culture. The final two lines might be puzzling and possibly controversial: they seem to refer to Wayne's death from cancer of the lung. What tone do you hear in them? Is it important to know that Wayne's final film, *The Shootist*, was about a gunfighter dying of lung cancer—in some ways a big-screen representation of his own terminal illness?

- The poem "I Was Sleeping Where the Black Oaks Move" quotes a couple of mystical phrases from a grandfather, explaining the ways of the natural world. How are those lines countenanced in this poem? As forgotten truth? Quaint foolishness? Something in between? If you hear mysteries invoked also in "Grief," in what spirit are they offered in this poem?

Cathy Song and Li-Young Lee

Once again, the value of thinking of these two Asian American poets together is to highlight their commonalities, their differences, and their complex and varied use of several traditions. Thanks to the popularity of haiku as a poetic form (and writer workshop exercise) through much of the past century, and of Japanese and Chinese prints as both art and decor in American galleries and hallways, Asian American poets may be linked, fairly or otherwise, to a tradition that is both a treasure and a burden.

Questions for discussion:
- That tradition of haiku is rich and subtle—but what are the dangers of echoing it or borrowing from it?
- If the canonical American tradition seems dramatically different from the Chinese or Japanese tradition in verse, what reconciliation or combinations are possible, without being typecast by a diverse contemporary audience?
- Ask students to compare two poems about solitude—Song's "The White Porch" and Lee's "Eating Alone." In each poem, what does each speaker describe herself or himself as being momentarily separated from? Family? Outsiders? The encumbrance of culture? What combination of separateness and connection are they yearning for in each poem?

Cluster: Writing in a Time of Terror: September 11, 2001

Even for the youngest students in our college classes, the experience of the 9/11 attacks is still fresh, kept so by a constant inflow of rebroadcast, dramatization, feature film, and retrospective commentary. The terrorist assault on the World Trade Center and Pentagon was the first American catastrophe seen by virtually everyone, in "real time" or something very close to it. For comparison: the slaughter at Gettysburg reached the American public as printed reports by correspondents, as engravings and lithographs in national journals, and as collections, in city galleries, of static black-and-white images made by Mathew Brady's photographers. Pearl Harbor came home as a spate of radio bulletins and a few minutes of grainy newsreel in the neighborhood movie theaters. But the destruction of the Twin Towers, caught "live" from every angle, was, and is, an avalanche of full-color trauma—and also an avalanche of words.

From the perspective of literature, 9/11 poses a responsibility and a challenge of several dimensions. With so many other ways of remembering, and with such a quick pileup of pontification and analysis in the press, in the bookstores, on line, and on film, what can be the cultural use of another poem or another essay? Immediately after such a morning, is a written response a sacred duty? A psychological compulsion? Some variety of usurpation or showing off? When national emotions are still running high, what useful or evocative originality is possible in a literary text—and how does the individual writer avoid exploitation of the event or self-indulgence? Our students have a stake in these questions, for all of them are continuing witnesses, and all of them face the predicament of reading and writing in a world inundated with response and of sorting out the honest and the original from the opportunistic and the canned. A class discussion about these issues can be especially lively and relevant.

Questions and issues for class discussion:

- Published almost three years after the attacks, the official *Report* from the National Commission is dispassionate, in keeping with the traditions and etiquette of documents that try to be definitive and exhaustive. In comparison, John Updike and several other writers published lengthy essays of evaluation and anguish in *The New Yorker* less than two weeks after 9/11, when the wreckage at the World Trade Center site was literally still hot. What vantage point does Updike begin with, and how does he close? Where and how does he address, directly or obliquely, the special challenge of this responsibility—to speak for us all? What do these introductory and closing paragraphs suggest about the personality and experience that Updike brings to the challenge of writing about a disaster seen firsthand?
- Ask students to read aloud portions of the poems in the cluster, searching again for tone, voice, and perspective. In which poems does the language seem mannered or affected—and which poems seem austere in their choice of words? Some of the poems are unmistakably about 9/11; others are more oblique. What is the effect of the obliqueness? Is it powerful understatement and an evocation of a shared memory? When a poem is published soon after a catastrophe, can subtlety seem coy or inappropriately "artsy"? Can it provide a new way of seeing when other ways seem exhausted?

- The cluster includes "On the Eve of Our Mutually Assured Destruction," published by C. D. Wright in 1986, and Naomi Nye's "Shoulders," published in 1994. Fifteen years before the attacks, Wright's poem refers directly to the Cold War strategy called "Mutually Assured Destruction," or MAD, in which each of the two superpowers, the United States and the Soviet Union, found some measure of safety in the knowledge that the adversary could not attack without suffering terrible losses. "Shoulders," in contrast, is a poem about the need for peace and makes no direct reference to geopolitical events. The cluster encourages us to read retrospectively, to consider the possible relevance of older poems to recent events. What is the aesthetic or psychological effect of reading Wright's poem and Nye's in this way? Does one poem seem fresher than the other? If so, why?
- In one of George Bernard Shaw's comedies, a professional critic says, "Tell me who wrote the play and I'll tell you how good it is." In an age of celebrity and notoriety, when the public image of an author can have a powerful effect (rightly or wrongly) on the valuation of his or her work, how does the fame of Updike, the relative obscurity of Wright and Nurske, the Vietnam-era affiliations of Ray, the New England pedigree and allusiveness of Galvin, or the minority ethnicity of Hahn and Nye influence the way you receive each work? With regard to these poems and essays, would you prefer to know less about the background and reputations of these writers—or more?
- With regard to 9/11, the end of the retelling, redramatizing, and response is nowhere in sight. How do you think the texts in this cluster will hold up as so many others accumulate in our libraries and archives?

Richard Powers

Powers has become famous as a master of the postmodern "novel of ideas," but unlike other writers of that sort he offers plausible and compelling characters and real emotional impact. Thoughtful and intensely literate (more about that intensity below), he takes us into dilemmas that haunt the enterprise of the course you are teaching, and he explores the complex underlying hope that the arts, imaginative experience, a reading of the "greats" in NAAL or out beyond it provides any kind of genuine wisdom, or even viable delusions to help us move through the turmoil and knowledge storms of contemporary life.

The only drawback I can think of to reading Richard Powers is that his breadth of curiosity and knowledge embarrasses nearly everything else you'll find on the jammed shelves of postmodern fiction. None of the narcissism and claustrophobia of the "little" story, the narrow personal experience pumped up suspiciously to signify something more; no parochial assumptions that a stack of literary texts, and a stack of laborious commentary on those texts, constitute an education worthy of the name. Powers believes deeply that the work of the novelist is to bring a reading public into hard thought about brute facts and discoveries that rarely cross the street into the humanities, neighborhoods, and that thinking about the human condition can no longer continue in the old tracks and pathways. New ways of telling are needed as well. The opening line of his novel *Galatea 2.2* is "*It was like so, but wasn't*"—and what follows that line is a narrative that blends truth with contemplations and imaginings that are one short step away. Did Mimi Erdmann, in "The Seventh Event," really exist? Well, no. Obviously she's something of an eponym, and even a pun: Erdmann, after all, means "earthman," and "Mimi" rings of the "me! me!" self-centeredness that this (sort of) fictitious cultural critic, and Powers along with her, struggle to transcend. The first name also suggests that the "me" we're listening to is Powers himself, that Erdman is a projection of his own thoughts or a side of himself.

But so what? The core issue that you might want to pursue with regard to this complex and fascinating semifactual semi-autobiographical work of fiction, or whatever it is, is how much is at stake here, and how well this kind of writing achieves those objectives.

Questions for discussion:
- From a glance, the story seems to be arranged backward. The title is "The Seventh Event" and the parts begin with "Six" and move down to "One." What's going on here?
- Over the course of the story, several direct quotations from Mimi are set off in a small font. There are other quotations in the same font from real flesh-and-blood authorities on various subjects: John Muir, Rilke, John Burdon Haldane, John Maynard Keynes. Take a step back from the whole group and talk about how we, as readers, contemplate quotations from sages as they come at us. In other words, how do we receive and assemble these bits of wisdom and pseudowisdom that come at us all the time?
- One of Mimi's strongest indictments of thinking in the humanities is found in the paragraph at the bottom of page 3222, beginning with the line "Criticism, she claimed, had treated American literature's centuries-long obsession with wildness. . . ." If there never was a Mimi Erdmann, how should we read this paragraph? As an evasive indictment from Richard Powers? As some other voice that we should attend to? If we listen, what are the consequences?
- With regard to our ability, as human beings, to imagine our situation, expand our awareness, and generally "think different," is this a hopeful story, or a pessimistic one?

WILLIAM T. VOLLMANN

Because Vollmann's "Red Hands" defiantly refuses to add up, and because its form seems to thrash and dodge on the page, your students might want to talk about the explicit resistance to form here and question of whether the narrative arrives anywhere. In keeping with the contrarian elements of "Red Hands," you might try reading the front and the back of the story together first, speculating your way toward the center.

Questions for discussion:

- The story ends with an ironic-sounding juxtaposition of a department store bombing, an act of terrorism, with the death of a mouse in a laboratory. The story was written in 1989. In light of September 11, 2001, what has happened to this attempt at irony?

- In the opening paragraph of the story there's line reminiscent of Hemingway, a pontification on human nature, phrased much as Hemingway would phrase it: "It is sometimes a hard thing to be a man and stand by the thing that you have done. He would have liked someone to take him out of the wind, but no one is supreme enough to do it." How do these lines work to establish our sense of the narrator, and his own sense of himself?

- There are chapters of this story that are only a few lines in length, but there is also a huge paragraph in chapter 5, beginning on page (3235) and extending all the way to page (3236). Why aren't there any breaks here? What is your sense of Vollman's decisions, or intuitions, about when to be stunningly brief in telling a part of a story and when to go on and on?

SHERMAN ALEXIE

One standard way to relegate Native Americans to secondary status in our collective cultural life is to confine them to a realm of nostalgia, to regard them as a people of the past; another strategy is to represent them as a people static and apart, untouched by or essentially oblivious to the action that rocks the world of everyone else. Just as Sherman Alexie's subjects rove far beyond sweat lodges and kivas and kachinas, his literary echoes and quarrels aren't limited to the reservation either. He shows us Native Americans living in the world, and he does so with literary voices that lay claim to much larger territory.

Questions for discussion:

- Starting with two of the poems, "Sister Fire, Brother Smoke" and "Crow Testament," look at the forms, listen to the voices, and think back through your own experience with Anglo-American poetry. "Sister Fire, Brother Smoke" is written in terza rima, a form that dates back to the Renaissance, a form that British and American modernists experimented with (including Dylan Thomas, whose famous opening line from a terza rima poem, "Do not go gentle into that good night," supplies the title for an Alexie story in the NAAL selection). Why might Alexie choose that old, confined, and thoroughly European form to work with here? Flip back to Wallace Stevens's "Thirteen Ways of Looking at a Blackbird" and read it alongside "Crow Testament." What echoes do you see and hear, and what do they suggest to you?

- Try reading "Marilyn Monroe" and "The Exaggeration of Despair" alongside poems by the Beats and other open-form poets of the fifties and sixties that your class may have looked at, especially shorter poems by Allen Ginsberg, Galway Kinnell, and James Wright. How does Alexie borrow from such voices, and how does he use them to establish a poetic voice of his own?

- The short narrative "Do Not Go Gentle" moves into dangerous country for a contemporary fiction writer of any background: developing contrasts between the Old Ways and the white man's New Ways, the story has to dodge sentimentality, powerless indignation, and cliché. Indians in a hospital, struggling against bureaucratic authority and scientific mystery: as a white man playing Indian, Ken Kesey has already tramped these sanitized hallways, and *One Flew Over the Cuckoo's Nest* may haunt any subsequent attempt, even by an actual Indian, to come in afterward. Try reading "Do Not Go Gentle" as a work of balance, of fine distinctions, complex observations—contrasted, perhaps, to the over-the-top dramatics of *Cuckoo's Nest,* if your students know that work. Where do you see these strategies of balance and modulation by Alexie, and how do they parallel or illuminate his skills and fine-tunings in other works in this set?

JHUMPA LAHIRI

"Sexy" is an easy and enjoyable work of postmodern fusion—not only of East and West, but also of the literary and the pop. Very quickly your students will figure out where they are, at least with regard to the mass-culture cousins of this story. Young women working in urban settings far away from home; chance encounters with enigmatic dark men and subsequent affairs, equally enigmatic; secrets in the cubicle next to you at the office; precocious children who spill the beans on the love life of parents—the lineaments of "Sexy" will recall, for your students, television shows like *Sex in the City* and *Desperate Housewives,* or *telenovelas* on Spanish-language cable channels, or any number of soaps and romance novels about love in the metropolis.

You might want to air these connections early in the discussion, to assure that your group understands that you're not wonderstruck by tropes and archetypes that they encounter out of class all the time, and to build a firm footing for launching into Lahiri's variations on standard themes. Good questions can put the story into bold relief against this background.

Questions for discussion:
- Lahiri herself is Bengali in her origins and Dev and Laxmi are Bengali as well—but the story is told from the point of view of Miranda, who is a white American from somewhere in Michigan, a woman who has been out of the United States only once. Why tell the story from her point of view? How convincing is Lahiri in assuming that perspective?
- To help situate Lahiri in an American literary tradition, you might read or circulate to the class the final paragraph of Hemingway's "A Very Short Story" or have them glance at the final page of "Babylon Revisited." How can we describe the mood of "Sexy's" ending? What seems to be unspoken in these final sentences?
- The visit to the "Mapparium" in Boston is fraught with symbolic implications. What are they, and how well does the scene work?

CHAPTER 12

Examination Questions and Essay Topics

In previous chapters, the teaching notes offer questions that can be adapted as writing topics. Similarly, the exam questions and essay topics offered in this chapter can work well as subjects for class discussion. Our intention here, however, is to suggest questions that encourage students to venture beyond the normal range of classroom presentations and conversations and to try their hand as individual readers and thinkers.

Within each historical period, the exam and essay questions are organized into two groups. "General Questions" addresses literary, historical, and genre connections among texts and authors. "Questions about Individual Authors and Works" focuses on the interpretation of specific texts and includes problems and topics that either situate these texts within their own literary traditions or promote comparisons across traditions.

Volume A: Beginnings to 1700

General Questions

1. The earliest literary works we have from this period, the Native American creation stories and trickster tales, come down to us in translation, and from cultures and times that can seem remote. Are there advantages to reading the creation stories as *one* narrative? What about the trickster tales? Write an essay about the value and drawbacks of combining the stories as we think about them and of seeing them as separate and distinct from one another.

2. Write an essay contrasting the Pima Stories of the Beginning of the World with creation stories from Egyptian, Greek, Chinese, or Norse mythology. Compare the mysteries that are explored by these stories and the emphasis they place on the importance of human beings in the larger scheme.

3. Most of these Native American narratives are received as anonymous works—attributed to a people rather than to a single author and historical moment. Most of the accounts by European voyagers and colonizers, however, have names and dates attached and often center on the adventures and thoughts of one author. Write an essay about these differences—the ownership of narrative, the concern with time—and how they might connect to different ways of perceiving the American landscape.

4. Wayne Franklin calls the period of European discovery and encounter a "many-sided process of influence and exchange." He also writes that "much of what was new . . . came about through struggle rather than cooperation." Choose either statement and write a short essay in which you comment on its accuracy by citing references to specific writers and narratives included in the period.

5. The period introduction discusses the purposes of European colonization. Referring to at least two of these purposes, describe how they are reflected and varied in individual texts from the time.

6. Much of the literature of encounter and discovery includes inventories of one kind or another. Choose inventories from three of the writers we have read, and describe what these inventories imply about the author's values and his conception of the New World and its inhabitants.

7. Choose several significant moments of encounter from different narratives included in this section, and describe the different perspectives from which Europeans and native peoples view each moment.

8. Research the myths of Doña Marina and Pocahontas and report on their cultural survival in Mexico and North America.

9. Viewing the encounters as moments of communication, interpret how each side views the other and what messages they convey in their own behavior. Ground at least part of your reconstruction in a reading of the Stories of the Beginning of the World.

10. Describe some of the central principles of Puritan ideology and illustrate their significance in specific literary works. Choose from among the following: (1) New World consciousness, (2) covenant theology, (3) typology, (4) innate depravity, and (5) irresistible grace.

11. Trace the connection between the Puritan reliance on written covenant, as in "[The Mayflower Compact]," and their uneasiness in their literature regarding personal vision.

12. Compare Bradford's metaphors to Morton's. Why does Morton resort to a different trove of analogies than Bradford does? What do these choices say about their temperaments and belief systems?

13. Identify and discuss literary texts that reveal stresses on Puritanism or that illustrate schisms within Puritan and colonial consciousness.

14. Describe the contrast between the personal and the didactic voice in Puritan and early colonial literature.

15. Trace the power of the written convenant in colonial and early American literature, beginning with "[The Mayflower Compact]."

Questions about Individual Authors and Works

Native American Stories of the Beginning of the World

1. Locate and read other Native American creation stories and discuss them in light of the Iroquois and Pima stories included in NAAL.

2. The Judeo-Christian accounts of the beginning of the world place emphasis on a grand design and purpose and on an essential order in the natural world. Do these Native American creation stories put similar importance on the centrality of humankind and on an overall plan? Where do you see similarities and differences in regard to this theme?

Native American Trickster Tales

1. Write about the concept of the trickster as a way of explaining or imagining the natural world. Is the trickster malevolent, an embodiment of evil? How is the landscape around the storyteller and listener transformed or energized by imagining the trickster as an abiding presence?

2. Write an essay in which you imagine the intended audience of these tales, and compare their culture-based expectations to those of a specific storyteller from the European tradition: Bradford, Mather, or some other white writer who narrates with a specific purpose and to a particular culture.

3. There are comic moments in these tales; but comedy and fear are often closely connected—sometimes we laugh at things that in some dimension frighten us. What might be frightening about these tales? What in the cosmology of the Native American teller and listener might be threatening about the trickster and the trouble he causes?

4. Write an essay about the mingling of irreverence and the sacred in two of these narratives. What does the bawdiness accomplish? Is it comic relief as in a Shakespeare drama or other European-style narrative? Or does the mingling of the irreverent, the scatological, and the sacred work in a different way?

Christopher Columbus

1. Discuss how Columbus's expectations, "thinking that I should not fail to find great cities and towns," reflect the contrast between European ideas of greatness and a more indigenous perspective on "great" civilizations in the New World.

2. Despite the fact that this material is translated and that five hundred years have passed since Columbus's voyages, can you discern a voice here or an imaginable personality? What moments in his letters give you those clues?

BARTOLOMÉ DE LAS CASAS

Write an essay about the moral outrage which Casas shows in his *Very Brief Relation*. Where is it grounded? Is it based in a traditional faith? In a kind of secular or nonsectarian humanism? Look at the details that he offers and the adjectives he uses, and try to describe his moral position.

ÁLVAR NÚÑEZ CABEZA DE VACA

Focusing on the texts of Cabeza de Vaca and Días del Castillo, write an essay that brings into focus the lives of native women in North America.

THOMAS HARRIOT

Locate moments in Harriot in which his intentions seem to be in conflict as he reports of the encounter between the English and Native Americans.

JOHN SMITH

1. The settlement of the Middle Atlantic lands is often contrasted with the settlement of Massachusetts Bay: the Virginia colonies are described as secular and materialistic in their purposes, rather than religious and spiritual. Where are the indications of Smith's motives and aspirations as he describes the Jamestown area to an English audience? What specifically excites him about the prospect of colonies in this region?

2. Near the beginning of the excerpt from the Third Book, Smith writes: "Such actions have ever since the world's beginning been subject to such accidents, and everything of worth is found full of difficulties, but nothing [is] so difficult as to establish a commonwealth so far remote from men and means and where men's minds are so untoward as neither do well themselves nor suffer others." What is he talking about? What assumptions is an observation like that based on? Can you think of modern intercultural misunderstandings that parallel the problem that Smith believes he is facing here?

3. At the end of the excerpt from the Third Book, Smith writes, "Thus you may see what difficulties still crossed any good endeavor; and the good success of the business being thus oft brought to the very period of destruction." Locate other passages in which Smith expresses his concern for the reputation of the business endeavor in which he is engaged or in which he uses metaphors from the world of work or business to describe his activities.

WILLIAM BRADFORD, THOMAS MORTON, AND JOHN WINTHROP

1. Write an essay comparing these three writers as literary stylists. What are the stylistic qualities that make Morton the odd man out in this group?

How can we differentiate Bradford and Winthrop from each other as Puritan writers?

2. Write an essay describing the Winthrop legacy in American public discourse, especially the president's Inaugural Addresses, State of the Union Addresses, and other speeches to the American nation. Find three recent addresses and compare their style and content to Winthrop's "A Model of Christian Charity."

Anne Bradstreet

1. Write a close reading of a single lyric poem. Depending on how much analysis you have already done in class, choose from among the following: "The Prologue," "The Flesh and the Spirit," "The Author to Her Book," "Here Follows Some Verses upon the Burning of Our House," and "As Weary Pilgrim."

2. Describe a sequence of stanzas from "Contemplations" and discuss the thematic and stylistic relationship between these stanzas and the entire poem.

3. Compare the imagery of "To My Dear and Loving Husband" with Taylor's "Huswifery." How does the imagery characterize each poet's work?

4. Discuss the extent to which Bradstreet's poetry reflects Puritan thinking. Analyze in particular the way Bradstreet reflects her own spiritual and metaphysical fears in the process of describing an actual event in "Here Follows Some Verses upon the Burning of Our House."

5. Describe the tonal and rhetorical differences among Bradstreet's three elegies for her grandchildren, and suggest reasons for these differences.

Michael Wigglesworth and Edward Taylor

1. Adapted from John Stuart Mill, a familiar assumption about poetry holds that "Rhetoric is heard; poetry is overheard." Compare the voices of Wigglesworth and Taylor. Does the distinction apply to either or both of these poets? Write an essay comparing the publicness and privateness of Wigglesworth and Taylor, and describe how their different intentions are reflected in their verse forms, imagery, and rhetorical style.

2. The first generations of New England Puritans are often remembered as people who favored plain speech and simple design. Write an essay about *The Day of Doom* as a Puritan poem—in its subject and also in its voice.

3. Write a close reading of any of the poems from *Preparatory Meditations*. Identify the central metaphor or series of related metaphors and describe the process by which Taylor develops each metaphor into an address to his own salvation.

4. If you have studied English Metaphysical poets (especially Donne, Jonson, Herrick, or Herbert), choose an interesting poem by one such poet and compare its theme and structure to a similar poem of Taylor's.

5. Discuss Taylor's use of objects from the natural world or of secular experience in "Upon Wedlock, and Death of Children"; "Upon a Wasp

Chilled with Cold"; or "A Fig for Thee, Oh! Death" and examine the relationship in the poem between earthly life and spiritual salvation.

6. Discuss the extent to which Taylor's poetry reflects specific concepts of Puritan theology.

Mary Rowlandson, Cotton Mather, and Robert Calef

1. In Rowlandson's *Narrative*, locate three passages that seem to vary or conflict in portraying her view of her captors. Write an essay discussing and accounting for these differences.

2. Rowlandson and Mather, following a Puritan pattern of thought, attribute certain worldly events to Divine Will or supernatural causes. Compare passages in which such attributions are made, and make distinctions about their thinking and their rhetorical style.

3. Write an essay about Robert Calef's "More Wonders" as a document within the New England Puritan tradition, rather than as a rejection of those values. What principles carry over into his indictment of Mather's argument?

Cluster: "A Notable Exploit": Hannah Dustan's Captivity and Revenge

1. Write an essay about the effects of intermediating time on perceptions of one historical event. What changes in cultural circumstances, in New England, might account for the differences among these accounts, especially between nineteenth-century accounts and ones closer to Dustan's lifetime?

2. Which of these six references to Dustan and her exploit are most surprising to you, and why? If you were selecting one or two of these passages as best representing this history, which ones would you choose—and why?

Volume A: American Literature 1700–1820

General Questions

1. Identify the literary forms available to eighteenth-century American writers. What limited their choice? How did they invent within these forms?

2. Describe some important differences between Puritan thinking and eighteenth-century deist thinking, and discuss literary works that illustrate these differences.

3. Describe the way the concepts of the self and of self-reliance develop and find expression in American literature of the eighteenth century and the Revolutionary period. Identify those specific figures or works that you see as significant and explain their contributions.

Questions about Individual Authors and Works

Sarah Kemble Knight and William Byrd

1. By modern standards, or even those of the nineteenth century, these travel writers do not travel far. Compare ways in which Knight and Byrd emphasize the oddness or otherness of the places they visit and how each traveler affirms the values and practices of home.

2. Write an essay in which you compare Byrd's *The Secret Diary* with a work by any of his New England contemporaries. What relationship does Byrd assume between the private and the public self? Between the worldly and the religious self? How do those relationships contrast with ones you see in major Puritan writers?

Jonathan Edwards

1. People often see "A Divine and Supernatural Light" as coming from a completely different sensibility than does "Sinners in the Hands of an Angry God." Do you agree? Do these works resonate with one another in any important way? Do they give indications of coming from the same theology and individual mind?

2. Discuss Edwards's manipulation of biblical language in "Sinners in the Hands of an Angry God." What specific transformations does he perform? And how does his use of language in the "Application" section of the sermon differ from and comment on the earlier doctrinal section?

3. Edwards and Franklin were contemporaries. Explain, with specific references to their works and more general comments on their ideas, why this fact might seem startling.

4. Write a brief comparative analysis of form and function in Taylor's poems and Edwards's sermons. Describe how each of these Puritans tried to demonstrate, or even "prove," in Edwards's case, spiritual salvation and how each associates being saved with finding the right language.

Benjamin Franklin

1. Explain why the eighteenth century was called the Age of Experiment and consider the relevance of this term as a description of Franklin's writing.

2. Evaluate metaphors that Franklin uses in Poor Richard's maxims in "The Way to Wealth." Count and categorize the metaphors; summarize your findings. What are their origins and how does he use them?

3. What is the "religion" Franklin "preaches" to his readers in Father Abraham's speech? How do you explain Franklin's use of religious metaphors in his writing?

4. Discuss several permanent contributions Franklin made to American life, ranging from the practical to the ideological.

5. Choose any single section or aspect of *The Autobiography* as the basis for analysis. Or contrast Franklin's choice of focus in its four parts; consider

the significance of his choice to address the book to his son; read closely the letters that begin "Part Two" and comment on their significance to *The Autobiography* as a whole; discuss Franklin's various practical attempts to alter his moral character.

6. Following notes from class discussion, explain the various ways in which Franklin's *Autobiography* may be seen as "self-invention."

7. How does the latter half of *The Autobiography* compare with the opening chapters with regard to essential themes? Which half seems more modern to you, and why?

JOHN WOOLMAN

Compared to Edwards's *Personal Narrative*, Woolman's *Journal* pays more attention to ordinary experience: family, town life, the details of growing up. How does Woolman give importance to these details? Why would they matter to him but not to Edwards? Choose two paragraphs from Woolman and two from Edwards, and compare them for language use and rhetorical style. Like the Puritans, the Society of Friends emphasized simplicity in ordinary life and personal deportment. Why then the differences in vocabularies and sentence structure?

SAMSON OCCOM

1. In his account of his life, Occom writes from two perspectives: as a minister and as a member of a minority group in the larger culture. Do these perspectives come into conflict in his narrative? Where and how?

2. Occom's narrative has come back into print only recently. In your opinion, what is the best way to read it: as a stand-alone work or as a work that converses with or responds to other autobiographies and personal narratives of the eighteenth century? If you feel that the work stands alone, then offer a close reading to support your position. If you see it as part of a conversation, then choose another autobiographical account and show how that dialogue enriches the reading of both authors.

J. HECTOR ST. JOHN DE CRÈVECOEUR

1. Witnessing slavery firsthand leads Crèvecoeur to lament the "strange order of things" in Letter IX from *Letters from an American Farmer*. How does he reconcile his view of slavery, and of the great contrast between lives of plantation owners and slaves in Charles-Town, with his portrait of America as a place where humankind can be renewed?

2. Crèvecoeur was one of the first writers to see America as a place where dogmatic disputes and sectarian violence could be permanently overcome—not by other idea systems but by the landscape and life within it. Describe his argument, the evidence he offers, and the European historical experience that he turns to for contrast.

3. Compare Woolman's and Crèvecoeur's understanding of "strangers" and their place in "American" society.

JOHN ADAMS AND ABIGAIL ADAMS

1. Compare one of Abigail's letters to John with one of Bradstreet's poems to her husband, "absent upon public employment." How are sentiments expressed and constrained in both of these texts?

2. The letters that pass between John and Abigail offer us a private view of the writing and signing of The Declaration of Independence. Examine the hopes these writers have for independence and describe those that are not explicit within the document itself.

3. How do the Adams letters reflect values in transition—changes that would reverberate in nineteenth-century American public and cultural life?

THOMAS PAINE

1. If Thomas Paine had written the opening paragraphs of the Declaration of Independence, what would they sound like? Experiment with writing those paragraphs in Paine's voice; then compare them to Jefferson's and explain the differences.

2. Paine and Franklin were both ardent believers in an "Age of Reason," but what differences in temperament do you sense between these two thinkers, as proponents of reason and logic?

THOMAS JEFFERSON

1. Write an essay about similarities you see between the rhetorical strategy of The Declaration of Independence and sermons, speeches, and public discourse from the American Colonial period.

2. Based on class discussion, recapitulate the ways The Declaration of Independence uses rhetorical style to achieve its power.

3. Describe the evidence of Franklin's interests in "self-invention" in *The Autobiography* and suggest ways in which Jefferson, with the assistance of Franklin, carries these interests into the political sphere of The Declaration of Independence.

4. Write about the rhetorical strategies used in the antislavery grievance from The Declaration of Independence, a section that the Continental Congress eliminated from its final version.

5. Describe the ways in which Franklin and Jefferson reflect the legacy of Puritan thinking.

OLAUDAH EQUIANO

1. Equiano's prose style is powerful. Choose one or two paragraphs and write an essay about the ways in which he structures his sentences, chooses analogies, and selects vocabulary. At times his prose is highly formal, even ornate. Why? How might his style reflect his situation, or predicament, as a writer?

2. For many years, Equiano lived in a paradoxical condition: as a slave in North America and virtually as a free man on his voyages and sojourns abroad. Do you see this strangeness reflected in the personality that he

constructs in his *Narrative* and in the language and style with which he writes it?

3. Reread in the early chapters of Bradford's *Of Plymouth Plantation* the portrait of life aboard the *Mayflower* with Equiano's account of life aboard the slave ship. Consider the various meanings different colonial authors attribute to the word *removal*.

CLUSTER: WOMEN'S POETRY: FROM MANUSCRIPT TO PRINT

1. Write an essay comparing poems by two of these writers, with special attention to elements of privacy or intimacy in the poems.

2. For you, what are the essential differences between private and public literary discourse? With reference to these poets, comment on how much we should respect the original intentions of writers when gathering their work into anthologies or other publications.

JUDITH SARGENT MURRAY

1. Write an essay about the different tones of voice you hear in "On the Equality of the Sexes." Where and how do you see these different tones established, and what is the overall effect of this variety on the essay?

2. Write an essay about the strengths and peculiarities of the epistolary novel, centering on Murray's use of this strategy in *Miss Wellwood*.

PHILIP FRENEAU

1. Although Freneau's "To Sir Toby" is ostensibly about a sugar planter on the island of Jamaica, examine the poem for evidence that Freneau is also writing about southern slavery. Locate references to slavery in his other anthologized poems and summarize the way slavery, for Freneau, contradicts eighteenth-century principles of reason and human rights.

2. Evaluate the language of Freneau's historical poems in comparison to specific passages in Paine or Jefferson, and speculate on the relative effectiveness of political and poetic voices within the context of American revolution.

PHILLIS WHEATLEY

1. Locate and discuss imagery in Wheatley's poems that directly or indirectly comments on her experience as a freed slave.

2. In the Wheatley poems that address others—students, General Washington, a painter, the earl of Dartmouth—how does Wheatley present herself? How does she create or suggest a personality within the formal context of these poems?

3. Should Wheatley's poetry be considered an important point of origin for African American verse? Why or why not? Can you talk about specific qualities or moments in Wheatley's poems to support your position?

Royall Tyler

1. How seriously should we take *The Contrast* as a social commentary? Write an essay about ways in which the play asserts itself as imbued with serious themes—and ways in which it undercuts or limits those implications.

2. Where does the legacy of *The Contrast* turn up in contemporary comedies, on either the stage or the screen? Select two of these recent plays or films and compare specific characters or plot situations to similar elements of Tyler's play.

Hannah Foster and Tabitha Tenney

1. Write an essay comparing *The Coquette* and *Female Quixotism* as works of suspense.

2. Write an essay comparing these novels as commentaries on gender roles in the early Republic.

Volume B: American Literature 1820–1865

General Questions

1. Why were the American landscape and political experiment especially suited to a flowering and transformation of European-style Romanticism? What problems did artists and writers face in adapting English romantic themes and tropes to the American scene?

2. Discuss the following statement with reference and relevance to specific literary works: The Puritans were typological, the eighteenth-century writers were logical, but the early-nineteenth-century writers were analogical in their way of knowing and expressing what it means to be an American.

3. Discuss changes in the concept of the American self in the early nineteenth century. Locate your discussion within specific works by Sedgwick, Bryant, Emerson, Thoreau, Hawthorne, and Melville.

4. Cite some key differences between early-nineteenth-century writers and their eighteenth-century predecessors. Focus on the concept of self-invention and, in specific literary works, discuss the early-nineteenth-century evolution of this concept.

5. Examine the work of one or more American Romantic and nineteenth-century painters (Thomas Cole, Albert Bierstadt, George Caleb Bingham, George Inness, Frederic Church), and discuss stylistic and thematic similarities that you see between the work of these painters and literary works of the period.

6. Consider literary portraits of women engaged in heroic struggle or of escaping slaves portrayed as heroic fugitives. Compare portraits by Stowe, Fuller, Jacobs, and Douglass with Hester Prynne in *The Scarlet Letter* or Thoreau's autobiographical narrator in *Walden*.

7. It may be possible to sort major writers of this period into two groups: those who advance particular doctrines and systems of thought, and those who question or critique those doctrines or who suspect any systematic or totalizing view of the world. Which of these writers seem to you most interested in arriving at some coherent view of experience? Which are temperamentally more interested in questioning such coherent views—and the possibility of seeing the world through what Fitzgerald would later call "a single window"?

8. American realists made different choices of language and genre than did their contemporaries and immediate predecessors. Write about a text by any of the following authors and explore elements of realism in their work: Stowe, Stoddard, and Davis.

Questions about Individual Authors and Works

WASHINGTON IRVING

1. What kind of relationship does Irving suggest between himself and the stories that he tells? Look at the end of "The Legend of Sleepy Hollow," and write an essay about how Irving offers his story to the American public. Why do you think Irving takes the stance that he does?

2. Compare Freneau's and Irving's uses of the historical situation as the subject of imaginative literature.

3. Discuss several different ways in which "Rip Van Winkle" addresses versions of the American Dream.

4. Compare Rip Van Winkle with Franklin's Father Abraham in "The Way to Wealth." What do the two have in common?

5. "Rip Van Winkle" is an early work that casts the American woman as the cultural villain. Analyze the character of Dame Van Winkle in the story and discuss the significance Irving attributes to her death.

6. What happens if we try reading "The Legend of Sleepy Hollow" as an allegory—about city ways and country ways, about common sense and "education"? Is that pushing the story too far for the sake of literary analysis? If the story does work as an allegory, in what spirit is it offered?

JAMES FENIMORE COOPER

1. In the Leatherstocking Tales (of which *The Pioneers* is one novel) Cooper is often said to be doing the traditional cultural work of an epic writer: helping a new culture to lay claim to an ancient or dying tradition. Where do you see this under way in these excerpts?

2. Write an essay about Chapter III ("The Slaughter of the Pigeons") as a critique of Old World and Native American ways of living in a natural context.

CATHARINE MARIA SEDGWICK

1. Compare Sedgwick's prose style to Cooper's. In the evolution of a vernacular suited to portraying ordinary American life, what are the advantages

of Sedgwick's strategy? If you compare her portraits of domestic life to Rowson's, what differences become clear?

2. In Sedgwick's work, do we see indications of the inadequacy of literary eras and "ages" (like the Age of Romanticism and the Age of Realism) for classifying and describing individual talents? In what ways might Sedgwick be ahead of her time? In what ways does she seem very much a writer of the early nineteenth century?

William Cullen Bryant

1. In his essays, Emerson calls for the emergence of an American poetics. Focusing on Bryant's "The Prairies," describe ways in which Bryant might meet Emerson's demand. In what ways does Bryant move away from imitating British poetry and address American themes? In what ways does he play by the familiar rules of the epic tradition?

2. Bryant is writing about a wilder and less imaginatively tractable landscape than Wordsworth and Coleridge wrote about in the early years of English Romanticism: the woods and prairies were not domesticated and were not haunted by "ghosts" of a kindred race and culture. Describe ways in which this situation proves advantageous to Bryant and difficult for him to work with.

William Apess

1. Write an essay in which you explore "An Indian's Looking-Glass for the White Man" as an American work. To what extent does it address familiar American themes? To what extent does the emergence of a Native American literature in the English language coincide with and contribute to the emergence of an indigenous (as distinguished from imitative) American tradition?

2. Compare Apess's "Indian's Looking-Glass" with Douglass's "What to the Slave Is the Fourth of July?"

3. Bryant wrote his poem "The Prairies" within a year of Apess's "Indian's Looking-Glass." Read "The Prairies" with Apess's perspective and comment on Bryant's portrait of "the red man" in light of Apess's text.

Caroline Stansbury Kirkland

Write an essay comparing Kirkland's prose style and treatment of subject matter to Sedgwick's. In what ways do these two writers resist modes of description and narration that you see in Irving and Cooper?

Ralph Waldo Emerson

1. Discuss what Emerson means in one of the following statements from *Nature*: (1) "The use of natural history is to give us aid in supernatural history. The use of the outer creation, to give us language for the beings and changes of the inward creation" or (2) "A man is a god in ruins. When men are innocent, life shall be longer, and shall pass into the immortal as gently as we awake from dreams."

2. Describe Emerson's thinking, image patterns, and particular forms of expression in one of the poems.

3. Compare an Emerson paragraph with an Edwards paragraph. What are the differences in structure? In argumentation? Does Emerson play by the rules that you were taught in composition classes? If not, then how does Emerson make his own strategy work?

4. Explain why the poet is so important for Emerson, summarizing his argument in "The Poet." Does his idea of a poet have a certain gender? Where do you see indications that it does or does not?

5. Discuss the way Emerson uses analogies. Choose several analogies he creates in *Nature* and explain their significance.

6. Explore any one of the following central concepts in Emerson's work in the context of your reading: the spiritual vision of unity with nature, the significance of language in achieving spiritual vision, basic differences between thinking and writing by means of analogy and by means of discursive logic, the theme of self-reliance, and the significance of self-expression.

7. Explain how Emerson's philosophy, as he expresses it in *Nature*, represents a culmination of what it means to be an American in his time and place.

Cluster: Native Americans: Removal and Resistance

1. Based primarily on direct references or inferences you can draw from the Cherokee Memorials, write an essay in which you describe the Cherokees' particular economic, cultural, and political situation in Georgia at the time of the writing of these Memorials. If you consult historical source(s) to verify your inferences, provide appropriate citations.

2. Summarize the argument or arguments that the Memorials urge on members of the Senate and House.

3. Compare the rhetorical strategies of Petalesharo, Boudinot, and the Memorials. Why might these strategies be especially effective in addressing their respective audiences?

Nathaniel Hawthorne

1. Explicate character, theme, language patterns, style, use of point of view, setting, or design in any particular short story or in *The Scarlet Letter*. (The problem with assigning one of these topics, of course, is that you then have to deal with the standard interpretations students are likely to find if they go straight to the library. If you use a version of this question, you might use it in in-class writing where the only book available is NAAL.)

2. What are the problems with assigning any of the following classifications to Hawthorne's work: Puritan, anti-Puritan, transcendentalist, anti-transcendentalist, romantic, realist? Cite specific works, characters, and passages to frame your answer.

3. Are some Hawthorne stories more fablelike than others? Choose two stories that illustrate your response to this question and write about them.

4. Explain what Melville means by Hawthorne's "blackness" in his essay "Hawthorne and His Mosses" and discuss it with specific reference to any two of the stories in the text (or any three with reference to specific characters in *The Scarlet Letter*).

5. Explore the moral ambiguity in any given Hawthorne character or work. What does reading "Rappaccini's Daughter" (or "The Minister's Black Veil" or "Young Goodman Brown") do to the reader's ability to discern "good" and "evil" characters?

6. Consider Hawthorne's presentation of women in his fiction. What attitudes inform his portraits of Beatrice Rappaccini or of Hester Prynne?

7. Consider the relationship between "The Custom-House" and *The Scarlet Letter*. Where does the narrator stand in each work? In what ways might we consider "The Custom-House" an integral part of the longer fiction? Consider the particular use of "The Custom-House" as a way of "explaining" or delaying the fiction: might "The Custom-House" serve as Hawthorne's "black veil" in facing his readers?

8. Given the autobiographical references in "The Custom-House," consider the possibility that each of the major characters in *The Scarlet Letter* might also be aspects of the narrator's own persona. Discuss ways in which Hester Prynne, Arthur Dimmesdale, Roger Chillingworth, and Pearl complement each other thematically.

9. Given your earlier study of Puritan literature, trace elements of Puritanism in Hawthorne's stories or *The Scarlet Letter* and discuss the extent to which Hawthorne himself embraces or critiques Puritan ideology. (Compare actual Puritans you have studied with Hawthorne's fictional characters: Anne Bradstreet with Hester Prynne; Edward Taylor with Arthur Dimmesdale; Jonathan Edwards with various ministers in Hawthorne, or with the narrator himself.)

10. Locate references to childhood in *The Scarlet Letter* and, focusing on Pearl, discuss Hawthorne's portrait of what it might have been like to be a Puritan child.

11. To lighten up the class a bit, screen a few scenes from the Hollywood film *The Scarlet Letter*. Ask students to comment on whether certain big (and unintentionally hilarious!) scenes catch the spirit of Hawthorne's novel. *Viewers' note*: the novel that you know doesn't start until about an hour into the film. The final ten minutes—featuring a big Indian fight, a bit of New Age catharsis by Dimmesdale, and an ending that you won't believe—can be a good place to start a lively conversation and inspire some comparative essays about characterization and major themes.

Henry Wadsworth Longfellow

Longfellow sought to be a poet for the American people: to inspire his nation, unite it, and help it imagine itself as a coherent culture with a historical legacy. Write about two of his poems in detail and talk about ways in which they make his poetic mission clear.

EDGAR ALLAN POE

1. Summarize Poe's theory of aesthetics as he expresses it in "The Philosophy of Composition" and discuss his application of that philosophy in "The Raven." Given Poe's delight in wit and practical jokes, do you think that he means everything that he says in "The Philosophy of Composition"? Are there elements of self-parody in "The Raven"?

2. Explicate a short lyric ("To Helen") and discuss Poe's creation of a persona.

3. Discuss "The Sleeper," "The Raven," "Annabel Lee," and "Ligeia" in light of Poe's statement in "The Philosophy of Composition" that "the death, then, of a beautiful woman is, unquestionably, the most poetical topic in the world—and equally is it beyond doubt that the lips best suited for such topic are those of a bereaved lover."

4. Explain what Poe means by his attempt to achieve "unity of effect," and trace the particular ways he manages this in "The Fall of the House of Usher," "The Man of the Crowd," or "The Masque of the Red Death."

5. Poe almost never writes about American settings or cultural contexts. Why not? Write an essay distinguishing his kind of Romanticism from that of Bryant, Whittier, or Longfellow.

ABRAHAM LINCOLN

1. Lincoln's prose style changed permanently the nature of American public speech. In the American literary tradition, what roots does he draw on and what traditions does he break from? Find passages from earlier public or political prose (Winthrop, Paine, Jefferson, Edwards) to make the comparison clear.

2. Comparing the 1858 "House Divided" speech to the Second Inaugural Address, do you see any differences in strategy, style, temperament? If so, describe those differences and speculate on causes and motivations.

MARGARET FULLER

1. Read Margaret Fuller's "The Great Lawsuit," published the year before Emerson published "The Poet." Focusing on comparison with Emerson, discuss Fuller's critique of the masculine assumptions of her generation of intellectuals.

2. At one point in "The Great Lawsuit," Fuller writes prophetically: "And will not she soon appear? The woman who shall vindicate their birthright for all women; who shall teach them what to claim, and how to use what they obtain?" Why was the time right for Fuller to expect an appearance "soon" of this new empowered woman? Had literary culture in some ways prepared the way? Had it created obstacles that Fuller's new woman would have to overcome?

3. Write an essay comparing Fuller's expository style to Emerson's or Thoreau's. Where does she draw on Transcendental modes of discourse? Where does she break radically from those modes, and why?

Harriet Beecher Stowe

1. Write an essay about Tom, whose fame has changed dramatically from the middle of the nineteenth century to now. Why might Tom have been an appropriate "hero" for the historical moment in which Stowe created him? Are the other African American characters in *Uncle Tom's Cabin* constructed in similar ways, for similar purposes? How do you account for variations?

2. Write an essay about the white characters in *Uncle Tom's Cabin*. Why would this particular array of characters serve Stowe's purposes?

Fanny Fern

Compare Fern's rhetorical strategies to those of Fuller, or compare both of them to Emerson. Is Fern implicitly criticizing a style of argument, as well as the subjugation of women? Cite and discuss specific passages in Fern's essays to support your answer.

Harriet Jacobs

1. Compare Linda Brent with Hester Prynne in *The Scarlet Letter*. See especially the following quotation from *Incidents*, which equates unwed motherhood with stigma: "My unconscious babe was the ever-present witness of my shame."

2. Write a paper comparing Jacobs and Douglass and based on the following central quotations from each narrative: "Slavery is terrible for men; but it is far more terrible for women" (Jacobs) and "You have seen how a man was made a slave; you shall see how a slave was made a man" (Douglass).

3. Explore the particular obstacles Linda Brent faces and their significance for women at the end of the twentieth century: sexual harassment, poor mothers' legal rights, and difficulties for advancement when faced with responsibilities and care for children.

4. Jacobs ends her narrative "with freedom, not in the usual way, with marriage." Comment on the implication here that freedom matters more to Linda Brent than marriage. To what extent does *Incidents* suggest that the "life story" is different for enslaved women than for free (white) women?

5. Identify the contradictions implied in Dr. Flint's promise to Linda that if she moves into the house he has built for her, he will "make her a lady."

Henry David Thoreau

1. Discuss one of the following statements from *Walden*: (1) "Every morning . . . I got up early and bathed in the pond; that was a religious exercise, and one of the best things which I did" or (2) "I fear chiefly lest my expression may not be *extravagant* enough, may not wander far enough beyond the narrow limits of my daily experience, so as to be adequate to the truth of which I have been convinced."

2. Cite several points of philosophical and stylistic connection and divergence between Emerson's *Nature* and Thoreau's *Walden*.

3. Discuss in detail one point of significant resemblance between Franklin's *Autobiography* and Thoreau's *Walden* and one point of contrast.

4. Explain specific ways in which Thoreau's *Walden* may be considered a "practice" of Emerson's theory. Emerson, whose philosophy influenced Thoreau, wrote that "words are also actions, and actions are a kind of words." Write an essay on *Walden* in which you demonstrate Thoreau's insistence on the truth of this statement or apply the same quotation from Emerson to "Resistance to Civil Government," paying particular attention to the relationship between self-expression and personal conscience.

5. Explore any of the following central concepts in Thoreau: the spiritual vision of unity with nature, the significance of language in achieving such a vision, the theme of self-reliance, the use of analogy as meditation (perhaps contrasting Thoreau with Edward Taylor), and the significance of self-expression.

FREDERICK DOUGLASS

1. Discuss the extent to which Douglass may be considered a Transcendentalist in his view of human nature and the future of the United States.

2. Compare Douglass's *Narrative* with Franklin's *Autobiography*, narratives about self-creation and about the possibilities open to the individual man or woman.

3. Douglass writes parts of his slave narrative as a series of incidents or adventures. Discuss ways in which those various incidents and adventures are made to cohere.

4. Compare Harriet Jacobs's *Incidents in the Life of a Slave Girl* with Douglass's *Narrative*. Was the model of "heroic fugitive" possible for female slaves? Jacob's *Incidents* depicts the network of relationships within the slave community and between black and white communities. Look for evidence of such a network in Douglass's *Narrative*. What explains Douglass's lack of attention to emotional connections?

5. In his prefatory letter to the *Narrative*, Boston abolitionist Wendell Phillips compares Douglass with the signers of The Declaration of Independence: "You, too, publish your declaration of freedom with danger compassing you around." Does the *Narrative* share formal similarities with The Declaration of Independence as well as rhetorical ones? Compare Jefferson's characterization of the British king and his itemizing of grievances with the design and structure of Douglass's *Narrative*.

6. Compare *A Narrative of the Captivity and Restoration of Mrs. Mary Rowlandson* with *Narrative of the Life of Frederick Douglass, an American Slave*. What formal, thematic, and historical continuities exist between these indigenous genres?

7. In "What to the Slave Is the July Fourth?" Douglass writes that the reformer's heart "may well beat lighter at the thought that America is young" and that "were the nation older," its "great streams" may dry up, leaving "the sad tale of departed glory." Explain why Douglass takes hope from America's youth, and contrast this expression with the

twentieth-century poet Robinson Jeffers's sentiments in "Shine, Perishing Republic."

8. Trace Douglass's views concerning the role of reform and dissent in the American republic in "What to the Slave Is the Fourth of July?"

Cluster: Section, Region, Nation

Write an essay in which you offer your views about "regions" as imaginative constructs or genuine geographic and cultural realities. When a region is conceived as such, how does that conception become self-fulfilling? In what ways do selections in this cluster contribute to the construction or subversion of these legacies?

Walt Whitman

1. Write an essay in which you describe the place and effect of "Facing West from California's Shores" within the context of *Leaves of Grass* ["Song of Myself"].

2. Focusing on the following two quotations, discuss thematic, philosophical, and technical connections between Emerson and Whitman: from *Nature*: "I become a transparent eyeball. I am nothing. I see all"; and from "Preface to *Leaves of Grass*": "[the greatest poet] is a seer . . . is individual . . . he is complete in himself. . . . What the eyesight does to the rest he does to the rest." Where does Whitman break with Emerson's practice, if not from Emerson's ideals and theorizing?

3. Compare Emerson's "The Poet" with "Preface to *Leaves of Grass*." In what ways does Whitman claim to embody Emerson's idea of the American poet?

4. Choose one of the following quotations from *Leaves of Grass* ["Song of Myself"] and discuss it by suggesting several ways in which it describes what Whitman is attempting in the poem: (1) "I know I am solid and sound, / To me the converging objects of the universe perpetually flow, / All are written to me, and I must get what the writing means"; (2) "I am an acme of things accomplish'd, and I am an encloser of things to be"; (3) "I know I have the best of time and space, and was never measured and never will be measured."

5. Discuss Whitman's poetry as a culmination in the development of American identity. How does Whitman contribute to the ongoing evolution of self-reliance? Of human freedom? Of concepts of democracy?

6. Write an essay about "Out of the Cradle Endlessly Rocking" and the traditions of the Anglo-American elegy. What rules and expectations does Whitman follow here? Which rules does he break, and how and why?

7. Trace Whitman's various responses to the Civil War throughout the poems anthologized from *Drum-Taps*. Compare and contrast Whitman's war poems with the anthologized lyrics from Melville's *Battle-Pieces*.

8. Do a study of Whitman's use of the catalog as a poetic device. Then illustrate, by means of close analysis, the effects Whitman achieves in a particular catalog from *Leaves of Grass*.

9. Alternatively, study and illustrate Whitman's use of parallel construction as a poetic device, and comment on its various effects.

HERMAN MELVILLE

1. Write an essay about "Benito Cereno" as expressing that "power of blackness" that Melville ascribes to Hawthorne's work. In pursuing that "blackness," what happens to the treatment of black slaves as characters in fiction?

2. Writing about "Benito Cereno," literary critic Newton Arvin noted that "the story is an artistic miscarriage, with moments of undeniable power." Evaluate the fairness of this statement given your own reading of the story.

3. How well is "Bartleby, the Scrivener" grounded in the actualities of modern-style work? Is the narrator himself a victim of the same misery that may have undone Bartleby? Write an essay about this story not as about "ah, humanity!" but as about the frustrations and balked emotions of the modern urban workplace.

4. Part of what fascinates the reader (and possibly Melville himself) about Bartleby is his inscrutability—and possible banality. Describe various "walls" that Bartleby may be trapped behind and explore ways in which the story's structure or design reinforces the reader's inability to penetrate those walls.

5. Choose any one of the following moments of dialogue in Melville and use it as a prism through which to "read" the work in which it appears: (1) "Ah, Bartleby! Ah, humanity!"; (2) " 'Follow your leader' "; (3) "God bless Captain Vere!"

6. If in some ways Billy is Adam or Jesus Christ and Claggart is Satan or the serpent, then is Vere to be understood as Pontius Pilate? What are the limits and complications of reading him that way?

7. Explore the two kinds of justice Melville sets in opposition in *Billy Budd, Sailor,* and discuss the moral, political, and thematic implications of Billy's execution.

ELIZABETH DREW STODDARD

1. Write an essay about "Lemorne *Versus* Huell" as a comedy. How fitting is that description for this story? How do comic moments in this narrative contribute to the development of major themes?

2. Compare "Lemorne *Versus* Huell" to any other nineteenth-century story or novel that you have read about independent young women in the city. How does Stoddard adapt motifs and themes from that tradition? Where do you see her move in original or surprising directions?

FRANCES E. W. HARPER

1. Write an essay about Harper as an experimenter with American English in poetry and prose. Where does she use different vocabularies, and how would you account for those variations?

2. How would you describe Harper's artistic relationship to the work of Harriet Beecher Stowe? In what ways does *Uncle Tom's Cabin* figure as an inspiration in Harper's work? Where might that famous novel seem like an obstacle for Harper to overcome?

Emily Dickinson

1. Read carefully a group of Dickinson poems with related themes—the natural world, death, traveling, private experience, art and its value—then write an interpretation of one of the poems that includes your expanded understanding of the way Dickinson uses the theme in other poems in the group.

2. Several of Dickinson's poems contain references to birds. Discuss how they are observed in each poem and variations in the thematic role that they play. If you like, you can do a similar essay centering on Dickinson's thinking about insects—bees, flies, butterflies.

3. Locate and discuss size, especially smallness, as a theme in Dickinson's poetry.

4. Many Dickinson poems illustrate change in the consciousness of the poet or speaker. Choose a poem in which this happens and trace the process by which the poem reflects and creates the change.

Rebecca Harding Davis

1. Compare the relationships between Hester and Dimmesdale in *The Scarlet Letter* and between Hugh Wolfe and Deborah in *Life in the Iron-Mills*.

2. Recall what Thoreau has to say in *Walden* about the "lives of quiet desperation" most men lead. Might Hugh Wolfe, like Thoreau, have chosen to simplify his life and retreat to a pond outside of town? Compare the conditions under which Wolfe makes his art with those Thoreau describes.

3. Study Davis's references to Deborah, who is generally depicted as being a "thwarted woman" who leads a "colorless life." Contrast her with the korl woman. Discuss the distance Davis creates between the real and the ideal woman in Wolfe's life.

Volume C: American Literature 1865–1914

General Questions

1. Compare the humor in Twain's "The Notorious Jumping Frog of Calaveras County," Harte's "The Luck of Roaring Camp," and Freeman's "The Revolt of 'Mother.'"

2. Writers following the Civil War put irony to new thematic uses. Compare the way in which irony is used in Bierce's "Occurrence at Owl Creek Bridge," James's "The Real Thing," and Crane's "The Open Boat."

3. Write an essay on point of view in regionalist and local-color fiction from this period. In which texts does the narrator look *at* the major characters from an omniscient perspective? In which texts does the narration unfold through the eyes of a character? What characters are excluded from sharing the point of view, and why? What effects do these varying strategies have on the fiction and its major themes?

4. Write an essay discussing differences in the portrayal of women characters and women's experience in the local-color writers Harte and Garland, regionalist writers Freeman, Jewett, and Chopin, the Asian American author Sui Sin Far, and the New York ethnic writer Cahan. Looking at these portrayals as a group, what generalizations occur to you about the status of women in various communities in late-nineteenth-century America?

5. Although this period was the heyday of Realism and Naturalism, many writers continued to use dreams and fantasy as important elements in their work. Discuss Bierce's "Occurrence at Owl Creek Bridge," Jewett's "A White Heron," Gilman's "The Yellow Wall-paper," and Wovoka's vision of the Messiah, focusing on how the use of dream, vision, or altered perception affects the realism of the fiction.

6. Many late-nineteenth-century writers wrote in response to contemporary social conditions. Present a composite picture of their concerns by discussing the following texts: Charlot's "[He has filled graves with our bones]" and Garland's "Under the Lion's Paw."

7. Examine political discourse of Cochise, Charlot, Washington, and Du Bois in the context of political discourse in earlier periods of American literature. What similarities and variations do you see? How do Washington and Du Bois respond, implicitly and otherwise, to new and prevailing literary styles of the late nineteenth or early twentieth centuries?

8. In your library, consult a standard literary history for its general discussion of local-color and regional writing at the end of the nineteenth century. These summaries are rarely more than a few pages long. Then analyze any story in NAAL by Jewett, Chopin, Freeman, Chesnutt, Harte, Garland, or Oskison in light of the historical commentary, and discuss differences you see between the story and the general descriptions.

9. Research a regional writer from this period (1870–1914) from your home state or region. Write an essay analyzing one of the sketches or stories by this writer.

10. Referring to Twain's "Fenimore Cooper's Literary Offenses," construct a theory of Realism that accommodates premises in several of these texts. Then choose one story by each writer, and see how thoroughly each plays by these rules.

11. Turn-of-the-century critics used the phrase *new realists* to describe the work of naturalists S. Crane, Dreiser, and London. Choose a work of fiction by any of these writers and consider the accuracy of the phrase. Based on your analysis, would you identify Naturalism as a new genre or a derivative one (a "new" Realism)?

12. Whether in anticipation of or in the general climate of Freud's *The Interpretation of Dreams* (1900), sexuality concerns several writers of the 1865–1914 period. Analyze sexual imagery or attitudes toward sexuality in several of the following works: James's "The Beast in the Jungle"; Jewett's

"A White Heron"; Chopin's *The Awakening*, "At the 'Cadian Ball," or "The Storm"; Freeman's "A New England Nun"; and Wharton's "Roman Fever."

Questions about Individual Authors and Works

For essay questions on Walt Whitman and Emily Dickinson, please see pages 310–311 and 312 above.

María Amparo Ruiz de Burton

1. Write an essay on the monologues in the excerpt from *The Squatter and the Don* and what they might imply about Burton's intentions in this novel.

2. Would you classify Burton as a realist? Why or why not? What characteristics of this excerpt figure in your thinking, and why?

Mark Twain

1. Many readers of *Adventures of Huckleberry Finn* consider the ending flawed—Hemingway, for example, said that Twain "cheated"—while others have praised it. Write an essay about the appropriateness of the novel's ending, focusing on Huck's treatment of Jim and on Huck's moral complicity with Tom.

2. The theme of pretending is one that unifies *Adventures of Huckleberry Finn*, although the word *pretending* takes on several meanings and levels of significance as the novel unfolds. Describe three of these, and illustrate each by analyzing a specific character, scene, or incident from the novel.

3. If one were constructing a list of "classic" American books, *Adventures of Huckleberry Finn* would probably appear on it. Write an essay about ways in which Twain explores American experience in new ways.

4. Explore the relationship between the possible symbolic importance of the river and the design and structure of the novel.

5. Analyze Twain's portrait of Jim in light of your reading of Douglass. Is *Adventures of Huckleberry Finn* in some ways a slave narrative? Does Twain use the discussion of slavery as a pretext to write about other issues?

6. Explore the novel as a presentation of mid-nineteenth-century attitudes toward children and child rearing.

7. Write an essay about Twain's humor, focusing on "The Notorious Jumping Frog of Calaveras County" or "Fenimore Cooper's Literary Offenses" and one or two incidents from *Adventures of Huckleberry Finn*.

8. Discuss Huck Finn's language in the opening passages of *Adventures of Huckleberry Finn*. Discuss how Twain uses Huck's style as a way to construct his character.

9. Compare Huck Finn's speech with dialects spoken by other characters in the novel. Compare Twain's depiction of dialect in general with that of Harte, Harris, or Jewett.

10. How does Twain portray Tom Sawyer? Is he model, rival, alter ego, or mirror for Huck? Does he develop in the novel?

11. Write an essay about the development of Jim as a character. Does he change over the course of the novel? Compare his portrait with portraits of black characters in the Harris tales or in Chesnutt's "The Goophered Grapevine."

12. Write an essay about the plot of *Huckleberry Finn*. If the novel were more tightly plotted, would it be better? In what ways is a loose structure advantageous?

13. For generations, *Huckleberry Finn* has been read as a moral breakthrough in American letters. Lately, that kind of reading has become more controversial. What are your own perceptions on this question, and where are they grounded in the novel?

BRET HARTE AND AMBROSE BIERCE

1. Write an essay comparing the use of irony in Harte and Bierce. How would you describe the differences in tone and temperament in these writers?

2. Write an essay comparing the prose of Harte and Bierce in the description of natural landscapes. What details do they focus on, and how? What word choices and techniques distinguish the style of each writer?

HENRY ADAMS

1. "The Dynamo and the Virgin," written at the turn of the twentieth century, was read for generations as a prophetic work on technology and civilization. Has the Information Revolution of the past twenty years confirmed Adams's projections, or rendered them obsolete?

2. As a nineteenth-century historian, Adams believes in the dialectical model—the organization of history and human experience into thesis and antithesis. Write an essay on "The Dynamo and the Virgin" as an example of dialectical thought, and write about the value and limitations of organizing the past and the present in this way.

3. What, finally, does Adams mean by "education"? Is he seeking the same kind of experience and wisdom that Emerson or Thoreau sought? Do his expectations determine his self-described "failure"?

NATIVE AMERICAN CHANTS AND SONGS

1. Write an essay describing resemblances between some of these chants and nineteenth-century poetry by white Americans.

2. When W. E. B. Du Bois turns to the "chants and songs" of African Americans as a focus for his meditations on being black in a predominantly white America, does he search for qualities similar to ones in these Native American texts? Write an essay on similarities you see between works in the Native American and African American folk traditions.

NATIVE AMERICAN ORATORY

1. Compare Charlot's rhetorical construction of "the white man" with rhetorical constructions of "King George" in The Declaration of Independence.

2. Write an essay about the role that Native American oratory can or should play in a history of modern American literature. What can be learned from these transcribed speeches? What stylistic and moral attention needs to be paid to them, and why?

CHARLOTTE PERKINS GILMAN AND HENRY JAMES

1. Write an essay comparing "The Yellow Wall-paper" to "The Real Thing," as meditations on the artifice of literary realism and the nature of reality. Which do you find more thoughtful about this paradox, and why?

2. Both "The Yellow Wall-paper" and "The Read Thing" are first-person narratives; the artist speaks of a personal experience pertaining to professional practice. Compare the prose with which these stories open and close. What does that prose suggest about the voice and personality of the speaker?

3. Compare Gilman's "Why I Wrote 'The Yellow Wall-paper'?" and James's "The Figure in the Carpet" as meditations on the importance and cultural work of imaginative fiction.

4. How does Gilman's realism differ from that of James? Does the narrator of "The Yellow Wall-paper" recognize any correspondence between her own perception and external reality?

5. Compare "The Yellow Wall-paper" to James's "Daisy Miller" as portraits of American women in peril. Compare the complicity of men in these crises.

6. Compare Gilman's narrator and Kate Chopin's Edna as potential artists. What kinds of perceptions empower them? What stands in their way?

7. In "The Art of Fiction," James writes, "A novel is in its broadest definition a personal, a direct impression of life." With this quotation as your point of reference, analyze the particular "impression" James is trying to create in "Daisy Miller," "The Real Thing," or "The Beast in the Jungle."

8. James has often been called a psychological realist who was more interested in the development of consciousness than in portraying character types and social reality. Discuss the extent to which this observation holds true in "Daisy Miller" or "The Beast in the Jungle."

9. Although "Daisy Miller" appears to focus on Daisy herself, a reader might argue that James's real interest is Winterbourne. Rethink the events of the story as Daisy herself might have viewed them, and suggest ways in which the author of "A White Heron" or "A New England Nun" might have differently handled both the story and the portrait of Daisy.

10. Reviewing the James stories for his interest in convention and social forms, write an essay on one or two scenes that exemplify James as a careful observer of social practices.

11. James is often credited with perfecting the use of point of view as a narrative device. Choose one incident from "The Beast in the Jungle," and analyze his use of point of view in that story. What does it reveal? What does

it conceal? How does it achieve its effectiveness? What is its significance in terms of the story's themes?

12. Write an essay about James as a writer of horror stories. As a realist, what Gothic or horror traditions does he draw on? How does he transform and modernize the idea of evil?

SARAH WINNEMUCCA AND MARY AUSTIN

1. Write an essay making a case for reading *Life Among the Piutes* as either an oral or a written document. Does this work seem to you to be from an oral tradition? Does it seem crafted for print and an audience of readers? Are those kinds of discourse blended here? Discuss the structure and prose of Winnemucca's account to support your case.

2. Compare Winnemucca and Austin as contributors to the literature of the American West. What experiments in form and narration do you see here that might be especially appropriate to the American landscape, populations, and history?

EMMA LAZARUS

1. Write an essay situating Emma Lazarus's poems in an American poetic tradition including Longfellow, Bryant, Whittier, and Whitman. In what ways does Lazarus stand outside that tradition?

2. Write an essay about point of view in "In the Jewish Synagogue at Newport" and "1492."

SARAH ORNE JEWETT AND HAMLIN GARLAND

1. Compare Jewett's Sylvy in "A White Heron" with any other heroine you have encountered in American realist fiction—for example, May Bartram of James's "The Beast in the Jungle."

2. Write an essay comparing the worlds of Jewett and Garland as those worlds are implied in "The White Heron" and "Under the Lion's Paw." What are the differences in the ways these worlds are observed and represented?

3. The tree, the hunter, the cow, and the heron all seem to possess mythical significance in "A White Heron." Choose one of these symbols to discuss in relation to Sylvy and explore the way Jewett combines elements of folk or fairy tale and literary realism.

4. Are these short stories, or fables? Using details from "The White Heron" and "Under the Lion's Paw," write an essay offering your perspective on this question.

KATE CHOPIN AND MARY E. WILKINS FREEMAN

1. These two authors are often classified as local colorists or regionalist writers. What do you see as the implicit emotional relationship between each of these authors and the place they write about? Are their ambitions the same? Do you find *local colorist* a descriptive term, or a limiting one, for describing these texts and authors?

2. *The Awakening*, "A New England Nun," and "The Revolt of 'Mother'" regularly appear as important moments in the history of American feminist literature. Compare the ways that each work investigates the predicament of a woman in a domestic setting.

3. Both "The Revolt of 'Mother'" and "A New England Nun" portray women who triumph over the material conditions of their existence. Describe the nature of that triumph and the process by which they achieve it.

4. Examine the use of the window and the barn doors as framing devices in the two anthologized stories. Compare form in Freeman's fiction with form in Gilman, James, or Jewett.

5. Describe the character of Mlle. Reisz in *The Awakening* and compare her with Louisa Ellis in Freeman's "A New England Nun." How does Chopin limit Mlle. Reisz's possibilities and influence on Edna in her novel?

6. Edna Pontellier is caught in the contradictions between the way others see her and the way she sees herself. Identify several moments in which this becomes apparent and show Edna's growing awareness of the contradiction.

7. Discuss the women of color in *The Awakening*. What does their presence and their treatment in the novel suggest about Edna's (and Chopin's) attitudes toward human development for nonwhite and poor women?

8. Some readers have described Edna's death in *The Awakening* as suicide; others view it as her attempt at self-realization. Argue the relative truth of both interpretations.

9. *The Awakening* contains elements of Regionalism, Realism, and Naturalism. Identify these by choosing exemplary characters or scenes from the novel and by basing your distinctions on close analysis.

10. In "At the 'Cadian Ball," Chopin explores the dimensions of sexual power and desire conferred by racial and class status and marked by dialect. Identify the numerous among the characters that can be understood in terms of power dynamics and explicate those dynamics.

ANNA JULIA COOPER

Write an essay about the variety of voices and rhetorical strategies that Cooper uses to make her case. What are the strengths and limitations of that variety?

CHARLES CHESNUTT, JOEL CHANDLER HARRIS, AND HAMLIN GARLAND

1. Consider the ending of "Under the Lion's Paw" and the ending of "The Wife of His Youth." Garland ties up the loose ends; Chesnutt leaves huge questions unanswered. Why do these stories conclude so differently? What does each ending suggest about the kind of "realism" espoused by each author?

2. After generations of dialect humor in American newspapers and magazines, what are the risks of Chesnutt's narration of "The Goophered Grapevine"? How successful is the story in overcoming those risks?

3. Explore the way in which Chesnutt manipulates point of view in "The Goophered Grapevine" and the effect this has on the story's ending.

4. Read the Uncle Remus stories by Joel Chandler Harris, and compare Chesnutt's use of the folk tale and the folk narrator with that of Harris.

5. Compare Washington Irving's use of folk materials early in the nineteenth century with Chesnutt's use of folk materials in "The Goophered Grapevine."

6. Write an essay about "The Wife of His Youth" as a possible act of resistance by Chesnutt against the relative innocuousness of the local-color tradition in which he usually worked and with which he was commonly associated. In what ways is this story a critique or confirmation of the idea that place determines identity? What difficult problems does it raise regarding the migration of African Americans to other regions and the establishment of new identities and social orders?

7. Compare Garland's portrait of the women in "Under the Lion's Paw" with Freeman's in "The Revolt of 'Mother.'" How does each author present women's ability to confront poverty?

8. Garland's narrator views his characters from the outside. Review specific scenes in the story to show how this outsider's view predetermines the reader's understanding of the characters' actions.

9. Are the characters in "Under the Lion's Paw" individuals or types? What would be the advantages or disadvantages of stereotyping in a story with these intentions?

BOOKER T. WASHINGTON, W. E. B. DU BOIS, AND IDA B. WELLS-BARNETT

1. Write an essay about the convention of regarding Washington and Du Bois as political opposites. How appropriate do you think that assumption is, and why? What aspects of these texts are you thinking about as you form your opinion?

2. The structure and rhetorical strategies of *The Souls of Black Folk* are markedly different from those favored by Washington in *Up from Slavery*. Write an essay describing some of these differences, and consider the relationship of these strategies to the intentions of each author.

3. In the canonical literature of African American experience at the turn of the twentieth century, Ida B. Wells-Barnett is a recently recovered author. In constructing an overview that would include Washington, Du Bois, and Dunbar, write an essay about Wells-Barnett's contribution to that dialogue.

EDITH WHARTON

Write an essay comparing Wharton and Sui Sin Far or Henry James as authors of realist fiction. Compare the challenges and complications of the setting that each author observes, and the challenge of making their narratives important to a broad audience.

CHARLES ALEXANDER EASTMAN

1. Research Elaine Goodale (perhaps by reading *Sister to the Sioux: The Memoirs of Elaine Goodale Eastman*, 1978, edited by Kay Graber), and construct a portrait of the young white woman who became missionaries to the American Indians in the West.

2. Calling the adherents of the Ghost Dance religion "prophets of the 'Red Christ,'" Eastman writes about what he calls this religious "craze": "It meant that the last hope of race entity had departed, and my people were groping blindly after spiritual relief in their bewilderment and misery." Set this comment against Captain Sword's account of the Ghost Dance religion and evaluate it in terms of the confusion that becomes evident among "hostiles" and "friendlies" during the Ghost Dance War.

ABRAHAM CAHAN AND SUI SIN FAR

1. In literary criticism, it's an interesting quirk that "ethnic" American writers from the turn of the twentieth century, writers like Cahan and Sui Sin Far, are often categorized apart from Wharton, James, Howells, Dreiser, Norris, and other "realists" and "naturalists." Write an essay about the advantages and drawbacks of merging Cahan and Far into one of these categories.

2. Some of the poignancy of "In the Land of the Free" stems from Far's portrayal of Chinese-American society as a hybrid, a mix of traditions and social practices. Write an essay about how the narrator situates herself with regard to the story, and compare that point of view to the perspective favored in "The Imported Bridegroom."

FRANK NORRIS AND THEODORE DREISER

1. Write an essay comparing the relationship of each author to his protagonist. What indications do you see of sympathy? Of condescension?

2. Write an essay comparing Norris and Dreiser as observers and describers of modern city life.

STEPHEN CRANE

1. Compare "The Open Boat" to *Maggie* as fables about the human condition. Which one seems more like a fable or a lesson? What differences do you see in the way in which irony is presented and handled in each narrative?

2. Write an essay about fate in the works of Stephen Crane, making reference to both the fiction and the poetry.

3. Compare Crane's *Maggie* to Chopin's *The Awakening* or Gilman's "The Yellow Wall-paper" as observations on the situation of women in America at the end of the nineteenth century? What are the strengths and weaknesses of Crane's representation of Maggie and "girls of the street"?

4. Does Crane's choice of the lyric poem allow him to develop aspects of his major themes that his fiction does not fully explore? How do his choices of language and form reflect his temperament and prevailing themes?

JAMES WELDON JOHNSON AND PAUL LAURENCE DUNBAR

1. Write an essay about Johnson and Dunbar as writers observing America from the margins, participating in group identity, and also resisting categorization.

2. Write an essay comparing the way Johnson and Ida B. Wells-Barnett engage the subject of lynching.

3. Write an essay about ways in which Johnson and Dunbar regard and make use of the tradition of the African American spiritual.

JACK LONDON

1. Write an essay in which you compare London's implicit motives, as a writer of fiction about contemporary American experience, to those of Dreiser, Freeman, Chopin, or Norris.

2. Write an essay about London's relationship to his own protagonists.

JOHN M. OSKISON

1. Write a research paper in which you locate "The Problem of Old Harjo" in the history of intervention in the lives of Native Americans in the nineteenth century. Cite evidence from other anthologized texts, including Apess's "An Indian's Looking-Glass," Eastman's *From the Deep Woods to Civilization*, Wovoka's vision, and Zitkala Ša's "Impressions of an Indian Childhood."

2. Explore Apess's figure of speech, the "Indian's looking-glass," as it applies to "The Problem of Old Harjo." To what extent does Harjo possess the cunning of the powerless? To what extent is Harjo the powerless character in the story?

NATIVE AMERICAN CHANTS AND SONGS

For most students writing about these transcribed oral works, the best strategy might be to read them in a broad context, rather than isolate them from each other or as a group away from the other materials in NAAL. In many cultures, chants and songs have done similar important kinds of cultural work: they can encourage resolve, peace of mind, a sense of group identity, connection with the past and with the divine. They also can provide solace or other sorts of escape from the verbal and psychological turmoil of ordinary life.

1. What, then, are the resemblances between some of these chants and nineteenth-century poetry by white Americans? Are some New England poets seeking these same values?

2. When Du Bois turns to the "chants and songs" of African Americans as a focus for his meditations on being black in a predominantly white America, does he search for qualities similar to ones in these Native American texts?

Volume D: American Literature 1914–1945

General Questions

1. At the end of Frost's poem "The Oven Bird," we find the following lines: "The question that he frames in all but words / Is what to make of a diminished thing." With reference to works by other poets and prose writers, explain how this statement expresses a common theme in twentieth-century American writing.

2. Compare an early-nineteenth-century poem (such as Bryant's "Thanatopsis") with an early-twentieth-century poem (Frost's "Directive" or Robinson's "Luke Havergal"). Discuss how these poems reflect shifts in perspective, and in ideas about what constitutes poetry.

3. Choose three twentieth-century works and show how they implicitly respond to the following quotation from Stevens's "Of Modern Poetry": "The poem of the mind in the act of finding / What will suffice. It has not always had / To find: the scene was set; it repeated what / Was in the script."

4. Explain the parallel concerns in the following statements: (1) "The poem is a momentary stay against confusion" (Frost, "The Figure a Poem Makes"), (2) "These fragments I have shored against my ruins" (Eliot, *The Waste Land*), and (3) "Poetry is the supreme fiction, madame" (Stevens, "A High-Toned Old Christian Woman").

5. Examine twentieth-century modernist lyric poems in traditional forms by Robinson, Frost, Millay, McKay, and Moore. How do these poets reconcile traditional forms with twentieth-century themes?

6. Many modernist lyric poems are themselves about poetic form and intention. Compare some of these poems by Frost, Stevens, Williams, Bishop, Wilbur, and Dove.

7. Examine the modern use of traditional metric forms. Analyze what Frost does to and with iambic pentameter in "Desert Places" or how Stevens uses it in "The Idea of Order at Key West."

8. In the headnote to Marianne Moore in NAAL, Mary Loeffelholz writes, "Pound worked with the clause, Williams with the line, H. D. with the image, and Stevens and Stein with the word; Moore, unlike these modernist contemporaries, used the entire stanza as the unit of her poetry." In an out-of-class essay, choose poems by each of these writers that will allow you to further explain the distinctions Loeffelholz creates in this statement. In British poetry, Robert Browning was a master of the dramatic monologue—a poem in which a speaker, different from the poet, reveals much about his or her own character in a speech to somebody else. Find and discuss dramatic monologues by three twentieth-century American poets. You might look at Stevens, Pound, Eliot, McKay, Hughes, and Wilbur for starters. Write an essay about how they adapt and develop the dramatic monologue as a form.

9. Several twentieth-century American poets have attempted to write epics. Research features of epic poetry, and write an essay about epic

characteristics in Pound's *The Cantos,* H. D.'s *The Walls Do Not Fall,* Eliot's *Four Quartets,* and Hart Crane's *The Bridge.*

10. Compare the realism of a twentieth-century story with the Realism of Twain, Jewett, James, or Wharton. Analyze Faulkner's "Barn Burning" or Ernest Hemingway's "The Snows of Kilimanjaro," paying particular attention to the twentieth-century writer's innovations in point of view or use of symbolism.

11. Several critics have suggested a progression from Moore and Millay to Plath, Sexton, and Rich in terms of a rising willingness to write poetry about women's experience. Choosing specific poems for your focus, trace this progression and comment about it.

12. Many writers between 1914 and 1945 wrote poetry that may have been influenced by the values of Modernism, but which reflects other artistic traditions and intentions. Write an essay about poems by Moore, Toomer, Sterling Brown, and Hughes that show a complex relationship to literary Modernism.

13. While writers like Pound and Eliot were concerned with tracing the origins of modernist consciousness in classical mythology, other writers were more interested in becoming assimilated into American society. Identify and discuss issues of importance to writers, fictional characters, or lyric voices who concern themselves with issues of immigration and assimilation.

Questions about Individual Authors and Works

BLACK ELK

1. Arnold Krupat (in "The Indian Autobiography: Origins, Type, and Function," *American Literature,* 1981) has written that "to see the Indian autobiography as a ground on which two cultures meet is to see it as the textual equivalent of the 'frontier.'" Write an essay in which you comment on this statement and its significance for understanding *Black Elk Speaks.* In writing your essay, pay particular attention to the way this text challenges the expectations of a white listener or reader.

2. In the second edition of *Black Elk Speaks* (1961), John Neihardt changed the title page of the text from "as told to John Neihardt" to "as told through John Neihardt." Explain the significance of this change and the relationship it suggests between Neihardt and Black Elk, and between Neihardt and *Black Elk Speaks.*

3. Compare this excerpt from *Black Elk Speaks* with two other American texts: Franklin's *The Autobiography* and the *Narrative of the Life of Frederick Douglass, an American Slave.* Focus on what constitutes a life-transforming moment for Franklin, for Douglass, and for Black Elk.

4. Compare Zitkala Ša's autobiographical writing and narrative voice with that of Black Elk. Both writers were Sioux; evaluate their respective roles as "holy man" and "teacher," comment on their different experiences with biculturalism, and compare the points at which they break off their autobiographical accounts.

Edgar Lee Masters and Edwin Arlington Robinson

1. Where does Masters seem to position himself in regard to the various voices in *Spoon River Anthology*? Does he seem to be among them? Above them? Where does Robinson seem to place himself, as observer, when commenting on Richard Cory and Miniver Cheevy? Write an essay comparing these points of view. What problems arise when an artist seeks to speak as or for the common man or woman, and how do Masters and Robinson engage with those problems?

2. Write about irony in *Spoon River Anthology* and the poems of Robinson. Does it have the same effect as irony in the works of Stephen Crane? Do the implications of the dramatic irony change from one poem to the next or over the course of several of these poems?

3. When these poets were writing, the legacy of Longfellow, Whittier, and Bryant as bards of the national experience loomed large in the American imagination. Write an essay about Masters and Robinson as extending that tradition, or quarreling with it.

Willa Cather

1. Write an essay about *My Ántonia* as a work in the realist or naturalist tradition. Where does the novel seem to ascribe to those values? Where does it seem to break away.

2. Write an essay about *My Ántonia* as a modern epic. What epic aspirations do you see here, and how are they developed or limited?

3. Walt Whitman's "Crossing Brooklyn Ferry" is a meditation on time; so is Frost's "The Wood-Pile" and Masters's *Spoon River Anthology*. Write an essay about Cather's novel as a work with similar moods and qualities.

4. "The Sculptor's Funeral" and "Neighbour Rosicky" tell of individuals in small communities, people who live out their lives without being understood, sometimes without companionship or love. Compare Cather's stories to other works which visit this predicament—poems of Robinson and Frost, stories by Freeman, Gilman, Chopin—and describe what is special or unique about Cather's experiments in this territory.

5. To what extent are these stories reflexive—in other words, stories about the predicament of the artist? Write an essay making a case for that kind of reading, and indicating the limits or qualifications that you think such a reading should have.

Amy Lowell and Carl Sandburg

1. Pound referred to Lowell's poetry as "Amygism," perhaps as a way of belittling its value, perhaps to distinguish it from "Imagism," a larger movement which Lowell helped to champion. Locate essays on Imagism in the influential magazine *Poetry* (for example, F. S. Flint, "Imagism," and Ezra Pound, "A Few Don'ts by an Imagist," both in the March 1913 issue), Lowell's own anthologies (see the NAAL headnote for Lowell), or other references that clarify the terms *Imagism* and *Amygism*. Compare Lowell's images with those of Pound and W. Williams. What qualities or tastes distinguish Lowell's verse from these others?

2. As American Modernist poets, should Lowell and Sandburg be seen as opposites? Are there moments where Sandburg's verse shows the influence of Imagism, moments where Lowell, like Sandburg, responds to the legacy of Whitman? Write an essay comparing the styles of Lowell and Sandburg, and speculating on causes for these differences and similarities.

3. Sandburg may continue a poetic tradition that begins with Whitman, but does he also draw on experimentation by other American poets? Locate moments in the Sandburg poems where you see influences from other American poets and talk about how Sandburg blends them.

GERTRUDE STEIN

1. Write an essay comparing Stein's avowed purposes, as a writer, to Whitman's in the opening stanzas of *Song of Myself*.

2. Write an essay describing the implicit relationship of Stein to ordinary American experience.

3. Discuss Stein's sentence structures in the excerpts from *The Making of Americans* and *Tender Buttons*. Locate similar sentences, identify points of transition in the prose, note the appearance of new and startling words, and comment on this prose as an aesthetic experiment or an act of persuasion.

ROBERT FROST

1. Write about the narrator's perceptions about death in "After Apple-Picking"; "Stopping By Woods on a Snowy Evening"; "Home Burial"; "'Out, Out-'"; and "An old Man's Winter Night." How does each poem serve as a buffer against mortality and meaninglessness?

2. Write about two of the following poems to show how Frost's poetic techniques serve as his own "momentary stay against confusion": "Desert Places," "Mending Wall," "The Wood-Pile," or "Design."

3. Illustrate how Frost's statement in "The Figure a Poem Makes" applies to "Home Burial": "The possibilities for tune from the dramatic tones of meaning struck across the rigidity of a limited meter are endless."

4. Discuss Frost's use of the sonnet form in the following poems: "Mowing," "The Oven Bird," and "Design."

5. One of the most striking characteristics of Frost's poetry is his creation of a speaking voice. Examine the following poems and describe the relationship between speaker and hearer: "The Pasture," and "The Tuft of Flowers."

6. Examine the motive of the loss of Paradise, or the Fall, in "Fire and Ice," "The Oven Bird," and "After Apple-Picking."

7. Choose one of the following poems not anthologized in NAAL for further close analysis: "A Minor Bird," "The Investment," "The Hill Wife," or "The Cow in Apple-Time."

8. "Directive" advises its readers to get lost to find themselves. How does this poem reflect Frost's twentieth-century worldview? What are the relative values of disorientation and reorientation? How does "Directive" offer a modern version of the American dream?

SUSAN GLASPELL AND SHERWOOD ANDERSON

1. Do you see modernist concerns in *Winesburg, Ohio* and *Trifles*? Or would it make more sense to think of Anderson and Glaspell as a latter-day local-colorists or realists? In answering this question, make specific reference to the selections in NAAL.

2. To what extent are Anderson and Glaspell writing as outsiders, introducing their readers to communities and ways of life unknown to many of them? What strategies do these writers employ to engage this larger, uninitiated American audience?

WALLACE STEVENS

1. One of the most famous lines from Stevens, and one of the most enigmatic, appears in "Sunday Morning": "Death is the mother of beauty." Summarize the thinking process by which the speaker in this poem transforms Sunday morning from a day of Christian religious observance for the dead into a very different kind of celebration.

2. Both "Anecdote of the Jar" and "Study of Two Pears" center on an inanimate object. Discuss the meaning these two poems share, and the syntactic and semantic techniques Stevens uses to create that meaning and make pears and a jar interesting as subjects for poetry.

3. Discuss the technical experiment in Stevens's "Thirteen Ways of Looking at a Blackbird." How do other Stevens poems help us understand what this poem is about?

4. "The Idea of Order at Key West" contains two poems or singers: the woman who sings, and the poem's speaker. Describe the relationship between them, and comment on Stevens's use of these two voices—one of which is heard, the other only described.

5. Compare poems of Frost and Stevens, focusing on one of the following pairs: Frost's "Desert Places" and Stevens's "The Snow Man" or Frost's "Directive" and Stevens's "A Postcard from the Volcano." In what ways do Frost and Stevens contribute to modernist ways of knowing the world?

6. Examine poems in which you see activities of (1) looking at things or (2) playing musical instruments or singing, and explore the significance of the activity in Stevens's poems.

MINA LOY AND WILLIAM CARLOS WILLIAMS

1. Write an essay about voice, comparing Loy's voice in "Lunar Baedeker" and "Parturition" to Williams's voice (or voices) in any three poems in the set.

2. Loy's "Brancusi's Golden Bird" and Williams's "The Dance" are both poems about works of art. Write an essay about how these poems emulate qualities found in the work that is the subject of each poem.

3. At the end of "To Elsie" Williams writes, "No one to witness and adjust, no one to drive the car." Describe how he arrives at this image; then comment on how this image addresses Frost's concerns in "The Oven Bird" or "Desert Places" and Stevens's in "A High-Toned Old Christian Woman" or "Of Modern Poetry."

4. In "A Sort of a Song," Williams writes, "No ideas but in things." Write an essay about the anthologized poems that appear to be about things rather than ideas: "The Red Wheelbarrow," "Death," and "Burning the Christmas Greens." What do these poems achieve?

5. Some of Williams's poems directly or indirectly address the writing of poetry. Discuss what the following poems tell us about his poetic theory: "Portrait of a Lady," "Spring and All," and "The Wind Increases."

6. Discuss Williams's word choices in "To Elsie."

7. Describe the form Williams invents in "The Ivy Crown." Discuss the effects this form has on the reader. How does the form contribute to a reader's understanding of the poem?

8. Compare the two Williams poems that derive from paintings by Brueghel: "The Dance" and "Landscape with the Fall of Icarus." Locate copies of these paintings in your library or on the Web, and look at them carefully. Why might these works interest a contemporary American poet? What relationship does Williams achieve between the visual and the verbal experience? Is it necessary to know these paintings to understand and appreciate the poems?

EZRA POUND AND H. D.

1. Write an essay comparing Pound's "Hugh Selwyn Mauberley" to Eliot's "The Love Song of J. Alfred Prufrock," as portraits of modern ineffectuality. Don't just compare themes—look for variety and moments of risk-taking in the form and rhetoric of these poems.

2. Pound affected an ardent masculinity in many of his poems; when H. D.'s poems are compared to Pound's, do feminine or feminist qualities in her poetry come into focus. Compare the way that these two poets engage with worldly experience.

CLUSTER: MODERNIST MANIFESTOS

1. Each of these overt or implicit literary manifestos responds to a cultural moment, a perception that times have changed and that literature must change as well. Write an essay comparing three of these excerpts for plausibility and freshness. Which of these pronouncements has held up best over the years, and why?

2. Write a brief experimental manifesto of your own, for a literary or artistic form or genre that you care about, responding to your own cultural moment or circumstance as you understand it. Because manifestos often quarrel (fairly or otherwise) with the cultural past, choose one of the writers in this cluster and reply in the course of your own manifesto.

MARIANNE MOORE

1. Moore's work resembles that of Stevens in its interest in ideas. Choose one of the following pairs of poems, focusing on your analysis of Moore, and discuss the resemblance: "The Idea of Order at Key West" and "A Grave" or "Of Modern Poetry" and "Poetry."

2. Moore experiments with form and line lengths in "The Mind Is an Enchanting Thing." Write about this poem, paying close attention to the relationship between form and meaning. How does "O to Be a Dragon" serve as a postscript to such a discussion?

3. Study Moore's work for explicit statements about what poetry is and does. Evaluate these statements in light of class discussion and construct a prose version of her poetic theory.

4. In 1858, Oliver Wendell Holmes published a short poem called "The Chambered Nautilus," which became famous for its intricacy and romantic themes. Take a look at Holmes's poem, and comment on how Moore responds to it in "The Paper Nautilus," in form as well as theme.

5. Discuss one of the following poems by Moore with the aim of describing the poem's form and demonstrating the relationship between form and meaning in the poem: "To a Snail," "Poetry," and "The Paper Nautilus," and "Nevertheless."

T. S. ELIOT

1. Eliot writes, in "Tradition and the Individual Talent," that the individual personality and emotions of the poet recede in importance and his meaning emerges from his place in cultural tradition. He writes that "no poet . . . has his complete meaning alone." Examine his use of classical allusions in "Sweeney among the Nightingales." What does a modern reader need to know to understand the allusions and how does that understanding enhance our meaning of the poem?

2. Describe the progression and interconnection of images and themes in *The Waste Land,* locating the central image in each of the five sections of the poem.

3. Eliot himself considered *The Waste Land* to be "a poem in fragments." Explain why this is an appropriate description of the poem, how it addresses Eliot's twentieth-century worldview, and how he attempts to resolve the fragmentation at the end of the poem.

4. Describe carefully the persona of the speaker in "The Love Song of J. Alfred Prufrock" by examining the way he sees the world.

5. Like Williams, Eliot tried to achieve exactness and compression in creating his visual image. Find "Preludes" in the library and analyze Eliot's use of the image in that poem.

6. Eliot dedicates *The Waste Land* to Ezra Pound, who offered suggestions for revision. Read Pound's "Hugh Selwyn Mauberley," published just before *The Waste Land,* and locate similarities between the two poems.

Eugene O'Neill

1. Discuss what O'Neill's character Edmund calls "faithful realism" in *Long Day's Journey into Night*. Is this play a work of realism? In what way does it extend or transform the concerns of the earlier realists to include twentieth-century concerns?

2. O'Neill suggests that modern life is more difficult for women than for men. Discuss continuities between the predicament of Edna Pontellier in Chopin's *The Awakening* and Mary Tyrone in *Long Day's Journey into Night*.

3. If you have studied early-nineteenth-century American literature, try reading *Long Day's Journey into Night* as the culmination of themes and concerns that have set a direction in American fiction from "Rip Van Winkle" on. What does the play have to say about versions of the American Dream, about individual identity, about self-reliance, about social exclusion, and about the development of consciousness?

Claude McKay

Write an essay in which you discuss ways in which McKay refreshes and personalizes traditional poetic forms. Is it legitimate to call McKay a modernist poet? Why do you think so? Make reference to specific poems in preparing your answer.

Katherine Anne Porter

1. One of Porter's recurring themes is the alienation or disconnection of the self—particularly of intelligent and independent women—from the rest of the world and a lack of genuine understanding or companionship or trust. Compare the predicament of one of Porter's heroines to that of some other isolated or misunderstood women we have looked at recently: Daisy Miller, May Bartram, Edna Pontellier, Mary Tyrone. Are there differences? Are men or is a male-dominated world the fundamental cause of the disconnection of Porter's women?

2. Write an essay comparing Porter's prose style and rhetorical strategies to those of Chopin, another Southern writer who wrote of women in grim predicaments. What differences to you see in the ways they handle expository prose and begin, pace, and end a narrative?

Zora Neale Hurston

1. Write an essay about the ways in which Hurston makes use of myths and archetypes. What emotional or psychological impact does mythology bring to "The Eatonville Anthology" and "How It Feels to Be Colored Me"?

2. Compare "The Gilded Six Bits" to Mark Twain's "Notorious Jumping Frog of Calaveras County" or a "Mr. Rabbit" story by Joel Chandler Harris. At what points in "The Gilded Six Bits" does Hurston emulate or pay homage to these older tales? At what points does she seem to resist or transform a literary folktale tradition dominated, up to that time, by white men?

3. During her lifetime, Hurston enjoyed a measure of fame, followd by a long eclipse. She died in poverty and obscurity. How do you account or this rise, fall, and posthumous rise in her reputation? How does her literary work reflect or conflict with the narrative or the American civil rights struggle or with the establishment of an African Amreican voice in our literary history?

Nella Larsen

1. Write an essay about Helga as an American protagonist. What do you see as her literary ancestry? In what ways is she an unprecedented or daring creation?

2. Write an essay about this question: Does Larsen achieve sufficient artistic distance between herself and her own heroine? Choose, analyze and evaluate specific moments which support or complicate your answer.

3. Write an essay about the way that *Quicksand* concludes. Compare its ending to the final scenes of *The Awakening*.

Edna St. Vincent Millay

1. Write an essay about wit and irony as a presence in poems of Millay. Compare the effects and the inferences, and speculate on the advantages, and risks, of wit as a rhetorical strategy in poems by modern American women.

2. When Millay writes about sex, does she see her own predicament as a natural one or as culturally inflected? Write an essay describing the differences you observe between Millay's perspectives and those of two other women authors who have engaged with gender and sexuality.

E. E. Cummings and John Dos Passos

1. Write an essay comparing Cummings to Sandburg and Whitman as observers of ordinary American life. Pay special attention to the implicit attitude conveyed with regard to middle-class or working-class people as subjects in the verse.

2. Throughout his career, Cummings attempted to distinguish his verse by ignoring or defying conventions in punctuation and capitalization. Write an essay that looks carefully at passages where you see this strategy at work, and comment on the effects—in regard to the specific lines you choose, and overall as a hallmark of Cummings's poetry.

3. Do you see similarities between Dos Passos's stylistic experiments in "The Big Money" and the voices achieved by Cummings and Sandburg? Write about the similarities and differences, and speculate on the large—scale cultural forces to which these authors might be responding together.

Jean Toomer

1. What is the literary analogue in Toomer's *Cane* for Du Bois's "double consciousness"? How does Toomer evoke "the souls of black folk" in this excerpt from *Cane*?

2. Place Fern herself in the context of other works by American male writers, such as Poe's "Ligeia" or Anderson's "Mother." How does this tale continue or transform a conversation between American writers and the larger culture, about the valuation of women?

F. SCOTT FITZGERALD

1. Write an essay about Fitzgerald as a nostalgic author. With what mix of emotions does he describe a personal and collective past? What moments in personal experience does he find most evocative? How does he make this nostalgia interesting or important to readers in different historical periods, with different backgrounds?

2. Fitzgerald is famous as a prose stylist whose sentences can convey conflicting perspectives, tension between romantic and cynical inclinations. Write an essay about the opening paragraphs of "Winter Dreams" and "Babylon Revisited." Analyze the prose and describe the complexity of the voices that you find there.

3. In Hemingway's "The Snows of Kilimanjaro," the narrator/protagonist recalls his friend Julian, a signifier for Fitzgerald, and his friend's fascination with the rich. Hemingway writes, "He thought they were a special glamorous race and when he found they weren't it wrecked him just as much as any other thing that wrecked him." Consider Hemingway's description of Fitzgerald as an interpretation of what happens in "Babylon Revisited." Fitzgerald made an often-quoted remark that "There are no second acts in American lives." Is this a theme in "Babylon Revisited"? If so, how is it developed and made interesting?

4. Compare the opening page of "Winter Dreams" to the opening page of a Porter story or Hemingway's "The Snows of Kilimanjaro." Describe the differences and suggest what they imply about the different ways in which these writers worked as modern artists.

WILLIAM FAULKNER

1. Keep a journal of your thoughts, frustrations, and insights as you read *As I Lay Dying*. In particular, note your use of visual reading skills. Does the novel allow you to develop visualization as a reading technique, and if so, how? Pay close attention to Faulkner's effects on your actual reading process.

2. A journey in a novel often fosters and symbolizes character development. Which character(s) develop markedly in *As I Lay Dying*? Consider carefully the evidence of character development, or lack of it, and write about the thematic implications of this growth or stasis.

3. Faulkner said that he wrote *As I Lay Dying* from start to finish in six weeks, and that he didn't change a word. While Faulkner was known to exaggerate, he conveys an essential fact about this novel: that he wrote it easily, quickly, and as if it were the product of a single action. Explore the ironies inherent in such a description of the novel's creation. Compare Faulkner's description of how he wrote *As I Lay Dying* with Addie's statement "I would

think how words go straight up in a thin line, quick and harmless, and how terribly doing goes along the earth, clinging to it, so that after a while the two lines are too far apart for the same person to straddle from one to the other."

4. Throughout *As I Lay Dying*, Faulkner's characters use measurement and geometry as a way to depict the world, and Faulkner himself created a map of Jefferson County that "located" the Bundrens' journey within the larger world of his fiction. Find the map on the flyleaf of an edition of *Absalom, Absalom!* Consider Faulkner's use of spatial form and spatial relations as a unifying element in *As I Lay Dying*.

5. In class we have discussed *As I Lay Dying* as an epistemology, a set of ways of knowing the world. Explore the idea of the novelist as a carpenter and *As I Lay Dying* as one of the tools—rather than one of the products—of Faulkner's trade.

6. Critics have often commented on Faulkner's use of comedy in *As I Lay Dying*. Think about the various meanings of comedy and evaluate the extent to which *As I Lay Dying* may be considered a comic novel.

7. Examine *As I Lay Dying* from the point of view of family dynamics or social process. Is "Bundren" an identity these family members all share? What is the ontology, the way of being a Bundren? To what extent is Faulkner commenting on the American, especially the southern, family? Evaluate the perspectives with which the outsiders in the novel view the Bundrens. Which is reality? How does Faulkner demonstrate his characters constructing it?

8. Critics often associate Faulkner's portrait of the Snopeses with his perception that the "New South" following Reconstruction had lost its values. Consider this proposition with regard to "Barn Burning."

HART CRANE

1. Write an essay about Crane's use of the sacred. Compare this usage to the role of the sacred in poems of Eliot or Stevens.

2. Crane's verse forms are enormously varied. From two poems, choose stanzas that seem antithetical in their formality, and write about them, describing the advantages and difficulties of each strategy, and possible relationships between form, tone, and theme.

ERNEST HEMINGWAY AND THOMAS WOLFE

1. Write an essay comparing the prose style of Wolfe to that of Hemingway. What are the crucial differences? Could the story of "The Lost Boy" be told in a Hemingway style? What would be the effects? What about the possibility of "The Snows of Kilimanjaro" retold in the style of Wolfe? What conclusions do you draw about the suitability of each style to each narrative?

2. In writing workshops and literary magazines after World War II, the Hemingway legacy was much more palpable than Wolfe's. Write an essay suggesting reasons why Hemingway became the more influential stylist.

STERLING BROWN

1. In the midst of an era of free verse, Brown chose to write in rhyme and favored tight stanzaic forms. Write an essay about Brown as a contrarian: speculate on why he resisted the trend away from traditional form. How does his prosody reflect his key interests and values and his conception of what modern poems are and should accomplish?

2. In "Mister Samuel and Sam" and "He Was a Man," Brown uses personae. Write about ventriloquism in these works and the stylistic and thematic advantages of assuming these voices.

LANGSTON HUGHES AND COUNTEE CULLEN

1. Write an essay about the poems of Hughes and Cullen as representations of their respective theories of poetry.

2. Place Hughes's work in the context of black musical forms invented in Harlem in the early twentieth century. Is black poetry the way Hughes writes it, like jazz, a new genre? What are its characteristics? If "black poetry" is a genre, does Countee Cullen write in it?

3. Hughes's poetry is open to the experiences of women. Analyze "Mother to Son," "Madam and Her Madam," and "Madam's Calling Cards," and explore the ways he transforms women's experiences into emblems of African American experience. Is Cullen's poetry distinctly gendered? If so, how, and to what effect?

4. Would you describe these two poets as modernist in their themes, use of images, and styles? Locate specific points at which you can see Hughes's and Cullen's modernism, and describe those moments in an essay.

RICHARD WRIGHT AND JOHN STEINBECK

1. Although Wright's work appeared later than that of the poets of the Harlem Renaissance, he reflects some of their concerns. Trace the theme of manhood in poems by Sterling Brown and in Wright's "The Man Who Was Almost a Man." What do these texts suggest about manhood as an American experience?

2. Wright's story makes significant use of dialect; even the title, in its original form, was in dialect. What are the challenges of writing in this voice, and how does the legacy of American fiction support or complicate that strategy?

3. Like Wright, Steinbeck is often regarded as a modern practitioner of literary naturalism. Write an essay comparing the narration of "The Leader of the People" to the narration of "The Man Who Was Almost a Man." What differences do you see in the way these narratives are told? What indications do you see of the author or narrator's relationship to the major characters?

4. Wright and Steinbeck were both writing in an age of film, and both of these authors had firsthand experiences with studios and movie-making. Write an essay about "camera work" in these two narratives: panoramic shots, close-ups, sudden changes of angle and perspective. How would you compare the cinematic style of these two writers?

Carlos Bulosan

Write an essay that reads Bulosan as continuing a legacy extending back to Cahan and Chesnutt. What are his contributions to a tradition of narratives about American minority experience?

Volume E: American Literature since 1945

Although the teaching notes for this period include questions that can work either as discussion openers or as essay topics, ambitious papers about postwar and contemporary literature may gravitate toward several important and open-ended questions:

- The continuing relevance of genres, modes, and literary traditions: where do we see their continuation and development? Where do we see indications that this legacy is being rejected or radically reconstructed?
- The coexistence of the printed word with other media. It is no secret that since the 1960s, many electronic-based arts and entertainments have entered the competition for our time and attention. How has written literature adapted? How has it implicitly or explicitly recognized this revolution—as competition, complication, or enhancement?
- Canons, continuity, and diversity. The recognized diversity of American culture creates enormous richness and vitality in our literary life—but it obviously poses challenges for the construction of conventional literary history. What efforts do writers make to cross boundaries and reach different communities of readers? How is American literary culture avoiding fragmentation?

General Questions: Prose

1. Explore the variety of themes and techniques by which late-twentieth-century writers of fiction depict their own life stories in imaginative literature. You might include the following authors in your discussion: Ralph Ellison, Saul Bellow, Jack Kerouac, Toni Morrison, Rudolfo Anaya, Amy Tan, Annie Dillard, N. Scott Momaday, Sandra Cisneros, Julia Alvarez, and Richard Powers.

2. Is heroism possible in contemporary society, as it is portrayed by our fiction writers? Discuss the possibilities for heroism in the following heroes or antiheroes: Miller's Willy Loman, Roth's Sargeant Marx, Baldwin's Jesse, Erdrich's Fleur, selected characters in Spiegelman's *Maus*, and Kingston's Wittman Ah Sing.

3. In their efforts to record and understand the mysteries of life, many contemporary writers show special interest in the grotesque, the inexplicable, or the fantastic. Discuss this dimension of the following works: Welty's "Petrified Man," Malamud's "The Magic Barrel," O'Connor's "The Life You Save May Be Your Own" or "Good Country People," Pynchon's "Entropy," and Le Guin's "Schrödinger's Cat."

4. White middle-class suburban life and marriage become a central subject for several contemporary writers. Discuss the different treatment of this subject in the following works: Cheever's "The Swimmer," Updike's "Separating," Apple's "Bridging," and Beattie's "Weekend."

5. While contemporary writers no longer take upon themselves the responsibility for "defining" what it means to be an American, many continue to reflect on what Norman Mailer once described as "the forces now mounting in America" and "the intensely peculiar American aspect" of contemporary life. Discuss commentaries on recent or current American life in the following works: Ellison's *Invisible Man,* Miller's *Death of a Salesman,* Baldwin's "Going to Meet the Man," Reed's "The Last Days of Louisiana Red," Erdrich's "Fleur," and Mamet's "Glengarry Glen Ross."

6. Betrayal by mothers—or by sisters—is one variation of the exploration of the influence of family on contemporary life. Stella, at the end of *A Streetcar Named Desire,* cries, "'Oh God, what have I done to my sister?'" Explore relationships between women in (for example) Welty's "Petrified Man," T. Williams's *Streetcar,* O'Connor's "The Life You Save May Be Your Own" and "Good Country People," Morrison's "Recitatif" and Walker's "Everyday Use."

7. Examine as a group the anthologized stories by these twentieth-century southern writers: Porter, Wolfe, Welty, and O'Connor. Do these writers alter the nineteenth-century concept of regionalism, and if so, how? If not, how do they extend the genre? How are twentieth-century regional writers also modernist writers?

8. Among contemporary writers, perhaps dramatists perceive most clearly the possibility for tragedy in American character and American life. The heroes and antiheroes of fiction seem to disappear, or take on tragic dimensions, in the work of Williams, Miller, Baraka, Shepard, and Mamet. Describe carefully one of the characters from their plays as a tragic hero, paying particular attention to the way the dramatic form enhances or frustrates such a reading.

9. Is it possible, and useful, to talk about a Native American voice in contemporary poetry and fiction? What would you say are thematic and stylistic characteristics of that voice? If you write about contemporary poets, consider especially Glancy, Harjo, Alexie, and Ortiz. If you write about prose, consider Silko, Vizenor, Alexie, and Erdrich.

10. Compare the way Williams constructs Blanche DuBois's southern speech with the way Faulkner, Welty, or O'Connor do for their southern characters in the anthologized stories.

11. A number of contemporary prose writers write about the challenge of writing, of being an artist within their own group or in and for the larger culture. What do these writers have to say about that challenge? What similarities in theme do you see among them? Consider Kingston, Bambara, Carver, and Reed.

12. Read a play by Lillian Hellman (*The Little Foxes, The Children's Hour*), Lorraine Hansberry (*A Raisin in the Sun*), Ntozake Shange (*For Colored Girls Who Have Considered Suicide*), Marsha Norman (*'Night,*

Mother), or Wendy Wasserstein (*The Heidi Chronicles*) and compare it with one of the plays in NAAL.

13. Locate and read one of O'Neill's earlier "expressionistic" plays written during the 1920s and compare it with *Long Day's Journey into Night*.

14. Read the anthologized selections by Cheever, Updike, Carver, Dillard, Barthelme, and Beattie. Based on these stories, identify formal and thematic features of these stories by writers who have appeared often in *The New Yorker*. Then read a short story published in *The New Yorker* during the past year and evaluate its similarities to these works.

15. One of the central questions for readers of *Black Elk Speaks* involves understanding the meaning of biculturalism. Explore the concept of biculturalism for contemporary Native American writers: Momaday, Silko, Vizenor, Alexie, and Erdrich. Alternatively, consider the meaning of cultural assimilation for members of minority groups in America and examine the following works and their treatment of assimilation: Ellison's *Invisible Man*, Walker's "Everyday Use," Silko's "Lullaby," and Anaya's "Bless Me, Ultima."

16. Write an essay comparing the excerpt from Tan's *The Joy Luck Club* with Paley's "A Conversation with My Father." Focus on what the younger narrators seem to learn from their interactions with older people. What remains mysterious in each of these narratives?

17. Write about ways in which Powers's "The Seventh Event" blurs the boundaries between fact and fiction, and why.

18. Write an essay about the implicit audience for Anaya's "Bless Me, Ultima" and Anzaldúa's "How to Tame a Wild Tongue." Whom do you assume these works were written for? What kinds of accommodation, or resistance of accommodation, do you see in each of these texts?

19. What are the pros and cons of grouping writers like Anzaldúa, Cisneros, Alvarez, and Anaya as "Latino writers," or Song and Tan and Lee as "Asian American writers"? Write an essay about this strategy, explaining and defending your views with reference to writers from early periods in American literature.

20. Readers have sometimes complained that the plays of Mamet and Shepard, the narratives of Carver, and other contemporary works sound too much like everyday life and language, or ordinary reportage, to qualify as "literary." Choose two contemporary texts from NAAL and comment on the mingling or the tension you see there in regard to artifice and truth.

21. American playwrights have often used siblings within a family to stand for divisions within the self or for two opposing forces. Consider the relationships between James Jr. and Edmund in *Long Day's Journey into Night*, Blanche and Stella in *A Streetcar Named Desire*, Biff and Happy in *Death of a Salesman*, and Lee and Austin in *True West*.

General Questions: Poetry

1. Based on your own careful reading of the selections in NAAL, affirm or challenge the accuracy of the following statements by and about poets in this section of the anthology:

- *Niedecker:* "Like other experimental American poets, she uses the space of the page to suggest the movement of the eye and mind across a field of experience."
- *Penn Warren:* "What poetry most significantly celebrates is the capacity of man to face the deep, dark inwardness of his nature and fate."
- *Oppen:* "Oppen's distinctive measure, with its hesitancies and silences, becomes itself a measure of language's capacity to say with clarity what is real."
- *Jarrell:* "He is master of the heartbreak of everyday and identifies with ordinary forms of loneliness."
- *Wilbur:* "The most adequate and convincing poetry is that which accommodates mixed feelings, clashing ideas, and incongruous images."
- *Ammons:* "Ammons has often conducted experiments with poetic forms in his effort to make his verse responsive to the engaging but evasive particularity of natural process. This formal inventiveness is part of the appeal of his work."
- *Levertov:* "Her overtly political poems are not often among her best, however; their very explicitness restricts her distinctive strengths as a poet, which include a feeling for the inexplicable, a language lyrical enough to express wish and desire, and a capacity for playfulness."
- *Rich:* "Our culture, she believes, is 'split at the root' . . . ; art is separated from politics and the poet's identity as a woman is separated from her art. Rich's work seeks a language that will expose and integrate these divisions in the self and in the world."
- *Snyder:* " 'I try to hold both history and wildness in my mind, that my poems may approach the true measure of things and stand against the unbalance and ignorance of our time.' Throughout his life Snyder has sought alternatives to this imbalance."
- *Plath:* "Seizing a mythic power, the Plath of the poems transmutes the domestic and the ordinary into the hallucinatory, the utterly strange."
- *Harper:* "Harper writes poems to remember and to witness, but at times the urgency of the content overpowers his form and his language cannot sustain the urgency the poem asserts."
- *Ortiz:* "His sense of contemporary life, especially its absurdities, is acute. But the America he travels conceals within it an older landscape, one animated by spirit."
- *Dove:* "The experience of displacement, of what she has called living in 'two different worlds, seeing things with double vision,' consistently compels this poet's imagination."

2. Niedecker and Oliver both present poetry about significant landscapes, poetry that might be called pastoral. Compare the technical or formal features of their attempts to create a spirit of place in their work.

3. Many of Bishop's poems concern themselves with loss and exile, yet the tone of her poems is often one of reserve, of detached observation. Is such a tone appropriate to Bishop's themes? Where do you see tone and theme combining (or contrasting) most effectively in these poems?

4. Brooks and Dove wrote sequences of poems based on life in African American communities. Compare Brooks's anthologized poems from *A Street in Bronzeville* and Dove's poems from *Thomas and Beulah*. How do these poets make use of the technique of collage? What are their technical and thematic differences?

5. Write an essay about four contemporary American poets, responding to Randall Jarrell's observation "the gods who had taken away the poet's audience had given him students."

6. What are the oppositions and tensions that energize and shape Robert Lowell's poetry? Do you see resemblances between his worldview and that of Henry Adams or other New England writers? Talk about specific poems that show these structures and conflicts.

7. Almost as if they were poetic "siblings," Levertov, Duncan, and Creeley trace their formative influences to William Carlos Williams and H. D. Choosing representative poems by each of these three, related by their choice of literary models, explore "family" influence. You may choose to trace the influence of Williams or H. D., or you may focus instead on the "sibling" qualities of Levertov, Duncan, and Creeley.

8. A number of American poets seem to favor austerity—short lines, sparse use of metaphor, a stance of cool detachment. Others have favored long lines, lavish use of images and allusions, and overt emotional intensity. Creeley, Jarrell, Simic, and Cervantes may seem to belong to the former group, Ginsberg, Lowell, Roethke, Graham, and Ortiz to the other. Write an essay about two contemporary poets who strike you as having markedly different, or even opposite, literary voices. Describe differences, making specific reference to poems by each writer, and then speculate on possible similarities.

9. Ginsberg's use of long lines was a deliberate experiment for him, the "long clanky statement" that permits "not the way you would *say* it, a thought, but the way you would think it—i.e., we think rapidly in visual images as well as words, and if each successive thought were transcribed in its confusion . . . you get a slightly different prosody than if you were talking slowly." Read *Howl* and other anthologized poems, paying particular attention to Ginsberg's use of the long line.

10. O'Hara wrote about his work, "The poem is at last between two persons instead of two pages." Explore your own sense of audience and connection with O'Hara's poems, then consider whether his statement also applies to other contemporary American poets.

11. Kinnell and Levine have written of Whitman's influence on their work and their influence on each other. Choosing specific poems as the basis for your commentary, examine thematic and formal connections between Kinnell, Levine, and Whitman.

12. Ashbery is often spoken of as associated with the "language" poets, including Charles Bernstein, Lyn Hejinian, and Michael Palmer. Locate the work of one of these poets and read representative poems in light of Ashbery's work.

13. Many of Charles Wright's poems depict in detail an actual American landscape. Close read one of Wright's poems and examine the relationship between internal and external "landscape" in his work. Would you call Wright a pastoral poet? Where are his roots and forebears in the American literary tradition?

14. When Collins was appointed as a poet laureate, there were comments about how "accessible" his poetry is—and sometimes the description was not intended as a compliment. Write about Collins as an accessible poet: what strengths do you discover in his clarity? When you read him in the context of other contemporary poets, does his work seem sufficiently rich and multidimensional? In framing your answer, develop readings of at least two of Collins's poems.

15. Write an essay comparing Robert Frost's "Directive" and Lowell's "Skunk Hour." Think about these poems as soliloquies or elegies, and comment on how their tone and implications vary.

16. Write an essay about the way the supernatural is invoked in Kunitz's "Quinnapoxet," and Graham's "The Dream of the Unified Field." Describe the mixture of belief and disbelief that you find in the work of each of these poets.

17. In one of the poetry seminars that Lowell taught at Boston University, both Plath and Sexton were students. All three of them knew Wilbur, who also frequented the Boston area in the fifties and sixties. Imagine that some or all of these people have gone out for coffee one night after class and write a conversation they might have had. What might they have had to say to each other about their work?

18. More than any other contemporary American poet, Rich has located and explicated women's lives and their relationships to each other, to their communities, to history. Her poems also reflect her "understanding of change as the expression of will and desire." Write an essay in which you trace the continuum of women's relationships to each other that appear in Rich's poetry and in which you also locate the poems along the timeline of composition dates that Rich provides, examining evidence of what she has termed, in an essay by the same title, "When We Dead Awaken: Writing as Re-Vision."

19. Consider the appropriateness of Lorde's own phrase to describe her poetry: "a war against the tyrannies of silence."

20. Locate Ortiz within the Native American tradition of literature as represented in NAAL. What themes, forms, and images link their work with earlier Native American writers or with contemporaries Silko, Alexie, or Erdrich?

21. Explore the themes of Ortiz's poetry: traveling, the power of storytelling, dislocations of American Indian identity, exploitation of the American land.

22. Explore the connections Dove draws between individual moments of her personal history and larger historical forces. Compare her use of black history with that of other anthologized black women poets: Brooks and Lorde.

23. The Latino and Latina writers included in NAAL intermix Spanish phrases and lines in their work. Choose one or more of these writers (Ríos,

Cervantes, Anzaldúa, Cisneros), and discuss the effects and effectiveness of the inclusion of Spanish in the work.

24. Like other contemporary American women poets (for example, Rich and Dove), Song writes about family ties and ancestors. Explore the power of family in Song's work.

25. Find examples of the use of traditional poetic or metric forms by post-1945 poets and describe the relationship between form and meaning. Choose, for example, the following sonnets or near sonnets: Jarrell's "Well Water" or Brooks's "kitchenette building."

26. The following poems all reflect the autobiography of the poet: Bishop's "In the Waiting Room," Lowell's "My Last Afternoon with Uncle Devereux Winslow," Ginsberg's "To Aunt Rose," Merrill's "The Broken Home," and Plath's "Lady Lazarus." Choose one of these poems for close analysis, locating it in the context of autobiographical poems by other writers.

27. Poems that are addressed to or are about family members tell us a great deal about differences between contemporary poets as well as family relationships in the twentieth century. Explore one of the following groups of poems: (1) mothers: Brooks's "the mother" and Rich's "Snapshots of a Daughter-in-Law"; (2) fathers: Roethke's "My Papa's Waltz," Berryman's *Dream Song* 384, Merrill's "The Broken Home," Wright's "Autumn Begins in Martins Ferry, Ohio," Plath's "Daddy," and Lee's "The Gift" and "Persimmons"; Komunyakaa's "Song for My Father"; and (3) sisters: Song's "Lost Sister."

28. Poems addressed to other contemporary poets, living or dead, can tell us about the poet writing the poem and the poet honored by the dedication. Choose any of the following poems for close analysis, working within the context of the anthologized work by the poet to whom the poem is dedicated or addressed: (1) Bishop's "The Armadillo," for Lowell; (2) Lowell's "Skunk Hour," for Bishop; and (3) Sexton's "Sylvia's Death," for Plath.

29. Contemporary poets have written about nature in many different ways. Explore some of the variations: does nature become the object of perception and the reason for precision in language? does it serve as the symbolic projection of human emotions and fears? does it provide an alternative world within which the poet can locate a coherent vision? Choose several poems from the following list: Bishop's "The Moose," Dickey's "The Heaven of Animals," Ammons's "Corsons Inlet," Wright's "A Blessing," and Plath's "Blackberrying."

30. Locate and read statements on poetry by post-1945 poets; then review particular poems in light of the poets' statements. Choose, for example, Levertov, "Some Notes on Organic Form," from *Poet in the World*; Snyder, "Poetry and the Primitive," from *Earth House Hold*; Rich, "When We Dead Awaken," from *On Lies, Secrets, and Silence*.

31. Poets often first publish their poems in small books or collections. Find and read one of the following titles, study the order of poems in the collections, and then analyze the poem included in NAAL within the context of the other poems with which it was originally published. The titles of the anthologized poems appear in parentheses.

- Bishop, *Geography III* ("In the Waiting Room," "The Moose," or "One Art")
- Lowell, *Life Studies* ("Memories of West Street and Lepke")
- Wilbur, *The Mind-Reader* ("The Mind-Reader")
- Brooks, *A Street in Bronzeville* ("kitchenette building" or "a song in the front yard")
- Wright, *The Branch Will Not Break* ("A Blessing")

32. Read the anthologized poems from one of the following connected poem sequences and describe intertextual connections within these sequences: Brooks, *A Street in Bronzeville*; Berryman, *Dream Songs*; Rich, *Twenty-One Love Poems*; or Dove, *Thomas and Beulah*. Or extend your reading to include all of the poems in the Brooks, Rich, or Dove sequences and consider them as a single connected work.

33. What do contemporary poets have to say about some of the traditional themes of poetry: love, death, loss, or the passing of time? Choose and discuss two or three poems from one of the following groups:

- Love: Niedecker, "[Well, spring overflows the land]"; Lowell, "Skunk Hour"; Creeley, "For Love"; Rich, "A Valediction Forbidding Mourning"; Clifton, "homage to my hips"; Snyder, "Beneath My Hand and Eye the Distant Hills," Your Body"; Wilbur, "Love Calls Us to Things of This World"; Komunyakaa, "Song for My Father."
- Death: Jarrell, "The Death of the Ball Turret Gunner"; Berryman, No. 384; O'Hara, "The Day Lady Died"; Merwin, "For the Anniversary of My Death"; Clifton, "The Lost Baby Poem"; Wilbur, "The Death of a Toad"; Sexton, "The Truth the Dead Know" or "Sylvia's Death"; Harper, "Deathwatch"; Wright, "The Appalachian Book of the Dead VI."
- Loss: Roethke, "The Lost Son"; Bishop, "One Art"; Jarrell, "Thinking of the Lost World"; Merrill, "Lost in Translation"; Merwin, "Losing a Language"; Levine, "Animals Are Passing from Our Lives"; and Song, "Lost Sister."
- The passing of time: Bishop, "In the Waiting Room"; Hayden, "Middle Passage"; Lowell, "Memories of West Street and Lepke"; Pinsky, "A Woman"; Wilbur, "The Beautiful Changes"; Graham, "The Dream of the Unified Field"; Collins, "Forgetfulness."

Questions and Topics Related to American Literary Traditions

1. In *Of Plymouth Plantation*, Bradford writes, "But here I cannot but stay and make a pause, and stand half amazed at this poor people's present condition; and so I think will the reader, too, when he well considers the same." With this quotation in mind, examine *Narrative of the Life of Frederick Douglass*. Look for patterns in the two prose texts: How does each construct an audience? On what terms does each writer convey a sense of beginning, of "new world," both in historical and in literary terms? What specific material and ideological circumstances oppress the writers of these texts? In what way does each text establish questions that later writers will address? How do the texts differently deal with the problem of literary authority? What are the didactic purposes of the narratives?

2. Bradstreet and Wheatley were the first white and black American women to publish poetry. Examine Wheatley's poems in light of Bradstreet's "The Prologue." Can you find any evidence of conscious encoding in Wheatley's poems? Is she aware, as Bradstreet was, that as a woman or an African American her poems might be "obnoxious" to "each carping tongue"? Compare in particular the formal elements of Wheatley's poems with some of Bradstreet's, especially stanzas from "Contemplations," "The Flesh and the Spirit," and "As Weary Pilgrim."

3. Consider the extent of Bradstreet's and Wheatley's acceptance of received theology by examining one of the following pairs of poems: "Contemplations" and "Thoughts on the Works of Providence"; "The Flesh and the Spirit" and "To the University of Cambridge, in New England"; and "As Weary Pilgrim" and "On the Death of the Rev. Mr. George Whitefield, 1770."

4. Polemical writers in each literary tradition use rhetorical language to move their audiences. Choose works from the following writers as the basis for cross-traditional analysis: Edwards, Occom, Jefferson, Apess, Fuller, Charlot, Washington, and Du Bois. Consider ideological similarities between Edwards's "great revival" thinking in "Sinners in the Hands of an Angry God" and Apess's looking-glass in "An Indian's Looking-Glass for the White Man," or discuss the radicalism (for their contemporaries) of Jefferson, Fuller, or Du Bois.

5. Show how the lyric poem develops across historical periods in the works of each of the following groups of writers: Bradstreet and Taylor; Emerson and Whitman; Wheatley, Brooks, and Lorde; Clifton, Glück, and Komunyakaa.

6. Demonstrate how concepts of black identity determine prose forms in works by the following writers: Douglass, Jacobs, Chesnutt, Hurston, Toomer, Ellison, and Walker.

7. The genre of autobiography reveals many differences between writers from separate literary traditions. Examine segments of some of the following autobiographical narratives, choosing figures from each tradition, and outline contrasts in social position and economic class, educational background, audience, or didactic purpose: Edwards's *Personal Narrative*, Franklin's *The Autobiography*, or Hawthorne's "The Custom-House"; Jacobs's *Incidents in the Life of a Slave Girl* or Hurston's "How It Feels to Be Colored Me"; Equiano's *The Interesting Narrative*, Douglass's *Narrative*, Eastman's *From the Deep Woods to Civilization*, or Momaday's *The Way to Rainy Mountain*.

8. Some writers, while not choosing the genre of autobiography, still include enough autobiographical allusions in their poetry or fiction to tantalize the reader or critic. Consider the use of autobiographical material in

literature outside the genre of autobiography from several traditions, perhaps choosing from among the following lists: Taylor, Thoreau, Whitman, Melville, or Robert Lowell; Bradstreet, Dickinson, Gilman, Porter, Levertov, or Rich; Wheatley or Brooks; Sterling Brown, Hughes, Ellison, or Harper; Dillard, Kerouac, Cisneros, Thompson, or Powers.

9. In an out-of-class essay, consider points of connection, useful contrasts, or central themes in each of several works that may be considered focal points for their respective literary traditions: Douglass's *Narrative*, Twain's *Adventures of Huckleberry Finn*, Chopin's *The Awakening*, and Momaday's *The Way to Rainy Mountain*.

10. Examine a play by Glaspell (such as *Trifles*) or Hansberry (such as *A Raisin in the Sun*) in the context of class discussion of O'Neill's *Long Day's Journey into Night*, Baraka's *Dutchman*, Mamet's *Glengarry Glen Ross* or Shepard's *True West*.

11. Choose an important writer in an American minority tradition, or in the tradition of American women authors. Write an essay in which you compare the perspective a reader achieves in examining a particular text within the context of the writer's literary tradition with the perspective he or she might have in placing the text within the context of the writer's white male contemporaries. Useful writers for this assignment include Jewett, Cather, or Welty; Hurston, Brooks, or Walker; Chesnutt, Brown, Hughes, or Richard Wright; or Eastman, Zitkala Ša, Momaday, or Erdrich.

12. Write an essay about the following lyric poems from different literary traditions: Frost's "The Gift Outright," Brooks's "kitchenette building," Wilbur's "Love Calls Us to the Things of This World," Rich's "Diving into the Wreck," Ortiz's "Poems from the Veterans Hospital," Ríos's "Madre Sofía," Cervantes's "Visions of Mexico," Song's "Beauty and Sadness," and Lee's "Persimmons." Focus on the disparate voices and perspectives the poems reveal.

13. Examine characters who have been created by writers of the opposite gender. Compare a male protagonist created by a woman writer, such as Mr. Shiftlet in O'Connor's "The Life You Save May Be Your Own," with a female protagonist in a male writer's fiction, such as Hawthorne's Beatrice Rappaccini, James's Daisy Miller, or O'Neill's Mary Tyrone.

14. Compare black characters created by white writers with black characters created by black writers, in pairings such as Melville's Babo and the autobiographical persona in Douglass's *Narrative*; Stowe's Eliza and Linda Brent in Jacob's *Incidents in the Life of a Slave Girl*; Twain's Jim and Chesnutt's Uncle Julius.

15. Compare women characters created by male writers, such as Irving's Dame Van Winkle, Hawthorne's Hester Prynne, James's Daisy Miller or May Bartram, O'Neill's Mary Tyrone, Toomer's Fern, Faulkner's Addie Bundren or Dewey Dell, or T. Williams's Blanche DuBois, with women characters created by female writers, such as Stowe's Eliza, Jewett's Sylvy, the narrator of Gilman's "The Yellow Wallpaper," Chopin's Edna Pontellier, Porter's Miranda, Walker's Mama, or the women of Tan's *The Joy Luck Club*.

16. Read works by writers outside the list of major authors in the literary traditions approach that illuminate questions of cross-gender or cross-racial interest or that increase our understanding of the development of literary traditions and explain how and why they are significant. Choose from the following list: Rowlandson's *A Narrative of the Captivity and Restoration* (to examine a Euro-American woman's view of Native American men), Poe's poems and stories about women, Davis's *Life in the Iron-Mills* (to raise issues of class and working conditions in pre-Civil War industrialism), Harris (for a white man's transcription of black folk life), H. Adams's "The Dynamo and the Virgin" from *The Education* (for a white male writer's sense of woman as a source of symbolism), Anderson's "Mother" from *Winesburg, Ohio* (to compare a woman character by a writer who deeply influenced Faulkner with one of Faulkner's own female characters), Williams's "Portrait of a Lady" (a poem that raises questions of literary convention), H. D.'s "Leda" or "Helen" (a woman poet's sense of woman as a source of mythology), Wolfe's "The Lost Boy" (another example of a writer using autobiographical material in a genre other than autobiography), Crane's "At Melville's Tomb," Berryman's "Homage to Mistress Bradstreet," Ginsberg's "On Burroughs' Work," and Sexton's "Sylvia's Death" (for questions of literary influence).

17. Write an essay about the southern tradition as represented in NAAL. Focus in particular on those writers who do not figure as major authors in any literary tradition, such as Smith, Byrd, Wolfe, Penn Warren, or Dickey. What generic or thematic concerns link some of these writers? Can you describe the development of southern literature in a chronological reading of the representative figures in NAAL? In examining writers from the literary traditions, to what extent are their works informed by southern history or identity? Consider minority writers in the context of their chronological contemporaries. Are Douglass, Hurston, or Richard Wright anomalous in their respective literary periods when we consider them as southern, rather than as black or women writers? Consider writers in different genres, such as Byrd and Jefferson, Poe and Douglass, Faulkner and Wolfe, Dickey and Warren, and Welty and Walker. Are these writers so diverse in form and theme that their southern ties become negligible, or does that southern heritage link them significantly despite their differences?

18. Define a literary tradition on your own according to genre or theme. Defend your list of writers and works, and choose for class analysis a particular work that both represents your larger list and illustrates its central concerns.

19. Study the Jewish writers represented in NAAL: Lazarus, Cahan, Malamud, Miller, Bellow, Roth, Ginsberg, and Spiegelman. Choose a representative text for close analysis and view it either within the context of other works in the tradition, with works by the writer's contemporaries from a variety of traditions, or paired with a significant work from another tradition.

20. Study the relationship between marginality and vision or social stigma and literary authority in works by white male writers: (1) The colonial period appears to be unique in American literature in that it did not produce white male writers who considered themselves marginal (with the exception of Williams and Woolman, who were not part of the Puritan community). Speculate on some of the reasons why this is the case. Might the absence of men who wrote against the established ideology have somehow made it easier for Bradstreet to write at all? (None of her contemporaries chose to establish himself or herself as marginal, perhaps leaving the possibility open to a woman; and in Puritan culture, where marginality might lead a man to predict his own damnation, a woman—a flawed version of an already flawed creation—might have less to lose by embracing marginality.) (2) Many white male writers in the early nineteenth century wrote as if they were marginal. Choose representative texts (by Irving, Hawthorne, Thoreau, Whitman, or Melville) and consider what the marginal characters in these fictions have to say about the relationship between white male authors and marginality. (3) Examine Twain's Huck Finn or James's John Marcher as representative of lonely, isolated, and marginalized characters. (4) Twentieth-century white male authors frequently explore the theme of social difference. Some created their most powerful fictions based on this theme. Examine the theme in Anderson, Jeffers, O'Neill, Faulkner, Bellow, or Tennessee Williams and speculate on the white male writer's fascination with marginality.

21. Beginning with Bryant's "Thanatopsis," Thoreau's *Walden,* and Fuller's *Summer on the Lakes,* and continuing up through Gary Snyder's poetry and Dillard's *Pilgrim at Tinker Creek,* write an essay on the evolution of American pastoral thought.

Index

*Page numbers in **boldface** indicate main discussions of works and authors.*